Studies of the New Testament and Its World

Edited by

JOHN BARCLAY
JOEL MARCUS
and
JOHN RICHES

The Social Ethos of the Corinthian Correspondence

The Social Ethos of
the Corinthian Correspondence

Interests and Ideology from 1 Corinthians to 1 Clement

DAVID G. HORRELL

T&T CLARK
EDINBURGH

T&T CLARK LTD
59 GEORGE STREET
EDINBURGH EH2 2LQ
SCOTLAND

First published 1996

ISBN 0 567 08528 7

British Library Cataloguing-in-Publication Data
A catalogue record for this book is available from the British Library

Typeset by Trinity Typesetting, Edinburgh
Printed and bound in Great Britain by Bookcraft, Avon

Contents

Preface

Unser Leben geht hin mit Verwandlung, Rilke says:
Our life passes in transformation. This is what
I seek to grasp in the theory of structuration.
    —Anthony Giddens, *Central Problems in Social Theory*

In recent years, New Testament scholars have experimented with a variety of new interpretative methods, among which sociological approaches have been prominent. This study seeks to consider critically the way in which sociological resources should be used, and to develop and employ a sociologically-informed approach to exegesis. Its principal theoretical resource is the work of the prominent social theorist Anthony Giddens, in particular his 'structuration theory'. The resources derived from Giddens' work provide the basis for a methodological discussion which moves from criticism of current methods to the construction of a theoretical framework for research (Part I of the study). This research framework then underpins the exegetical studies which follow (Part II). It will become clear that Giddens' work provides the basis for, indeed requires from the interpreter, an approach to the understanding of early Christianity which is diachronic, which studies the transformation that takes place as this new faith is reproduced through time in particular contexts by particular people in the light of particular problems. As this process of transformation is studied, a critical sociological approach should also, I suggest, again following Giddens, continually ask questions concerning the ideological dimensions of each reproduction of the Christian faith and the interests which it sustains and represents.

The study which follows is a revised version of my PhD thesis, submitted to Cambridge University in 1993. That thesis was the result of three years' research funded by the British Academy, and I am most grateful both to the British Academy and to the Methodist Church for the opportunity and financial support that made it possible.

The process of thinking through the ideas developed here has been greatly helped by a number of opportunities to present and discuss seminar papers: at the British New Testament Conference on 18 September 1992 (now in *JSNT* 50, 85–103); at Professor Hooker's Cambridge New Testament Seminar on 2 February 1993; and at Context and Kerygma: the St Andrews Conference on New Testament Interpretation and the Social Sciences on 2 July, 1994 (now in *Modelling Early Christianity*, edited by Philip Esler (Routledge, 1995), 224–36). I am grateful to everyone who on those occasions engaged in discussion or raised questions.

The scholars whose written work I am indebted to are acknowledged in the footnotes and bibliography. There are, however, a number of people who have helped me greatly in specific connection with this project and I wish to extend my gratitude to them. The original thesis was supervised with continual encouragement by Andrew Chester; Ivor Jones, Principal of Wesley House, read and commented on the whole thesis; Alison Horrell proof-read the entire text; and Lucy Coleman compiled the indexes. Others who generously gave of their time were Richard Andrew, Anthea Bethge, James Carleton Paget, Alberto Gallas, Anthony Giddens, Justin Meggitt, Philip Payne, Stephen Plant, John Proctor, Gerd Theissen, Geoff Thompson, Jo Thornton, Helen Watson, Nigel Watson and Dagmar Winter.

The work of revising the thesis for publication has been considerably helped by the comments and criticisms of my examiners, Chris Rowland and Andrew Lincoln, and especially by John Barclay, an editor of the series in which this work now appears, whose suggestions, criticisms and encouragement have been of great value. The inadequacies of the work naturally remain my own responsibility.

Unfortunately Dale Martin's book *The Corinthian Body* (Yale University Press, 1995) came to my attention after this manuscript was completed and I can therefore do no more than mention it briefly here. While Martin's major foci and framework of interpretation are quite distinct and different from those developed here, there are substantial areas in which our interests and conclusions are in broad sympathy; indeed, Martin's earlier work, especially *Slavery As Salvation* (Yale University Press, 1990), was influential upon the perspectives I develop, particularly in chapter 5. In *The Corinthian Body*, Martin is interested in ideological analysis (see pp. xiii–xv, 251, and *passim*), referring to the work of Anthony Giddens and John Thompson in this field (see p. 253 n. 4). Martin also believes that there is a diversity of socio-economic positions encompassed within the Corinthian congregation, though none of the members of this group were likely to have come from the elite of the city (pp. xv–xvii). He argues that much of the conflict within the Corinthian church owes its origin to the socio-economic divisions amongst its membership, and that Paul opposes the ideology of the Corinthian strong, the dominant ideology of Greco-Roman society. Paul challenges 'some' of the Corinthian Christians – the higher status members of the congregation – to imitate him in his voluntary self-lowering (see pp. 55–103, etc.). Except in relation to the male-female hierarchy, '[t]hroughout 1 Corinthians Paul attempts to undermine the hierarchical ideology of the body prevalent in Greco-Roman culture. He attempts to make the strong weak and the weak strong' (p. 248). The degree of correlation between these perspectives and conclusions, and those presented here (notwithstanding the differences), will be clear to readers of both books. (See further my review of Martin in *Journal of Theological Studies* 47/2, 1996.)

I consider that the issue of inclusive language is important and have avoided using masculine forms for non-gender specific references throughout. The English language, of course, lacks gender-inclusive third-person singular pronominal forms and my preference, where possible, has been to use 'they'/'their' etc., since the frequent repetition of 'he or she', 'his or hers', and so on, can be clumsy and tiresome.

To keep the footnotes as short as possible I have adopted the system of referring only to an author's name, followed by the date of publication and relevant page numbers. All of the names and items mentioned can be found in the bibliography. Translations of the New Testament and of 1 Clement are my own, except where otherwise attributed.

My final prefatory words must be ones of personal thanks. There are too many friends and relatives to name, whose love and encouragement have been important to me, but I am grateful to them all, especially to those friends who have supported me over the last year. This book is dedicated, however, to Alison, my companion through most of the time in which I have worked on this project.

August 1995

Abbreviations used in text

In addition to the standard abbreviations for biblical books, the following abbreviations are used in the text and footnotes. Full bibliographical details can be found in the bibliography.

N.B. Articles cited from TDNT are not listed in the bibliography

BAGD	Bauer, Arndt, Gingrich & Danker; A Greek–English Lexicon
Barn.	*The Epistle of Barnabas*
CD	Cairo (Genizah text of the) *Damascus Document;* Dead Sea Scrolls
1 Clem	1 Clement
2 Clem	2 Clement
Did.	*The Didache*
Dio Cassius *HR*	Dio Cassius, *Historia Romana*
Dio Chrysostom *Diss.*	Dio Chrysostom, *Discourses*
Ep.	*Epistulae*
Epictetus *Diss.*	Epictetus, *Discourses*
ET	English Translation
Eusebius *HE*	Eusebius, *Historia Ecclesiastica*
Hermas *Vis.*	The Shepherd of Hermas, *Vision(s)*
Hermas *Sim.*	The Shepherd of Hermas, *Similitude(s)*
IESS	International Encyclopedia of the Social Sciences, D. L. Sills (ed.)
Ignatius *Magn.*	Ignatius, *Epistle to the Magnesians*
Ignatius *Rom.*	Ignatius, *Epistle to the Romans*
LSJ	Liddell, Scott & Jones; A Greek-English Lexicon
LXX	Septuagint
NA[27]	*Novum Testamentum Graece*, E. Nestle & K. Aland
NAB	New American Bible
NIV	New International Version
NJB	New Jerusalem Bible

NRSV	New Revised Standard Version
OCD	Oxford Classical Dictionary, N. G. L. Hammond & H. H. Scullard (eds)
Origen *Cels.*	Origen, *Contra Celsum*
P. Oslo	*The Oslo Papyri*
P. Oxy.	*The Oxyrynchus Papyri*
P. Yale	*The Yale Papyri*
Polycarp *Phil.*	Polycarp, *Epistle to the Philippians*
1QS	*Rule of the Community, Manual of Discipline;* Dead Sea Scrolls
REB	Revised English Bible
RSV	Revised Standard Version
Strom.	Clement of Alexandria, *Stromateis*
Suetonius *Claud.*	Suetonius, *Lives of the Caesars; Claudius*
Suetonius *Dom.*	Suetonius, *Lives of the Caesars; Domitian*
TDNT	Theological Dictionary of the New Testament, G. Kittel (ed.)
TLNT	Theological Lexicon of the New Testament, C. Spicq
UBS	United Bible Societies *Greek New Testament*

Introduction

This project has developed out of an interest in sociological approaches to the New Testament. Social questions are certainly not new to the agenda of New Testament studies;[1] in the early years of this century a number of prominent scholars, Adolf Deissmann, Shirley Jackson Case, Karl Kautsky and others, devoted considerable attention to the social dimensions of early Christianity.[2] The form-critical school too, with its focus upon the *Sitz im Leben* of texts, promised a degree of social contextualisation, although it is often noted that this promise was hardly fulfilled.[3] Indeed, Gerd Theissen has suggested that a number of factors led New Testament studies away from a focus upon socio-historical context: dialectical theology's focus upon the *theological* content of the texts, Rudolf Bultmann's existential and individualising hermeneutic, redaction criticism's focus upon the individual author over and against their community, and the antihistoricism of some more recent structuralist approaches.[4]

However, since the early 1970s New Testament studies have witnessed a renewal of interest in 'the social description of early Christianity'.[5] An important stimulus to this revival of interest was in fact offered as early as 1960, by Edwin Judge.[6] But as well as increasing the attention given to what may be termed 'social history', many studies since the 1970s have made explicit and deliberate use of social-scientific

---

[1] Theissen 1979b, 3–6; see also Schütz 1982, 3–11; Domeris 1991, 216. For a perceptive analysis of the progress and stimuli of sociological research into the New Testament since 1870, focusing largely on the German experience, see Theissen 1993, 1–29.

[2] See Keck 1974, who reviews contributions from the earlier parts of this century.

[3] See Schütz 1982, 7–8; Theissen 1979b, 5–7; 1993, 9–10; Best 1983, 181–82; Esler 1987, 3; Horsley 1989, 3.

[4] Theissen 1979b, 6–9; see further 1993, 8–15. Cf. Moxnes 1988, 147–52.

[5] The title of Smith's (1975) early outlining of the possibilities and tasks in the field. See also Moxnes 1988, 143–47; Horsley 1989, 1–2; Barton 1992, 399–406; Theissen 1993, 15–21.

[6] Judge 1960a (also 1960b); note the comments of Theissen 1979b, 10 n. 25; 1993, 19 n. 23; MacDonald 1988, 20.

models and theories, seeking to explore the explanatory, as well as the descriptive, possibilities of the social sciences.[7]

Like many academic (including theological) movements, New Testament sociology has arisen partly as a reaction to perceived inadequacies in established methods; in this case the apparent failure of historical-critical research to deal with the social dimensions of the early Christian communities. The criticism is perhaps best summarised by Robin Scroggs:

> To some it has seemed that too often the discipline of the theology of the New Testament (the history of *ideas*) operates out of a methodological docetism, as if believers had minds and spirits unconnected with their individual and corporate bodies. Interest in the sociology of early Christianity is no attempt to limit reductionistically the reality of Christianity to social dynamic; rather it should be seen as an effort to guard against a reductionism from the other extreme, a limitation of the reality of Christianity to an inner-spiritual, or objective-cognitive system. In short, sociology of early Christianity wants to put body and soul together again.[8]

Certainly sociological approaches have widened the agenda of New Testament research, bringing new questions and issues to attention.[9] This is clearly the case in the essays by Theissen, published between 1973 and 1979, which use sociological perspectives to understand both the Jesus movement[10] and the Pauline church at Corinth.[11] Of all the sociological work that has emerged, Theissen's remains perhaps the most influential.

Other early and important studies include those by John Gager (1975) and Scroggs (1975). Seeking to understand the early Christian movement and to gain new perspectives upon it, Gager drew particularly upon

---

[7] See Richter 1984; Gager 1979, 175; 1982, 258–59; Kee 1989, 32–64.

[8] Scroggs 1980, 165–66; cf. Elliott 1981, 3–4; Best 1983, 181; Meeks 1983, 1–2; Gallagher 1984, 91; Holmberg 1978, 201–203; Tuckett 1987, 136–37; Moxnes 1988, 149–52; Horsley 1989, 3–4.

[9] Cf. Gager 1982, 265; Holmberg 1990, 156; Tuckett 1987, 136, 148, who is generally quite critical of the achievements of the 'new' approach (see 144–45, 147–48).

[10] Essays collected in Theissen 1979b, 79–197; ET now in 1993, 33–156; also, in more popular form, see Theissen 1978.

[11] Essays collected in Theissen 1979b, 201–317; ET in 1982, 27–174.

anthropological work on 'millenarian movements',[12] whereas Scroggs used the 'sect' model developed by Werner Stark.[13] The method pursued by Scroggs has proved influential: many sociological studies of the New Testament have since used 'sect' models or typologies in their work.[14] The church-sect distinction made by Ernst Troeltsch is an important precursor to such study,[15] but the more recent work of Bryan Wilson has been of especial influence.[16]

After the work of Theissen, the most influential and encompassing sociologically-orientated study of the Pauline Christians is Wayne Meeks' *The First Urban Christians* (1983). This book, while open to criticism,[17] is an impressive attempt to describe and understand the life, faith and worship of the ordinary urban Christians converted by Paul.[18]

Since the mid-1970s much work has been done using sociological perspectives and there has been a steady stream of review work, serving the purposes of assessment and bibliographical collation.[19] It is not my intention here to offer another extensive review. However, interaction with much of this work will be apparent throughout the study.

The most important theoretical resource for this project has been the work of Anthony Giddens. Giddens is one of the foremost contemporary social theorists, yet his work has to date seldom been referred to in biblical studies.[20] I hope to show that the use of Giddens' work as a theoretical resource may enable us both to reconsider the ways in which a sociological approach should be understood, and to formulate significant questions for exegesis to address, although I am certain that my

---

[12] Note the critical responses of Smith 1978; Bartlett 1978; Tracy 1978; and the review in Holmberg 1990, 78–81.

[13] See critical overviews by Holmberg 1990, 88–92; Barton 1993, 141–45. Another early and influential attempt to move towards a 'sectarian' view of early (in this case Johannine) Christianity is Meeks 1972 (see 49–72 and Barton 1993, 145–52).

[14] See Elliott 1981; Watson 1986; Esler 1987; MacDonald 1988; and critical discussions in Holmberg 1990, 88–114; Barton 1993.

[15] Cf. MacDonald 1988, 164–65; Troeltsch 1931, 331ff.

[16] See below p. 14–15 with n. 37.

[17] See Elliott 1985; Malina 1985; Tiryakian 1985; Schöllgen 1988.

[18] Note the positive comments of Theissen 1985.

[19] The most recent overviews are by Barton 1992; Holmberg 1990. Useful recent bibliographies are Elliott 1993, 138–74; Harrington 1988; Theissen 1988a, 331–70. Other significant reviews are Gager 1979; Harrington 1980; Judge 1980; Scroggs 1980; Edwards 1983; Richter 1984; Gallagher 1984; Kümmel 1985; Rowland 1985b; Venetz 1985; Domeris 1991; Garrett 1992; Elliott 1993. Brief introductions include Tidball 1983; Osiek 1984; Tuckett 1987, 136–50; Morgan with Barton 1988, 133–66.

[20] An exception is Mayes 1987, 45–46, 55, 57 n. 7, 58 nn. 37–39; 1989, 125–30.

approach represents only one possible way of taking up and utilising Giddens' perspectives. The Corinthian correspondence, including both the letters written by Paul and the letter known as 1 Clement, not only offers rich material for a study of the social ethos of early Christian teaching, but also – and this is important in the light of Giddens' work – enables a focus on a specific community and on change over time.

The following study is divided into two parts. The first draws upon Giddens' work in order to consider how one should conceive of a 'sociological' approach. It takes issue with the ways in which New Testament scholars have understood and presented such approaches (chapter 1) and draws on a variety of theoretical resources, including Giddens' 'structuration theory', in the attempt to formulate a framework for exegetical research (chapter 2). These theoretical reflections and the framework which is developed provide the basis and direction for the exegetical studies which follow in Part II. However, I hope that the methodological discussions have a value of their own, and contribute towards the task of formulating adequately a socio-historical approach to the New Testament.[21] Our methods and approaches, and the theoretical issues which surround them, should be carefully and critically considered.[22]

It will become clear that the primary focus of the exegesis presented in Part II is upon the social ethos that emerges from the Corinthian correspondence.[23] I explore the ways in which each formulation of Christian teaching arises from a particular context and attempts to shape the believers' social relationships. I aim also to assess the extent to which such teaching supports or legitimates the interests of dominant social groups in an ideological way.[24] After outlining the formation and composition of the Corinthian Christian community, I consider the variety of situations (revealed in 1 Corinthians) about which some socially significant information appears to be available (chapter 3). The purpose of this sketch is to provide the context in which to read parts of 1 Corinthians as Paul's response to these situations: chapter 4 considers the social ethos which is evident in Paul's responses to the problems he

---

[21] On the reasons for the use of the term 'socio-historical' as opposed to 'sociological', see §1.5 below.

[22] Cf. Stowers 1985, 149, 168; Horsley 1989, 7; Holmberg 1990, 143–44. Note the importance given to methodology by Theissen 1979b, 3–76; Kee 1989.

[23] The term 'social ethos' is defined in §2.5., p. 57.

[24] The term 'ideology' is discussed and defined in §2.4., p. 50–52.

perceives in the community. Chapter 5 assesses the ethos which emerges from the way in which Paul practises and portrays his role as an apostle, and relates this to the increasing conflict between Paul and the Corinthian church which comes to a head in 2 Cor 10–13 and is then to at least some degree resolved. Chapter 6 moves to a time about four decades later, when the role of instructing and informing the Corinthian community is taken on, at least on this epistolary occasion, by the church at Rome. I seek to assess the social ethos of the Roman church's letter (1 Clement), and to consider the ways in which, from a sociological perspective, its symbolic order[25] differs from that of Paul's Corinthian letters.

The inclusion of 1 Clement in this study should not be taken to imply a judgment that it is a particularly 'Pauline' document.[26] There is, however, a point in including it as part of a study of 'the Corinthian correspondence'. We know that Paul's Corinthian letters and 1 Clement were sent to the Christian community at Corinth and, therefore, that Clement filled the role that Paul once filled: as Paul responded to the problems in the Corinthian community around the middle of the first century so Clement addresses them some decades later. Clement, like Paul before, shapes the Corinthians' understanding of their faith. Indeed, Clement clearly takes up resources from 1 Corinthians and uses them for his own purposes, and sees himself as continuing the apostle's admonitory work. Thus an investigation of 1 Clement in conjunction with an investigation of Paul's Corinthian letters enables us to examine, in relation to one particular Christian community, the ways in which the symbolic resources of Pauline Christianity are taken up and transformed over

---

[25] On this term and the framework in which it is understood, see §2.5. below.

[26] There is considerable debate on this point. The extremes are represented by Sanders 1943, who stresses Clement's Paulinism and Hellenism, and Beyschlag 1966, who attempts to show Clement's dependence on Jewish and early Jewish-Christian traditions (see further Barnard 1967 and 1969, who approves of Beyschlag's work but suggests that 1 Clement cannot be so entirely severed from the Pauline tradition). Note also the debate between van Unnik 1970; 1972 and Beyschlag 1972. See also Jaubert 1964a; 1964b. Discussions of the sources of 1 Clement can be found in Harnack 1929, 66–87; Knoch 1964, 50–100; Jaubert 1971, 28–58; Fuellenbach 1980, 11–22. On the 'Paulusbild' and the use of Paul's epistles in 1 Clement, see Lindemann 1979, 72–82, 177–99 and 1990, with useful response by de Boer 1990. Hagner's study of the use of biblical material (including allusions to Pauline letters) in 1 Clement is useful and detailed, though he claims too much: 'Er sieht schwache begriffliche Parallelen in der Regel bereits als Indizien für unmittelbare literarische Abhängigkeit an' (Lindemann 1979, 179 n. 34; see Hagner 1973, esp. 236–37, 283).

time, to consider how the social ethos of Christianity may have developed and changed, and the potential impact of this upon social relationships, particularly within the Christian community.

Before the exegetical work can begin, however, the theoretical foundations must be laid. The first part of the study therefore considers how a sociological approach should be understood and outlines a theoretical framework within which exegesis may be attempted.

Part I

Methodology: sociology and New Testament study

1

What is a 'sociological' approach?

1.1. Introduction

Given the blossoming of interest in sociological approaches to the New Testament, it is important to reflect upon certain key questions: 'What is a "sociological" approach?' and 'How does a sociological approach differ from a historical one?'. In this chapter, I look at some of the ways in which New Testament scholars have characterised a sociological approach and argue that these often reflect particular and debatable conceptions of social science against which important objections can be (and in the social sciences have been) lodged. The challenging of some of these views of social science leads to the question concerning the difference between sociology and history. Here I argue, as some sociologists, social theorists and historians have done, that there is no appropriate methodological distinction to be drawn between sociology and history. This does not mean, however, that the introduction of 'sociological' perspectives has been a blind alley; for new methods, issues and questions have emerged which offer important and stimulating new directions for biblical study.

1.2. The use of models

New Testament scholars frequently equate a sociological approach with the use of sociological models. Thomas Best, for example, refers to 'the interpretive model' as 'the fundamental tool used by all sociological analysis'.[1] John Elliott too notes that 'models play a key role in social scientific analysis'.[2] Indeed, Elliott, Margaret MacDonald and Bengt Holmberg

---

[1]   Best 1983, 188.
[2]   Elliott 1986, 3.

all agree on the 'basic fact about models... that there is no choice as to whether or not we use them'.[3] It is interesting to note that the work of Thomas Carney explicitly underpins the arguments of all these authors.[4]

One's suspicions about this characterisation of sociology might initially be aroused by the discovery that a number of modern dictionaries of sociology devote very little space to the entry 'model'.[5] The massive International Encyclopedia of the Social Sciences does not have a general entry on models, although there is a relatively short article on the specific topic of 'mathematical models' which includes the comment that 'specific models are discussed in various articles dealing with substantive topics'.[6] Models are mentioned little in the extensive article under the entry 'sociology', which discusses the development, scope and methods of the discipline.[7] Recent introductions to sociology and the social sciences also make little mention of this supposedly fundamental social-scientific approach.[8] Models, it would seem, are not portrayed as a ubiquitous feature of sociological analysis, in contrast to the statements of the New Testament scholars cited above.

To some extent the disparity stems from variations in terminology (and also perhaps from differences between British and American sociology).[9] Bruce Malina, for example, gives the label 'model' to approaches which are generally known as 'theories', and this is noted by Elliott, who asserts his preference for the term 'theoretical perspectives' in these cases.[10] W. R. Domeris distinguishes between 'models' and 'perspectives' such as structural-functionalism (within which models are located), but then refers later to structural-functionalism as a model.[11] Similarly, Philip Esler

---

[3] Elliott 1986, 6; cf. Elliott 1993, 40–48; MacDonald 1988, 26, Holmberg 1990, 12–15; also Esler 1987, 9–16; 1994, 12; Chow 1992, 28–30.

[4] See Carney 1975, esp. 1–38.

[5] See e.g. Mann 1983; Mitchell 1979; Thompson and Theodorson 1970; Abercrombie et al. 1984; Slattery 1985 – not a dictionary as such but a series of short articles introducing the discipline, with no discussion of the topic of models.

[6] Bush et al. IESS 10, 378; 'Mathematical models', 378–86.

[7] Reiss et al., 'Sociology', IESS 15, 1–53.

[8] E.g. Coulson and Riddell 1980; Potter et al. 1981; Bilton et al. 1981; Giddens 1982b; 1989a (in this massive introduction to Sociology, models hardly feature during the book, nor do they receive an entry in the glossaries of basic concepts and important terms: see esp. 1–26, 657–753).

[9] American sociology has tended to be more 'scientific' and quantitative; see Reiss IESS 15, 4; cf. Moxnes 1988, 153.

[10] Malina 1982, 233; Elliott 1986, 7.

[11] Domeris 1991, 224 and 228.

uses Peter Berger and Thomas Luckmann's work as a 'model',[12] although it is generally referred to by the authors themselves as an exercise in 'theory'.[13] Some clarification of terminology is clearly necessary. Derek Gregory offers perhaps the most succinct definition of 'model': 'An idealized and structured representation of the real'.[14] A further definition might expand this conception: a model is 'a pattern of relationships, either conceptual or mathematical, which is found in some way to imitate, duplicate, or analogously illustrate a pattern of relationships in one's observations of the world'.[15] While models may contain an 'inner dynamic' or mechanism, as Esler suggests, this is not in my opinion a ubiquitous feature of what constitutes a model, and cannot be sustained as the decisive difference between typologies and models.[16] Rather, typologies are intended to offer a classificatory scheme (and therefore compare a range of examples) whereas models each summarise, represent or analogise one type of situation (even though they may be used for comparative purposes). Thus, to illustrate, Bryan Wilson's typology of sects classifies a range of observed sectarian forms, any one of which could be formulated as a model.[17]

Models generally arise as a result of empirical studies (even if they are then applied to other contexts). This is the case with models arising from the sectarian research of Wilson and others, from studies of millenarian movements, and with the classic geographical models of Von Thünen, Christaller and Lösch, Burgess and Hoyt and so on.[18] On this view, and cohering with the definitions given above, a model, initially at least, represents a researcher's attempt to simplify, generalise or abstract their findings. Certainly this may be in the interests of wider application, though it need not be so. However, the 'models' offered by Elliott in his article on the subject are of a different kind; they do not simplify or generalise, rather, like Carney's, they are formulated with regard to knowledge of the specific arena of research and provide a framework *into* which re-

---

[12] Esler 1987, 9, 16; cf. 1994, 4–18; also MacDonald 1988, 11; Maier 1991, 9.

[13] Berger and Luckmann 1966, 7, 207, 209; Berger 1967, v, vi.

[14] Gregory 1986, 301. Cf. Malina 1982, 231, although see §1.4. below for objections relating to the use of models for 'prediction and control', as Malina summarises their purpose.

[15] Thompson and Theodorson 1970, 261.

[16] Esler 1987, 9, drawing a distinction between typology and model. Cf. Holmberg 1990, 14 n. 38, 115 n. 94.

[17] E.g. MacDonald 1988, 25. On Wilson, see further below p. 14–15 with n. 37.

[18] Cf. Gregory 1986, 301.

search material may be organised.[19] This kind of framework both draws upon empirical knowledge of the area of study, and facilitates further research. Such 'models', *contra* Esler, are neither prior to, nor independent of, empirical research, nor are they 'stripped of temporal and spatial markings'.[20] This kind of heuristic framework also depends upon theoretical perspectives which, Elliott insists, should be explicated and clarified.[21] However, in the light of social-scientific definitions, I would suggest that such 'models' are better labelled 'research frameworks'. Interestingly, Carney often describes his 'models' as 'frameworks' or 'frames of reference'.[22] These research frameworks are located within larger and more encompassing theories, inappropriately, in my view, labelled 'models' by Malina, Esler and Domeris.[23] Theories in turn are located within a 'paradigm', a term used after T. S. Kuhn to denote the assumptions and approach shared by convention in a scholarly community, although Kuhn later proposed that 'disciplinary matrix' was a more appropriate term.[24] Models and research frameworks are not identical, according to the definitions offered in social-scientific literature: the latter derive from theoretical perspectives and delineate an approach to research, whereas models are formulated as the fruit of such research and in turn facilitate further research and investigation. These terms and relationships may be set out in diagrammatic form:[25]

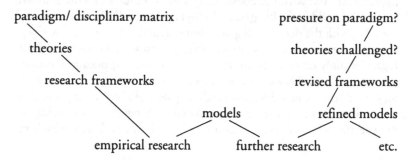

Fig.1: Research terminology

[19] Elliott 1986, 14, 18–19. The model on p. 14 follows Carney explicitly.
[20] Esler 1987, 14.
[21] Elliott 1986, 9, 11, 26 n. 29.
[22] Carney 1975, 4, 5, 7, 47, 52, 72, 73, 75, 83, 160–61, 321, 349, etc.
[23] Malina 1981, 18–22; 1982, 233; Esler 1987, 9, 16; Domeris 1991, 228.
[24] Kuhn 1970, 175–76, 182; cf. Elliott 1986, 7; Barbour 1990, 32.
[25] Cf. Barbour 1990, 32.

It may be that New Testament sociology will be able to develop models of its own, models which are idealised and simplified reflections of our analyses of the early church.[26] However, the most common approach at present is one which uses models developed in other (often modern) contexts. Comparisons between different contexts may of course be instructive and important, but the use of models derived from distant contexts may not be the most apposite form of comparative study.[27] Moreover, such a use of models often reflects a concern with the 'typical' and with generalisation which may itself be subjected to criticism (see §1.4. below).[28] Indeed a model-based approach and the conception of the research process outlined in the diagram above are founded upon a strongly scientific paradigm which many would argue is an inappropriate paradigm for the social and human sciences (see further below).

Cyril Rodd and Edwin Judge are among those who have questioned the propriety of using contemporary sociological models for the study of ancient societies.[29] Judge criticises Holmberg's *Paul and Power* in this respect, suggesting that

> it couples with New Testament studies a strong admixture of modern sociology, as though social theories can be safely transposed across the centuries without verification... Until the painstaking field work is better done, the importation of social models that have been defined in terms of other cultures is methodologically no improvement on the 'idealistic fallacy'. We may fairly call it the 'sociological fallacy'.[30]

Malina too, while committed to the use of models in research, has insisted that the models used should be cross-cultural and appropriate to the context in which they are employed;[31] though the idea that models must (or even can) be 'cross-cultural' is at least questionable (see further §1.4. below).

---

26 Cf. Best 1983, 191; Holmberg 1990, 154–55.
27 Cf. Craffert 1992, 226: 'a contemporary sociological model can just as readily result in anachronism and ethnocentricism as a contemporary theological or literary model.' Note that Theissen draws his comparisons from movements contemporary with early Christianity; 1978, 3, 14–15, 21–22, etc.
28 For a critique of the assumption of 'commensurability' between ancient and modern societies and of using 'law-like generalizations', see Stowers 1985, 150–51, 169–70.
29 Rodd 1979, 469; 1981, 104–105; 1990, 639; Judge 1980.
30 Judge 1980, 210.
31 Malina 1979, 178; 1982, 240–41; 1981, 22–24: the whole of this book uses models intended to illuminate the 'foreign' culture of the New Testament era: see Richter 1984, 83.

Esler's response to Judge criticises the latter's apparent empiricism, and insists that models are necessary tools, in order to make explicit and open the framework with which the subject is approached. 'It is quite impossible', he maintains, 'to collect facts without... already subscribing to a whole range of theoretical presuppositions'. Carney is therefore quoted with approval: 'Models bring values – in the subject matter and in the analyst – out into the open'.[32] Models, many New Testament sociologists suggest, are heuristic and exploratory devices which explicitly guide research but do not predetermine it.[33] Any use of models to 'fill in the gaps' in the evidence is generally rejected.[34]

However, there are two main problems here, which in part relate to the issue of terminology. The first concerns empiricism. One must agree, I believe, that all historical inquiry is guided by the choice of questions, by the approach, presuppositions and commitments of the researcher. It is never merely the collection of facts. Indeed Carney's opening point is that we all view reality from particular 'perspectives'. These 'organisational frameworks' should be chosen consciously and explicitly rather than remaining in the realm of the intuitive.[35] However, the question is whether the use of a *model* is the appropriate, or the only, guard against the illusions of empiricism (the myth of 'immaculate perception', as Carney puts it).[36] Such a conclusion is problematic not least because models frequently arise initially *from* empirical investigations. Wilson's typology of sects, which forms the basis of a number of models used by New Testament sociologists, arose from his own field work, which began with a study of three sects in Brit-

---

[32] Esler 1987, 15; cf. MacDonald 1988, 25–26. MacDonald follows Esler quite closely here and uses a number of the same theoretical perspectives; compare also Esler 1987, 16 and 228 n. 66 with MacDonald 1988, 10–11 and 240 n. 16.

[33] Esler 1987, 14; 1994, 12–13; Holmberg 1990, 15; cf. MacDonald 1988, 27, 240 n. 16; Watson 1986, ix–x, whose models are discussed on 19–20, 38–41.

[34] Scroggs did suggest the possibility of models being used in this way (1980, 166; cf. 1975, 14), a method criticised by Rodd 1981, 104; 1990, 639. Gager also hinted that 'new "data" may come in the form of new models' (1975, 4). Such a use of models is explicitly rejected by Esler 1987, 12, 14, and Holmberg 1990, 15.

[35] Carney 1975, 1, 4.

[36] Carney 1975, 1.

ain.[37] Furthermore, Wilson himself has objected to any use of such typologies in which,

instead of being useful short-hand summaries of crucial elements in *the empirical cases they are meant to epitomise*, they become caricatures remote from empirical phenomena...
Sociology in such a condition ceases to provide explanations, and becomes the ready vehicle for ideologies and ready-made formulae that do not explain the world, but rather obscure its richness and diversity.[38]

The idea that the use of models avoids the errors of empiricism also ignores the fact that one has to have some prior assessment of the field of study in order to make a decision as to which models may be appropriate. This decision is not arbitrary, of course.[39] Indeed, Carney's models are frameworks constructed on the basis of detailed knowledge of the period of study.[40] This approach is quite different from the ways in which models developed in contemporary social science, often from comparatively recent social situations, have been 'applied' to the New Testament world.[41] A rejoinder that 'models may be used heuristically' needs to face a second problem, or caveat, namely that *'each model reveals and orders reality from a particular perspective'.*[42] We cannot therefore be adequately satisfied with the conclusion that the evidence appears to fit the model:[43] we must also ask how the model has *shaped,* prioritised and interpreted

---

[37] Miller 1979, 161; see Wilson 1961; 1963. Used, for example by Elliott 1981, 74–78, 102–106, Esler 1987, 46–70, Watson 1986, 19–20, 38–41; MacDonald 1988, 25, 34 42; Jeffers 1991, 160–87; see reviews by Holmberg 1990, 92–108; Barton 1993. Watson does not discuss the sociological work on sectarianism directly but adopts Esler's framework: see Watson 1986, 184 n. 25 and Esler 1987, 46ff (esp. 58–70); cf. Holmberg 1990, 105. Despite Esler's distinction between typology and model (9) the sectarian typology of Wilson forms the basis of models used by New Testament scholars and referred to as such; e.g. MacDonald 1988, 25; Watson 1986, 19, 38.

[38] Wilson 1967, 2, my italics; cited in part by Best 1983, 190.

[39] Cf. Bartlett 1978, 118.

[40] See Carney 1975, 47–369; for example note the frameworks on 314–16.

[41] E.g. Gager 1975, esp. 20–65; Esler 1987, 10–12; MacDonald 1988, 25.

[42] Thompson and Theodorson 1970, 261, my italics. Cf. Elliott 1986, 5: 'Models are the media by which we establish the meaning of what we allow ourselves to see.'

[43] *Contra* Carney 1975, 35; 'data themselves will tell us whether the model is a good one. If it is they will fit it, if it isn't, they won't.' This is a remarkably empiricist statement. Esler 1994, 13, also adopts a rather pragmatic approach: 'it is inappropriate to debate whether a model is "true" or "false", or "valid" or "invalid". What matters is whether it is useful or not ...'

the evidence. And models developed in distant modern contexts are likely to put a quite specific shape upon the New Testament evidence.[44] The mere fact that a model is used does not, *contra* Esler and Carney, bring 'values into the open'.[45] This only happens when we clarify the theoretical perspectives and commitments upon which particular models are based. Indeed, it is at this level that the naïvety of empiricism is to be avoided.

One of Jonathan Smith's criticisms of John Gager's work in *Kingdom and Community* was that he constructed a model based on the work of three anthropologists without being aware of 'the deep theoretical differences among these three scholars'.[46] In addition, situations which Gager had taken to be independent of Christian influence were not in fact so, and thus his model contained a degree a self-confirming circularity.[47] (We might also note that the model has again been derived from empirical fieldwork elsewhere.) Indeed, one of the major problems in applying millenarian and sect models derived from recent contexts to early Christianity is the extent to which the chronological reversal involved leads to a certain circularity. Thus Holmberg comments that

> All later millenarian movements have been influenced by Judaeo-Christian apocalyptic... [One should therefore note] the amount of circular reasoning specifically inherent in the attempt to explain the strongly apocalyptic early Christianity with the help of a set of characteristics, i.e., a model, found in strongly apocalyptic movements, which all stand under the influence of the Judaeo-Christian heritage.[48]

Similarly, he points out that later Christian sectarian movements are to a degree imitative of early Christianity.[49]

Modern sociological models may perhaps 'fit' the New Testament evidence, but we must be aware of the particular way in which they *shape* this evidence. The use of such models may not be the most appropriate way to attempt a sociology of early Christianity. This is not to suggest that our approach should be naïvely empirical. Rather it is to suggest

---

[44] Cf. Craffert 1992 esp. 235–36.
[45] Esler 1987, 15.
[46] Smith 1978, 127. See also the discussion in Holmberg 1990, 78–81.
[47] Smith 1978, 127–28.
[48] Holmberg 1990, 86. For a critical discussion of the use of 'sect' models, see Barton 1993.
[49] Holmberg 1990, 109–10.

that a self-conscious choice of questions and priorities, and a theoretical framework, carefully elaborated, may further our understanding of the New Testament more than a particular 'model' based upon a very different cultural context. What the use of sociological and anthropological models from whatever cultural context has offered, however, is alternative perspectives from which to view texts which have all too often been interpreted in the light of sub-consciously theological and ecclesiastical commitments. A major concern of social-scientific study of the New Testament has been to avoid and to correct 'ethnocentric' readings.[50] Nevertheless, these new perspectives must themselves be critically assessed.

A final but important reason for caution over the use of models arises from the extent to which they are often allied to an approach to sociology based primarily upon that of natural science.[51] Aspects of this approach include the use of models for comparison, prediction and control,[52] the testing of hypotheses in 'experimental' manner, the search for 'laws', or at least for generalisations, and for causal explanations. *A model-based approach often reflects a specific and debatable form of social science,* one which is cast within a strongly 'scientific' frame. Gregory, for example, notes some human geographers' critique of, and reaction against, model-building and its theoretical and philosophical framework.[53] Of course the relation between natural and social science continues to be a matter of debate and there are those who propose to retain a much more 'scientific' conception of sociology, a conception which certainly goes back to Auguste Comte and the origins of sociology as a science of society.[54] However, for reasons which will become clear in the following sections, it is not a conception I can share.

In summary: models, correctly understood, are not an ubiquitous feature of sociological analysis, although they may sometimes be valid and useful tools. Models are the result of empirical study and not its precur-

---

[50] See esp. Malina 1981; Elliott 1993, 9–59; and cf. the concern of Nineham 1976, 1–39; 1982.

[51] Some of the work cited in connection with the use of models is primarily concerned with natural science or with the relation between natural science and theology; e.g. Barbour and Kuhn, cited by Elliott 1986, 4 and Fiorenza 1979, 412 n. 6. Esler tends to favour the 'scientific' approach to sociology; 1987, 6–9.

[52] Malina 1982, 231.

[53] Gregory 1986, 302.

[54] See §1.3. and §1.4. below, and esp. Ryan 1981.

sor, though once models have been developed their main use is to facilate further research and comparative investigation. It is questionable, however, whether a model-based approach is necessarily the most apposite method of sociological study and whether the models used should be drawn from distant cultural contexts. Certainly the application of a model derived from a modern social context is not the *only* way to approach the New Testament sociologically. Indeed, it is a method which has serious weaknesses. Moreover, we should recognise that the use of 'models' often reflects a (perhaps unintentional) commitment to a specific form of social science, one which is open to significant criticisms. Some confusion arises from terminological imprecision. New Testament scholars apply the term 'model' to a wide range of approaches not known as models in the sociological literature, where the term is used in a more restricted and specific sense. In my opinion the framework with which an investigation is approached should in most cases be termed a theoretical or research framework. Theoretical frameworks should not be incorrectly labelled models. Nevertheless it is true that every researcher approaches the subject from a particular (theoretical) perspective which should be clarified and made explicit. My criticisms of a model-based approach to the New Testament should not be taken as a plea for a merely empirical method which claims to stick only to the facts and to be innocent of theoretical presupposition.[55] However, I have argued that it is an explicit exploration and clarification of theory that is needed rather than the adoption of a model. In this work I therefore propose to outline carefully a theoretical basis and a research framework derived from it. I shall not use specific models, as understood above, nor will my approach be comparative (see further §1.4. below). I maintain that my work does not thereby forfeit the right to the label 'sociological'.

1.3. Determinism and causal explanation

It is often asserted that sociology proper, contrasted with 'social history', 'proto-sociological' or descriptive approaches, is concerned with 'explanation'.[56] This is probably one of the main reasons why 'reductionism' is

---

[55] Cf. the comments of Garrett 1992, 92.
[56] Gager 1979, 175, 179; Elliott 1981, 3; Best 1983, 185; Richter 1984, 78; Holmberg 1990, 4; Domeris 1991, 217, 219.

so often discussed when social science enters the domain of New Testament 'theology'.[57] Social science, it would seem, aims to explain human behaviour on the basis of social causes and thus compromises theological claims and any doctrine of human 'free will'.[58] I do not intend to challenge the idea that we should be interested in 'explanation', but rather to suggest that the term may carry either a 'weak' or a 'strong' (more deterministic) implication. Explanation also inevitably involves theoretical decisions as to what is of fundamental or basic influence, and here there may be grounds for conflict between sociology and theology.[59] Social-scientific research, particularly when cast within a strongly 'scientific' frame, may tend towards the stronger conception of explanation, or causality. Malina, for example, confirms this assumption:

> It should be quite clear, [he asserts], that the social sciences are indeed deterministic, but only in the sense that they are sets of models that seek out the 'that,' 'how,' and 'why' of meanings imposed on human beings... *From the social science point of view, human beings are socially determined.* Yet unless used reductionistically, the social sciences do not preclude other avenues of approach to our data set.[60]

Malina suggests, as do other New Testament sociologists, that a social-science model or theory explains human behaviour with reference to social causes or determinants.[61] Reductionism, according to Malina, would be a legitimate criticism only if the possibility of other perspectives or approaches were denied. However, a deterministic view of human behaviour is in no way an ubiquitous feature of social science; indeed, the determinism of *some* forms of social theory is precisely one of the inadequacies which modern attempts to reformulate such theory are seeking to overcome.

---

[57] Malina 1982, 237–38; Meeks 1983, 2–4; Esler 1987, 12–13; Holmberg 1990, 149–50; cf. Theissen 1979b, 58–60; 1983, 318.

[58] Cf. Esler 1987, 6.

[59] See Milbank 1990, 4, 101–43, 249 etc.

[60] Malina 1982, 238, my italics.

[61] Gager 1982, 263, misrepresents the sociology of knowledge as being based on the premise that 'beliefs and actions are determined by social circumstances'. This is not an accurate appraisal of Berger and Luckmann's work, to which Gager refers (263 n. 29). Berger and Luckmann regard 'knowledge' and beliefs as social constructions, *human products*, but this is not the same as saying that they are socially *determined; contra* Gill 1977, 22, 24; 1987, 148. For more accurate assessments see Berger 1977, 126; Scroggs 1980, 175–76; also Horrell 1993, 87–89.

Even within the contemporary natural sciences there is debate as to how the notion of 'cause' should be understood. A strict notion of deterministic causality leads to a view in which everything becomes a tautologous 'working out' of what was already 'contained within', and thus was inevitable from, the beginning.[62] Scientists seem to be recognising a degree of openness, or *indeterminacy*, within even the fundamental processes of the physical world (a recognition which has resulted in renewed theological reflection upon the nature of God's interaction with the world).[63]

In the social and human sciences the notion of cause is even more problematic, given that their subject is human beings. Certainly the social sciences have been influenced by strongly deterministic schools of thought, emanating both from the Comtean origins of sociology as a latecomer on to the scientific scene and from structuralist theoretical traditions.[64] However, we do not need to resort to theological apologetic in order to criticise this conception of social science; an increasingly important voice within these sciences themselves is asserting the need to overcome the inadequacies of determinism and a concern for 'human agency'.[65] This emphasis has long been rooted in sociology, at least since Max Weber set out to oppose Karl Marx by exorcising 'the spectre of collective conceptions' from the discipline.[66] Modern developments in social theory are sensitive to criticisms of Weber's voluntarism, subjectivism and individualism, but seek just as strongly to reject the opposite tendency: 'an objectivist type of social theory, in which human agency appears only as the determined outcome of social causes'.[67] They reject determinism of cultural, social, structural, economic or geographical derivation and insist that people are capable and knowledgeable agents who actually *act*; who make real choices and decisions within the constraints and opportunities they encounter.[68] Human action cannot be

---

[62] Polkinghorne 1989, 1–2; Barbour 1990, 95–104, 172–76; Milbank 1990, 83.

[63] See further Polkinghorne 1989; Barbour 1990.

[64] See Giddens 1977, 9–10, 29ff; 1979, 50–52, 155–60, 234–59; 1982a, 29–30, 68ff (on Comte); 1984, 207–21, 227–28; also Ryan 1981.

[65] See Giddens 1979, 2; 1982a, 8; 1982b, 10–12; Bryant and Jary 1991, 22; Archer 1990, 73–74. Note similar developments, for example, in human geography; see Gregory 1981, esp. 1–5.

[66] Cited in Eldridge 1971, 25, on Weber's 'methodological individualism'.

[67] Giddens 1982a, 8; cf. 1979, 49–53; 1982a, 28–30; 1984, 217–20.

[68] See Giddens 1976, 160; 1979, 5, 253–57. However, the possibility of physical laws limiting human action is certainly recognised; Giddens 1979, 244.

understood without some appreciation of the awareness and intentions of the actors themselves. 'What people do depends on what they know and what they want; these vary unpredictably'.[69] 'One thing is clear:', Giddens asserts, *deterministic views of human agency, which explain human action as the result of social causes, are to be rejected*'.[70] Such views, Giddens insists, are untrue to our experience of what it is to be human, and amount to 'a derogation of the lay actor'.[71] Human beings are not 'cultural dopes'.[72]

A concern for 'human agency' within the social sciences is of course of significance for theology, just as recent developments in natural science have been. Although the development is by no means completely unopposed, my own conviction, primarily on sociological grounds, is that a degree of emphasis upon the (limited) capability of human beings to 'act' (that is, to function as agents in the world) is of fundamental importance and validity, in opposition to any view of them as merely obedient to structural dictates and social determinants. As Marx once commented, 'people make their own history, but not in circumstances of their own choosing'.[73] The aim of a 'sociological' investigation, as I see it, is not to 'explain' human behaviour on the basis of social determinants, but to consider the context and conditions within which human action takes place, the knowledge and intentions of the actors themselves, and the consequences of their action.[74] This is still a form of 'explanation' but one which avoids the imperialism of determinism.

This contemporary approach to social science thus calls into question the frequent distinction drawn by New Testament scholars between social history or social description and sociology 'proper'.[75] If we should

[69] Ryan 1981, 30; cf. 20–25, 28–33.
[70] Giddens 1982a, 15 (my italics); cf. 1979, 253: 'In the cruder versions or applications of naturalism in sociology, conduct is explained merely as the outcome of social causes.'
[71] Giddens 1979, 71; 1982a, 38; 1984, 217. Cf. also Giddens 1987, 3.
[72] A phrase of Garfinkel's, quoted by Giddens 1979, 52 and 1982a, 30, 199.
[73] Cited by Giddens 1984, xxi and Cohen 1987, 273.
[74] This is linked with the question as to whether explanation is 'contextual' or whether sociological study aims to explain human behaviour on the basis of generalisations or laws which apply across time and space; on which see the following section. It is also important to note that the non-deterministic formulation above, unlike some forms of interpretative sociology, does *not* imply that the context and conditions can be reduced to those of which the actor is aware, or the consequences to those which are intended: cf. Giddens 1976, 160; 1982a, 28–29.
[75] See n. 56 above and Osiek 1984, 4–5; Tuckett 1987, 139, (though note his caution on 148 n. 8); Malina 1979, 178.

21

reject both the possibility of 'theory-free description', and the validity of deterministic explanation, then any distinction between 'descriptive' and 'explanatory' studies will unavoidably be blurred. Indeed John Milbank's critique of causation suggests that all 'explanation' is a form of redescription or renarration in terms of the factors which are deemed to be most significant.[76] If sociology does not *necessarily* imply either the use of models or the search for social determinants, then descriptive social studies (although never of course without at least an implicit theoretical framework) may certainly warrant the label 'sociological'. Contemporary practitioners of sociology engage in descriptive, investigative and empirical studies which never forfeit their right to be called 'sociology'.[77] However, the challenge to clarify one's approach applies equally to all such study.

1.4. Sociology and the 'typical'

Another assertion frequently found in presentations of sociology by New Testament scholars is that, in contrast to history, sociology is concerned with the 'typical': 'The main differences between history and sociology are that history attends to the individual and particular, sociology to what is general or typical.'[78] This characterisation stems from two main assumptions about the nature of sociology. One is that sociology is intrinsically committed to a 'comparative' approach which therefore implies that the 'commonalities' between various situations will be sought.[79] The second is that sociology is a science whose purpose, ideally, is to formulate laws of human behaviour. Although there is widespread recognition that such 'laws' may be difficult or impossible to discern, it is still considered the aim of sociological investigation to seek 'generalisations' which apply across different arenas of human interaction.[80] Holmberg, for example, states that 'sociological analysis proper

---

[76] Milbank 1990, 83.
[77] See for example Giddens 1989a, 657–89; Haney et al. 1973; Marsh 1978.
[78] Morgan with Barton 1988, 139, also 140. Cf. Malina 1982, 238; Holmberg 1990, 9, 10, 155; Theissen 1978, 4; 1979b, 16, 272 (=1982, 121); Elliott 1981, 9.
[79] Malina 1982, 238; Scroggs 1980, 167–68; Esler 1987, 9–12.
[80] Cf. Stowers 1985, 150, who is critical of the idea that any such generalisations could be applied across ancient and modern contexts: see also 169–70, and Garrett 1992, 92–93, on the problem of incommensurability.

begins only when we proceed from the description of the interaction to a classification of its type and a subsuming of its genesis under the general laws of social behaviour'.[81]

However, once more, these assumptions may be challenged; again, from a sociological perspective rather than a theological one. The first assumption is somewhat misleading on two counts. First, because not all sociology adopts a comparative approach. Whilst comparative studies are certainly frequent and important, many sociological studies investigate one particular study area, albeit with the use of broader theoretical categories, without comparative models or studies.[82] Second, because the equation of 'comparative' with the search for the 'typical' does not necessarily follow: comparative study can equally aim to illuminate the *distinctiveness* of each particular socio-historical context.[83] Indeed, Giddens asserts that one of sociology's major responsibilities is to consider the uniqueness of the modern age, and the unique challenges which modernity poses: 'We live today in a world system that has no parallel in previous ages.'[84]

The second assumption certainly has a long sociological pedigree, emanating from the discipline's origin as a 'science of society'. Although a latecomer onto the scientific scene, it was hoped that sociology could discover the laws of human social behaviour in the same way that natural science had apparently discovered laws of the physical world.[85] This aim, it should be noted, cannot be viewed as solely an 'academic' one. On the contrary, as with the physical sciences, it included prediction and control (as Malina, interestingly, summarises the purpose of models).[86] The physical sciences sought mastery over nature, whereas sociology sought control over society. This is clearly formulated in Comte's famous phrase, *savoir pour prévoir, prévoir pour pouvoir*, generally translated, 'to know in order to predict, to predict in order to control'.[87]

---

[81] Holmberg 1980, 197. Note however his more recent caution; 1990, 12–13, 116.
[82] E.g. Haney et al. 1973; Marsh 1978; cf. also §1.2. above.
[83] Cf. Holmberg 1990, 114.
[84] Giddens 1982b, 16; cf. 9, 13–22.
[85] See Giddens 1977, 9, 29ff; 1979, 237–38, 240–42; Ryan 1981, 9–13.
[86] Malina 1982, 231.
[87] See Giddens, 1977, 32; 1982b, 10; also Giddens 1982a, 71–72; Ryan 1981, 10, 13–14. MacIntyre 1981, 84–102, explores and criticises the aim of social science to predict and control, maintaining that 'systematic unpredictability' in human action renders such prediction and control, based upon 'law-like generalizations', impossible.

This sociological tradition is assessed in various ways today. There are those, notably Jonathan Turner, who continue to insist that sociology's aim should be to seek the causes of human behaviour and to express these in 'laws and precise models'.[88] (Note the explicit conjunction of laws and models within a particular conception of social science.) However, such views are shared, according to Hans Joas, 'with but few of his contemporaries'.[89]

Some reject such a view primarily because it seems unattainable and unrealistic. It is 'too difficult' a task to expect success but remains something of a broad aim: laws may not be discernible, but typical and general patterns of behaviour can be discovered. The term 'generalisation' reflects the awareness that our findings cannot (yet) warrant the status of 'law'.[90]

However, other sociologists question the search for law-like generalisations much more decisively. Giddens, for example, rejects both the idea that sociology should be modelled on the natural sciences and any conception of sociology as merely a latecomer on to the scientific scene or a poor relative of these sciences.[91] Its conception of laws is therefore logically and profoundly different. Any 'laws' in social science 'are *historical* in character and in principle *mutable* in form'.[92] This means that even regularised and typical forms of social conduct may be transformed and replaced through human action.[93] Human subjects possess limited knowledgeability and capability on the basis of which they act. New knowledge and awareness may enable those subjects to 'monitor' their behaviour differently, and so to alter it. Social-scientific findings, even 'laws', can be taken up and interpreted by human subjects, whose social behaviour may thus be reshaped.[94] In a later work Giddens therefore concludes that 'it is preferable not to use the term [law] in social

---

[88] Turner 1990, 113; also 1987, 156–94, esp. 156–61.
[89] Joas 1990, 112; cf. Giddens and Turner 1987, 7; Turner 1987, 191.
[90] See Esler 1987, 6; note the comments of Stowers 1985, 150.
[91] Giddens 1979, 240–42. See also the discussion by Ryan 1981, 9–13, 20ff. MacIntyre 1981, 89–95, argues that four areas of 'systematic unpredictability' prevent the formulation of law-like generalisations.
[92] Giddens, 1979, 243, 244; also 1982a, 15; 1984, 343–47.
[93] Cf. Giddens 1979, 243–45.
[94] See Giddens 1979, 242–45; 1982a, 13–14; 1984, xxxv, 341–54. This is one of the consequences of what Giddens terms the 'double hermeneutic'; see further 1976, 162; 1982a, 7–8, 11–14; 1984, 374.

science',[95] since human action is always contingent and changeable according to the capability and knowledgeability of the agents. '*Explanation*', he maintains, '*is contextual*', and 'most "why?" questions do not need a generalization to answer them'.[96] Indeed, Nigel Thrift suggests that the 'nub' of Giddens' argument is that 'social theory must become more *contextual*'.[97] Deterministic and nomological forms of social science, on the other hand, portray human agents as subject to social causes and laws. They therefore depreciate the possibilities of human action and minimise its transformative potential. Politically they disempower human subjects, whose behaviour is presented as determined, and for whom acquiescence in the status quo therefore appears the only option. Such an approach fails adequately to theorise human agency. (There is perhaps some irony in the fact that the concern for human agency, surely an issue of some theological relevance, has been prominent in social-scientific debates but not in sociological approaches to the New Testament.)

These issues are not irrelevant to historical study, even though the subjects of such study are, of course, unable to reinterpret or change their behaviour in the light of the findings of research.[98] An approach which assumes that first-century behaviour was determined by sociological laws must presumably assess contemporary action in the same way. Historical studies are important not least because they help us to understand and to reinterpret ourselves. When the object of study is one of such profound and enduring influence as Christianity, then our theoretical conceptualisations of it are of even greater significance.

Social scientists themselves, then, argue that a 'sociological' approach must take due account of the specificity inherent in each particular context. Many of them would reject the idea that sociology should seek to formulate law-like generalisations explaining human behaviour. Many New Testament scholars would agree that the specificity of any historical situation must be respected, even when 'sociological' perspectives are employed, but sometimes see this in terms of a contrast between the historian's interest in particularity and the sociologist's search for 'gen-

[95] Giddens 1984, 347.
[96] Giddens 1984, xviii–xix, my italics.
[97] Thrift 1985, 610.
[98] Cf. Giddens 1984, 341.

eral laws of human behaviour'.[99] In this section we have seen that it is invalid to maintain such a contrast between the concerns of historians and sociologists: many social theorists, for theoretical reasons, reject the idea of sociological laws and insist on the importance of *contextual* understanding.

1.5. Sociology and history: same difference?

The critical discussions above lead almost inevitably to the question concerning the difference between sociology and history. Already I have questioned any distinctions drawn on the basis of sociology's supposed commitment to scientific models, general laws and causal explanations, in contrast with history's supposed concentration upon particularity, detail, and descriptive narration.[100] While such contrasts may have some basis in what has actually been the case, they cannot provide a legitimate distinction between sociology and history.

It may be accurate, for example, to draw some contrast between the theoretical constructions of the sociologists and the descriptive details of the historians. Among early social theorists, Herbert Spencer, for example, 'declared that sociology stood to history "much as a vast building stands related to the heaps of stones and bricks around it"'.[101] However, any distinction between a 'theoretical' discipline and a supposedly 'untheoretical', descriptive one cannot stand as legitimate, not least because of the impossibility of 'detached', purely objective, theory-free description: 'all data are theory-laden'.[102] It is increasingly accepted that the presuppositions and perspective of the historian shape both the form of the inquiry and the interpretation of the evidence. There can never be simply a collection of the facts, for interpretative decisions are always involved when deciding which questions are worth asking, and which

---

[99] Meeks 1982a, 266 (cf. 1983, 1–7 esp. 5–6), who describes himself therefore as a (social) historian. Cf. Ste. Croix 1981, 34.

[100] For such characterisations see Malina 1985, 346; Morgan with Barton 1988, 139–40; cf. also Jones 1976, 295. See also the list of contrasts between historical and social-scientific research in Elliott 1993, 107–109.

[101] Burke 1980, 19, with the quotation from Spencer.

[102] Barbour 1990, 33.

facts are significant.[103] Moreover, our assumptions, methods and perspectives derive from particular conventions and paradigms even though they may be unacknowledged.[104] Certainly 'theoretical' perspectives can be ill-formed and implicit, but if their ubiquity is acknowledged then scholars are increasingly obliged to elucidate and justify them. Once these points are conceded then history can no longer be viewed as a discipline concerned merely with the collection and descriptive presentation of facts. Thus Gareth Stedman Jones, for example, argues that history must become a self-consciously theoretical discipline, rejecting the notion that it could remain theoretically vacuous.[105]

In a recently published thesis Andrew Clarke argues against the use of Weberian social theory by New Testament scholars. He includes a lengthy quotation from Clifford Geertz in support of his rejection of such theory in favour of 'the proto-sociological work of historical description'.[106] Clarke maintains that: 'The theoretical advantages of one sociological method over another have long been argued. The value of adding to the discussion here is limited. Instead, in this study descriptive-historical work will be undertaken.'[107] While Geertz is certainly complaining about an apparent dependence on the 'classics' of social theory in anthropological research, he cannot justifiably be cited in support of an approach which eschews the use of theory altogether. Indeed, what Geertz highlights is the need for ongoing creative theoretical work which will continue to invigorate and inform social-scientific research. The passage quoted in part by Clarke includes the following observations (with my emphases):

> Two characteristics of anthropological work on religion accomplished since the second world war strike me as curious... One is that it has made *no theoretical advances of major importance*. It is living off the conceptual capital of its ancestors, adding very little, *save a little empirical enrichment*, to it. The second is that it draws what concepts

---

[103] See Ste. Croix 1981, 81–82; Judge 1960a, 49; Meyer 1979, 14; Caird 1980, 203: 'Sources are only sources in virtue of the questions which the historian addresses to them, and he to some extent creates his own past by his choice of questions.'

[104] Cf. Kuhn 1970.

[105] Jones 1976, 295–96, 304. Jones is arguing for the adoption of Marxian and not sociological theory, although he is not in principle against a close relationship between the two disciplines; 296, 304; cf. Abrams 1980, 4; 1982, x, 300.

[106] Clarke 1993, 5; see 3–6; quotation from Geertz 1966, 1–2.

[107] Clarke 1993, 6.

it does use from a very narrowly defined intellectual tradition. There is Durkheim, Weber, Freud, or Malinowski,...[108]

In the passage which follows that quoted by Clarke, Geertz argues that the way forward is 'not to abandon the established traditions of social anthropology in this field, but to widen them... they are starting-points only. To move beyond them we must place them in a much broader context of contemporary thought than they, in and of themselves, encompass'.[109] That is one of the reasons for the extensive discussion of theory in this study and for the focus upon one of the foremost *contemporary* social theorists. Any attempt, whether it is labelled 'history' or 'sociology', to concentrate upon 'the facts' and to avoid discussion of theory is likely to be an approach which merely conceals its own presuppositions and commitments.

Another distinction between history and sociology which has some basis in the actual practice of the two disciplines is that history's approach is diachronic whereas sociology's is synchronic. Thus Robert Morgan suggests that 'whereas history describes (and occasionally explains) the past in terms of its extension and change through time (diachrony), sociology looks at societies as systems or structures frozen at a particular moment (synchrony)'.[110] Yet once more, as a legitimate distinction between the two this must be questioned. Certainly there are sociological approaches which may rightly be called synchronic, most notably functionalism, but the validity of such an approach has been challenged by social scientists. Their assertion is that *time* is so fundamental to all social interaction that any adequate analysis cannot 'bracket' it out. Philip Abrams, for example, insists that any understanding of 'the process of social structuring' must 'conceive of that process chronologically; at the end of the debate the diachrony-synchrony distinction is absurd'.[111] Giddens likewise argues that time (and space) must be incorporated into the heart of social theory, and that this 'involves breaking with the synchrony/diachrony' division.[112] For Abrams and Giddens, a

---

[108] Geertz 1966, 1.
[109] Geertz 1966, 2.
[110] Morgan with Barton 1988, 139–40; cf. Scroggs 1980, 168. Note Malina 1981, 19, who makes it clear that this approach is essentially that of 'structural-functionalism'.
[111] Abrams 1982, x, cited by Holmberg 1990, 9. Cf. Abrams 1980, 5, 14; 1982, xvi–xviii; Giddens 1979, 7–8; 1981, 17; 1984, 355.
[112] Giddens 1979, 198ff; cf. also 53ff; 1984, esp. 110ff.

synchrony-diachrony division, whilst characteristic of some forms of social science, is a weakness, a decisive error in social theory, which must be overcome and not assumed as a perennial distinction between sociology and history.

This question, then, looms large: if we cannot legitimately continue to contrast sociology's concern with the typical, the synchronic, and the 'grand' scale of structure and theory, with history's focus upon the unique, the detailed, and an untheoretical concern with diachronic narration, then what does distinguish the two disciplines? An influential body of both historians and sociologists agree on an answer: nothing. 'There simply are no logical or even methodological distinctions between the social sciences and history – appropriately conceived.'[113] Indeed, if we look back to the great figures of Weber and Marx, for example, who could categorise them as *either* historians *or* sociologists?[114] For various reasons the disciplines did become increasingly separate, yet the legitimacy of continued separation may be questioned:

> What some of us would like to see, what we are beginning to see, is a social history, or historical sociology – *the distinction should become irrelevant* – which would be concerned both with understanding from within and explaining from without; with the general and with the particular; and which would combine the sociologist's acute sense of structure with the historian's equally sharp sense of change.[115]

Abrams insists that all socio-historical analysis must be 'an analysis of structuring situated in process in time... once that is conceded the separation of history from sociology ceases to have meaning'.[116]

There seem to be only two justifiable reasons for continuing disciplinary separation, both of which are to an extent pragmatic. Firstly, Giddens argues that sociology's concern is with modern industrialised societies: its particular *raison d'être* and its contemporary responsibility are to analyse and respond to the conditions and challenges of 'modernity'. Anthropology's focus is upon contemporary non-industrialised societies,

---

[113] Giddens 1979, 230; cf. 1984, 355ff; Burke 1980, 30; Abrams 1982, x–xi, xviii, 17, 200–201 etc, Milbank 1990, 80. See also Holmberg 1990, 8–9, although Holmberg does not pursue the implications of the argument; indeed, almost immediately he reiterates sociology's concern with the typical (9–10).

[114] Cf. Burke 1980, 20; Skocpol 1984, 1–2.

[115] Burke 1980, 30, my italics; see further 21–30.

[116] Abrams 1982, xviii; see further x–xviii, 3, 8, 16–17, and Abrams 1980.

whereas history's concern is with the past.[117] While even these boundaries of subject area are unavoidably imprecise and inadequate, Giddens' main point is that there should be no *methodological* differences between the disciplines.[118] He believes 'social theory' to be a theoretical discipline relevant to a range of disciplines including the three mentioned above.[119]

Secondly, Peter Burke, in a review of Abrams' *Historical Sociology*, suggests that the practical reality of separate faculties, methods of training, terminology and so on, may continue to keep the disciplines apart, at least to some extent.[120] However, this restriction does not, or need not, apply to those who work in the area of biblical studies and seek to develop the most appropriate and adequate methodologies for their task.[121] Thus, I argue, we should abandon the unsustainable attempt to distinguish and separate historical and sociological research. Such a division is both intellectually untenable and practically unhelpful. The value of 'sociological' approaches, I suggest, is not to stand as an alternative, but rather to challenge, to broaden and to reformulate the methods of historical criticism. (Scroggs' criticism of 'methodological docetism' would be equally relevant as a call for better *history*, which should also keep 'body and soul' together!)[122] For example, recent work seeking to understand Paul's view of the law in its historical context also employs 'sociological' concepts such as group boundaries and membership markers, and focuses upon the 'social functions' which the law performs.[123] There would be no value in an attempt to distinguish the 'historical' from the 'sociological' in such approaches or to insist that the two should somehow be kept separate. Certainly sociological resources offer new perspectives, emphases and terminology, some of which reflect the sociological tendency to categorise and generalise in a manner which facilitates comparison: analysing circumcision, for example, in terms of its function as a marker of group membership is clearly to place it into a wider category into which many other specific forms of social practice

---

[117] See Giddens 1982b, 9–10; 1984, xvii; 1991, 207; Held and Thompson 1989, 1, 10–11.

[118] Giddens 1979, 230. He makes the same point about human geography; 1984, 368.

[119] Giddens 1982a, 5–6; cf. 1989b, 295. On the unity of history, sociology and anthropology, cf. Burke 1985, 907 and Giddens 1987, 23, 37–41.

[120] Burke 1985, 907–908.

[121] Cf. Craffert 1991, 140, who argues against an opposition between historical and sociological approaches and for an interdisciplinary approach in New Testament studies.

[122] Scroggs 1980, 165–66; quoted above, p. 2.

[123] E.g. Dunn 1990a, 215–41.

could be placed.[124] However, all historians need to use concepts and terms other than those intrinsic or native to a particular practice or culture if they are to analyse or interpret in an interesting and enlightening way, and indeed, if they are to make a foreign context intelligible to their readers.[125] To speak of power, or conflict, or exploitation, or protest, is to move to a macro-level of analysis which uses terms and concepts which could be utilised in other contexts too. The 'opening up' of historical criticism to the methods and perspectives of sociology offers the opportunity for it to be substantially broadened and reorientated, and thus for new interpretations of biblical texts to be offered. The resources which the social sciences offer should be seen as complementary rather than alternative to historical investigation.[126] I therefore suggest that such research should most appropriately be termed 'socio-historical', a term which indicates both a continuity with the discipline of history and the additional breadth of 'sociological' perspectives.[127]

1.6. Conclusion

The discussions of this chapter have been more critical than constructive. They have attempted to question some of the ways in which a 'sociological' approach is often characterised and to show that no legitimate distinction can be drawn between sociological and historical methods. This does not mean, however, that sociological resources have nothing to offer. On the contrary, as I suggested above, they bring new questions, issues and theoretical perspectives to the agenda of historical research.

Any historical or exegetical study is inevitably guided by the approach which is taken and the questions which are asked. Therefore a responsi-

---

[124] I am grateful to John Barclay for this point.
[125] Anthropologists refer to 'emic' and 'etic' terms, those 'internal' and 'external' to a culture, respectively, both of which are necessary in critical analysis.
[126] Cf. Garrett 1992, 90; Esler 1994, 2: 'The social sciences are best seen as a necessary adjunct to established forms of criticism. In dealing with the past they must inevitably collaborate with history.' He then refers, however, to history's focus on 'the novel, the unique and the particular'. I would prefer to speak of the amalgamation of sociology's and history's theoretical and conceptual resources, in recognition of the fact that there are no justifiable methodological distinctions to be made or sustained.
[127] Cf. MacDonald 1988, 23; whose subtitle describes her work as 'a socio-historical study'.

ble and critical choice of questions and approach is infinitely preferable to one in which such crucial decisions remain implicit and unexplored. In this chapter I have sought to clarify what I understand by a 'sociological' – or rather, in view of the above, a 'socio-historical' – approach and my reasons for conceiving of this in a particular way. After the critical discussions of this chapter, the next chapter seeks in a more positive way to make my approach and priorities clear. Its purpose is to draw upon some of the theoretical resources which the social sciences offer, including Giddens' structuration theory, in order to establish a framework for the exegetical studies which follow.

2

Theoretical resources

2.1. Introduction

A comprehensive review of the range of theoretical resources which the social sciences offer would obviously be impossible in the space available here. I therefore focus upon just two theoretical traditions which have been influential in sociological studies of the New Testament and which are significant in forming my own approach, and upon Giddens' work, which is as yet relatively unknown in biblical studies. I recognise that this leaves many avenues unexplored, for example, the methods specifically associated with cultural anthropology,[1] but the purpose of this (and the previous) chapter is not to offer a comprehensive survey but to develop and justify the particular approach taken in this study. The two theoretical traditions explored below – functionalism and Berger and Luckmann's sociology of knowledge approach – I suggest, offer important emphases yet are also open to significant criticisms. While drawing upon Giddens' work, I hope to retain some of their valuable perspectives but to avoid their apparent weaknesses.

2.2. Functionalism

Functionalism, in various forms, has been one of the most dominant forms of sociological theory in the twentieth century.[2] An important influence upon its development was Émile Durkheim, although more

---

[1] Used in New Testament studies, for example, by Malina 1981; 1986; Barton 1986; Neyrey 1986; Atkins 1991. The work of the anthropologist Mary Douglas has been particularly influential.

[2] Cf. Abrahamson 1978, 7; Alexander 1987, 40; Giddens 1982a, 2–3.

complex neo-functionalist formulations have been proposed by later theorists such as Talcott Parsons and Robert Merton.[3]

It is probably the biological analogies which provide the clearest way of understanding functionalism in sociological theory.[4] Indeed, Giddens states that 'the origins of functionalism, in its modern form, are bound up with the advances made within biology in the nineteenth century'.[5] Social entities (society, sectarian group, etc.) are viewed as some kind of system in which various aspects of social activity perform functionary roles in maintaining the whole.[6] Thus, A. R. Radcliffe-Brown stated that 'the function of any recurrent activity is the part it plays in the social life as a whole'.[7] A functionalist approach, then, analyses aspects of social activity in terms of what they *do*, in other words, what their function is. This mode of explanation is common, of course, in the kind of biology from which functionalism was derived: to take a simple example, the parental response to the inquisitive child's question 'why have I got a heart?' will probably be something like 'to pump the blood around your body'. Viewing the body as a functioning system, the heart's presence is explained in terms of what it does; the function it performs in the maintenance of the whole. A focus upon the 'needs' of the 'system' is therefore often characteristic of functionalist methodology;[8] an aspect of social activity will be considered in terms of what need it meets, what 'function' it fulfils.[9] Thus the task for a functionalist investigation of religious practice and belief is to ask of each component, 'what is its social function?', or 'what need does it fulfil?'.

Given the dominance of functionalism in sociological theory we would expect to discover its influence upon sociological studies of the New Testament. Indeed, two of the foremost exponents of a broadly sociological approach, Meeks and Theissen, explicitly employ a functionalist perspective.

Meeks does not devote much space to an elaboration of his theoretical perspectives (hence the criticisms of reviewers such as Elliott and Malina)[10]

---

[3] See Abrahamson 1978; Turner 1974, 15–76; Riis 1988, 164–74.
[4] Cf. Turner 1990, 103–105.
[5] Giddens 1977, 96.
[6] Cf. Stowers 1985, 152; Horsley 1989, 27.
[7] Cited by Lyon 1975, 39 and Riis 1988, 166.
[8] Giddens 1981, 16–19; Turner 1990, 105–107; Gregory 1986, 165–67.
[9] Cf. Theissen's summary of functionalist theory; 1979b, 60–62; Horsley 1989, 37, 149.
[10] Elliott 1985, 332–34; Malina 1985, 347.

but declares his approach to be that of a 'moderate functionalist', referring in a note to the work of Ernest Gellner.[11] Thus, 'the sort of questions to be asked about the early Christian movement are those about how it worked. The comprehensive question concerning the texts that are our primary sources is not merely what each one says, but what it does.'[12]

Theissen devotes considerably more space to theoretical and methodological discussion, believing that methodological reflections form an important part of the task of establishing the validity of sociological approaches to the New Testament.[13] While Theissen draws upon a number of theoretical perspectives,[14] the functionalist approach is prominent, particularly in his theoretical essay of 1974(a). He suggests that a functionalist approach can combine aspects of phenomenological and 'reductionalist' theories of religion and also avoid the problems of a reductionism which claims to 'explain' religious phenomena on the basis of social factors.[15] This, according to Theissen, is because it does not focus upon the essence, truth or 'cause' of religious phenomena, but rather upon the impact, or effect of these phenomena upon society:[16] 'Approaches inspired by Marxism ask about the influence of society upon religion; functionalist approaches investigate rather the influence of religion upon society.'[17]

The influence of functionalism may also be found in other New Testament studies; explicitly, for example, in Robert Atkins' recent book, which draws upon Merton's work (without noting or responding to the criticisms of functionalism),[18] and implicitly, I would suggest, in Francis

---

[11] Meeks 1983, 7, 198 n. 15; Gellner 1962.
[12] Meeks 1983, 7.
[13] Theissen 1979b, 9; see 1–76. It is thus unfair, I consider, to criticise Theissen's 1978 *The First Followers of Jesus* for its lack of explicit theoretical foundation when this intentionally 'popular' book depends upon the theoretical perspectives outlined in Theissen's earlier theoretical essays (1974a; 1975a). For criticism of Theissen see Elliott 1986, 11; Horsley 1989, 9–10. Horsley's critique of Theissen (see 15–64, 147–70), while often valuable and perceptive, takes very little account of Theissen's (then untranslated) theoretical essays (esp. 1974a (ET now Theissen 1993, 231–54); 1979a), though they are noted (see 27, 29 n. 5, 156, 165 n. 2).
[14] See Theissen 1979b, 23; 1988b (revised version in 1993, 257–87); 1993, 256.
[15] See Theissen 1979b, 57–58, 60; also Riis 1988, 161–64.
[16] Theissen 1979b, 60; cf. Elliott 1986, 23 esp. n. 8.
[17] Theissen 1979b, 30: 'Marxistisch inspirierte Ansätze fragen nach der Einwirkung der Gesellschaft auf die Religion; funktionalistische Ansätze untersuchen eher die Einwirkungen der Religion auf die Gesellschaft.'
[18] Atkins 1991, 39–51.

Watson's analysis of the 'social function' of Pauline theology, viewed as fulfilling a sect's need for 'an ideology legitimating its separation from society'.[19]

However, in the social sciences functionalism has been subjected to sustained critique and is widely regarded as 'outdated'.[20] Indeed, these criticisms have been elaborated by a number of New Testament scholars.[21]

Perhaps the most basic question concerns the status of functionalist 'explanation'. 'The question; is functional analysis causal analysis? is one that has frequently cropped up in the functionalism debate.'[22] Many years ago, for example, Durkheim asserted that the 'causes which give rise to a social fact must ... be identified separately from whatever social functions it may fulfil'.[23] Functionalist approaches often imply that an understanding of 'function' is a sufficient explanation of existence. There are two particular problems here; one is what Turner calls 'illegitimate teleology'.[24] In other words 'the unintended or unanticipated consequences of a form of social conduct cannot be used *a posteriori* to explain its existence in the first place'.[25] The second is that functionalism often relies upon a concept of 'needs' in order to explain the phenomena which arise to fulfil a function; their function is to satisfy certain needs. However, such a formulation of needs is both ontologically fallacious (an error based on the use of an analogy between society and a living organism) and also explains nothing about how and why needs are met in some cases and not others.[26] For example, consider a Marxian statement like: 'the function of racism is to divide the interests of the working

---

[19] Watson 1986, 40; cf. 19–20, 106ff. Watson suggests that the separation from the Jewish community came about for pragmatic and not 'theoretical' reasons; see 28–38. *Contra* Watson, Campbell 1989, 462 is surely right to insist that 'for the apostle theology was as much a *cause* as a *consequence* of the existing social reality'.

[20] See Giddens 1977, 96–134; Turner 1990, 103–14; Riis 1988, 168–69, 172–73, 178; Horsley 1989, 30.

[21] See Elliott 1986, 11–25; Stowers 1985, 172–76; Horsley 1989, esp. 30–42, 147–55; also Riis 1988; Milbank 1990, 110–33. Note Theissen's recent comments in defence of his form of functionalism; 1993, 254–56.

[22] Giddens 1977, 109; see 109–12.

[23] Giddens 1971, 91; see 90–91.

[24] See Turner 1974, 21–27, 52, 72–73; 1990, 106.

[25] Gregory 1986, 166.

[26] See Giddens 1977, 110; 1981, 18; Elliott 1986, 23. Cf. Theissen's comments on the 'basic aims' (*Grundaufgaben*) and 'chief concern' of *society*, 1978, 98; see also 1979b, 61ff; 1988b, 209, 217, and Horsley's critique, 1989, 28, 37, 149.

class'. However much this statement may illuminate some of the *consequences* of racism it certainly does nothing to explain how and why racism arises and continues, a process which must be examined historically;[27] unless, of course, one is satisfied with the explanation that racism exists because it is 'necessary' for the survival of capitalism, an entirely spurious 'explanation'. To speak of the function of a biblical text, in relation to the need for legitimation and so on, may be similarly problematic. Functional terminology seems to suggest that an understanding of function is sufficient explanation of existence. The term 'function' is at least ambiguous. To return to the biological analogy mentioned above, the 'explanation' that 'the heart exists to pump blood around the body' explains the function of the heart, but explains nothing about how the heart as an organ came to evolve, nor why the heart takes the form it does.

The conception of the needs of a social 'organism' also contributes to functionalism's failure adequately to theorise human agency.[28] Functionalist approaches often focus upon the unintended consequences of social activity, suggesting that these consequences function to meet a need entirely beyond the awareness or intentions of the human actors involved. Certainly the consequences of social activity go beyond those which are intended,[29] but it is unsatisfactory to close out so completely the conscious and practical awareness which human agents possess with regard to their own activity and to that of others.[30]

Finally, functionalism adopts an essentially static view of society (see further §1.5. above).[31] Because the term function is used, often in relation to supposed needs, a social activity is regarded as 'acting back', 'fulfilling a function', in the setting in which it arose. Indeed this failure to incorporate the temporal nature of social interaction characterises Gellner's essay, cited by Meeks. Gellner defends functionalism by suggesting that 'each functional explanation be as it were, *read backwards*', reasserting that a functional approach must view a society as a functioning 'whole'.[32] However, it should be clear that a study of the *consequences*

27 This example is discussed by Wright and Giddens; see Wright 1989, 78–82; Giddens 1989b, 260–62; cf. also Giddens 1981, 18.
28 Gregory 1986, 166; Giddens 1977, 106.
29 Cf. Theissen 1979b, 59; Giddens 1979, 59.
30 Giddens 1977, 106–109, 121; 1981, 18; cf. Stowers 1985, 152ff, 175–76; Horsley 1989, 27.
31 For criticism on this point, see Martins 1974, 246–47; Giddens 1981, 17.
32 Gellner 1962, 118; see 117–18.

of a form of social activity is not identical with a study of the conditions and context which gave rise to the activity. The consequences, be they intended or unintended, *become* the conditions on which subsequent activity is based. Social life is an intrinsically *ongoing* historical process, and a focus upon 'functions' obscures this.

Significant and fundamental though these criticisms are, it should not be thought that functionalism incorporates nothing of value. According to Giddens, functionalism's focus upon the impact, the (often unintended) consequences of social activity is of basic importance.[33] This is an important corrective to forms of sociology which have restricted the focus of their inquiry to the intentions and perceptions of actors.[34] Hence the significance of Meeks' statement that 'the comprehensive question concerning the texts that are our primary sources is not merely what each one says, but *what it does*'.[35] However, Giddens' 'structuration theory' (to which I shall turn in §2.4.) aims to incorporate this focus upon the unintended consequences of social activity while at the same time being self-consciously a 'non-functionalist manifesto'.[36] Indeed the very word 'function' is one which Giddens regards as unhelpful.[37] His own theory attempts to attend to the impact of social activities without viewing such activities as fulfilling a function in the context in which they arose, but instead regarding them as a part of an ongoing process whereby the consequences of actions, both intended and unintended, become the conditions (some acknowledged, some unacknowledged) on which subsequent activity is based. In the exegetical studies which follow, considerable attention will be given to the potential impact of various texts upon social groups and relationships within the Christian community. The question about what these texts *do* will indeed be of importance. Following Giddens I believe it is possible to incorporate the main strength of functionalist approaches while departing decisively from the functionalist paradigm.

---

[33] See Giddens 1977, 100–10; 1979, 59; 1984, 12, 296. Cf. Stowers 1985, 156.
[34] Cf. Giddens 1982a, 28–29.
[35] Meeks 1983, 7, my emphasis; cf. Watson 1986, 22.
[36] Giddens 1979, 7.
[37] Cf. Giddens 1981, 16.

2.3. The sociology of knowledge: Berger and Luckmann[38]

In a review of the state of sociological interpretation of the New Testament, Scroggs stated that: 'For some of us... the single most important approach within the field of sociology comes from the sociology of knowledge.'[39] Dennis Nineham also suggested that the sociology of knowledge offered great potential as a 'partner' for theology.[40] From this area of sociology, the most influential work has almost certainly been Berger and Luckmann's *The Social Construction of Reality*, first drawn upon, to my knowledge, by Meeks, but employed since in a variety of works.[41] Also influential is *The Social Reality of Religion* (USA: *The Sacred Canopy*), by Berger alone, which elaborates Berger and Luckmann's theoretical perspectives specifically in relation to religion.[42]

Berger and Luckmann's project consists of an attempt to understand social reality as a human construction:[43] The reality which people generally take for granted as 'the way things are', is in fact a human product.[44] Every human society represents an enterprise of 'world-building' in which behaviour and interaction are shaped by socially-constructed norms.[45] This socially-constructed world gives order and meaning to life. The construction of social worlds is a human attempt to make life meaningful in the face of the ever-present threat of chaos, anomy and death.[46] Berger and Luckmann identify three inseparable moments in the dialectical process by which human beings produce society which

[38] Some of this section has already appeared in print; see Horrell 1993, 87–93. The material is reproduced here by kind permission of Sheffield Academic Press. Private correspondence with Philip Esler has helped me to clarify further my criticisms of Berger and Luckmann.

[39] Scroggs 1980, 175. For assessments of the sociology of knowledge in relation to New Testament study, see Berger 1977; Remus 1982; Holmberg 1990, 118–44.

[40] Nineham 1975.

[41] See Meeks 1972, 70; Scroggs 1980, 175 n. 38; Esler 1987, 16–23; 1994, 4–18; MacDonald 1988, 10–18; Maier 1991, 9, 108–35 etc.

[42] Berger 1967; for use of Berger's perspectives, see Gager 1975, 9–12; Kee 1980, 23–25, 30–53; Theissen 1983.

[43] Cf. Berger and Luckmann 1966, 13.

[44] On the theological issues that such a projectionist theory raises (Berger sees it as 'methodological atheism'), see Berger 1967, 179–88 and 1969 (a remarkable attempt to offer a theological 'reply' to his own sociological work). The theological interest and implications of Berger's work are discussed by Cairns 1974 and Gill 1974; see also Gill 1975, 29–34 and 1977, 16–22.

[45] Cf. Berger 1967, 3; Berger and Pullberg 1966, 62.

[46] Berger and Luckmann 1966, 121: '*All* societies are constructions in the face of chaos.' Cf. Berger 1967, 52, 53–80.

produces human beings: externalisation, objectivation and internalisation.[47] In a Feuerbachian sense society is a human projection which is externalised such that it becomes, for each individual, objectified.[48] Thus, 'society confronts man as external, subjectively opaque and coercive facticity'.[49] Through the process of socialisation, individuals 'internalise' this social world, making it their own. This process of internalisation is generally unconscious and hidden from critical scrutiny: 'The social world intends, as far as possible, to be taken for granted. Socialization achieves success to the degree that this taken-for-granted quality is internalized.'[50]

Every social construction of reality, Berger and Luckmann stress, requires legitimation, 'that is, ways by which it can be "explained" and justified'.[51] The most comprehensive level of legitimation is offered by 'symbolic universes'; 'bodies of theoretical tradition' that 'encompass the institutional order in a symbolic totality'.[52] These symbolic universes have a definite social significance: 'They are sheltering canopies over the institutional order as well as over individual biography. They also provide the delimitation of social reality; that is, they set the limits of what is relevant in terms of social interaction.'[53] It is on such a level that religion is generally to be understood; as a 'sacred canopy' which legitimates the social order upon which a society is built and as a fundamental provider of meaning.[54]

Berger and Luckmann's work offers a number of elements which are of considerable value to a sociological approach to the New Testament. Of fundamental importance is their focus on the way in which human self-understanding and social interaction are shaped by a socially-constructed symbolic universe. From this perspective we may view Pauline Christianity as a symbolic order which shapes the believers' world-view and gives order to their social interaction and community relationships

---

[47] Berger and Luckmann 1966, 78–79, 149; Berger 1967, 3–4, 81–85; cf. also MacDonald 1988, 10–11.
[48] See Berger 1967, 89 and 203 n. 20 for his use of the term 'projection' and its derivation from Feuerbach.
[49] Berger 1967, 11.
[50] Berger 1967, 24; cf. Berger and Luckmann 1966, 149–82.
[51] Berger and Luckmann 1966, 79; see further 110–46.
[52] Berger and Luckmann 1966, 113; see further 113–22.
[53] Berger and Luckmann 1966, 120.
[54] Cf. Berger 1967, esp. 26–28, 32–52, 87–101.

(see further §2.5. below). Also important is their emphasis upon legitimation;[55] that is to say, upon the ways in which a symbolic universe serves to sustain and legitimate a certain ordering of reality and of social relationships, offering ways in which a pattern of social life can be 'explained and justified'.

However, I also believe that their theory suffers from serious shortcomings and that the fundamental insights which they have developed can be better utilised within the kind of framework which Giddens' structuration theory provides. As with functionalism I consider that Giddens' work offers at least one way of taking up and retaining the insights of this theoretical perspective while avoiding its apparent weaknesses. Work like Berger and Luckmann's remains of enduring importance, but it was published almost thirty years ago (in 1966) and New Testament scholars need to consider the ways in which contemporary social theory offers more adequate theoretical resources.

The first shortcoming, I believe, arises from the extent to which Berger and Luckmann stress the objectivity which the social world attains. While they appreciate the dialectical way in which human beings simultaneously produce and are produced by society,[56] and stress society's humanly constructed nature,[57] their concepts of externalisation and objectivation lead to a view of the social order as *external* to human activity. Thus: 'An institutional order is experienced as an objective reality.'[58] 'Social structure is encountered by the individual as an external facticity.'[59] 'Above all society manifests itself by its coercive power. The final test of its objective reality is its capacity to impose itself upon the reluctance of individuals.'[60] In my opinion, this formulation obscures the extent to which social order is continually reproduced only in and through the activities of human subjects, and hence neglects the important relationship between reproduction and transformation.[61] Berger, for

---

55 Taken up especially by Esler 1987, 16–23; also Maier 1991, 122–35.
56 See Berger and Luckmann 1966, 78–79, 208–209; Berger 1967, 3, 18–19, 189 n. 2.
57 See Berger and Luckmann 1966, 69–70, 78; Berger 1967, 6–9; Berger and Pullberg 1966, 62. See further the discussion in Thomason 1982, 114–61. Alienation, according to Berger, occurs when people 'forget' that they are the producers of their own social world; see Berger 1967, 81–101; Berger and Pullberg 1966, 61, 64.
58 Berger and Luckmann 1966, 77.
59 Berger and Pullberg 1966, 63.
60 Berger 1967, 11; cf. also 24–25.
61 This concern is at the heart of Giddens' 'structuration theory', on which see §2.4. below.

example, illustrates the social world's objectivity with a reference to language, whose 'rules are objectively given'.[62] While partially true, quite obviously, one may contrast this emphasis with Giddens' use of the linguistic illustration as an analogy of social structure: For Giddens, every use of language both *draws upon* the rules of that language *and* at the same time reproduces them. Thus, in every act of reproduction the possibility of transformation is at hand. Language, like society, is not simply objectively 'given', but is reproduced and transformed in and through ongoing human activity (see further §2.4. below). Such a shift in emphasis is, I believe, of considerable socio-political significance. It is important to realise that a symbolic order does not have some 'reified' existence external to the human subjects who sustain and reproduce it. It is maintained, transformed, and contested by various human individuals and groups, and the issue of power is crucial: certain groups and classes have greater power to influence and shape the ongoing reproduction of the symbolic order. What a Berger and Luckmannian perspective may portray as 'protection' of a symbolic universe may in fact be an attempt to reproduce and transform it in a certain direction, an attempt perhaps made by those in power and contested to a degree by those who are not.[63] The fact that a social order may be experienced as 'coercive power' by many is not necessarily to be explained by the notion that it is 'externalised' and 'objectified' but rather by the fact that certain groups have power and others do not. Berger and Luckmann present as a feature of the construction of social reality what is in fact a feature of the unequal distribution of power.

The concept of an externalised and objectified social world gives rise to a second shortcoming: namely, that, with such a conceptualisation of the dominant social order, critique and alternative, indeed *change* itself, are all-too-easily conceived of as threatening and destructive.[64] Ideally, individuals are 'successfully socialized' into the 'reality' which confronts them as 'objective'. The dominant social order requires legitimation and maintenance: its continuance provides security against chaos and anomy.

---

[62] Berger 1967, 12; Berger and Pullberg 1966, 63–64.

[63] Cf. my critique of the use of a Berger and Luckmann perspective to interpret the Pastoral Epistles; Horrell 1993, 89–103.

[64] Berger and Luckmann 1966, 121: 'The constant possibility of anomic terror is actualized whenever the legitimations that obscure the precariousness [of all societies] are threatened or collapse.' The analysis of 'de-reification' is deemed to be beyond the framework of their concerns (109), though on this see Berger and Pullberg 1966, 69–70.

Such a theory can easily form a legitimation of the status quo, suggesting that its maintenance and continuation are essential for human well-being. Challenges to the social order are *portrayed* as marginal activities which threaten to cause chaos, and increase the need for legitimation. Berger and Luckmann speak, for example, of the 'problem' caused by 'deviant versions of the symbolic universe'.[65] Note too Berger's description of threats to the social world:

All socially constructed worlds are inherently precarious ... they are constantly *threatened* by the human facts of self-interest and stupidity. The institutional programmes are *sabotaged* by individuals with conflicting interests. Frequently individuals simply forget them or are incapable of learning them in the first place. *The fundamental processes of social control, to the extent that they are successful, serve to mitigate these threats.*[66]

The idea that the continuance of the social order is necessary for the well-being of society is all the more dangerous given the insistence that the social world intends, as far as possible, to remain unquestionable. 'It is not enough', Berger writes, 'that the individual look upon the key meanings of the social order as useful, desirable, or right. It is much better (*better, that is, in terms of social stability*) if he looks upon them as *inevitable*, as part and parcel of the universal nature of things.'[67]

What this approach, based on the concept of an externalised social order, fails to highlight, is that the symbolic order is always being reproduced in and through ongoing human action; it will often, therefore, be being transformed albeit in subtle and almost imperceptible ways. The *labelling* of some forms as 'deviant' may be a strategy of dominant social groups to portray themselves as defenders of the social order while stigmatising and externalising others. But Berger and Luckmann's theory tends to suggest that such defence of the symbolic order is necessary in order to protect the precarious socially-constructed world. It may thus (unintentionally) legitimate the use of power by groups who are in fact seeking to transform the symbolic order in the direction in which they wish it to go (the way which serves their interests?). A symbolic order can never exist apart from the lives of those who inhabit it; it must be

---

[65] Berger and Luckmann 1966, 124.
[66] Berger 1967, 29, my italics; see further 29–32 and cf. Berger and Luckmann 1966, 87.
[67] Berger 1967, 24, my italics; cf. Berger and Luckmann 1966, 77–85, 149–57.

continually reproduced. While it may indeed by challenged by an 'alternative' order, most often it is the power struggles among those who inhabit the same symbolic social world but who seek to transform it in different directions which must be acknowledged and illuminated. What Berger and Luckmann present as 'social order' versus 'chaos and anomy' is in social life more often a contest between different versions of what the social order should be.

Indeed, a third shortcoming concerns their inadequate attention to issues of interests and ideology.[68] Giddens asserts that 'their approach ... completely lacks a conception of the critique of ideology'.[69] In other words, there is no adequate consideration of the ideological dimensions of the construction of social reality: whose interests are served by the social order and how are inequalities and exploitation concealed as 'natural' in such a construction of 'reality'? Any consideration of the 'construction' of social reality must give due attention to the ways in which the dominant reality which is constructed may reflect the interests of certain groups and legitimate and conceal the exploitation of others. Moreover, the emergence, sustenance *and transformation* of a dominant social order is inextricably connected to the issue of power. As Berger and Luckmann themselves comment: 'He who has the bigger stick has the better chance of imposing his definitions of reality.'[70] But what this means is that one of the crucial things to examine in connection with any social construction of reality is the ways in which power is used by some, to serve certain sectional interests and to legitimate the domination of others.

As was the case with functionalism these shortcomings, I believe, are sufficient to require us to look elsewhere for a social theory which will enable an adequate framework for research to be developed. Nevertheless, again as with functionalism, there are important strengths and insights which must be retained. Berger and Luckmann's conception of a symbolic universe which shapes and informs the lives of those who 'inhabit' it underpins my conceptualisation of Pauline Christianity and thus forms a significant part of my theoretical framework. Also of fundamental importance is their emphasis upon the way in which such symbolic

---

[68] On the way in which the term ideology is used by Giddens, and throughout this study, see below pp. 50–52.

[69] Giddens 1979, 267 n. 8.

[70] Berger and Luckmann 1966, 127.

orders legitimate certain patterns of social life and interaction. However, these valuable insights must, it seems to me, be linked with a critical focus upon the ways in which the symbolic universe may serve the interests of certain social groups and legitimate the exploitation of others, and with an approach which views the symbolic universe not as an externalised objectivity but as a human construct which is continually produced and contested, reproduced and transformed, in and through ongoing human activity.

2.4. Giddens' structuration theory[71]

Although Giddens' work underpins much of the presentation thus far, an attempt to review it in its entirety would be both overwhelming and often irrelevant.[72] I intend to use 'structuration theory' (itself only a part of Giddens' work) as a theoretical resource and will draw upon aspects of it which seem to illuminate this particular area of research. It is not a 'theory' in the sense of something which could be taken up as a precise framework and 'applied' to a particular area of investigation, nor does it offer models or explanatory generalisations which could be tested against the evidence. For the reasons stated in chapter 1, such a conception of social theory is one which I follow Giddens in rejecting. Rather, structuration theory seeks to offer conceptual resources – or, an 'ontological framework'[73] – with which to approach the study of social activities. Thus Giddens suggests:

> The concepts of structuration theory, as with any competing theoretical perspective, should for many research purposes be regarded as sensitizing devices, nothing more. That is to say, they may be useful for thinking about research problems and the interpretation of research results.[74]

Giddens does 'not think it useful, as some authors have tried to do, to "apply" structuration theory as a whole in research projects',[75] preferring

---

[71] A shorter resumé of §2.4. and §2.5. may be found in Horrell 1995d, 224–27.
[72] See the bibliographical appendix below for references to Giddens' work on topics relevant to this study.
[73] Giddens 1991, 201; see also Cohen 1989, 1–8.
[74] Giddens 1984, 326–27; see further 1984, preface, xvii–xix; 1990, 310–11; 1991, 202–206.
[75] Giddens 1990, 311.

those studies 'in which [its] concepts ... are used in a sparing and critical fashion'.[76] Indeed, Giddens' substantive orientation towards modern industrialised societies means that any use of his work in relation to a distant historical context must be selective and judicious. Nevertheless, he claims that his work in the field of social theory is relevant to any study of human social activity.[77] In Jon Clark's words, 'structuration theory is a general social theory which aims to advance our understanding of human agency and social institutions, but with a sociological bias in that much of its substantive focus is upon "advanced" or modern societies.'[78]

In order to understand structuration theory, it is necessary to appreciate the dualism which it seeks to transcend. This dualism essentially concerns the relation of action to structure: a 'fundamental problem [which] stalks through the history of sociological theory'.[79] On one side of this dualism are those sociological traditions which 'have stressed the primacy of object over subject, of social structure or social system over the purposeful, capable social actor'.[80] On the other are 'subjectivist' and individualist traditions which have restricted their attention to the intentional aspects of human behaviour.[81] Fundamentally, then, the theory of structuration is 'an attempt to move beyond the apparent opposition between perspectives which emphasise structure and perspectives which emphasise action':[82] an 'opposition between voluntarism and determinism', as Giddens puts it.[83] A recognition that this opposition needs to be overcome is widespread, and Allan Pred speaks of an 'emerging consensus' over the shape which a resolution should take, mentioning Berger and Luckmann, Roy Bhaskar, and Giddens, among others.[84] Derek Gregory represents diagrammatically a number of these attempts to overcome the dualism between action and structure[85] but 'prefer[s] to draw largely on Giddens' own version because it is the most fully

---

[76] Giddens 1991, 213; cf. 1989b, 294.
[77] See Giddens 1982a, 5–6, 197; 1984, xvii; 1989b, 295.
[78] Clark 1990, 24.
[79] Archer 1990, 73; cf. Outhwaite 1990, 63; Thompson 1989, 56; Giddens 1982a, 28.
[80] Giddens 1982a, 29.
[81] See Giddens 1982a, 28–29; 1979, 49–50; 1984, 213–21.
[82] Held and Thompson 1989, 3–4.
[83] Giddens 1979, 2.
[84] See Pred 1982, 158–63; Urry 1982, 100–101; Bhaskar 1979, 39–47; Berger and Luckmann 1966, 78–79, 208–209; Berger 1967, 3, 18–19, 189 n. 2.
[85] Gregory 1981, 11; cf. Bhaskar 1979, 39–47.

developed'.[86] And Giddens himself notes the 'strong convergence between [his] standpoint and those worked out largely independently by other authors', referring specifically to Bhaskar (1979) and John Thompson (1981).[87] Talk of consensus, however, should not be taken to imply a lack of disagreement and debate, not least concerning Giddens' own proposals.[88] Criticism of Giddens has come from those defending an approach to sociology which he criticises,[89] from those attempting to develop new alternative schemes,[90] from those who find structuration theory irrelevant to empirical research,[91] and from those who are basically sympathetic but seek to clarify or improve the theory.[92] It is clear, however, that Giddens is at the centre of debate in contemporary social theory and that to choose his work as a theoretical resource is to choose a resource of acknowledged importance.

The key conception with which Giddens seeks to transcend the opposition between voluntarism and determinism is that of the *duality of structure*:

> The dualism of subject and object ... must cede place to recognition of a *duality* which is implicated in all social reproduction, the *duality of structure*. By the 'duality of structure' I refer to the essentially recursive character of social life: the structural properties of social systems are both medium and outcome of the practices that constitute those systems.[93]

To illustrate this conception, Giddens cites the analogy of language:

> When I utter a sentence I draw upon various syntactical rules ... These structural features of the language are the medium whereby I generate

---

86 Gregory 1980, 335; cf. 1981, 8; Thompson 1989, 57.

87 Giddens 1982a, viii and ix n. 3.

88 See esp. Held and Thompson 1989; Clark, Modgil and Modgil 1990; Bryant and Jary 1991. For a concise overview of the areas of contention, see Giddens 1990, 297–301 (esp. 299–300). Clark's (1990, 26) three point summary of the 'main criticisms' is far too limited, focusing entirely on structuration theory's relation to empirical research, only one area of contention. For Giddens' most recent responses to critics, see Giddens 1989b; 1990.

89 E.g. Turner 1990, 107–10, 112–14; 1986, esp. 969, 975–77; 1987, 157, 160; who defends a more nomological, scientific and model-based approach to sociology (cf. ch. 1 above); Callinicos 1985 (note Giddens' response; 1985) and Wright 1989 (note Giddens' response; 1989b, 259–67), who defend Marxism against Giddens' critique.

90 E.g. Archer 1990 ('Morphogenesis'). Cohen 1989, 56–83 develops a critique of morphological approaches from a position sympathetic to structuration theory.

91 E.g. Gregson 1989; Stinchcombe 1990; note Giddens' response to this issue; 1984, 281–354; 1989b, 293–301; 1990, 310–15.

92 E.g. Thompson 1981, ix, 144; 1984, vii, 128, 148–72 (=1989, 56–76); Cohen 1987; 1989.

93 Giddens 1982a, 36–37, cf. 10; 1976, 121, 127–28; 1979, 69–70; 1984, 25.

the utterance. But in producing a syntactically correct utterance I simultaneously contribute to the reproduction of the language as a whole. This view rejects the identification of structure with constraint: structure is both enabling and constraining.[94]

The rules and resources of language simultaneously structure communication and are reproduced in that very communication. They are both the medium which permits meaningful communication and the outcome of that communication. They are both enabling – they facilitate communication – and constraining – they define and limit meaningful communication. Moreover, these linguistic 'rules and resources' have no 'existence' external to or independent of the language itself. Thus, 'in the theory of structuration, "structure" refers to rules and resources instantiated in social systems, but having only a "virtual" existence'.[95] Giddens divides structures into three types: structures of signification, of domination, and of legitimation, while stressing that these are separable only analytically and are always linked in social institutions.[96]

It should be clear, not least from the linguistic analogy, that Giddens' conception of the duality of structure brings *reproduction* into central focus. Ira Cohen considers that this is perhaps the main achievement of structuration theory: 'Giddens has succeeded in bringing the production and reproduction of social life into the centre of concerns in social theory.'[97] The act of speaking or writing is not only structured by the rules of language but is also the means whereby those rules are reproduced. Similarly, social structures are reproduced in and through human activity. The central term *'structuration'*, then, refers essentially to a *process*, to 'the structuring of social relations across time and space'.[98] As communication is structured by the rules of language, so *social practices are structured by the rules and resources embedded in social systems yet*

---

[94] Giddens 1982a, 37. Cf. 1976, 103–104, 118–29, 161; 1984, 24. Thompson's criticisms (see n. 92 above) focus on the appropriateness of this analogy. Giddens has always stressed that the linguistic analogy is a limited one, and does not depend on the view that society is like a language. Nevertheless, language is a central feature of social life and hence does illustrate aspects of social interaction more generally; see Giddens 1985, 169; 1989b, 259.

[95] Giddens 1982a, 9.

[96] See Giddens 1984, 28–34.

[97] Cohen 1987, 306; cf. 1989, 287.

[98] Giddens 1984, 376, cf. 25; 1982a, 35; 1979, 66. Giddens first introduced the term in 1973 (see Giddens 1973; 1991, 202). However, the theory of structuration was first developed in Giddens 1976.

are simultaneously the means by which these rules and resources are reproduced.[99]

A further inextricable connection must also be stressed, namely that between reproduction and *transformation*. Again the linguistic analogy makes the connection clear; language is transformed as it is used. Thus:

Every act which contributes to the reproduction of a structure is also an act of production, a novel enterprise, and as such may initiate change by altering that structure at the same time as it reproduces it – as the meanings of words change in and through their use.[100]

... with a conception of structuration, the possibility of change is recognised as inherent in every circumstance of social reproduction.[101]

Such an emphasis clearly reflects Giddens' concern not to allow human action to be viewed as merely the outcome of social causes, or of structural determination (see §1.3. above). However, one must be quick to point out that this does not become a naïve individualism or voluntarism, another version of the thesis that society is merely constituted by intentional action.[102] Giddens always maintains that human agency is 'bounded', limited:[103] what actors know, their awareness of their social context, is clearly restricted,[104] as is their capability, which is limited by the power and resources they are able to command. Human agency is bounded, in another sense, 'by the unacknowledged conditions of action on "one side", and its unintended consequences on the other'.[105] Although actors are partly aware of what they are doing and why they are doing it, they will generally be unaware of some of the conditions which affect their action and will not intend some of its consequences.

---

[99] Cf. Abrams 1982, 3: 'this shaping of action by structure and transforming of structure by action both occur as processes in time.'

[100] Giddens 1976, 128.

[101] Giddens 1979, 210. Cf. also 1979, 114; 1981, 27.

[102] Cf. Giddens 1976, 156.

[103] Cf. Giddens 1976, 160; 1984, 27.

[104] However, Giddens makes the important point that what actors 'know' must not be restricted to what they can articulate, to 'discursive knowledge'. They also possess vitally important and significant stocks of 'practical knowledge', knowledge by which they are able to 'go on' in social life. These two levels of knowledgeability are distinguished from the unconscious, from which certain motivations clearly come: see 1982a, 9, 31; 1984, 6–7.

[105] Giddens 1982a, 32. As noted above (p. 38), Giddens sees the main strength of functionalism to be its focus upon these unintended consequences, though the label 'function' implies that these consequences are the true 'purpose' of the social activity and obscures the temporal dimension of all social activity.

Subsequent awareness of these unintended consequences may of course influence future activity. This is one of the ways in which Giddens brings temporality into the heart of his social theory, for the consequences of human activity *become* the conditions on which future action is based.[106] However, unintended consequences may or may not be 'noticed' and so, as conditions of action they may or may not be acknowledged.

Giddens' emphasis upon the 'capability' of human actors 'connects in an immediate way to the significance of *power* in social theory'.[107] Power, Giddens suggests, may be defined, in its broadest sense, as 'the *transformative capacity* of human action'.[108] Differentials of power mean different levels of influence over the reproduction and transformation of the rules and resources which structure social life. Symbolic orders define and shape the social world, and a position of power implies influence over the formulation and reproduction of these symbolic orders. Thus, '"*what passes for social reality*" *stands in immediate relation to the distribution of power*'.[109] The powerful, therefore, are potentially in a position to shape social life in a way which serves and legitimates their own sectional interests. Particular interests may be expressed within, and at the same time concealed by, particular symbolic orders. In other words, symbolic orders may be *ideological*, in the sense in which Giddens uses the term.

'The term "ideology" has been used in so many different senses that one might despair of using it in any precise manner at all.'[110] It is therefore necessary to clarify the sense in which it is used above, and throughout this study. The term is used, as Thompson points out, in 'two fundamentally differing ways' in contemporary thought.[111] One is based on what Thompson calls a 'neutral' conception of the term and uses 'ideology' as a descriptive term to refer to any system of thought, or of belief.[112] The second is a 'critical' conception which links ideology 'to the process of sustaining asymmetrical relations of power – that is, to the process of maintaining domination'.[113] Both Thompson and Giddens

---

[106] See Giddens 1979, 59; 1984, 5, 8, 27.
[107] Giddens 1982a, 9; see also 1979, 88–94; 1976, 110–13.
[108] Giddens 1976, 110.
[109] Giddens 1976, 113, my emphasis.
[110] Berger and Luckmann 1966, 228 n. 100. Cf. Lash 1986, 124.
[111] Thompson 1984, 3.
[112] Thompson 1984, 4. Cf. the use of the term by Elliott 1981, 268.
[113] Thompson 1984, 4. Eagleton 1991, 43, refers to Raymond Geuss' 'useful distinction between "descriptive", "perjorative" and "positive" definitions of the term ideology'.

argue for the second conception, and I propose to follow them in this, as this seems to give the term a sharp and useful meaning, rather than an over-generalised one. Giddens makes his own use of the term clear:

> Ideology is not a distinctive type of symbol-system, to be contrasted with others, such as science. As I conceptualise it, ideology refers to the *ideological*, this being understood in terms of the capability of dominant groups or classes to make their own sectional interests appear to others as universal ones.[114]

For Thompson, to study ideology is 'to study the ways in which meaning (or signification) serves to sustain relations of domination'.[115] Terry Eagleton refers to Thompson's definition as 'probably the single most widely accepted definition of ideology'.[116] Eagleton maintains, however, that some flexibility in the use of the term is required and argues 'that both the wider and narrower senses have their uses, and that their mutual incompatibility ... must be simply acknowledged'.[117] Nevertheless, he maintains that the 'force of the term ideology lies in its capacity to discriminate between those power struggles which are somehow central to a form of social life, and those which are not'.[118] 'Not everything, then,' he insists, 'may usefully be said to be ideological. If there is nothing which is not ideological, then the term cancels all the way through and drops out of sight.'[119] He also suggests that an analysis of ideology cannot proceed merely on the basis of the words which are said or written but must consider the context and manner, the form of *discourse*, in which they are employed.[120] To cite but one of his many witty illustrations: 'A breakfast-time quarrel between husband and wife over who exactly allowed the toast to turn that grotesque shade of black need not be ideological; it becomes so when, for example, it begins to engage questions of sexual power, beliefs about gender roles and so on.'[121]

---

[114] Giddens 1979, 6.
[115] Thompson 1984, 4, 130–31, 134, 141, 146; note the general discussion on 126–47.
[116] Eagleton 1991, 5.
[117] Eagleton 1991, 7; cf. 221. He later refers to 'six different ways' of defining ideology, ranging from the most general to more specific and critical conceptions (28–31). Thompson's definition comes closest to Eagleton's definitions four and five (29–30).
[118] Eagleton 1991, 8.
[119] Eagleton 1991, 9.
[120] 'It is a matter of "discourse" rather than of "language" ...', Eagleton 1991, 223.
[121] Eagleton 1991, 8; see further 8–9.

Giddens suggests that there are three principal ideological forms; the representation of sectional interests as universal ones, the denial or transmutation of contradictions, and the naturalisation of the present (reification).[122] Similarly, Thompson lists as three central 'modes by which ideology operates', *legitimation, dissimulation* (that is, concealment or denial), and *reification* (that is, 'representing a transitory, historical state of affairs as if it were permanent, natural, outside of time').[123] It is perhaps in this third form that religion is most likely to feature, for it has a particular opportunity to legitimate and sustain forms of social organisation; elevating such forms above the status of merely human products and reifying or naturalising them by rooting them in the divine will.[124]

As noted above, Giddens' stress upon the capability and knowledgeability of human actors is balanced by an emphasis upon the fact that human agents do not always, or even generally, understand fully the conditions upon which their action is based; nor do they intend, or foresee, all of its consequences. Human action takes place in the context of a set of conditions, some of which are unacknowledged, and it produces a range of consequences, some of which are unintended.[125] To link this with the ideological question is to state that the legitimation of relations of domination, or of sectional interests, may not be the intended consequence of a particular action, though it may be a consequence nonetheless. Texts, in particular, Giddens suggests, may 'escape' the intentions of their authors and take on new meanings in new contexts. He proposes that:

> One of the main tasks of the study of the text, or indeed cultural products of any kind, must be precisely to examine the divergencies which can become instituted between the circumstances of their production, and the meanings sustained by their subsequent escape from the horizon of their creator or creators.[126]

So from a structuration theory perspective, texts will be viewed as a form of social action in which the rules and resources which comprise a

---

[122] Giddens 1979, 193–96.
[123] Thompson 1984, 131. Cf. Eagleton 1991, 51–61, who mentions as 'ideological strategies', rationalisation, legitimation, universalisation, naturalisation, and reification.
[124] Cf. Berger 1967, 33: 'Religion legitimates social institutions by bestowing upon them an ultimately valid ontological status.'
[125] Cf. Giddens 1984, 5, 8, 27.
[126] Giddens 1979, 44.

symbolic order are produced and reproduced. A text is produced in the context of a particular set of circumstances and it has an impact – a range of consequences – in that context and beyond it. Texts both arise from and act within a social setting and thus play a role in the process of structuration – in the structuring of social relations across time and space. The elements of structuration theory presented above are clearly at a high level of theoretical abstraction. Nevertheless, they form the basis of my approach to research in this study. The following section seeks to draw upon these theoretical resources, and upon the positive aspects of those presented previously, in order to formulate a more specific framework for the exegetical research which follows. It should be stressed, however, that this framework and the studies which follow do not represent the only use to which Giddens' theoretical resources might be put, nor the only kind of framework which might be derived from structuration theory.

2.5. A framework for exegetical research

Structuration theory seems to me to offer two important and basic resources from which to build an approach to the Pauline and post-Pauline epistles: firstly, a theoretical framework with which to analyse the ongoing reproduction and transformation of Pauline Christianity, and secondly, within this, a critical focus upon issues of power, interests and ideology.

In using these theoretical resources to construct a framework for exegetical research I begin with the relatively straightforward assertion that Pauline Christianity may best be understood as a 'symbolic order';[127] categorised by Giddens as an institution in which structures of signification, domination and legitimation are all instantiated, but where structures of signification are especially dominant.[128] That is to say, it is a coagulation of symbols (embodied in rituals), a linguistic framework, a

---

[127] I prefer the term 'order' (used by Giddens; see 1984, 31, 33) to 'universe' (used by Berger and Luckmann 1966, 110–46) as the latter tends to underemphasise both the extent to which a number of conflicting symbolic orders may influence people's lives and the extent to which alternatives and reformulation constantly reshape and reconstruct any particular symbolic order. See further §2.3. above.

[128] Cf. Giddens 1984, 31, 33; where he categorises institutions according to the types of structures which are dominant.

collection of rules and resources, which shapes the life of particular communities. Pauline Christianity offered to its converts new symbols, images and rituals – structures of signification – with which to 'understand' and to shape their lives. Clifford Geertz suggests that a religious system comprises 'a cluster of sacred symbols, woven into some sort of ordered whole'.[129] These 'religious symbols', moreover, 'dramatized in rituals or related in myths, are felt somehow to sum up, for those for whom they are resonant, what is known about the way the world is, the quality of the emotional life it supports, and the way one ought to behave while in it'.[130] In one sense, then, Rudolf Bultmann was right to assert that the Christian gospel offers a new self-understanding.[131] What Bultmann suggests may readily be formulated in sociology of knowledge terms: all human living is shaped by the socially-constructed world and symbolic order in which it is located. The gospel offers an alternative symbolic order; if one accepts it then one accepts a new way of understanding one's life. However, it is Bultmann's existential individualism which is inadequate, for it isolates the gospel from any socio-historical context and formulates it only as a word to the individual.[132] A symbolic order, on the contrary, is always a phenomenon shared and sustained by a group of people. A new self-understanding comes not to an isolated individual but in the context of a social group and is always, therefore, at the same time, a new understanding of others.[133] Indeed a symbolic order can only exist insofar as it is 'lived' and embodied, insofar as it shapes people's understanding and interaction. As a somewhat fuller definition I therefore suggest that Pauline Christianity may best be understood as *a symbolic order embodied in communities.*[134]

In contrast to Berger and Luckmann's theory, I reject the view of this order as an 'externalisation'; a universe which people 'enter' and which is then 'sustained' and 'protected'.[135] Instead, drawing upon Giddens'

---

[129] Geertz 1957, 424.

[130] Geertz 1957, 422.

[131] E.g. Bultmann 1960, 73, 75–76, 81; 1969, 236.

[132] Cf. Kee 1989, 4–5.

[133] On the need and potential for developing Bultmann's thought in the direction of a more socially and politically based theology, see Sölle 1974, 2, 22, 38 etc; Rowland and Corner 1990, 69–74; Jones 1991, esp. 185–92, 203–208.

[134] Cf. Gager 1975, 10: 'the process of generating a sacred cosmos or a symbolic universe is always rooted in concrete communities of believers.' On the 'community-forming' dimensions of fundamental Christian symbols, see Barton 1982; 1984.

[135] See further §2.3. above.

notion of the duality of structure, I suggest that this symbolic order – the symbols, rules and resources of Pauline Christianity – is both medium and outcome of the community's life. It is produced and reproduced in the activities of those who comprise the community. It structures the life of the community and is at the same time the outcome of that life. The symbolic order shapes the lives of the believers, yet at the same time is reproduced (and transformed) by members of the Christian community, predominantly those with the power and position to do so.

Indeed, to speak of the reproduction of the symbolic order of Pauline Christianity should immediately raise the question of power. Who was in a position to reformulate the faith and thus to shape the community's life? Clearly Paul, of course, until his death, but even during his lifetime other leaders too were able to exert some influence, particularly as Paul travelled from place to place and was therefore most often a leader *in absentia*.[136] In the Corinthian context other visiting leaders, such as Apollos and Cephas, were of significance, and local figures within the Christian community also exercised leadership and influence. After Paul's death, the prime responsibility for reproducing and reinterpreting the symbolic order to the believers at Corinth fell to others, one of whom was a prominent figure in the Christian community at Rome (see chapter 6).

Linked with the question of who has the power to reformulate the faith and thus to shape the symbolic order and its social embodiment, we must ask whose interests the symbolic order reflects.[137] Whilst such a question in no way reflects an assumption that such symbolic orders are always a concealed expression of class domination or a legitimation of exploitation, it does reflect a willingness to explore the possibility that the Christian symbolic order might at times be formulated on the basis of sectional interests and therefore become 'ideological'. By this I mean that it may become a means whereby domination is concealed, reinforced and/or legitimated.[138] 'Symbolic orders and associated modes of

---

[136] Schreiber 1977 explores the group-dynamic aspects of the Corinthian community's development, giving particular attention to the impact of Paul's absence; see esp. 117–46, 174–80. Note however the critical comments of Kümmel 1985, 342–43 and Meeks 1983, 221 n. 1.

[137] Cf. Mosala 1989, 13–42, who argues that biblical scholars should attempt to appreciate the ideology which underpins any particular text and be prepared to see those texts as the expression of particular class interests.

[138] See Mayer 1983 and Ste. Croix 1975 (esp. 19–24) and 1981, 103–11, 416–41, for this kind of (Marxist) criticism directed primarily at Pauline Christianity. See Theissen 1979c, 6–27, for a review of and response to the 'ideological criticism' of religion.

discourse', Giddens maintains, 'are a major institutional locus of ideology.'[139] A critical sociological approach, for me, is not one which assumes that such ideological characteristics are always contained within religious orders, but is one which is prepared at least to ask the questions which may reveal their presence. As the Christian symbolic order develops and evolves we must seek to assess its trajectory[140] and to consider the interests which influence its ongoing transformation.

Adopting the critical conception of ideology outlined above, there are two different ways in which the symbolic order of Pauline Christianity might be regarded as ideological: the first is in terms of the ways in which its resources of signification are used by leaders such as Paul to sustain and legitimate their own power and position. This is one sense in which it might be said to sustain relations of domination. The second relates to the ways in which its resources might be used to legitimate the dominant social order of Greco-Roman society, to sustain the position of dominant social groups or classes and to legitimate the exploitation and domination of others. In the first century, of course, there is no sense in which Christianity is a religion exerting significant influence over the social life of the empire, though an analysis of the ways in which it shapes and legitimates the relations between different social groups in its own congregations is itself significant. Moreover, such an analysis may be relevant to the question as to why Christianity was eventually adopted as the religion of the empire. I shall seek in the study which follows to be aware of both of these ideological dimensions, but it is the second to which I give closest attention as it seems to me to be of greater sociological significance. Giddens, we recall, speaks of ideology in terms of 'the capability of *dominant groups or classes* to make their own sectional interests appear to others as universal ones'.[141] It is the potential of the Christian symbolic order to add ideological legitimation to the position of various social groups and to the dominant social order with which I am primarily concerned. Nevertheless, we should not ignore the significance of the ways in which the Christian symbolic order may be used, even if it contrasts with and challenges the dominant social order, to sustain its own ecclesiastical

---

[139] Giddens 1984, 33.

[140] An emphasis which Robinson and Koester sought to develop (see 1971, esp. 1–19, an essay by Robinson).

[141] Giddens 1979, 6, my italics; see §2.4. above.

hierarchy which then becomes, in some senses, a parallel to the hierarchy of society.[142]

The exegetical studies which follow focus primarily upon the 'social ethos' expressed within the symbolic order of Pauline Christianity. The term 'ethos' is defined by Geertz in the following way: 'A people's ethos is the tone, character, and quality of their life, its moral and aesthetic style and mood; it is the underlying attitude towards themselves and their world that life reflects.'[143] I use the term 'ethos' in order to focus upon the 'shape' which Pauline Christianity gives to the life of particular communities. It refers to their 'life-style'[144] and is thus deliberately chosen as a broader term than 'ethics', which is generally used to refer more specifically to discussions about behaviour and conduct. I use the adjective 'social' in order to focus particularly upon the ways in which Pauline Christianity shapes relationships within the community, upon the ways in which it leads the believers to view and to interact with one another and with their wider society.

In other words, the following studies explore what the symbolic order of Pauline Christianity as found in the Corinthian correspondence 'does', or attempts to do – its potential impact upon social relationships and various groups within the Christian community – and ask whether it expresses or promotes the interests of any particular social group. A question of crucial sociological significance is: When and in what ways might the Christian symbolic order be said to offer a religious ideology, theologically legitimating the dominant social order (in relation, say, to the institution of slavery, or to the power and position of the *paterfamilias* as head of his household)?

Giddens' notion of the duality of structure portrays forms of social structure not as externalised or rigid creations with an existence 'outside' of human action, but as 'rules and resources' which are continually produced, reproduced and transformed in and through the actions of human subjects. The linguistic analogy provides probably the clearest way of grasping this idea (see §2.4. above). In a similar way the Christian symbolic order is continually reproduced, reinterpreted and transformed over time, by new people and in new contexts. The re-presentation of Christian teaching is an ongoing process enmeshed in the practical

---

[142] Cf. Boff 1985, 47–64.
[143] Geertz 1957, 421; cf. 1966, 3.
[144] Cf. Keck 1974, 440: 'Ethos refers to the life-style of a group or society ...'

demands of each particular context. A focus on this ongoing reproduction might ideally encompass an attempt to 'tell the story' of the interaction between Paul (and later leaders) and the Christian community at Corinth in as much detail as possible, beginning with the presentation of the gospel in the missionary situation and its impact upon the first believers.[145] The available evidence, however, is sufficient to allow only a limited view of the interaction which occured prior to the writing of 1 Corinthians, which is sketched in chapter 3 below as a part of the process of outlining the context within which 1 Corinthians must be understood. It must be acknowledged that the texts we possess permit only glimpses of Pauline Christianity at certain points in time. There are gaps not only before the writing of 1 and 2 Corinthians but also afterwards; we have no information relating specifically to the Corinthian community on developments after the death of Paul until the writing of 1 Clement.

The following exegetical studies, then, are necessarily limited in scope. They first build up a picture of the context to which 1 Corinthians is addressed and then explore the social ethos which is conveyed by the teaching of this letter, by Paul's presentation and practice of his role as an apostle in 1 and 2 Corinthians, and by the admonition of 1 Clement.

The theoretical orientation of this study may be summarised thus: the conceptual framework is drawn from structuration theory's approach to social structure and reproduction. From this perspective Pauline Christianity is viewed as a symbolic order which, like a language, comprises rules and resources which are drawn upon, reproduced and transformed over time. The lives of those who are members of the Pauline communities are shaped by this symbolic order, as it is encapsulated and expressed in the texts which are addressed to the particular context in which each community is located. I seek to focus upon the 'shape' – the social ethos – which various formulations of this symbolic order give to the relationships and social interaction of the Pauline Christians at Corinth. The critical orientation of this approach implies that I shall seek throughout to be aware of the extent to which these formulations may reflect or

---

[145] The most detailed attempt to work out the conversation between Paul and the Corinthians prior to and including 1 Corinthians is Hurd 1965, though Hurd's detailed reconstruction of the Corinthians' letter to Paul and his previous letter to the Corinthians is open to criticism and doubt (see further §3.6. below). For another attempt to reconstruct the Corinthians' letter to Paul, see Findlay 1900.

sustain the interests of particular social groups and may be ideological – insofar as they use the symbolic and theological resources of the developing Christian tradition to legitimate or sustain forms of social domination.

Part II

The Corinthian correspondence: exegetical studies

3

The Corinthian community

3.1. Introduction

In the light of the theoretical framework outlined in the previous chapter, the exegetical studies in the following four chapters seek to investigate some aspects of the way in which the symbolic order of Pauline Christianity is reproduced and transformed over time in relation to, and in the context of, a particular community, the Corinthian one. Giddens' approach demands that we view Pauline Christianity not as a system frozen at a moment in time, but as a set of rules and resources, a symbolic order, which, like a language, is continually produced, reproduced and transformed over time, through the activities of the human subjects who both shape and are shaped by this symbolic order. The symbolic order is produced in the context of a set of conditions, some of which are unacknowledged, and its reproduction produces a range of consequences, some of which may be unintended. These consequences form a part of the context in which further reformulation takes place. I am interested especially in the 'social ethos' of the Corinthian correspondence,[1] in the potential impact of Christian teaching upon various social groups and upon their relationships ἐν ἐκκλησίᾳ, and I seek throughout to be aware of the interests and ideology which the symbolic order may convey.

The purpose of this chapter is to set the scene for the chapters which follow, and specifically for the analysis of 1 Corinthians in chapter 4. In this part of the study my dependence on the work of others, especially Theissen, will be clear. In terms of the theoretical framework, this chapter outlines the context and conditions which form the basis for Paul's reformulation of the symbolic order in 1 Corinthians, and also attempts to sketch at least an outline of the previous interaction between Paul and

---

[1] This term is defined above, p. 57.

the Corinthian Christian community. I begin by outlining the wider context, that of the city of Corinth and of the Roman empire. Then I explore the most likely contexts for Paul's missionary activity and some aspects of his message; developments between the founding mission and the time of 1 Corinthians; and the social composition of the Corinthian congregation. Most attention, however, is given to considering the evidence (from 1 Corinthians) concerning social tensions and divisions within the community. The reason for such a focus is that Paul's responses to such situations are clearly the most important sources for an investigation of the social ethos of his teaching: if there are problems which stem from tension between social groups, or which concern social interaction and behaviour, then the way in which Paul formulates a Christian response to those situations will be of especial interest.

3.2. Social context: first-century Corinth and the Roman Empire

Centuries before Paul visited Corinth it was a thriving Greek city, its growth and prominence due in large part to its strategic location on the isthmus which formed the gateway to the Peloponnesian peninsula. Corinth's two ports, Lechaeum and Cenchreae, facilitated and handled a large volume of trade.[2] However, its history was decisively interrupted in the second century BCE when the city's inhabitants joined the Achaean league in war against Rome. Military victory was won by the Romans under Lucius Mummius, and they ransacked the city of Corinth in 146 BCE, burning buildings and slaughtering the inhabitants.[3] A century later, in 44 BCE, the city was refounded as a Roman colony by Julius Caesar. While complete destruction and desolation in the period 146–44 BCE should not be assumed,[4] 44 BCE clearly marked a significant new beginning in Corinth's history. Not only did it mean the establishment of Roman administration but also the settlement there of a new population, colonists from Rome comprising freedpersons, urban plebs and

---

[2]   For the ancient description of Corinth and its formative (often mythical) history see Pausanius *Description of Greece*, Book 2; Strabo *Geography* 8.6.20–23; see further Murphy O'Connor 1983, for ancient texts and commentary. Various location maps and a detailed overview of Corinth's history from 228 BCE – 267 CE may be found in Wisemann 1979.

[3]   See Pausanius *Description of Greece* 2.1.2; Vitruvius *On Architecture* 5.5.8; Strabo *Geography* 8.6.23; Wisemann 1979, 461–62.

[4]   See Wisemann 1979, 491–96 (esp. 494); Willis 1991; Oster 1992, 54–55.

possibly army veterans.[5] The Roman province of Achaia was formed in 27 BCE and Corinth most probably served as capital of the province.[6] With its favourable and strategic location, refounded Corinth offered great opportunities for business and trade, and thus for money to be made.[7] Indeed, the city expanded rapidly during the first two centuries after its resettlement, reaching a peak in the second century, and a great deal of impressive building work took place during this time of growth.[8]

Corinth, in the first century CE, is a city whose social and administrative structures are a part of the wider social, economic and political system of the Roman empire. The social structure of the empire as a whole is probably best visualised as a large pyramid; a representation of a system in which power, wealth and status are concentrated heavily within a tiny ruling elite who comprise at most around one per cent of the empire's population.[9] Below the emperor himself, this ruling elite comprised three main orders (*ordines*), the *ordo senatorius*, or senatorial order, the *ordo equester*, or equestrian order, and the *ordines decurionum*, the orders of decurions, the ruling elite in each city. 'The high offices in the administration of the empire and in the command of the military were reserved for senators and *equites*, while the adminstration of the civic communities was reserved for the local elites gathered in the *ordines decurionum.*'[10] Among the qualifications for entering the elite strata wealth was highly important; there were levels of wealth specified as the requirement for joining the *ordines*, the higher the order, the greater the sum required.[11] Also important were birth, legal status (possession of Roman citizenship) and place of origin. In particular, high social position was often

---

5   See Strabo *Geography* 8.6.23; Plutarch *Life of Caesar* 57.5; Appian *Roman History* 8.20.136; Engels 1990, 16; Furnish 1984, 7; Wisemann 1979, 497.
6   See Wisemann 1979, 501–502.
7   Engels 1990, 17, speaks of 'an excellent chance to prosper' and notes that by the first century CE Corinth had grown from a small colony to become the first city of Greece (24).
8   See Wisemann 1979, 509ff; Engels 1990, 43–65, 170–71.
9   See esp. Alföldy 1986; 1985, 146, for diagrammatic representations of the social structure of the empire (taken up also by Theissen 1988b, 209–10; 1993, 269–71) and discussion of this subject; Alföldy 1985, 147, for the figure of 1 per cent. For further discussions of the social structure of the Roman empire, see Gager 1975, 96–106; Alföldy 1985, 94–156; 1986, 69–81; Garnsey and Saller 1987, 112–18; and, in favour of a class-based analysis, Ste. Croix 1981, 31–111 (contrast Finley 1973, 35–61). Batomsky 1990 offers an illuminating analysis of the vast gap between rich and poor, in comparison with Victorian England.
10 Alföldy 1985, 108.
11 See further MacMullen 1974, 89–91; Alföldy 1985, 115–31.

inherited, while humble origins were generally a barrier to progress and a social stigma, even for an individual who managed to amass considerable wealth.[12]

The decurional order comprised the ruling elite in each particular city; 'the members of the council and the magistrates, deliberately set apart from the *plebs* of the city'.[13] In Corinth the chief magistrates of the city were two annually elected officials who were given the title *duoviri* and were effectively the heads of the city community for that year. Also elected annually were two aediles, immediately below the *duoviri* in position. 'The city councillors, *decuriones*, were appointed from among ex-aediles and *duoviri* and held office for life.'[14] Normally, rich freedmen, though economically among the elite of a city, could not be elected into such offices. However, at Corinth this restriction did not apply,[15] perhaps because of the recent refounding of the city and the large numbers of manumitted slaves among the colonists who populated it.

There was considerable diversity among the lower strata in the empire. One important division was between city and country (it is interesting that Pauline Christianity in its early years is apparently an urban phenomenon),[16] and in both these spheres there were three main categories of people within the lower strata; slaves (*servi*), freedpersons (*liberti*), and the freeborn (*ingenui*).[17] While the lowest legal status was that of the slave,[18] slaves cannot simply be lumped together and assumed to form a stratum or class at the bottom of the pyramid. Certainly many slaves on rural estates endured harsh treatment and were forced to work for very long hours in inhumane conditions, yet there were also many rural peasants who faced the problems of extreme poverty, malnutrition and debt. In the urban setting, the status and position of slaves depended in large part upon who they served and in what capacity.[19] Being a slave of a reputable owner and being given a position of some responsibility

---

[12] See further Alföldy 1985, 111–15; MacMullen 1974, 88–120.

[13] Alföldy 1985, 127.

[14] Wisemann 1979, 499; on the administrative structure of Corinth and the other elected offices, see 497–502.

[15] Wisemann 1979, 498; for the normal situation see Alföldy 1985, 131.

[16] Cf. Meeks 1983, 9–16; Ste. Croix 1975, 1–9; Alföldy 1985, 94–156.

[17] See Alföldy 1985, 133–49, esp. 146; Theissen 1993, 269.

[18] Cf. Stambaugh and Balch 1986, 113; Westermann 1943, 26–27.

[19] See further Martin 1990, 1–49; 1991a, 107–11.

could bring a degree of status and possibly even wealth.[20] Freedpersons often remained bound to their former owners and obligated to them, while hoping perhaps to benefit from their patronage.[21] Independent artisans and traders, while perhaps more free from the direct dominion of another, lacked therefore the security of provision which slaves received.

The diversity within the lower strata meant that there was never sufficient commonality of interest for a revolutionary class consciousness to develop.[22] Protests were generally restricted to the concerns of a particular group in a particular locality. The well-known slave revolts all took place in the first two centuries BCE, two in Sicily (139–132 and 104–100 BCE) and one in Italy (the famous revolt led by Spartacus, 73–71 BCE), when conditions and treatment were particularly bad.[23] Fear of revolt and rebellion plagued slave owners. Conditions in the first century were different, and no large scale revolts occurred,[24] though this change may be linked as much with the lack of opportunity for group cohesion as with any improvements in treatment. Pronouncements by the emperors Claudius and Domitian, for example, reveal a certain limited concern for slaves, but also surely reveal that cruel treatment was relatively common:[25]

> When certain men were exposing their sick and worn out slaves on the island of Aesculapius because of the trouble of treating them, Claudius decreed that all such slaves were free, and that if they recovered, they should not return to the control of their master; but if anyone preferred to kill such a slave rather than to abandon him, he was liable to the charge of murder. (Suetonius, *Claud.* 25.2.)

> He [Domitian] prohibited the castration of males, and kept down the price of the eunuchs that remained in the hands of the slave dealers. (Suetonius, *Dom.* 7.1.)

---

[20] The most prominent examples being those slaves employed in senior positions in the *familia Caesaris* (cf. Phil 4.22).

[21] Suetonius *Claud.* 25.1. reports that Claudius 'reduced to slavery again such [freedpersons] as were ungrateful and a cause of complaint to their patrons'.

[22] Cf. Alföldy 1985, 153; MacMullen 1974, 123–25.

[23] See Finley OCD, 996; Koester 1982a, 61; Ste. Croix 1981, 146, 409; Westermann 1955, 66, 140; Alföldy 1985, 67–73.

[24] Bartchy 1973, 71, 24 n. 66.

[25] See further below, on the treatment of slaves within the legal system.

Wider class unity was also dissipated by the many 'vertical' links which bound slaves and freedpersons not to one another but to their patrons and their households. As well as the direct tie of ownership which slavery represented, vertical links were also sustained through patron-client relationships.[26]

The traditional head of the Roman household was the father, the *paterfamilias*, who possessed the power of dominion (*patria potestas*) over the other household members: wife, children and household slaves.[27] It is difficult to ascertain precise figures concerning the average composition of households in first century Corinth, and still harder to do so for those which were a part of the Pauline ἐκκλησία, but there is sufficient evidence to reveal that among the Pauline Christians in Corinth there were certainly both householders and slaves (see further §3.7. below). David Verner has estimated that 'it is unlikely that more than twenty-five percent of households included slaves, even in the slave centers of the empire ... a large majority of the population could not have afforded to buy and keep slaves'.[28] Some of the wealthy elite possessed large numbers of slaves, while many lesser households contained much smaller numbers.[29]

The main source of slaves during the period of Rome's expansion as a republic was war; conquered 'foreigners' were enslaved in their thousands.[30] As expansion slowed, however, this source became less significant and other sources became important. One such source was the offspring produced by those who were already slaves (outside the legal context of marriage, since slaves were not allowed to marry).[31] Such offspring were automatically the property of the parents' owner. Indeed, it has been suggested that the production of a new generation of slaves could go some way towards encouraging the manumission of older

---

[26] See further Chow 1992; Saller 1982; Alföldy 1985, 101, 148, 153.

[27] See further Saller 1991; Lassen 1991, 128–29; Verner 1983, 27–81.

[28] Verner 1983, 61. Bloch 1947, 204 therefore exaggerates somewhat when he writes: 'Dans le monde romain des premiers siècles, l'esclave était partout: aux champs, à la boutique, à l'atelier, à l'office. Les riches en entretenaient des centaines ou des milliers; il fallait être bien pauvre pour n'en posséder au moins un.'

[29] See Alföldy 1985, 137; Westermann 1955, 84–90. Pedanius Secundus, a leading Roman senator, had 400 slaves in 61 CE, according to Tacitus *Annals* 14.43. On the prices paid for slaves see Jones 1956, 9–10; Westermann 1955, 100–101.

[30] Cf. Koester 1982a, 59.

[31] Westermann 1955, 81.

slaves.[32] Other new slaves included those who were forced by debt to sell themselves or family members into slavery.[33] The practice of exposing unwanted or unsupportable infants may also have provided a source of slaves for those prepared to rear an abandoned child.[34]

The achievements of the Roman empire, especially in the legal and administrative spheres, are often regarded with admiration. The time of the empire is described by E. Gibbon, for example, in his famous *Decline and Fall of the Roman Empire*, as 'the period in the history of the world when the condition of the human race was most happy and prosperous'.[35] However, from the perspective of a *critical* socio-historical inquiry, without ignoring or denying the positive elements within this social system, it must also be regarded as a system built upon and sustaining particular forms of domination.[36]

Most obviously the empire was built upon military domination. The blunt truth about the might of Rome is well expressed by Josephus:

> The might of the Romans was irresistible ... To scorn meaner (ταπεινοτέρους) masters might, indeed, be legitimate, but not those to whom the universe (τὰ πάντα) was subject. For what was there that had escaped the Romans, save maybe some spot useless through heat or cold? Fortune, indeed, had from all quarters passed over to them, and God who went the round of the nations, bringing to each in turn the rod of empire, now rested over Italy. There was, in fact, an established law, as supreme among brutes as among men, 'Yield to the stronger' and 'The mastery is for those pre-eminent in arms.' (Josephus *War* 5.364–367.)

The ruling elite, however, describe their achievements ideologically as an establishment of peace and justice (see further below). The perspective of the dominated is perhaps revealed in the remarkable speech which Tacitus puts into the mouth of Calgacus the Briton:

---

[32] MacMullen 1974, 92: 'Their children they might have to leave in their master's house to endure in turn some decades of servitude – a fair exchange, since many of them came into their condition as the price for life itself, having been abandoned by their parents at birth and reared by their finders for later sale.' On the widespread practice of manumission, see further below, §4.3.1. excursus on 1 Cor 7.21b.

[33] Cf. Ste. Croix 1981, 165–70; Alföldy 1985, 141; 1 Clem 55.2.

[34] Cf. MacMullen 1974, 92 (quoted above, n. 32); Alföldy 1985, 138.

[35] Quoted by Ste. Croix 1981, 13.

[36] Cf. Wengst 1987, 5.

To plunder, butcher, steal, these things they misname empire; they make a desolation and they call it peace. Children and kin are by the law of nature each man's dearest possessions; they are swept away from us by conscription to be slaves in other lands. (Tacitus, *Agricola* 30.5–31.1, cited by Wengst 1987, 52–53.)

In part as a result of military conquests and the associated plundering, a small elite in the empire amassed huge levels of wealth.[37] A record of the division of spoils at Pompey's triumph reveals the concentration of rewards upon those of higher rank. For example, his 20 staff officers received around 800,000 denarii each, while 32,000 legionary privates received about 1,500.[38] Military and economic domination were also closely linked through the imposition of taxation upon the provinces.[39] Even the 'charitable' distributions (often of grain) which took place in many cities were skewed towards those of higher position: 'cash or food was handed out by rank.'[40] In Giddens' terms we see structures of domination operating through both military and economic spheres, and controlling the allocation of resources.

The Roman legal system – structures of legitimation, Giddens suggests, operate primarily through legal institutions[41] – also supports the social hierarchy established and sustained by military and economic power. The upper strata had greater access to the courts owing to the benefits brought by their financial position and social status, especially in cases of civil litigation (see further §3.8.3. below). Although all people were liable to punishment for committing crimes,[42] evidence was extracted and valued in various ways, depending on the standing of the witness. 'Torture traditionally was reserved for slaves', although during the second century BCE it became acceptable to torture witnesses of humble position, even if they were free persons or citizens.[43] When Pliny was endeavoring to find out about the Christians it is notable that he chose

---

[37] See MacMullen 1974, 88–120; Batomsky 1990.
[38] See MacMullen 1974, 94.
[39] Sherwin-White 1963, 12, refers to three decisive aspects of Roman rule in relation to the provinces: permanent military occupation, regular taxation, and Roman supervision of public order, including jurisdiction and municipal government.
[40] MacMullen 1974, 118; cf. further Ste. Croix 1981, 195–97.
[41] See Giddens 1984, 28–34.
[42] Cf. Suetonius, *Claud.* 25.2, quoted above, where killing a slave is explicitly said to be murder.
[43] Garnsey, quoted in Ste. Croix 1981, 459; cf. 454.

'to extract the truth by torture from two slave-women' (*Ep.* 10.96; c.112 CE).

In the punishments meted out under the law we encounter what G. E. M. de Ste. Croix terms a '*dual penalty system*, in which the privileged groups receive a lighter penalty than the lower classes'.[44] As the most degrading and painful punishment 'crucifixion was usually reserved for slaves and particularly vicious prisoners of war'.[45] The harsh treatment of members of the lower classes, and especially of slaves, may be illustrated by the case of Pedanius Secundus, a prominent Roman senator, who was murdered by one of his slaves in 61 CE. This incident led to a notable discussion over appropriate punishment.[46] The normal punishment was for all the victim's slaves to be executed, as a warning to others, for, as the lawyer Gaius Cassius said, in a revealing comment, 'you will never coerce such a medley of humanity except by terror' (Tacitus *Annals* 14.44). So, although some of the senators were concerned about the loss of innocent life and in spite of protests by the populace, the 400 slaves of Pedanius Secundus were duly executed.[47]

A third category of structures mentioned by Giddens is structures of signification, by which he refers to the symbolic orders, interpretative schemes, or 'modes of discourse' which operate within a social system.[48] Here, Giddens suggests, we are most likely to find the operation of ideology, as language is used to describe and legitimate the dominant social order in particular ways.[49] Caesar Augustus, for example, described his achievements as the establishment of peace:

I extended the boundaries of all the provinces which were bordered by races not yet subject to our empire. The provinces of the Gauls, the Spains, and Germany, bounded by the ocean from Gades to the mouth of the Elbe, I reduced to a state of peace (*pacavi / ἐν εἰρήνῃ κατέστησα*). The Alps, from the region which lies nearest to the

---

[44] Ste. Croix 1981, 458–59; cf. also Wengst 1987, 39–40; Garnsey 1970, 199–203.

[45] Stambaugh and Balch 1986, 35–36. The earlier slave revolts had of course been severely punished, perhaps the most well known punishment being the crucifixion of 6,000 slaves who were lined along the *Via Appia* from Rome to Capua (see Ste. Croix 1981, 409; Wengst 1987, 231 n. 5).

[46] Tacitus *Annals* 14.42–45; see also Ste. Croix 1981, 409.

[47] For another such incident see Pliny *Ep.* 3.14.

[48] See Giddens 1984, 28–34.

[49] Cf. Giddens 1984, 33.

Adriatic as far as the Tuscan Sea, I brought to a state of peace without waging on any tribe an unjust war. (*Res Gestae* 26.)[50]

To describe military domination as the establishment of peace is clearly to use a particular interpretative discourse to describe the action. Klaus Wengst identifies 'peace and security' as one of the central slogans of the empire (a slogan quoted by Paul in 1 Thess 5.3).[51] Aelius Aristides, a second-century orator, praising the achievements of the empire, asserted: 'But now a universal security (ἄδεια) which is clear to all has been given to the earth and to all who dwell upon it. And they seem to me to be fully free from the suffering of evil, and on the other hand to have received many opportunities to be governed well.'[52] And Wengst quotes Seneca on the benefits of Nero's reign, including 'a security deep and abounding, and justice enthroned above all injustice'.[53] Such phrases clearly present the empire as an establishment of order, peace, security and justice.

Within this established order was a social hierarchy in which rank and position were strongly defined and displayed. Wealth, legal standing, and family origin were all important, as we have already noted. Ramsey MacMullen has explored in some detail this sense of hierarchy, which, he argues, 'ruled behaviour'.[54] From the perspective of those near the top of the pyramid, manual and wage-labour were degrading, and slaves were despised. The poor, it seems, were held in contempt basically because they were poor. 'Poverty in and of itself is "vile", "dishonoured", "ugly" …'[55] As MacMullen's 'lexicon of snobbery' shows, there were specific groups of words used to describe those who were worthy of honour and respect, in contrast to those who were not. These words 'indicate the range of prejudice felt by the literate upper classes for the lower'.[56] Dinners, banquets and other social occasions were, as MacMullen shows, occasions on which social distinctions could be, and were, made clear.[57]

---

[50] Quoted also in Barrett 1956, 3. On Caesar's military conquests, see further *Res Gestae* 25–35.

[51] Wengst 1987, 19–21.

[52] Aristides *Eulogy of Rome* 104, cited in part by Wengst 1987, 19.

[53] Wengst 1987, 38; Seneca *De Clementia* 1.1.8.

[54] MacMullen 1974, 112; see 104–120.

[55] MacMullen 1974, 116; see 115–16.

[56] See MacMullen 1974, 138–41.

[57] See MacMullen 1974, 110–11; Pliny *Ep.* 2.6; Juvenal *Satire* 3.153ff; *Satire* 5; see further §3.8.1. below.

The steep social hierarchy represented by the pyramid was sustained, then, not only by economic and military might and by the operations of the legal system, but also by the ideology of elite discourse and its social expressions.

This, then, is a brief sketch of the social context in which the Corinthian community was located, and of the dominant social and symbolic order of the time. Into this context Paul came, proclaiming his message concerning God's action through his son, Jesus Christ, the crucified and risen Messiah.

3.3. Paul's mission at Corinth

Paul was clearly the founder of the Corinthian Christian community,[58] although precisely when he did so is a matter of some dispute. Generally, the dating of Paul's mission at Corinth (and of 1 Thessalonians) is based upon the evidence of Acts 18.1–17, the passage where Luke describes Paul's arrival and eighteen-month ministry in the city. There are two points of reference within the Acts passage which permit correlation to be made with external evidence and thus allow an absolute dating to be attempted. The first of these references is to the edict of Claudius, recorded by Suetonius, expelling Jews from Rome who had rioted 'at the instigation of Chrestus'.[59] This edict is dated by Orosius, a fifth-century ecclesiastical historian, to 49 CE, and, until recently, this has been almost universally accepted as correct. The second crucial reference comes in Acts 18.12, where Gallio is named as proconsul of Achaia (Γαλλίωνος δὲ ἀνθυπάτου ὄντος τῆς 'Αχαίας). An inscription referring to Gallio as proconsul of Achaia has been reconstructed from a number of fragments, discovered during excavations at Delphi, which has allowed the year in which Gallio held office to be determined as 50–51 or 51–52 CE.[60] Thus Paul's eighteen-month stay in Corinth has traditionally been

---

[58] See 1 Cor 3.6, 10; 4.15; 2 Cor 10.14ff; Acts 18.1ff, though Prisca and Aquila were probably Christians before they came to Corinth: it was those involved in the 'Chrestus' controversy who were evicted by Claudius; see Suetonius *Claud.* 25; Lüdemann 1984, 166, 170; Wiefel 1991, 92–93.

[59] Suetonius *Claud.* 25; Acts 18.2: διὰ τὸ διατεταχέναι Κλαύδιον χωρίζεσθαι πάντας τοὺς 'Ιουδαίους ἀπὸ τῆς 'Ρώμης.

[60] On the Gallio inscription, see Barrett 1956, 48–49 and esp. Murphy O'Connor 1983, 141–52, 173–76, who suggests that 51–52 is most likely to have been Gallio's year of office (149).

dated sometime between 49 and 52 CE.[61] However, Gerd Lüdemann has argued in some detail that the edict of Claudius should be dated to 41 CE and that the account in Acts 18.1–17 is a conflation of accounts relating to two visits by Paul to Corinth (the other being hinted at in Acts 20.2).[62] The Gallio incident would therefore relate to the second of these visits and not to the founding mission. Lüdemann therefore dates the beginning of Paul's mission to around 41 CE, almost ten years earlier than the generally accepted date.[63] John Knox, accepting much of Lüdemann's argument, favours 43 CE.[64] Jerome Murphy O'Connor, while agreeing that 41 is the most likely date for the edict, rejects the conflation theory of Acts 18 and argues that 49/50 remains the most likely date for Paul's arrival in Corinth.[65] Others reject Lüdemann's argument that the edict was issued in 41 CE and support the traditional date of 49.[66] My own judgment is that Lüdemann's argument regarding the date of the edict and the redaction of Acts[67] is highly plausible, and that Paul's mission at Corinth may therefore have begun between 41 and 44 CE.

Information about Paul's method of mission is usually derived primarily from Acts, as Paul's letters give few concrete indications. In Acts, Paul is most frequently found preaching in the synagogues[68] but also in the open air, the most famous example being in the Areopagus (Acts 17.16–34). However, there are problems with both of these Lucan presentations.

With regard to the first, preaching in the synagogues, Paul nowhere *explicitly* mentions the synagogue – though the synagogue discipline mentioned in 2 Cor 11.24 presumably reveals a considerable degree of

---

[61] See, for example, Fee 1987, 4–5; Barrett 1971a, 5.

[62] Lüdemann 1983, 292, 302–303; 1984, 6–18, 157–77. Lüdemann builds his chronology primarily on the evidence of the epistles; see esp. 1984. Knox's work (1950) is influential on such an approach. For Knox's critical approval of Lüdemann's work, see Knox 1983, 359–61.

[63] Lüdemann 1984, 262. It is significant that Lüdemann does not give weight to the Aretas incident (2 Cor 11.32f; Acts 9.23–25) as offering a secure chronological datum, as Jewett (1979, 30–33) does (see Lüdemann 1984, 31 n. 10; note also the caution of Knox 1983, 357–58). Jewett dates the incident to 37–39 CE. See overview by Wedderburn 1980.

[64] Knox 1983, 358. Cf. Murphy O'Connor 1982, 88: 'At the earliest ... Paul could have reached Corinth in AD 44.'

[65] See Murphy O'Connor 1982, 85–90; 1983, 130–40; 1984, 148. Cf. Hyldahl 1986, 124.

[66] E.g. Watson 1986, 91–94.

[67] See further Lüdemann 1989.

[68] See Acts 13.5, 13ff; 14.1; 17.1f, 10, 16f; 18.4f, 19; 19.8.

contact over some time with that community[69] – and it seems likely that the emphasis upon it as the major *locale* of Paul's missionary activity is a Lucan one, reflecting Luke's belief that mission goes first to the Jews, and then, after rejection by the Jews, to the Gentiles.[70] However, at least in the case of Corinth, it would be equally implausible to argue that Paul had no contact with the Jewish population. The likelihood of there being a Jewish population at Corinth in Paul's time is suggested both by the discovery of the lintel bearing the rough inscription [Συν]αγωγη Ἑβρ[αιων][71] (although problems of dating prohibit the conclusion that it was contemporary with Paul)[72] and by the mention of a Jewish colony there in Philo's *Legatio ad Gaium* (281) written around 39–41 CE.[73] Paul's contact with a synagogue at Corinth is unprovable, but his reference to being more than once on the receiving end of Jewish synagogue discipline (2 Cor 11.24), together with the evidence for the existence of a Jewish community in Corinth and for Jewish members among the Pauline Christians makes it highly probable.[74] The Corinthian Christian community certainly contained both Jews and Gentiles (see §3.7. below), though mostly the latter (1 Cor 12.2).

The image of Paul as a great orator lecturing in public places may owe more to Luke and to Acts 17 in particular than to historical recollection. Ernst Haenchen refers to the Areopagus speech as 'a Lucan creation and not the shortened report of a Pauline sermon'.[75] Conservative scholars too allow that the precise words of the speeches of Paul in Acts owe much to Luke's hand.[76] Moreover, as Stanley Stowers points out, 'this picture of Paul the public orator is not even typical of Acts'.[77]

In recent years, some attention has been given to Paul's missionary activity and lifestyle, in particular by Ronald Hock.[78] Focusing upon

---

69 See Watson 1986, 28–32, who argues for the temporal priority and subsequent abandonment of the mission to the Jews. On the reasons for the punishment of flogging and its administration see Mishnah *Makkoth* 3.1–15; Bell 1994, 326.

70 See esp. Acts 13.46; 18.5–7; cf. Rom 1.16; 1 Cor 9.20f.

71 'Synagogue of the Hebrews'. See Wisemann 1979, plate 5 no. 8; Deissmann 1927, 16 n. 7; Barrett 1956, 50.

72 Cf. Furnish 1985, 352; Murphy O'Connor 1983, 78; Oster 1992, 55–58.

73 See Murphy O'Connor 1983, 77–78. Wisemann 1979, 503 n. 255: 'there were Jews in Corinth at least as early as the reign of Caligula'. On Jews in Corinth see also Richardson 1986, 60–63.

74 Cf. Stowers 1984, 64.

75 Haenchen 1971, 529.

76 E.g. Marshall 1980a, 41–42.

77 Stowers 1984, 61; see further 59–62.

78 See Hock 1979; 1980.

Paul's manual work as a σκηνοποιός, tentmaker,[79] Hock describes the workshop as a plausible setting for missionary activity, for contact and conversation with passers-by. In Corinth many such shops were around the busy ἀγορά (market-place), so contact with people would have been frequent, especially if word got round that someone with a new message or 'philosophy' had come to town.[80] It is also likely that Paul's first and most obvious point of contact would be with people of the same trade, particularly if they were of Jewish origin (Acts 18.2f).

The home in which Paul was staying may also have provided missionary opportunities. Whether with Prisca and Aquila, Titius Justus or Gaius, Paul would doubtless have shared his message in the context of the household:[81]

> The private house was a center of intellectual activity and the customary place for many types of speakers and teachers to do their work ... The speaker might use his own home or be invited to speak or teach in another home. These were private affairs and audiences came by invitation.[82]

Such 'invitation only' meetings, however, would probably have been organised by rather well-to-do households. But whatever the social level of the household where Paul stayed, it would presumably have provided opportunities for him to share his 'good news' with various people. In this context, the baptism of households is clearly understandable (1 Cor 1.16), as are the ways in which a believing community might grow through personal contact and invitation.

---

[79] A fact we learn only from Acts 18.3 (and omitted in D and gig). There is no reason, however, to doubt it; certainly Paul practised some trade working with his hands (1 Thess 2.9; 1 Cor 4.12; cf. 1 Cor 9.3–19).

[80] See Murphy O'Connor 1983, 24–25, 167–70.

[81] See Acts 18.2f, 7; Rom 16.23. Paul only mentions Gaius as his host at Corinth (Rom 16.23). Titius Justus is unknown except in Acts; the identification with Gaius which is sometimes suggested (see e.g. Klauck 1984, 22–23) – the full name would be Gaius Titius Justus – is uncertain and purely conjectural. Accommodation with Prisca and Aquila seems likely; their presence in Corinth at one time may explain why they send special greetings from Ephesus to the church at Corinth (1 Cor 16.19); there was an ἐκκλησία in their house both in Ephesus and Rome (Rom 16.3–5; 1 Cor 16.19), assuming Rom 16 to be addressed to Rome and not Ephesus. Gamble 1977 seems to have convinced many of this, though for the opposite view see Koester 1982b, 138–39.

[82] Stowers 1984, 65–66, who notes mention of such invitations in Epictetus *Diss.* 3.21.6; 3.23.6, 23, 28, 35; Pliny *Ep.* 3.18.

There seems, then, no reason to doubt the essence of Luke's account of Paul's arrival at Corinth in Acts 18.1–4, even if the suggestion of regular speaking in the synagogue 'on every sabbath' (κατὰ πᾶν σάββατον; 18.4) is exaggerated. There were therefore three social settings for Paul's missionary activity at Corinth, the workshop, the house and probably the synagogue.[83]

3.4. The central resources of the faith: a new symbolic order

In these various settings Paul proclaimed his gospel message. What follows is an attempt to sketch the basic outline of Paul's missionary message at Corinth, the fundamental 'rules and resources' which comprise the symbolic order of Pauline Christianity as expressed to the Corinthians. A comprehensive and detailed reconstruction is impossible due to the lack of available evidence: we have no record of Paul's original teaching at Corinth, or elsewhere, and are therefore dependent on the information given in letters written at the time of that first visit to Corinth (1 Thessalonians)[84] or later. In this respect 1 Corinthians is of great value, particularly when it explicitly recalls previous instruction.[85] The developments in thought and expression which no doubt occured during Paul's career should make us wary of using later letters (Romans, 2 Corinthians etc.) to reconstruct an outline of Paul's gospel as it may have been presented at Corinth in the 40s CE. I doubt that Paul's thought underwent decisive changes at particular points in time, as has sometimes been argued,[86] but certainly his perspectives change and the variety in his letters reflects a contingent particularity which means that each epistle is deeply shaped by the context which it addresses.[87] We may, however, state with confidence that Paul's message centred upon the death and resurrection of Christ. When he reminds the Corinthians of his gospel, stressing also the fact that he received the message from

---

[83] Cf. Hock 1979, 450. Stowers 1984, 64–65, 81, emphasises the home and the synagogue.

[84] It is generally agreed that 1 Thess was written from Corinth during Paul's first visit there; see Best 1972, 7, 11; Bornkamm 1971b, 241; Kümmel 1975, 257–60.

[85] However it will not be assumed here that the issues raised in that letter facilitate a reconstruction of Paul's original teaching in the manner outlined by Hurd 1965; for criticism see Barrett 1971a, 6–8; Ford 1966; Kümmel 1966; and further §3.6. below.

[86] Famously by Dodd 1933; 1934.

[87] Cf. Beker 1980; 1991; Dunn 1990b, 21–26.

others, he recalls: 'For I handed on to you among the first things, what I also received, that Christ died for our sins according to the scriptures, and that he was buried, and that he was raised on the third day according to the scriptures' (1 Cor 15.3f).[88] Paul's central convictions concerning Christ's death and resurrection are set within a wider symbolic order.[89] The one, true God has acted in Jesus Christ and, through the resurrection, has vindicated him and declared him to be Lord, κύριος.[90] The declaration or confession κύριος 'Ιησοῦς is of central significance, especially for non-Jews, to whom the term Χριστός may have conveyed little (1 Cor 12.3; 16.22; Rom 10.9; 2 Cor 4.5). Negatively, the message of Jesus' lordship announces that the world is under God's judgment because of its sin, but through the saving action of God in Christ, believers may be rescued from 'the present evil age' (Gal 1.4). People should turn from sexual immorality, idolatry and other sins and be washed and sanctified through Christ, who saves them from the wrath to come (1 Thess 1.9f; 1 Cor 6.9–11). It is relatively clear that Paul's initial instruction would have included some guidance on the 'vices' which were to be shunned and the 'virtues' to be cultivated (1 Thess 4.1ff).[91] Referring to 1 Thess 4.1–8, Meeks suggests that 'it belongs to the catechetical instruction which new Christians received either before or after their baptism'.[92]

Some idea of the instruction Paul is likely to have given his Corinthian converts may be gained from a comparison of 1 Thess 4.1–12 and the vices mentioned in the traditional lists in 1 Cor 5.10f and 6.9–11.[93] The

---

[88] Cf. Hengel 1986, 222–27. 1 Thess 1.9b–10 cannot be taken as a summary of Paul's early missionary preaching, at least not if taken to imply a lack of attention to Christ's death. The 'fact' of Christ's death 'for us' is taken for granted in 1 Thess 4.14; 5.10; 1 Cor 1.13; 8.11 as well as in the traditional kerygma in 1 Cor 15.3ff. Cf. Munck 1963, 104–106, who notes the prominence of Christ crucified in 1 Cor 2.1–5 and Gal 3.1–5. But note also Thrall 1975, who rightly sees Paul's *emphasis* upon Christ crucified in the Corinthian letters as polemical and corrective.

[89] For a brief analysis of the central claims of Paul's gospel, see Sanders 1991, 21–24.

[90] See 1 Cor 8.4, 6; Phil 2.6–11; Rom 1.4. Cf. Meeks 1983, 165–70; Beker 1980, 351–67; who stresses the theocentricity of Paul's thought; Sanders 1977, 442, 447; 1991, 22–23, who expresses Paul's gospel with a focus on *God's* action in Christ.

[91] Cf. Gal 5.21; 1 Cor 5.10–11; 6.9–11. Vielhauer 1975a, 56: 'Die schriftliche Paränese ist Erinnerung und Wiederholung der mündlich „überlieferten" Paränese. Diese wurde also schon gleich zu Anfang mit der Missionspredigt erteilt.' Cf. also Marshall 1983, 105; Tomson 1990, 91.

[92] Meeks 1983, 100; cf. Carrington 1940, 89; Hunter 1961, 130; McDonald 1980, 88.

[93] On the traditional nature of the catalogues of vices and virtues see Conzelmann 1975, 100–101; Ellis 1986, 483–84; Schrage 1991, 386–88; it is widely agreed that they are no new

fundamental theme underlying such material is the change from ἀκαθαρσία (impurity) to ἁγιασμός (holiness), from the old ways to the new, a transformation brought about by the Spirit.[94] Three vices emerge consistently from 1 Cor 5 and 6; πορνεία (sexual immorality), πλεονεξία (greediness) and εἰδωλολατρία (idolatry). Other vices listed fall broadly under one of these headings, as expansions of it. Hans Conzelmann suggests that 'πορνεία and πλεονεξία are the two cardinal points of the paraenesis in 1 Thess 4.1ff.[95] Εἰδωλολατρία admittedly does not feature in 1 Thess 4.1ff, but in 1.9 turning 'from idols' appears as a fundamental description of the Thessalonians' response to the gospel. The positive themes in Paul's paraenesis centre upon love, which is prominent in 1 Thess 4.9ff, specifically as φιλαδελφία, and in 1 Cor 13, as ἀγάπη (cf. also 1 Cor 14.1; 16.14). Other positive qualities associated with love are μακροθυμία (patience), χρηστότης (kindness) and εἰρήνη (peace) (cf. 1 Thess 5.13f; 1 Cor 13.4; 2 Cor 13.11).

God's decisive action in Christ demonstrates for Paul that the end is near and that the world in its present form is passing away (1 Cor 7.31). J. C. Beker puts it concisely: 'The Christ-event is the turning point in time that announces the end of time.'[96] Paul views himself and the believers as those 'upon whom the end of the ages has come' (1 Cor 10.11). His message is based upon the conviction that the death and resurrection of Christ had inaugurated the new age (though Paul never uses this term)[97] which was shortly to be consummated at the parousia.

For Paul the most important sign of the inauguration of this new age is the Spirit.[98] The gospel is preached in power and in the Spirit (1 Cor 2.4; 2 Cor 12.12);[99] believers are baptized and 'washed' 'in the Spirit' (1 Cor 6.11; 12.13); and receiving the Spirit is the essential mark of being in Christ (1 Cor 12.3; Gal 3.2; 4.6; Rom 8.9). The Spirit is active in the worship meetings of the believers (1 Cor 12–14) and should not be quenched (1 Thess 5.19). Believers should no longer live κατὰ σάρκα, 'according to the flesh', but κατὰ πνεῦμα, 'according to the Spirit',

Christian creation, but have roots in both Jewish and Greco-Roman moral traditions; so Vielhauer 1975a, 53; Carrington 1940; Hunter 1961, 52–57; Furnish 1968, 25–51.

94 See 1 Thess 1.9; 3.13; 4.3, 5, 7; 5.23; 1 Cor 6.11; 12.2; 2 Cor 6.14–7.1; Gal 5.19–25 etc.
95 Conzelmann 1975, 102 n. 76; cf. Holtz 1986, 162.
96 Beker 1980, 362.
97 Grayston 1990, 23.
98 Cf. Rowland 1985a, 209; further Dunn 1975, 197–342.
99 Sanders 1991, 24–25, suggests that miraculous signs, δυνάμεις, accompanied the proclamation of the gospel.

(Rom 8.1ff; Gal 5.13ff): a mark of Paul's disappointment with the Corinthians is his judgment that he cannot address them as πνευματικοί but only as σαρκικοί (1 Cor 3.1).[100] The Spirit is one mark of the transfer of believers from one sphere to another: they are no longer 'in darkness' but are 'sons of light' (1 Thess 5.4f). They are members of a new community, the gathering of those who belong to Christ. Paul reminds the Corinthians of this in 1 Cor 6.20 and 7.23 with 'what looks like a familiar dictum', τιμῆς ἠγοράσθητε, 'you were bought with a price'.[101]

These are the central pillars of the Pauline message as we may suspect that the Corinthians heard it. But how did those who accepted this new faith signify their conversion and how were their new beliefs enacted, symbolised and embodied (recalling the definition offered in §2.5., that Pauline Christianity may be defined as a symbolic order embodied in communities)? What did they *do*? To answer this question we must look at ritual.[102]

3.5. Ritual: enacted faith

Ritual, as I understand it here, is an activity in which religious faith is 'enacted'.[103] Rituals, in other words, are forms of behaviour – 'consecrated behaviour', as Geertz puts it[104] – which express and embody the symbols and stories central to a religion. Ritual activities are repeated and recognised by a group; they are rule-governed in the sense that their procedures are generalised and repeatable.

There are many things that the Corinthians did together about which we know very little. We know that they met for worship, most likely weekly,[105] and it seems probable that each gathering included the Lord's supper.[106] We know that they met together in houses,[107] though it is

---

[100] οἱ πνευματικοί is a term applied not hypothetically to some of the Galatians (Gal 6.1).
[101] Grayston 1990, 32.
[102] Cf. Meeks 1983, 140–63; 1993, 91–101.
[103] Cf. Geertz 1957, 422.
[104] Geertz 1966, 28; cf. MacDonald 1988, 62.
[105] Suggested by 1 Cor 16.2: κατὰ μίαν σαββάτου.
[106] 1 Cor 11.18 describes the divisions that occur when they gather ἐν ἐκκλησίᾳ and 11.20 describes the intention of 'the same' (τὸ αὐτό) gathering as κυριακὸν δεῖπνον φαγεῖν. On the possible pattern of events including the Lord's Supper and the worship described in 1 Cor 12–14 see Lampe 1991; cf. also Moule 1961, 62–63.
[107] Rom 16.5; 1 Cor 16.19; Phlm 2; Col 4.15; Meeks 1983, 75–77, 221 n. 2. On the early 'house churches', see Banks 1980; Klauck 1981.

impossible to say how many 'house churches' came together when 'the whole church' (ἡ ἐκκλησία ὅλη) gathered, or how often this would have happened.[108] We know from 1 Cor 11.2–16 that both women and men were free to participate in the worship gatherings[109] and that such gatherings would have included prayers, psalms, prophecies, revelations, tongues, interpretations, etc., as well as teaching and exhortation, perhaps through the reading of scripture or of Paul's letters, which presumably were read when they assembled together.[110] But the details of these assemblies we can only imagine. What did it *mean* to have a λόγος σοφίας ('word of wisdom') or a λόγος γνώσεως ('word of knowledge'; 1 Cor 12.8), and how would the χαρίσματα ἰαμάτων ('gifts of healing'; 12.9) be exercised, and so on?

Given the lack of evidence it is perhaps tempting to 'discover' liturgy and ritual scattered throughout Paul's letters. Thus P. Vielhauer, as many others, interprets 1 Cor 16.20b and 22 as parts of the 'entrance liturgy of the Lord's supper', used, he suggests, to mark the end of the public worship service and the beginning of the eucharistic celebration (the holy kiss, the curse on those not loving the Lord, the cry of 'maranatha' and the blessing of 'the grace of the lord Jesus').[111] Similarly, many parts of Paul's letters have been seen as liturgical or hymnic fragments and assigned to baptismal or other contexts.[112] Meeks devotes considerable attention to what he calls 'minor rituals' such as singing, praying and speaking in tongues, gleaning information from the scattered hints in the Pauline texts.[113]

Unfortunately we really cannot be so sure that such texts actually reveal liturgy and ritual. Thus Stowers suggests: 'Much of Meeks' discussion of ritual is brilliant. He just finds too much of it ... Metaphors too easily become rituals'.[114] We can, however, be certain about

---

[108] 1 Cor 14.23; Rom 16.23. Cf. Moule 1961, 28–29; Meeks 1983, 143.

[109] A practice which seems to be in line with the tradition Paul passed on to them (11.2).

[110] Cf. 1 Thess 5.27; Meeks 1983, 143. On the Corinthians' worship see esp. 1 Cor 14.26ff with the discussions of gifts etc in chapters 12 and 14. Cf. further Moule 1961; Meeks 1983, 142–50; Lampe 1991.

[111] 'die Eingangsliturgie des Herrenmahls'; Vielhauer 1975a, 37–39. Cf. Moule 1961, 43–44; Bornkamm 1969, 169ff.

[112] See discussion in Moule 1981, 31–43. Note the criticism of such an approach in Dunn 1990b, 141–48.

[113] Meeks 1983, 142–50.

[114] Stowers 1985, 174.

the practice of the two 'major ritual complexes':[115] baptism and the Lord's supper. Although these rituals do not receive a great deal of attention in the Corinthian letters, when they are mentioned their practice is assumed. While we lack precise knowledge about the nature of the believers' meetings, we do know that these two rituals must have been performed in the context of a gathering of some sort. They therefore form crucial foci for the sharing, enacting and embodying of Christian faith.

3.5.1. Baptism

Whatever the origins of Christian baptism and Paul's understanding of it,[116] it is clear that it served as the 'rite of initiation' into the Christian community.[117] Certainly the baptism of believers at Corinth is presumed by Paul's question 'or were you baptised in the name of Paul?' (ἢ εἰς τὸ ὄνομα Παύλου ἐβαπτίσθητε; 1 Cor 1.13; cf. 1.15). Paul is unconcerned about who does the baptising and emphasises his own role as a proclaimer of good news not a baptiser. The last thing he wants is a faction whose claim is that *Paul* baptised us (1.13–17). But clearly they were baptised by someone.

Their baptism, as far as we can tell, would have involved immersion in water (Rom 6.4)[118] and probably the unclothing and reclothing of the initiate.[119] As a rite of initiation, baptism symbolised 'the separation of the baptizand from the outside world' and their 'integration ... into another world'.[120] But the believers' understanding and interpretation of their baptism would obviously have depended on the teaching or message which made sense of the physical actions for them. What ideas would the Corinthian converts have been given to understand what was happening at this 'rite of initiation'?

An answer to this question must be cautious, not least because of the relatively late date of much of the Pauline and deutero-Pauline material on baptism. For example, the idea that baptism symbolised or enacted a

[115] As Meeks 1983, 150, labels them.
[116] Questions much debated in the literature: see for example Wagner 1967; Wedderburn 1987.
[117] Cf. Hunter 1961, 66; Dunn 1990b, 159; Meeks 1983, 150–57; Wedderburn 1987, 357; Barrett 1985, 68.
[118] Matthew and Mark both imply that Jesus' baptism by John (thus John's baptism generally) involved immersion; Mark 1.10 describes Jesus ἀναβαίνων ἐκ τοῦ ὕδατος; cf. Matt 3.16:... ἀνέβη ἀπὸ τοῦ ὕδατος.
[119] Meeks 1983, 151, 155; Dunn 1970, 110.
[120] Meeks 1983, 156.

'dying and rising with Christ', which was once widely accepted as a reflection of Paul's understanding,[121] is best regarded as a later development, reflected in Col 2.12 and rejected as a heresy in 2 Tim 2.18.[122] In the undisputedly Pauline letters, resurrection is always a future hope and Alexander Wedderburn has in my view established that the belief in an already realised resurrection is not the most likely explanation for the denial of the resurrection by the Corinthians.[123] Paul did not teach the Corinthians that in baptism they would die and rise with Christ.

From 1 Cor 1.13 and 15 we may be sure that the Corinthians' baptism was administered 'in the name of Christ [Jesus?]' (εἰς τὸ ὄνομα Χριστοῦ ['Ιησοῦ]). This was probably understood as signifying their coming to belong to Christ, as a 'change of ownership'.[124] Baptism marks the end of one form of life and the beginning of a new one (cf. 1 Cor 6.9–11). Paul may have taught the Corinthian converts to understand their descent into the waters of baptism as an identification with Christ's death and burial, and thus as the end of the old life, but as this idea only appears explicitly in Rom 6.3ff it may well be a later 'development in Paul's theology of baptism' and not one current at the time of the Corinthian mission.[125]

Our attention is directed in 1 Cor 12.13 to the importance of the Spirit in connection with baptism. While James Dunn argues that here 'Paul is thinking of baptism in the Spirit; he is not speaking about water at all', C. K. Barrett comments that: 'There is no reason to think that *we were baptised* refers to anything other than baptism in water (together with all that this outward rite signified)'.[126] Indeed the close similarity between 1 Cor 12.13 and Gal 3.27f, where baptism is also mentioned,

---

[121] See Tannehill 1967; Hunter 1961, 66, 70, 135; Barrett 1971a, 288; and discussion in Wedderburn 1987, 1ff.

[122] Cf. Wedderburn 1987, 1–89; Petersen 1986, 217–18; Horsley 1978b, 203–204.

[123] See 1 Cor 15.12ff; Wedderburn 1987, 6–37. Note the future hope of resurrection in Rom 6.5, 8; (cf. 8.23); Phil 3.10–12.

[124] Dunn 1970, 117–18; cf. 1 Cor 6.20, 7.23.

[125] Dunn 1970, 144; cf. Barrett 1985, 69. The ἢ ἀγνοεῖτε ὅτι of Rom 6.3 may imply that such an understanding of baptism was common and widespread (Wedderburn 1987, 40–43) or be 'the polite teacher's manner of passing on new knowledge' (Dunn 1970, 144 n. 17). The idea of the believer's death with Christ is, however, more widespread in Paul; Gal 2.19b; 2 Cor 5.14; Rom 6.5–8.

[126] Dunn 1970, 129; Barrett 1971a, 289. Dunn's sharp (antisacramentalist?) separation between Christian *experience* of Christ and the Spirit, and the ritual 'act' of baptism, does not to me seem sustainable. Dunn insists that baptism is a metaphor and not a spiritual reality; see 1970, e.g. 129–33, 142 etc.

strengthens the latter argument.[127] The gift of the Spirit is the essential mark of the believer's new status (1 Cor 12.3ff; Gal 3.2; Rom 8.9). Paul did not teach the Corinthians that the new life they were beginning was to be understood as resurrection life but rather that it was life 'in the Spirit'. In 1 Cor 12.13 it is stressed that this entry is into a community in Christ, εἰς ἓν σῶμα, (a point which Paul builds on in the following verses). Through baptism believers all become members of one body.

The oneness of believers in Christ is also proclaimed in Gal 3.28b: 'for you are all one in Christ Jesus' (πάντες γὰρ ὑμεῖς εἷς ἐστε ἐν Χριστῷ Ἰησοῦ).[128] Indeed, further information about the teaching with which the Corinthians understood their baptism, I suggest, may be found here in Gal 3.26–28. The strong parallels between Gal 3.27f, 1 Cor 12.13 and Col 3.10f, noted by many writers, suggest that the material was widely used.[129] The extra-canonical parallels strengthen this case.[130] Since baptism is explicitly mentioned in both Gal 3 and 1 Cor 12 we may reasonably assume a connection between this material and the rite of baptism. Whether the material is rightly termed 'liturgical'[131] may be debatable but in some way this interpretation of what was going on in the act of baptism would have been communicated.

Crucial questions, of course, concern the earliness of this baptismal teaching and the phrase οὐκ ἔνι ἄρσεν καὶ θῆλυ ('there is no longer male and female') which appears only in the Galatians passage. Would Paul's Corinthian converts have heard these or similar words? The earlier one dates Galatians, naturally, the more likely is an affirmative answer to this question,[132] yet there are additional grounds on which to argue that the three pairs Jew/Greek, slave/free, male/female represent

---

[127] On Gal 3.27f, Dunn 1970, 109–13 again draws a sharp distinction between spiritual reality and ritual act, claiming that Paul's words in Gal 3.26ff are metaphors drawn from the rite of baptism.

[128] Note the stress on 'all' at the beginning and end of the short section in vv. 26–28; Πάντες γάρ ... πάντες γάρ ... On the structure see Betz 1979, 181.

[129] E.g. Paulsen 1980, 78–79; MacDonald 1987, 5–6. Cf also Rom 12.5 and 1 Cor 10.17.

[130] See esp. Betz 1979, 182–84; Meeks 1974; Paulsen 1980, 80–85; MacDonald 1987, esp. 17–63.

[131] So Betz 1979, 181, 184.

[132] Dates for Galatians vary widely and are dependent in part on a decision as to the precise destination of the epistle; see overviews and arguments for an early date in Fung 1988, 9–28; Dunn 1993, 1–19; Longenecker 1990, lxxii–lxxxviii.

the earliest Pauline form of this material.[133] That the ideas precede the letter to the Galatians is suggested strongly by the fact that the two pairs slave/free and male/female, and the religious, social or conventional distinctions between the opposites, play no significant part in Paul's argument in the letter.[134] Indeed, Paul's extensive use of slave/son and slave/free imagery in his argument draws a sharp distinction between those who are slaves and those who are free/sons (Gal 4.1–31), in contrast to the statement that 'in Christ there is no longer slave and free' (which presumably refers to 'real' slaves and freepersons). The occurrence of Jew/Greek and slave/free in 1 Cor 12.13 and Col 3.11 strengthens the argument for a widespread tradition including these two pairs, but what of male/female?

On the basis of the literary structure of Gal 3.26–28, H. D. Betz argues that οὐκ ἔνι ἄρσεν καὶ θῆλυ is 'a secondary addition to an earlier version of the saying', noting that 'it is not found in the parallels in 1 Cor 12:13 and Col 3:11'.[135] This literary argument depends upon the change from οὐδέ (connecting the first two pairs) to καί (between ἄρσεν and θῆλυ) and the fact that the third phrase 'stands in the neuter' while the previous two 'are masculine'.[136] However, Betz fails to note the most likely reason for these facts, namely the probable echo of Gen 1.27, although he does discuss this verse elsewhere.[137] Further support for the early conjunction of all three pairs within Paul's theology is offered by the fact that all three are found in 1 Cor 7: while discussing 'male/female' issues, Paul illustrates his point (that each one should continue in their calling) using the pairs circumcised/uncircumcised and slave/free, even though, once again, they are of no direct relevance to the situation he is addressing (1 Cor 7.17–24).[138] Thus Scott Bartchy argues

---

[133] It is often suggested, quite plausibly, that the material is pre-Pauline (e.g. Scroggs 1972, 291; MacDonald 1987, 5–16; Betz 1979, 181). However the argument here is only concerned with its use by Paul; cf. Paulsen 1980, 88; Bruce 1982, 187.

[134] Betz 1979, 182; Longenecker 1990, 151. The use of material shaped prior to the passage in which it appears may also be signalled by 'the change from first person to second person plural' between vv. 25 and 26; Betz 1979, 185, with other commentators listed at n. 29.

[135] Betz 1979, 182.

[136] Betz 1979, 182.

[137] Betz 1979, 182, 198–99. The LXX reads ἄρσεν καὶ θῆλυ ἐποίησεν αὐτούς. If MacDonald is right in his argument that the most original form of the saying is found in the Gospel of the Egyptians then the male/female pair is the one original pair. It is certainly prominent in the material MacDonald cites; see 1987, esp. 17–63, 113–26.

[138] *Contra* Lührmann 1975, 61; Gayer 1976, 112ff.

that Gal 3.28 is the source of Paul's thought pattern here.[139] Finally, in view of the extent to which Paul, at the time of 1 Corinthians, regards male/female issues as problematic at Corinth,[140] it seems most likely that the phrase οὐκ ἔνι ἄρσεν καὶ θῆλυ was regarded by Paul as a cause of too much misunderstanding and social disruption, and therefore was dropped from his formulation of the 'all one in Christ' saying.[141]

Gal 3.26–28 also announces that believers are those who through baptism have 'put on Christ' (Χριστὸν ἐνεδύσασθε – v.27). Whether or not Paul specifically drew the analogy (such language does not appear in 1 Corinthians), the metaphor of unclothing and reclothing arises naturally from 'the baptisand's action of unclothing before and reclothing after baptism'.[142]

Many of the central ideas of the Pauline gospel, then, would have been passed on to the Corinthians, symbolised and enacted, in the context of baptism. Baptism enacted and dramatised the believers' transfer from the old life to the new, their escape from the wrath to come and their entry into the community of those who are 'one in Christ'. 'In Christ', they were told, 'there is neither Jew nor Greek, there is neither slave nor free, there is no longer male and female'. Their new status was confirmed by the gift of the Spirit, who now dwelt in them (1 Cor 3.16; 2.12–15; 12.1).

3.5.2. The Lord's Supper

The paucity of texts offering direct evidence concerning early Christian practice is even more obvious in the case of the second major ritual, the Lord's Supper. Indeed, without 1 Cor 10.16–17 and 11.17–34 we would know virtually nothing about how the Lord's Supper was celebrated in New Testament times.[143] Fortunately for this study the texts do relate directly to the Corinthian community and reveal that the Lord's Supper

[139] Bartchy 1973, 162ff; Witherington 1988, 26–27. Gayer 1976, 112ff, argues that there was an emancipatory movement among slaves at Corinth. As Kümmel (1985, 340) comments this is definitely 'nicht sicher' and Gayer fails to take Bartchy's study into account (noted by Kümmel 1985, 341 n. 14).

[140] See further §3.8.5.; §4.3. below.

[141] Cf. Paulsen 1980, 90 n. 94; Lührmann 1975, 60; Barton 1986, 234. However, the saying continued to influence Christian thought in other places and 'schools'; see n. 130 above.

[142] Dunn 1970, 110; cf. Moule 1961, 52. The idea of being clothed with Christ is specifically present in Gal 3.27 and Rom 13.14 (cf. v. 12); cf. also 2 Cor 5.3; Col 3.10–12; Eph 4.24, 6.11, 14.

[143] Cf. Marshall 1980b, 16.

was an established part of the Corinthian believers' practice. But since Paul's major concern in both texts is with particular issues which have now come to his attention, our approach to the Lord's Supper as inaugurated at Corinth must once more be cautious. However, Paul does cite traditions which, he tells us in language close to that used in 1 Cor 15.3, he has previously delivered to them.[144] We may safely assume that the (probably weekly) celebration of this meal was established by Paul during his mission to Corinth.

It is clear from the account in 1 Cor 11.17ff that 'the basic act [was] the eating of a common meal'.[145] However, Paul did not simply instruct the Corinthian believers to get together regularly for a meal. They were to understand their meal as an imitation of the meal of Jesus with his disciples 'on the night in which he was betrayed' (11.23).[146] In particular the meal was to include the sharing of bread and wine, understood as a sharing (κοινωνία) in the body and blood of Christ (11.23–25; 10.16). The fundamental *rationale* for the gathering was as a 'memorial' of Jesus. It proclaimed his death 'until he comes' (11.26). They heard Jesus' command as addressed to them: 'do this in memory of me' (11.24). Again, central elements of the Christian story – the self-giving death of Christ – are recalled, enacted and embodied in this ritual celebration.

Whether or not 11.23–25 is strictly 'liturgical', it seems most reasonable to assume that the 'words of institution', or similar, would have been spoken at the appropriate points during the meal, to give the bread and the cup their particular meaning.[147] During his time at Corinth it was most probably Paul who did this; initially at least this must have been the case, since he was the origin of the tradition. It is interesting, though, that we find no explicit concern in the letters with who fulfilled this role in his absence. The householder who served as 'host' to the gathering seems the most likely guess, although other figures in the community may (sometimes or always) have performed such tasks: teachers, prophets or others appointed to the service of the saints.[148] We simply do

---

[144] Paul had probably not visited Corinth since his founding mission, though he had written a letter (1 Cor 5.9). On the technical language of tradition used in 11.23 see Ellis 1986, 481; Tomson 1990, 145–146 and cf. 1 Cor 11.2; 15.3.

[145] Meeks 1983, 158.

[146] Cf. Meeks 1983, 158.

[147] *Contra* Barrett 1971a, 264, whose scepticism on this point Meeks finds 'excessive' (1983, 239 n. 72).

[148] On the role of hosts as leaders, cf. Filson 1939, 111–12. We know little about the roles of the other figures mentioned; see 1 Cor 16.15; 12.28; 1 Thess 5.12.

not learn about any specific arrangements in this. regard, because it was not an issue on which Paul felt the need to write.

As baptism enacted the believers' entry into 'the body' (1 Cor 12.13), so the Lord's Supper symbolised their κοινωνία within this body: 'because there is one bread, we many are one body, because we all share in the one bread' (ὅτι εἷς ἄρτος, ἕν σῶμα οἱ πολλοί ἐσμεν, οἱ γὰρ πάντες ἐκ τοῦ ἑνὸς ἄρτου μετέχομεν – 10.17). Their sharing together of bread and wine embodied concretely their common membership of the group. Indeed it is significant that the two most important rituals established by Paul in the Corinthian community, rituals which recall and enact central stories and symbols of the Christian faith, are both seen by Paul as a demonstration of the fact that believers have been made one in Christ – an essentially social and communal, as well as religious, affirmation.

3.6. Between founding mission and 1 Corinthians

If Lüdemann's dating of Paul's Corinthian mission is broadly correct (let us say, between 41 and 44 CE),[149] then a considerable period of time passed between this founding visit and the writing of 1 Corinthians (for which Lüdemann suggests a date of 49 or possibly 52 CE).[150] On any conventional dating at least two to three years elapse between the original mission and 1 Corinthians.[151]

There are certain things which we know about the interaction and developments which took place during this time. Other preachers had visited Corinth: certainly Apollos and quite possibly Cephas, or at least some who aligned themselves with Cephas and the Jerusalem church.[152] The extent of the influence of these other preachers is much debated (see §3.8.4. below). Clearly on at least some points, criticism of Paul is based upon comparisons between him and others, notably Cephas (1 Cor 9.1ff; see further §5.3.). Paul, it seems, had not visited the Corinthians in the

---

[149] See §3.3. above.
[150] Lüdemann 1984, 263.
[151] It is generally assumed that Paul left Corinth in 51 or 52 CE (see §3.3. above). 1 Corinthians is dated to late 53 or early 54 by Barrett 1971a, 5; to spring 54 or 55 by Kümmel 1975, 279 (cf. also Fee 1987, 4–5).
[152] See n. 170 below.

meantime,[153] but he had written them a letter, to which he makes reference in 1 Cor 5.9. From 1 Cor 5.9 we learn that in this letter Paul had instructed the Corinthians 'not to mix with the sexually immoral' (μὴ συναναμίγνυσθαι πόρνοις). Paul's clarification of his point in 1 Corinthians indicates that he intended them to separate *not* from the sexually immoral in the world – 'for then you would have to come out from the world' (5.10) – but from anyone who calls themselves an ἀδελφός but is guilty of such immorality (5.11). What Paul's first letter actually said we can hardly know – it is perhaps somewhat unfair to accuse the Corinthians of deliberately misunderstanding it[154] – though it has been suggested that a portion of it is preserved in 2 Cor 6.14–7.1, a passage which seems to intrude upon and interrupt its canonical context.[155] Certainly this passage, about which there has been much debate (including the suggestions of non or anti-Pauline origin),[156] urges Christians not to be 'unevenly yoked' (ἑτεροζυγοῦντες) with unbelievers (ἄπιστοι), and draws sharp contrasts between believers and unbelievers, righteousness and lawlessness, light and dark, Christ and Beliar, and so on. Such exhortation could easily have been understood in the way the Corinthians seem to have understood Paul's previous letter, and the hypothesis that it is a portion of that first letter is in some ways attractive. It has always been hard to see, however, why such a passage, if not originally a part of 2 Corinthians 1–8, should have been inserted into such an apparently inappropriate context.[157]

Precisely what else was included in the 'previous letter' is impossible to say, though it seems reasonable to suggest that the Corinthians' letter to Paul (1 Cor 7.1) was at least in part a reply to it.[158] Gordon Fee suggests that idolatry was another subject dealt with in the letter.[159] John Hurd's detailed reconstruction of Paul's first letter is vulnerable; partly due to the weight he places upon the apostolic decree (recorded in Acts

---

153 2 Cor 2.1–3 refers to the 'painful visit' made after the writing of 1 Corinthians, and 2 Cor 13.1 announces a third visit; see further appendix 1 and §5.4. below.
154 Cf. the comment of Harris, quoted with approval by Barrett 1971a, 130.
155 Hurd 1965, 135–37; Taylor 1991, 71, 75–78. It is regarded as an interpolation into 2 Cor also by, among others, Watson 1984, 331 esp. n. 57, 335; Hyldahl 1973, 289.
156 For bibliography and discussion see Kümmel 1975, 287–88; Martin 1986, 181–95; Scott 1992, 187–220; Thrall 1994, 25–36.
157 A point made by Fee 1977, 140–47; see also the defence of integrity by Thrall 1978.
158 Cf. Fee 1987, 7.
159 Fee 1987, 7.

15.20, 29) as providing the content and the occasion for Paul's letter; partly because he seems to make insufficient allowance for misunderstanding of Paul's teaching, assuming, for example, that asceticism among the Corinthians must have arisen from a direct instruction of Paul's on this matter.[160]

However, Hurd's reconstruction of the list of subjects raised in the Corinthians' letter to Paul remains highly plausible. Hurd suggested that each of the sections on 1 Corinthians which begins with the words περὶ δέ represents Paul's reply to specific points or questions from their letter.[161] Margaret Mitchell has recently questioned Hurd's argument, by showing that in Greek letters the words περὶ δέ do not necessarily indicate the beginning of a response to an issue raised in a previous letter, but only the introduction of a new subject known to both writer and reader(s).[162] But these observations, valuable though they are, do not entirely undermine Hurd's case. It is only in 1 Corinthians and twice in 1 Thessalonians (1 Thess 4.9; 5.1), that Paul uses περὶ δέ to introduce successive topics of discussion, and in 1 Corinthians the first of these clearly marks the beginning of a response to the Corinthians' letter (περὶ δὲ ὧν ἐγράψατε ... 1 Cor 7.1). Six times in 1 Corinthians the phrase is used to introduce new topics (7.1; 7.25; 8.1; 12.1; 16.1; 16.12). The likelihood that these subjects are ones raised in the Corinthians' letter is increased by the observation that, as Hurd suggested, Paul seems to deal in a calm and reasoned way with these subjects, whereas his response to oral reports is forceful and indignant (this is certainly the case in 1.10ff (cf. 4.18–21); 5.1ff; 11.17ff).[163] But exactly how each of these subjects came to be an issue for the Corinthians is hard to say. The collection project, for example, is certainly something about which the Corinthians already know and have probably asked Paul for further information about in their letter (1 Cor 16.1–4); but we do not know whether it was introduced to them in Paul's first letter (so Hurd),[164] or by Titus and others on their visit to Corinth.[165]

---

[160] Hurd 1965, 275–76, further 240–70; note the criticism of Barrett 1971a, 6–8 and see n. 85 above.
[161] See Hurd 1965, 65–74.
[162] Mitchell 1989.
[163] See Hurd 1965, 75–82.
[164] Hurd 1965, 293.
[165] See further appendix 1.

It is clear that 1 Corinthians has a double occasion: it is a response to the Corinthians' letter to Paul, quite possibly brought to Paul by Stephanas, Fortunatus and Achaicus (1 Cor 16.17), and a response to the oral reports which Chloe's people have passed on to Paul (1 Cor 1.11; cf. 5.1; 11.18). Many of the specific subjects raised, whether in written or verbal form, will be dealt with further below.

Without attempting to spell out the details of this previous interaction any further, it is important to take note of the extent to which, prior to the writing of 1 Corinthians, there has already been an extended process of interaction between Paul and the Corinthians. Paul has been engaged in the task of presenting and representing what it means to be Christian, in the light of the reactions and (sometimes unintended) consequences which his original message drew forth. He has shaped the Corinthians 'world view' and their 'ethos',[166] their beliefs and their actions and relationships. In the remainder of this chapter, I shall outline further the context to which 1 Corinthians is addressed, before focusing in some detail (in chapter 4) on the further reformulation of the Christian symbolic order which 1 Corinthians represents.

3.7. The social composition of the Christian community at Corinth

Before we explore the various aspects of the Corinthian church's life in which social factors play some part, it is important to develop some appreciation of the composition of the Corinthian ἐκκλησία. Our understanding of Paul's response to this community will depend, to some extent, on the picture we have of the range of people who were members of this group.

Certainly by the time of 1 Corinthians, the congregation contained both Jews and Gentiles. From 1 Cor 12.2 (ὅτε ἔθνη ἦτε ...) we must assume that it was composed largely of Gentiles, some of whom may previously have been 'Godfearers',[167] but a Jewish presence within the community should not be denied.[168] According to Luke, Crispus and

---

[166] Geertz's terms; see §2.5. above.
[167] Assuming some such people to have existed, see Finn 1985; Esler 1987, 36; Levinskaya 1990; *contra* Kraabel 1981; 1986. Theissen 1982, 102–104, emphasises the importance of Godfearers for the Pauline mission.
[168] Cf. Fee 1987, 4. Tomson 1990, 59–62, 242 argues that the Corinthian church, as most Pauline congregations, was an exclusively Gentile church.

Sosthenes were ἀρχισυνάγωγοι, leaders of the synagogue, and Aquila was a Jew. All three names occur in 1 Corinthians and there is no reason to doubt the Jewishness of Crispus and Aquila, although the two Sosthenes mentioned may well be different people.[169] Visits to Corinth by Apollos and possibly by Cephas increase the probability that there were Jewish converts within the ἐκκλησία; whether Cephas had been there or not, there were certainly some who aligned themselves with him (1 Cor 1.12).[170] Furthermore, in Rom 16.21 Paul names Lucius, Jason and Sosipater, probably all members of the Corinthian ἐκκλησία, as οἱ συγγενεῖς μου, which is most likely to mean 'fellow Jews' (cf. Rom 9.3; 16.7, 11).[171] Finally, Paul's illustration in 1 Cor 7.18f strongly implies a Jewish presence among the believers, or it would have been without significance to them.[172] But what of the social level of the converts? From which strata of Corinthian society did they come?

Celsus, 'the first pagan author we know of who took Christianity seriously enough to write a book against it',[173] claimed that the religion attracted only 'the foolish, dishonourable and stupid, and only slaves, women and little children'.[174] Origen's reply includes an early example of the exegesis of 1 Cor 1.26 which points out 'that Paul's words are not "*no* wise man after the flesh", but "not *many* wise men after the flesh"'.[175] However, early in the twentieth century, the consensus view still lay close to that of Celsus. Deissmann in particular popularised the view that early Christianity was essentially a movement among the lower classes.[176]

---

[169] On these characters see Acts 18.2, 8, 17, 18, 26; Rom 16.23; 1 Cor 1.1, 14; 16.19.

[170] On Apollos see Acts 18.24ff; 19.1; 1 Cor 1.12; 3.4ff; on Cephas, 1 Cor 1.12; 3.22; 9.5; 15.5. Barrett 1963 argues that Cephas had visited Corinth; see also Richardson 1986, 64.

[171] BAGD, 772 ('fellow Jew' or 'relative') – but the number of people Paul relates it to in Rom 16 makes the meaning 'relative' unlikely. See also Meeks 1983, 216 n. 29, otherwise Judge 1960b, 137 n. 25.

[172] Cf. Lührmann 1975, 61. Watson 1986, 80–87 is, however, right, I believe, to argue that Judaizers were never a problem at Corinth. Richardson 1986, 65–74, exaggerates the extent to which Jewish issues were problematic at Corinth.

[173] Meeks 1983, 51.

[174] Quoted by Origen *Cels.* 3.44. Note, however, that Pliny *Ep.* 10.96 reports that Christians came from 'omnis aetatis, omnis ordinis, utriusque sexus'.

[175] Origen *Cels.* 3.48, my italics.

[176] Deissmann 1927, 143–45, 250–51, 385 etc. Cf. also Engels (in Marx and Engels 1957, 330–32) who interestingly argues that the lack of common interests among the early Christians led to the transference of their hope into a heavenly realm. Note also the comments on the 'old consensus' of Wuellner 1973, 666; Kreissig 1967, 94–96; Malherbe 1983, 31; Theissen 1982, 69; Meeks 1983, 51–52.

In recent years this consensus has been challenged, to the extent that a 'new consensus' is spoken of, namely that 'the social status of early Christians may be higher than Deissmann had supposed'.[177] Judge and Theissen have particularly focused attention on the small but influential number of Christians of relatively high social status within the Corinthian community.[178] Abraham Malherbe's study focuses on the conclusions which may be drawn from the literary character of the New Testament writings, arguing that Deissmann aimed too low,[179] and Meeks has attempted to draw together much of the available evidence, prosopographic and indirect, in an investigation of 'the social level of the Pauline Christians'.[180] Meeks concurs with the 'emerging consensus' reported by Malherbe: 'a Pauline congregation generally reflected a fair cross-section of urban society'.[181] Meeks is criticised by D. Engels, an ancient historian, who argues that the vast majority of Paul's converts came from among the 'urban poor'. However, he agrees that 'Chloe may have been well-to-do, as was Gaius ... and Erastus the aedile'.[182] Another ancient historian, D. Kyrtatas, concurs to a considerable extent with the 'new consensus' in New Testament scholarship. He notes the dominance by the end of the nineteenth century of 'the theory that early Christianity was a religion of the oppressed classes' and suggests that in the twentieth century, this general consensus held increasing sway: 'It is only in recent years', he observes, 'that the tide has begun to turn'.[183] Kyrtatas concludes:

> The early Christian communities, it is now accepted, had complex social structures, drawing members of both sexes from all ages and social classes (as Pliny had noticed in the early second century). In the large cities of the Roman empire, such as Rome and Alexandria, there

---

177 Malherbe 1983, 31; cf. also 118; Meeks 1983, 52. Scroggs 1980, 170–71, raises some questions concerning the new consensus to which Judge 1980, 208–209, responds. Kreissig 1967, 96–100, also offered an early challenge to the old consensus, arguing that the early Christians were spread mostly 'in den städtischen Kreisen wohlsituierter Handwerker, Händler und Angehöriger freier Berufe', though there were poorer adherents too (99). Dissenting voices include Gager 1979, 179–80; 1982, 262–63; Schottroff 1985. For overviews see Holmberg 1990, 21–76; Kidd 1990, 35–75.

178 Judge 1960a, 59–60; 1960b, 127–34; 1972, 28; Theissen 1982, 69, 73, 95–96; 1988b, 210–11; also Sänger 1985, 285–86, 291 n. 39; Chow 1992; Clarke 1993, esp. 42–57.

179 Malherbe 1983, 29–59.

180 Meeks 1983, 51–73.

181 Meeks 1983, 73; cf. Filson 1939, 111 cited below p. 101.

182 Engels 1990, 108, see also 229–30 n. 57.

183 Kyrtatas 1987, 24; see 21–24.

seem to have been many more of the educated and of the upper classes than was once thought.[184]

Much of the New Testament evidence relating to the earliest Pauline Christians centres upon Corinth, and Georg Schöllgen criticises Meeks for overgeneralising about Pauline congregations in a variety of urban settings:[185] 'The Corinthian community is surely the only one for which hope exists of coming to a sustainable conclusion.'[186] The particularity of the Corinthian context should also be borne in mind (see §3.2. above). For example, the social disadvantages normally suffered by freedpersons may have been less significantly felt in Corinth, where the freedpersons made up an important part of the new population.

Unfortunately, however, we must face the fact that there is little available information to enable us to ascertain with any degree of exactitude or representativeness the social positions of the Corinthian Christians, despite the fact that we are better informed about this Pauline community, at this early date, than any other. We have virtually no precise information on their levels of income or wealth, their occupations, size of households, numbers of slaves owned, official *ordo*, and so on, and therefore cannot allocate people confidently to particular classes or socio-economic groups.[187] The specific information we do have is for a very few individuals and even then gives little indisputable evidence with respect to their socio-economic position. The point of these observations is not to encourage despair, but rather to stress the need for caution and for conclusions congruent with the nature and extent of the evidence. Meeks and Theissen have both been criticised for too readily taking certain indices to indicate wealth and social status. Schöllgen, for example, highlights the dangers involved in overstretching the limited evidence and using it to support hypotheses whose weight it cannot bear.[188] Nevertheless, their work remains valuable and provides the basis for the more cautious sketch which follows. Theissen's basic thesis is that 'the

---

[184] Kyrtatas 1987, 185; see 184–85.
[185] Schöllgen 1988, 72–74. Theissen has, however, argued that there are reasons for the social structure of the Corinthian community which may allow the results to be generalised; 1982, 69–70, 102–106.
[186] 'Die korinthische Gemeinde ist wohl die einzige, für die Hoffnung besteht, zu einem tragfähigen Ergebnis zu kommen.' Schöllgen 1988, 74.
[187] On the social structure of the Roman empire, see §3.2. above.
[188] Schöllgen 1988; see also Pleket 1985; Malherbe 1983, 73 n. 27.

Corinthian congregation is marked by internal stratification. The majority of the members, who come from the lower classes (*aus den unteren Schichten*), stand in contrast to a few influential members who come from the upper classes (*aus der Oberschicht*)'.[189]

It is not my intention here to offer an extensive or original study of the social composition of the Christian community at Corinth, but to establish and sketch the diversity within it. Given the limited evidence it is impossible, I believe, to do much more than this without going beyond the level of detail which the data permit. Nevertheless the establishment of the result that there was a considerable degree of social diversity encompassed within the community is of significance.

In 1 Cor 1.26, it is implied that the majority of the Corinthian believers were of humble position, and also that there were a few who were powerful, wise and well-born.[190] A number of other general references within the Corinthian correspondence also allow the conclusion that some of the members of the congregation had a degree of wealth and social power. The references in 1 Cor 4.8ff to the Corinthians being already full and rich are generally understood theologically, as a reflection of their 'realised eschatology',[191] but Paul's description of their present abundance (2 Cor 8.14) in contrast to the poverty of the Macedonian believers (2 Cor 8.2), in a context which certainly refers to material things, suggests that at least some of the Corinthians seemed quite prosperous. Similarly 1 Cor 11.17–34 clearly shows that some in the community could afford lavish amounts of food and drink, in a way which contrasted them with other community members who are described as τοὺς μὴ ἔχοντας, 'the have-nots' (1 Cor 11.22). 1 Cor 6.1ff reveals that some of the Corinthian believers were pursuing cases of litigation, a legal procedure most likely to have been pursued by those with some degree of wealth and status (see §3.8.3. below).

---

[189] Theissen 1982, 69; German from 1979b, 231; cf. Theissen 1988b, 210–11; 1993, 268–71. *Schicht* should strictly be translated 'stratum' and not 'class'; cf. the translation of Alföldy's work, where *Schicht* is generally rendered 'stratum'; compare 1984, 85–132 with 1985, 94–156 and see Alföldy's discussion of terminological issues in 1986, 72–78. On the methodological issues involved here, see esp. Rohrbaugh 1984; Martin 1991a.

[190] A point made by Origen *Cels.* 3.48; Filson 1939, 111; Judge 1960a, 59; Theissen 1982, 72–73. Robertson and Plummer 1914, 25, warn against taking οὐ πολλοί to mean more than 'very few'; similarly, Schrage 1991, 209–10.

[191] See esp. Thiselton 1978; and further §3.9. below.

Prosopographic evidence may add specificity to these general observations.[192] Paul specifically mentions the household of Stephanas, which he baptised (1 Cor 1.16), and it may be that Stephanas was the head of a household of some size, including slaves as well as his wife and children. Fortunatus and Achaicus may be among his slaves or dependent workers (1 Cor 16.17).[193] Theissen argues strongly that reference to an οἶκος generally implies more than just parents and children.[194] Owning slaves does not necessarily place one among the Corinthian elite, but Stephanas may be comparatively wealthy, if he has been able to acquire and support slaves;[195] certainly his social level is different from that of his own slaves. His financial position may also be indicated by the fact that he was able to travel to meet Paul (1 Cor 16.17), particularly if Fortunatus and Achaicus are slaves or dependant workers of his who travelled with him.

It is probable that Gaius too was a person of some means, since he served as host not only to Paul but to ὅλης τῆς ἐκκλησίας, 'the whole church' (Rom 16.23; also 1 Cor 1.14). The fact that people met in someone's 'house' may imply little about that person's social status – Schöllgen's warning not to assume that reference to a house implies relative wealth is important[196] – but if a number of smaller house-fellowships combined on occasions when Gaius acted as host, then he most probably possessed a house of some size.[197]

One of the ἐκκλησίαι which may have come to Gaius' house on occasion is the one at Cenchreae, one of Corinth's ports, of which Phoebe was διάκονος. This woman may also have been a person of some financial means, for she had become a patron of many (προστάτις πολλῶν), including Paul.[198] She is obviously travelling to Rome[199] and Paul

---

[192] For detailed use of prosopographic evidence see Theissen 1982, 73–96; Meeks 1983, 55–63; Clarke 1993, 46–57.

[193] See Theissen 1982, 92; Fee 1987, 3, 829, 831–32; Fiorenza 1987, 392–93.

[194] Theissen 1982, 85–87. The distinction between οἶκος and οἰκία, as Theissen points out, cannot be used to distinguish between the small family unit and a larger household. Both terms are used of Stephanas' household; cf. 1 Cor 1.16 and 16.15 and further Michel TDNT 5, 130–31.

[195] Cf. above p. 68 with n. 28.

[196] Schöllgen 1988, 74.

[197] See discussion of accommodation size in relation to meetings of the church in Murphy O'Connor 1983, 153–59.

[198] Rom 16.2; cf. Meeks 1983, 60; Judge 1960b, 128–29. On Phoebe and the translation of προστάτις, see Whelan 1993.

[199] Or possibly Ephesus, depending on the destination of Rom 16 (see above n. 81).

commends her to the believers there (Rom 16.1), requesting that 'you supply her with whatever practical help she may need' (παραστῆτε αὐτῇ ἐν ᾧ ἂν ὑμῶν χρῄζῃ πράγματι; 16.2). Theissen suggests that 'the statement could be understood as a recommendation to support Phoebe in her "worldly" business. This support would reciprocate Phoebe's service to Paul and others.'[200]

If 'Chloe's people' (οἱ Χλόης; 1 Cor 1.11) are slaves or dependent workers attached to Chloe (perhaps as members of her household), then Chloe too must be considered to be a person of some wealth and social position.

Among the believers at Corinth is the one and only person whose civil office Paul mentions; Erastus, ὁ οἰκονόμος τῆς πόλεως, 'the city treasurer' (Rom 16.23). Evidence for this person's social position centres around the term οἰκονόμος and the discovery of an inscription on pavement slabs, probably first-century CE, which records that

[praenomen nomen] Erastus pro aedilit[at]e s. p. stravit

Erastus in return for aedileship laid [the pavement] at his own expense.[201]

The identification of the Erastus Paul mentions with the Erastus who became an aedile of Corinth, while hardly provable beyond doubt, seems highly likely, especially as the name is relatively uncommon.[202] Theissen concludes that the term οἰκονόμος referred to the office of *quaestor*, from which Erastus later rose to the position of aedile.[203] However, in a recent thesis, Clarke argues that Paul may well have used the term οἰκονόμος as an equivalent to aedile.[204] Either way it seems likely that Erastus was a person of wealth and social position, if the pavement inscription refers to the Erastus of Rom 16.23. The term οἰκονόμος alone can hardly prove this, as it may refer to a position held by a slave (albeit an important one).[205]

---

[200] Theissen 1982, 88.
[201] See Kent 1966, 99–100, no. 232 ; Theissen 1982, 80. 'S. p.' is a common abbreviation for *sua pecunia*.
[202] See further Clarke 1993, 46–56; 1991; Gill 1989.
[203] Theissen 1982, 75–83.
[204] Clarke 1993, 49–56.
[205] Cf. Lane Fox 1986, 293; Pleket 1985, 194; Cadbury 1931 (who argues that the identification of the two Erasti is unlikely).

Apart from Erastus (and even here the evidence is not indisputable) we can hardly state with confidence that the most socially prominent members of the Corinthian congregation belong to the 'elite', the 'ruling class', of Corinth, as Clarke does.[206] Nevertheless, there do seem to be at least some members of the ἐκκλησία who are relatively well-to-do, who are the heads of households which include slaves, the owners of accommodation of some size, and people with some wealth at their disposal. Paul's own words seem to be trustworthy: there are a few, though perhaps only a few, who are 'wise, powerful, and well-born'.

The search for evidence of members of the lower strata within the Corinthian congregation may also begin with 1 Cor 1.26, which seems to imply that the majority of the believers will recognise their position as the 'nobodies' in society.[207] But again, specific evidence is hardly plentiful. The division at the Lord's Supper (1 Cor 11.17–34) may again be cited to show that some of the community could be described as τοὺς μὴ ἔχοντας, 'the have-nots', in contrast to those who seem to have plenty (see §3.8.1. below). There must certainly have been slaves among the members of the ἐκκλησία, or the illustration and advice Paul gives in 1 Cor 7.21ff would have been utterly irrelevant.[208] Chloe's people, for example, 'are probably slaves or dependent workers',[209] although they might possibly have been members of the Ephesian church who travelled to Corinth rather than members of the Corinthian congregation.[210] However, 'the fact that Paul expects the name to be recognised by the Corinthian Christians suggests that Chloe lived there'.[211] It is also

---

[206] Clarke 1993, 59, 88, 130. Cf. also Gill 1993 (e.g. 336: 'There is a hint that Stephanas is a member of the élite as his household is mentioned.') and his entirely positive review of Clarke 1993 ('If there is one criticism of this book, it is that it restricts itself to 1 Cor. 1–6.' Gill 1994, 679).

[207] Cf. Theissen 1982, 70–73; Schrage 1991, 208–210; Schottroff 1985. *Contra* Wuellner 1973, who seeks to eliminate any sociological implications from 1 Cor 1.26–29 (see esp. 672). He argues that the ὅτι in v. 26 is interrogative and expects a positive affirmation; 'yes, we are endowed with wisdom, power and noble heritage'! (see 667–68). Wuellner explores the origins and traditions of the 'wise-powerful-noble' triad in 1978 and 1982; see also Gibbs 1978.

[208] Though on the variety even within the positions of slaves, see Martin 1990, 1–49; 1991a, 107–11.

[209] 1 Cor 1.11; Theissen 1982, 93, 115 n. 53; cf. Klauck 1984, 10. Kreissig 1967, 99, considers that slaves are implied. Fiorenza 1987, 394–95, argues that 'the expression "those of Chloe" means "the people or followers of Chloe" in Corinth' and thus that 'they were the official messengers of the community'.

[210] Cf. Fee 1987, 54.

[211] Meeks 1983, 59.

possible that Stephanas' companions, Achaicus and Fortunatus, were slaves, probably among the members of his household whom Paul baptised and refers to as 'the firstfruits of Achaia' (ἀπαρχὴ τῆς᾽ Ἀχαίας; 1 Cor 16.15; 1.16), though they might be family members, or simply travelling companions.[212] Their names are the kind of names we might expect of slaves or freedmen, though this does not necessarily tell us much about their socio-economic status at the time when Paul wrote 1 Corinthians. They do, however, lend 'weight to the possibility that these two men are attached to Stephanas in some way'.[213] The conversion of households may have been one of the main ways in which slaves and other dependent workers became members of the community (1 Cor 1.16; Acts 18.8). Nevertheless, we should not assume that all conversions happened *en bloc* with a household. 1 Cor 7.12ff suggests that some of the wives and husbands Paul addresses were believers without their partners so being, and later evidence shows that slaves might be Christians without having believing masters (1 Tim 6.1f).

Prisca and Aquila, according to Luke, were artisans, σκηνοποιοί, as Paul was.[214] This occupation ranked them fairly low on the social scale, but their social position is hard to gauge. They may well be representatives of the numerous artisans among the 'urban poor', but they might have been people of some wealth and power, who employed other slaves and workers; we simply do not know. Certain factors might indicate that they were not poor: offering accommodation to Paul, being able to host an ἐκκλησία in three cities and to travel from place to place.[215] In addition, 'the fact that Prisca's name is mentioned before her husband's once by Paul and two out of three times in Acts suggests that she has higher status than her husband'.[216] Other individuals who are mentioned also allow only guesses as to their social position. Tertius, for example, Paul's scribe when he wrote Romans from Corinth (Rom 16.22), may have been a slave-scribe or a scribe of some social position.[217]

---

[212] See p. 96 above.
[213] Fee 1987, 831.
[214] In Acts the couple are called Πρίσκιλλα καὶ ᾽Ακύλας (Acts 18.2, 18, 26) whereas Paul calls the woman Πρίσκα (Rom 16.3; 1 Cor 16.19; also 2 Tim 4.19).
[215] Cf. Meeks 1983, 59.
[216] Meeks 1983, 59.
[217] See Theissen 1982, 92.

There are other named individuals connected with the Corinthian congregation about whom only Acts offers any details. We must therefore be wary of concluding much about the social composition of the Corinthian community from Luke's references to Crispus (ἀρχισυνάγωγος and converted with his whole household; Acts 18.8, 1 Cor 1.14), Sosthenes (also ἀρχισυνάγωγος and *possibly* the Sosthenes mentioned in 1 Cor 1.1; Acts 18.17) and Titius Justus (whose house Paul used; Acts 18.7). Undoubtedly Theissen and Meeks at times push limited evidence too far. Meeks' hypothesis that Pauline Christianity was particularly attractive to those characterised by 'status inconsistency' is especially vulnerable.[218] As Schöllgen points out, this hypothesis is potentially of considerable significance for understanding the spread of Christianity.[219] However, not only is the evidence insufficient to establish the necessary details about enough people's situations,[220] but Meeks also fails to consider the statistical information necessary to make such a hypothesis sustainable. What percentage of people in the Roman empire generally, or in Corinth particularly, could be said to have a degree of status inconsistency (given, for example, the frequent manumission of slaves; the refounding of Corinth only a few generations before)?[221] If, for sake of argument, a majority of the population suffers a degree of status inconsistency, then *even* the firm conclusion that a majority of the Pauline Christians had this characteristic is of no significance in explaining their conversion: the majority of 'status inconsistents' in the Pauline congregation would merely reflect their frequency in society as a whole.

Nevertheless, as far as the evidence allows, we can confidently conclude that the Christian community at Corinth included a range of

---

[218] See Meeks 1983, 72–73, 191. Meeks explains the term in the following way: 'In every society the status of a person, family, or other group is determined by the composite of many different clues, status indicators.' Where there is a high degree of disparity, or 'criss-crossing', between these various indicators in relation to a particular person, they may be said to experience 'status inconsistency' or 'status dissonance' (22–23).

[219] Schöllgen 1988, 78.

[220] Schöllgen, 79–80; note also the criticisms of Pleket 1985, 193–96.

[221] On social mobility in the Roman empire, see Theissen 1983, 320–26 (=1993, 190–96). Alföldy 1985, 137, speaks of 'great internal mobility among the urban lower strata ... a very large percentage of the lower strata of the population – at least in the larger cities – consisted of persons of servile origin'. Similar problems arise in relation to Gager's 'relative deprivation' thesis; see Gager 1975, 25–28; 1979, 179–80; 1982, 262–63; for criticism see Meeks 1983, 215 n. 20; Kidd 1990, 39; Rohrbaugh 1984, 525–26. Note also Milbank's criticisms of Meeks (1990, 117–18).

people from Corinthian urban society. Some were slaves and household servants, others were probably householders of some wealth and position.[222] A considerable degree of social diversity was encompassed within the community. This broad conclusion, widely accepted at present among New Testament scholars, was summarised long ago by F. V. Filson:

> Once we recall that Gaius ... Erastus ... Crispus ... and Stephanas all lived at Corinth, we realise that the words 'not many mighty' in 1 Corinthians 1.26 must not be taken to mean 'none'. The apostolic church was more nearly a cross section of society than we have sometimes thought. The fact that the poor predominated must not obscure this truth; the poor have always outnumbered the wealthy.[223]

3.8. Social tensions in the community: background to Paul's response

Having outlined the social diversity encompassed within the Corinthian community, I now seek to outline a number of situations revealed in 1 Corinthians in which there is some evidence that social distinctions or social factors play a part in creating the problems which Paul addresses.[224] This is not to deny that sociological factors may have played some role in other aspects of the church's life which Paul addresses, nor that theological factors are also bound up in the situations of social tension and conflict. Indeed, in a short section below (§3.9.) I attempt to sketch one way in which theological and sociological perspectives on the Corinthian believers might be fruitfully brought together. In the following, however, I focus upon situations about which some socially significant evidence seems to be available.

As we attempt to explore these situations, it is important to remember that our information is worse than second hand; it comes from some of the Corinthians to Paul and is only accessible to us through his response to their questions and situation. However, the sketches which follow will enable us in the next chapter to consider Paul's responses; to investigate the way in which he draws on the Christian symbolic order to

---

[222] Cf. Fee 1987, 3–4.

[223] Filson 1939, 111.

[224] In some cases they may not have been problems for the Corinthians, though they were for Paul; probably, for example, 11.2–16.

address these situations, and to assess whether his responses reflect the interests of any particular social group.

3.8.1. Division and the Lord's Supper: 1 Cor 11.17–34

One of the oral reports Paul received concerned the Corinthians' behaviour at the Lord's Supper (11.18). This central Christian ritual had been established by Paul during his mission to Corinth (παρέδωκα ὑμῖν; 11.23).[225] However, it was now reported to Paul that when they gathered ἐν ἐκκλησίᾳ, to eat the Lord's Supper, there were divisions, σχίσματα, among them (11.18, 20). These divisions resulted from the fact that 'each goes ahead with their own supper' (ἕκαστος ... τὸ ἴδιον δεῖπνον προλαμβάνει – v. 21).

Theissen has made a number of suggestions in an attempt to clarify the details of the situation Paul alludes to here: προλαμβάνει may indicate that some of the Corinthians began eating 'before the commencement of the congregational meal'.[226] In addition, the phrasing of v. 21 may suggest that while the Lord's Supper is going on (ἐν τῷ φαγεῖν), some are also enjoying their own private food (τὸ ἴδιον δεῖπνον προλαμβάνει): 'So it may be that with the words of institution, not all of the food on hand was shared with the congregation, but a certain portion of it was claimed as "private".'[227] Theissen suggests that during the Lord's Supper not only were different *amounts* of food consumed, but different *types* of food too.[228]

Such practice would certainly not have been exceptional in its sociohistorical context. A number of ancient writers describe banquets and meals at which the quality and quantity of a person's fare depends upon their social status and relationship to the host.[229] Pliny, for example, describes a dinner with a man whose friends are all 'graded', at which 'the best dishes were set in front of himself and a select few, and cheap scraps of food before the rest of the company'.[230] Three different qualities of wine are allocated to the various guests. Pliny recounts a conversa-

---

[225] See §3.5.2. above.
[226] Theissen 1982, 153; see 151–53.
[227] Theissen 1982, 153.
[228] Theissen 1982, 153–59.
[229] Theissen surveys much of this evidence; 1982, 156–59.
[230] Pliny *Ep.* 2.6.

tion with his neighbour at table in which he outlines his own preference for treating guests as equals. The neighbour seems surprised that Pliny included even the freedmen in this practice. Slaves, presumably, would not have been among the guests invited to such occasions, although we must assume that they attended the Corinthians' celebrations of the Lord's Supper. Pliny's account comes from someone who belongs to the privileged social group; at the dinner in question he and the host are among those who receive one sort of wine (the best, by implication), while lesser quality wines are allocated to the 'lesser friends' and the freedmen. Much more critical and satirical accounts are found in the writings of Juvenal and Martial, who represent, in Theissen's words, the view 'from below'.[231] Although all these writers are generally critical of such customs, they provide evidence that they were not uncommon. Moreover, as Theissen points out, 'those who were in agreement with a practice had little reason to express themselves on the subject'.[232] In an important survey of Roman social relations, Ramsey MacMullen stresses the extent to which distinctions of rank and status were displayed and reinforced in Roman society (and Corinth was a Roman colony).[233] Dinners and banquets were occasions at which such distinctions were made explicit[234] and Theissen suggests that the Corinthian believers' gathering was no exception. He argues that we should not expect the wealthy Corinthians to have felt that the nature of their gathering was self-evidently 'sinful' or inappropriate. On the contrary: 'In all likelihood wealthy Christians probably did not suffer from a guilty conscience in this entire matter. It is more likely that they thought of themselves as having supported the poorer Christians in generous fashion by providing a meal.'[235] After all, the hosts in particular had opened their houses to the entire gathering and at least bread and wine was available for all. Would it not be entirely 'normal' for the hosts to offer better food and drink to those of their own social circle, from whom reciprocal invitations to dine might also be received?[236]

An alternative reconstruction has recently been offered by Peter Lampe, who also seeks to illuminate the Corinthian situation with evidence

---

[231] Theissen 1982, 157. Juvenal *Satire* 5; Martial *Epigrams* 3.60; cf. 1.20; 6.11.
[232] Theissen 1982, 156.
[233] MacMullen 1974, 106–20.
[234] Cf. MacMullen 1974, 111.
[235] Theissen 1982, 162.
[236] Cf. Theissen 1982, 160–62.

concerning contemporary practice and custom. Lampe suggests that the evening would have begun with a meal – a *prima mensa* (first course), followed by a *secunda mensa* (second course) – followed by a *'symposion'* (drinking party) in which conversation and music would have been enjoyed.[237] This latter time, Lampe suggests, probably corresponded to the time of worship described in 1 Cor 12–14.[238] Lampe concentrates, however, on the time *before* the sacramental Lord's Supper, that is, on the *prima mensa*.[239] He argues that the custom indicated by the reference to ἴδιον δεῖπνον is one in which people each bring some food with them. The meal is not therefore a banquet furnished only by the host or by a few wealthy Christians. The problem Paul confronts is primarily a *temporal* one;[240] certain Christians arrive before others and get on with (προλαμβάνει) their food, while those who come later receive insufficient food for a satisfying meal.[241] Thus 'one goes hungry and another gets drunk' (ὃς μὲν πεινᾷ ὃς δὲ μεθύει – v.21). Moreover, those who arrived earliest would probably have filled the *triclinium* (dining-room) of the house where the meal took place, leaving the latecomers to find places in the *atrium* (hall) and *peristylum* (colonnade), thus forming definite divisions among them.[242]

In the context of the present discussion, the most important point is that both authors, along with many others, agree that the 'division' is essentially between rich and poor.[243] Theissen places most emphasis upon the ways in which the wealthier members of the congregation enjoy a meal of better quality and quantity *during* the Lord's Supper,[244] whereas Lampe stresses not only the ability of the rich to bring better quality food with them, but primarily their arrival *before* the lower class members of the community.[245] The latter group, especially the slaves, would obviously have had less control over their time and no doubt less free

---

[237] See Lampe 1991, 186ff.

[238] Lampe 1991, 188–91.

[239] Lampe 1991, 191ff.

[240] See Lampe 1991, 192–93, for criticism of Theissen and 194–97 for Lampe's own suggestions.

[241] See Lampe 1991, 194–201.

[242] Cf. Lampe 1991, 197, 201; Murphy O'Connor 1983, 153–61.

[243] Theissen 1982, 151; Lampe 1991, 192; Klauck 1982, 293; Barrett 1971a, 261; Fee 1987, 531–45; Engberg-Pedersen 1993, 109.

[244] See Theissen 1982, 147–51, 153, 155–62.

[245] Lampe 1991, 192, 197, 201. The interpretation of ἐκδέχεσθε (v. 33) has important bearing on this debate; see below p. 153 with nn. 141–142.

time in total.[246] The people Paul criticises in verse 22, on the other hand, are clearly the better-off members of the congregation who were free to gather together earlier. These people had houses where they could eat and drink and were evidently able to provide themselves with ample food and drink in a way which Paul sees as bringing shame on τοὺς μὴ ἔχοντας.[247] The report which reached Paul may well have expressed the dissatisfaction of the poorer members of the community with the way in which the community meal was being conducted.[248] However, both Theissen and Lampe stress that the conduct of the wealthier Corinthian believers was by no means exceptional in its socio-historical context.[249]

3.8.2. Disagreement about εἰδωλόθυτα: 1 Cor 8–10

Class-based variations in diet and social practice may also have contributed to the tension and disagreement evidenced in the Corinthians' question 'concerning food offered to idols' (περὶ τῶν εἰδωλοθύτων – 8.1; cf. 8.4). Theissen argues that 'members of the lower classes seldom ate meat in their everyday lives' and would therefore have been more likely to associate eating meat with ceremonial religious feasts.[250] Peter Tomson similarily states that, 'In antiquity meat was expensive and very difficult to keep ... it was eaten only at special events such as festivals and ceremonies, certainly by the lower classes ... fish, bread, vagetables [sic], cakes and fruit were the regular diet.'[251] The wealthy, however, would have been more accustomed to accepting dinner invitations and eating meat in a variety of settings, and would indeed have risked losing their position within a social circle if they had 'rejected all invitations where "consecrated meat" might have been expected'.[252]

Theissen applies the terms 'strong' and 'weak' to the two groups whose views are contrasted in 1 Cor 8–10, though only the latter term is actually used here by Paul.[253] The strong, he suggests, are to be found among

---

[246] Cf. Schweitzer 1967, 5; Bornkamm 1969, 126; Klauck 1984, 81; Lampe 1991, 192.

[247] Cf. Theissen 1982, 150–51; Klauck 1982, 293.

[248] Cf. Theissen 1982, 162–63, 57.

[249] Theissen 1982, 160–62; Lampe 1991, 198–202.

[250] Theissen 1982, 128; see further 125–29.

[251] Tomson 1990, 189; cf. Barrett 1982, 48–49; Jeffers 1991, 6. On the inscriptional evidence showing the presence of a meat market at Corinth, see Gill 1992.

[252] Theissen 1982, 130, who makes this point specifically with reference to Erastus.

[253] But cf. Rom 15.1; Willis 1985a, 89. On the links between 1 Cor 8–10 and Rom 14–15 see Karris 1973. For the use of the terms 'strong' and 'weak' in the Corinthian context see

the socially prominent members of the Corinthian church, who had no compunction about eating meat that had been offered to idols, since they ate meat relatively often and were involved in the social circles where invitations to various kinds of banquets and celebrations were offered and received. The weak, on the other hand, whom Theissen identifies with 'the socially weak of 1:26–27', are those who were too poor and lowly to be involved in such social circles and thus associated idol-meat with the few occasions on which a particular ceremony or festival occurred.[254] Indeed, 8.1–8 is widely agreed to reflect the argument of some of the Corinthians (the 'strong') that they have the right (ἐξουσία – see v. 9) to indulge freely in such eating; a right based upon their 'knowledge' and strong 'consciousness' (συνείδησις).[255] The weak, on the other hand, regarded such action as a participation in idol sacrifice. Verse 10 might seem to tell against the class-based interpretation, suggesting as it does that the 'weak' 'may be encouraged to eat idol-food' (οἰκοδομηθήσεται εἰς τὸ τὰ εἰδωλόθυτα ἐσθίειν). However, Paul could well mean that if they see the wealthy eating idol-meat and attending banquets on a regular basis, they will be encouraged to join in the few occasions when an invitation is extended to all, even though they are conscious of the idolatrous nature of the event.

One challenge to such an interpretation comes from the work of Hurd, recently reiterated (with differences) by Peter Gooch. Hurd and Gooch maintain that there is no disagreement at Corinth over the issue of idol-food, and that the only conflict is between Paul and the Corinthians. The 'weak' are an entirely hypothetical group and it is Paul himself who has a problem with idol-food and wishes to warn the Corinthians of its dangers.[256] Gooch differs from Hurd in arguing that

Theissen 1982, 121–43; Murphy O'Connor 1978b, 545ff; Horsley 1978a, 581ff; Gardner 1994.

[254] Theissen 1982, 125; see 121–43, followed by Martin 1990, 119–20; Chow 1992, 141–57. Fee 1987, 431, agrees that the term 'weak' is 'probably a more purely sociological category than a socio-religious one.' Dodd 1953, 134 saw the weak as 'morbidly scrupulous' people; Black 1983, 241; 1984, 118–19, loses the specific identity of the weak by making the term 'a broad and general description of those Paul seeks to win for Christ' and over-spiritualizing the term (cf. the criticism of Fee 1987, 431 n. 49). For Barrett 1971a, 215, the weak 'are Christians not yet fully emancipated from legalism'; Tomson 1990, 193–98, sees them as 'delicate', 'pagan neophytes who had difficulties with the power of idolatry' (195). Gardner 1994, deals with the 'strong' and the 'weak' in entirely 'religious' terms (cf. Horrell 1995e).

[255] Cf. Murphy O'Connor 1978b, 545ff; Horsley 1978a, 577–85; 1981; Hurd 1965, 115–31; Willis 1985a, 83–87.

[256] Hurd 1965, 117–25; followed by Fee 1980, 175–76; Gooch 1993, 61–72.

Paul did not himself eat idol-food when at Corinth (both argue from silence in 1 Cor 9 here!) and he rejects Hurd's argument that Paul's problem results from a change in policy brought about by his acceptance of the Apostolic Decree. Gooch suggests that Paul's policy had always been to avoid idol-food.[257] He points to the hypothetical nature of the objections of the weak mentioned in 8.9 and 8.13 to support the argument that 'in 8.7–13 we hear not weak Christians but Paul'.[258] However, he does not deal with the fact that 8.7 is not a hypothetical statement. Moreover, as Gooch recognises, 8.10 is hypothetical in form too, which leads him to some doubt as to whether the Corinthians were actually visiting idol temples at all.[259] Paul's concluding advice in 10.31–11.1 clearly reiterates the themes of avoiding offence and consideration for others – themes which run throughout these chapters – but on Gooch's view the only one likely to be offended is Paul. We may, with most scholars, doubt the plausibility of assuming that there is no conflict over this issue at Corinth.[260]

Gooch offers further criticisms of Theissen, however, which are perhaps more important. He offers two reasons for doubting Theissen's argument that the 'strong' and the 'weak' in 1 Cor 8–10 may be divided along social class lines on the basis that the former ate meat regularly while the latter did not. The first is that Theissen 'assumes that idol-food refers exclusively to meat', whereas in fact 'all kinds of food ... could be and were sanctified ... even the simplest meal might become idol-food'.[261] Gooch does accept, however, that Paul's use of the word κρέα (meat) in 8.13, 'shows clearly that the idol-food Paul has in mind most readily is meat'.[262] The second is that the evidence does not support Theissen's view of 'the stark difference in the social use of food ... between social classes'; archaeological excavations suggest that the lower classes made use of the dining rooms at various sacred and temple sites.[263] These observations are also supported by the work of Justin Meggitt, who has explored the evidence concerning the eating of meat by the lower classes

---

[257] See Gooch 1993, 93–95, 140–43; Hurd 1965, 278–80, 290, 240–70.
[258] Gooch 1993, 66.
[259] Gooch 1993, 66–67. Hence Tomson's argument that the *strong* are a hypothetical group! (Tomson 1990, 193, inaccurately citing Hurd in support of such a view at n. 31.)
[260] See further Horrell 1995a; Murphy O'Connor 1978b, 544; Willis 1985a, 92ff.
[261] Gooch 1993, 149; cf. 53–55.
[262] Gooch 1993, 53. Cf. Gardner 1994, 15 n. 3: 'κρέα (8:13) indicates that meat was the issue'.
[263] Gooch 1993, 149–50; cf. 3.

in non-sacred settings. Meggitt argues that meat 'was more regularly eaten by the non-elite than [Theissen] allows', particularly in the 'cookshops'.[264] His evidence (unavoidably, perhaps) is drawn largely from Rome, but it is enough to add further doubt concerning Theissen's thesis.

There are, however, further points which offer some support to the thesis that the Corinthian division over this issue may be at least partly along social lines, remembering that within the Corinthian congregation we are dealing more with social diversity within the lower strata than with an elite/non-elite division.

First, there is the observation, often made, that the Corinthian letter to Paul reflects the perspective of the 'strong' and may have been occasioned partly by the complaints of the weak.[265] Those who have produced such a letter must be among the literate members of the community. Literacy was not widespread among the non-elite and may be taken to reflect a measure of education and social standing.[266]

Second, there is the implication from Paul's response that the 'strong' are those who may expect to receive invitations to dine (10.27). Again, we may suspect that such people may be among the more well-to-do members of the community; it is hard to imagine slaves having the opportunity to invite one another to dinners. The papyri offer many examples of invitations to a variety of events, but Theissen is surely right to question whether such invitations would be found among the poor.[267]

Third, the socially prominent members of the Corinthian congregation have much more to lose from opting out of the social circles and occasions which are so important for maintaining their social status.[268] It is not unlikely, then, that they are largely the group seeking to defend their right to continue to enjoy this social interaction.

None of these arguments is compelling, though taken together, and in conjunction with the wider evidence from the letter which supports this kind of social scenario, they attain a reasonable level of plausibility. However, when in the next chapter I explore the social ethos of Paul's instruction on this matter, I shall exercise caution with regard to this particular hypothesis.

---

[264] Meggitt 1994, 138.
[265] Cf. Murphy O'Connor 1978b, 551–56; Gardner 1994, 52–54.
[266] Cf. Young 1994, 80; further Harris 1989.
[267] For examples of invitations see *P. Oxy.* 110, 523, 1484, 1485, 1755, 2791; (some are cited by Willis 1985a, 40–42). Theissen 1982, 128; cf. also Lang 1986, 107.
[268] Cf. Gooch 1993, 150.

Whatever the extent of the disagreement at Corinth over this issue, some of the company, probably among the socially prominent members, assert their right to eat 'food offered to idols' whether 'in a temple' (ἐν εἰδωλείῳ) or elsewhere. This is hardly some new-found freedom based upon Christian 'enlightenment' but rather an insistence upon their right to retain the social contacts to which they were accustomed, justified from a 'Christian' perspective.[269] Indeed, 'the probability is that those who ate simply were unwilling to remove themselves from normal social life'.[270]

3.8.3. Believers engaged in litigation: 1 Cor 6.1–8

'Normal' social behaviour, by which I mean behaviour which is relatively common in its socio-historical context, is also evidenced in 1 Cor 6.1–8.[271] It seems certain that Paul heard of this situation through oral report; his angry and sarcastic response scarcely suggests that it stems from a question put to him by the Corinthians.[272] It is less clear whether one particular case is in view or a common practice among the Corinthians.[273] Τις (v. 1) may mean 'a certain one' (of you) or 'anyone',

---

[269] See Barclay 1992, 57–60 on the lack of social dislocation among the believers at Corinth. Contrast Gardner 1994, 54 (critique in Horrell 1995e).

[270] Willis 1985a, 266; cf. Murphy O'Connor 1978b, 554. Willis stresses the social character of pagan meals against the common 'sacramental' interpretation (see esp. 7–64). It is disappointing that he does not pursue the sociological aspects suggested by Theissen, but simply states: 'I am unable to assess his sociological arguments' (266 n. 2). Tomson 1990 does not mention Theissen either, nor does Gardner 1994, 2–10, in his review of hypotheses as to the 'background' to 1 Cor 8–10, though he refers to Theissen on 78 n. 66, 174 n. 371.

[271] Vischer 1955, 6–7, and Dinkler 1952, 169, divide vv. 1–11 into three sections; 1–6, 7–8, 9–11; Fuller 1986, 98, prefers a twofold division between 1–8 and 9–11. Fee 1987, 239–40 argues against a sharp break between vv. 1–8 and 9–11, seeing v. 9f as a warning to the brother who has cheated the other. Derrett 1991, 33–34, also argues against a break, interpreting vv. 9–11 as indicating that the saints are not guilty of these faults and thus are fit to judge disputes fairly. Seeing 9–11 as a *warning* against unrighteous behaviour is, I think, more plausible, linked with 1–8 especially through the ἀδικ– words (vv. 1, 7, 8, 9). However, it is in 1–8 that the specific situation is directly addressed; 9–11 contain traditional lists of vices, on which see Conzelmann 1975, 100–101; Ellis 1986, 483–84; Schrage 1991, 386–88.

[272] Cf. Fee 1987, 228 esp. n. 1; Watson 1992c, 54; Fuller 1986, 98. Hurd 1965, 74, 82, argues that Paul seems to react angrily to the oral reports and calmly to the questions raised in the Corinthians' letter.

[273] In 5.1ff an individual case is clearly in view. Murphy O'Connor 1981, 605, argues that 7.10f refers to 'a crisis situation involving one particular marriage', but this is hardly convincing: the words ἐὰν δὲ καὶ χωρισθῇ are more likely to refer to a general conditional possibility (cf. Fee 1987, 295).

'someone'.[274] Barrett assumes that lawsuits (plural) are taking place, as do a number of commentators,[275] but Fee treats the report as concerning two particular men, one of whom is taking the other before the civil magistrates for allegedly defrauding him.[276] A plurality of cases may well be evidenced by the use of plural forms in verses 7 and 8. Fee's explanation that here Paul 'turns his attention directly to the two men involved in the litigation, but speaks to them in such a way that the entire community is also addressed', is somewhat unconvincing.[277]

The cases involved are probably civil litigations. Such cases do not fall under the criminal law of the Roman empire, but are initiated by a plaintiff when some 'wrong' is claimed to have been suffered.[278] This is suggested primarily by the fact that the cases involved are instigated by one person against another and are described as κριτηρίων ἐλαχίστων, 'trivial cases' (NRSV, v. 2),[279] and is assumed by most commentators.[280] The precise nature of the cases is impossible to discern. The only textual clue, from the verb ἀποστερέω, is that they involve 'defrauding' (v. 7f). Richardson's argument that 6.1–8 concerns sexual matters is possible but not entirely convincing.[281] Fee suggests 'that some kind of property or business dealing is the problem', but even this level of generality is not certain.[282] Many aspects of personal or party rivalry, including perhaps the sphere of sexual relations, could be involved. 'In the ancient world parties engaged in

---

[274] BAGD, 819–20.
[275] Barrett 1971a, 135, 139; Robertson and Plummer 1914, 110; Conzelmann 1975, 104; Schrage 1991, 404.
[276] Fee 1987, 228–30, 239. Watson 1992c, 54, follows Fee.
[277] Fee 1987, 239.
[278] See further Garnsey 1970, 181–218; Kelly 1966; Winter 1991; Clarke 1993, 59–68.
[279] Cf. Winter 1991, 560.
[280] Robertson and Plummer 1914, 108–11; Orr and Walther 1976, 195; Barrett 1971a, 135; Fee 1987, 228–29. Stein 1968, made the improbable suggestion that the Corinthians were resorting to Jewish arbitrators (see rejection by Conzelmann 1975, 105 n. 23; Fee 1987, 236 n. 32). Fuller 1986, 100–101, 103–104, suggests that 'the (Gentile) Christians were resorting to their pagan neighbours (not officially appointed judges) and inviting them to act as arbitrators'. This seems most unlikely to me, and is motivated (a) by the force of καθίζετε implying 'appointment' (on which see below pp. 139–40) and (b) by a desire to remove from the passage 'any negative assessment of the Roman judicial system' and therefore any conflict with Rom 13 (but on this see Winter 1991, 559–60 and below pp. 275–76).
[281] Richardson 1983. Note the criticisms of Fee 1987, 228 n. 2, 241 n. 14 and Schrage 1991, 405.
[282] Fee 1987, 241.

strife regularly made use of the courts as a means of attacking their political opponents.'[283]

Although we can say little with certainty about either the precise nature of the cases or the identity of the litigants, it seems likely, due to the prejudices of the Roman legal system, that the accusers would have been people of some wealth and social position. Wealth and social status carried considerable advantages in the courts[284] and in cases of civil litigation the accuser had to bring a proper act of accusation, a procedure which was 'elaborate and expensive'.[285] It was generally forbidden for sons and freedmen to sue parents or patrons and for people of low status to sue those of high status.[286] 'A humble prosecutor might be rejected merely because of the quality of his opponent.'[287] The social position and character of the plaintiff and the accused, as well as of witnesses, were all taken into account in forming judgments,[288] and the severity of any penalty imposed would vary according to the social position of the accused.[289] The use of torture to extract or 'validate' the testimony of witnesses was generally reserved for slaves.[290] 'Social status and legal privilege were closely connected in the Roman empire.'[291] J. M. Kelly argues that lawsuits were generally conducted among equals or were brought by a powerful plaintiff against someone of lower status.[292] The relative powerlessness of the lower strata may be illustrated by the account written by the elder Seneca, in which a rich man taunts a poor man, due to the latter's inability to prosecute him successfully, though he believes that the rich man had his father murdered.[293] 'In general', Peter Garnsey concludes, 'the unequal distribution of wealth, influence, and knowledge of the law prevented the lower orders from making full use of the legal system.'[294] It therefore seems most likely that the instigators of litigations

---

[283] Welborn 1987, 107. Note Schrage's general and cautionary comment (1991, 405).

[284] See Winter 1991, 564–66.

[285] Sherwin-White 1963, 1; cf. 17–18.

[286] See Garnsey 1970, 182; Winter 1991, 561; Justinian *Digest* 2.4.2, 4; 4.3.11.1.

[287] Garnsey 1970, 187.

[288] See Garnsey 1970, 209–13.

[289] See Garnsey 1970, 199–203 and more generally on the 'dual penalty system' in Roman law; Ste. Croix 1981, 458–59; Garnsey 1970, 178; Wengst 1987, 39–40; §3.2. above.

[290] See Garnsey 1970, 213–16; Ste. Croix 1981, 454, 459.

[291] Winter 1991, 566.

[292] Kelly 1966, 62–68.

[293] Seneca *Controversiae* 10.1.2,7; see Winter 1991, 565; Garnsey 1970, 216–17.

[294] Garnsey 1970, 277.

among the Corinthian believers were among the 'not many wise, powerful and well-born' in the community.[295]

3.8.4. Factions among the believers: 1 Cor 1–4

The divisions which are described in 1 Cor 1.10ff are one of the most widely discussed features of the Corinthian church. However, much of this discussion has focused upon theological questions, seeking to locate the origin of the divisions in conflicting theological 'schools'.

In his classic interpretation of the 'parties' at Corinth, F. C. Baur argued that the opposition was essentially between two groups, one of which represented Pauline Christianity (Paul and Apollos), the other Petrine Jewish Christianity (Cephas and Christ).[296] Thus, 'Baur was able to integrate the Corinthian controversy into a comprehensive view of the earliest history of Christianity which he found to be determined by the tension between Paulinists and Petrine Judaizers.'[297]

Others have argued that Paul's main 'opponent' at Corinth (at least at the time of 1 Corinthians) was Apollos, and that Paul's attack on wisdom in the opening chapters of the letter is directed to 'those adherents of Apollos who despised Paul's simple preaching and were striving after wisdom'.[298] Apollos is seen as the source of a Philonic type of Hellenistic Judaism in which wisdom plays a prominent role.[299]

Thus, in a variety of ways which cannot be explored further here, the parties at Corinth are seen primarily as expressions of theological disagreement; non-Pauline theology has been introduced and is opposed by Paul in 1 Corinthians.

However, there are problems with such views. There is no evidence of any judaizing activity at Corinth[300] and no explicit mention of any

---

[295] Cf. Theissen 1982, 97; further Mitchell 1993. They may, of course, have been involved in trials with non-Christians as well; cf. Conzelmann 1975, 106 n. 29; Schrage 1991, 414.

[296] Baur 1831; see Hyldahl 1991, 19; Munck 1959, 135, whose essay is intended to refute Baur's position; see further 69–86 etc. This view of the opposition at Corinth has recently been revived by Goulder 1991. Vielhauer 1975b also explores the importance of the Cephas party at Corinth.

[297] Dahl 1967, 313–14.

[298] Munck 1959, 143; cf. Weiss 1910, 24.

[299] See e.g. Hyldahl 1991, 20–23; Horsley 1978b, 207; Sellin 1982, 74; 1987, 3015; Murphy O'Connor 1987, 66; 1991b, 42. Munck 1959, 143–44, points out that assumptions about Apollos' theology may only be drawn from Acts 18.24ff and that this is insufficient evidence to establish that he was a proponent of the kind of theology which flourished there. Note also the critical comments of Fee 1987, 13–14; Barclay 1992, 64–65 n. 29.

[300] Watson 1986, 81–87; Fee 1987, 57.

distinctively 'Petrine' theology. Indeed Cephas is only mentioned twice in connection with the divisions and we learn nothing of any distinctive views held by those who claimed ἐγὼ Κηφᾶ ('I am of Cephas'; 1.12; 3.22). Similarly we are never explicitly told of any 'false' theology taught by Apollos or held by his faction. Paul never expresses disapproval of Apollos but describes the two of them as 'one' (3.8), and as συνεργοί, co-workers (v. 9), engaged in the complementary tasks of planting and watering (3.5ff). And in 4.6 Paul states that the reason for his 'applying' the preceding ideas to himself and Apollos is so that the Corinthians may learn not to be puffed up for the one against the other.[301] Finally, if Paul felt that Apollos had introduced dangerous and misleading ideas, his attempt to persuade him to return to Corinth is incomprehensible (16.12).[302] It must be conceded that we learn little about theological differences in connection with the σχίσματα at Corinth. 'Paul refuses to analyse the opinions of the various factions, but speaks to the community as a whole.'[303] Indeed, Johannes Munck asserts that 'Paul is not arguing in chs. 1–4 against false doctrine'.[304] We should therefore consider the possibility that the causes of the divisions may be social as much as theological.

Paul's first observation is that there are divisions (σχίσματα) among the Corinthian believers (1.10). This has been reported to him by some of Chloe's people (v. 11) and he knows it to be the case because of their slogans: 'I am of Paul, and I of Apollos', etc. (ἐγὼ μέν εἰμι Παύλου, ἐγὼ δὲ 'Απολλῶ ... κτλ. – v. 12). The slogans clearly reveal that in some way the various teachers are 'rallying points' for the divisions.[305]

---

[301] The phrase τὸ μὴ ὑπὲρ ἃ γέγραπται is notoriously enigmatic and much disputed; cf. Sellin 1987, 2983, 3013 n. 378 ('4,6 ist leider eins der ungelösten exegetischen Rätsel des NT'). Murphy O'Connor 1986, 84–85, takes it as a scribal gloss pointing to the addition of a μη in the following clause. Some take it as a reference to scripture; e.g. Goulder 1991, 519, 526; RSV. Note also the suggestions of Marshall 1984, 279–81 and Fitzgerald 1988, 123–27. But whatever its meaning, the purpose of learning τὸ μὴ ὑπὲρ ἃ γέγραπται is explicitly (ἵνα) so that they may learn not to be puffed up for one against the other; cf. Sellin 1982, 75.

[302] Sellin argues that chapters 1–4 and 16 belong to different letters; see 1982, 72; 1987, 2964–82; 1991, 554. I do not find partition theories of 1 Corinthians convincing; cf. Merklein 1984; Barrett 1971a, 11–17; Murphy O'Connor 1986, 81.

[303] Welborn 1987, 89; see 88–89; further Mitchell 1991.

[304] Munck 1959, 152; cf. Dahl 1967, 332; Koester 1982b, 121; Hyldahl 1991, 23; Schrage 1991, 142–52, who emphasises the lack of evidence for conflict with Apollos or Cephas (143–46) '...wissen wir im Grunde über die einzelnen Gruppen so gut wie nichts'.

[305] Fee 1987, 48; cf. Theissen 1982, 54. The slogan ἐγὼ Χριστοῦ has led to much discussion over whether there was such a party at Corinth. Fee's comment is apt: 'The grammar of the

Paul's vocabulary demonstrates that 'wisdom' is in some way connected with the Corinthians' situation and self-understanding,[306] and in his view they are guilty of boasting and pride.[307] In addition some criticism or judgment of Paul seems to have been evident; hence Paul's statement that their judgment of him is of no importance to him (4.3f), his portrayal of his apostolic experience in 4.8ff, and his defence of his apostolic lifestyle in 9.1ff (see further ch. 5).[308]

But apart from the postulation of theological differences causing the divisions, are we able to understand them any further? We may perhaps begin by observing that the lack of information about theological differences of opinion reinforces the fact that the 'problem', in Paul's view, is *division* itself (1.10–13).[309] Moreover, these divisions are evidence for Paul that the Corinthians are acting in a 'human', fleshly way:

ὅπου γὰρ ἐν ὑμῖν ζῆλος καὶ ἔρις, οὐχὶ σαρκικοί ἐστε καὶ κατὰ ἄνθρωπον περιπατεῖτε; ὅταν γὰρ λέγῃ τις· ἐγὼ μέν εἰμι Παύλου, ἕτερος δέ· ἐγὼ Ἀπολλῶ, οὐκ ἄνθρωποί ἐστε;

for wherever there is jealousy and strife among you, are you not being fleshly and living in a purely human way? For whenever anyone says: 'I am of Paul' and another, 'I am of Apollos', are you not being mere humans? (1 Cor 3.3–4)

'What threatened the survival of the community of chosen people was not seductive gnostic theology or infectious Judaistic propaganda, but the possibility that its adherents might "behave like ordinary men" (3:3).'[310] The behaviour Paul condemns appears to him to be all-too-human and worldly, involving rivalry, jealousy and strife. Thus L. L.

---

passage seems to demand that there were in fact Corinthians saying such a thing. But beyond that all is speculation' (1987, 58–59). Cf. Sellin 1982, 73 who attempts an answer on 92–96. *Contra* Vielhauer 1975b, 343; 1975a, 135–37; Lampe 1990, 117 n. 2.

[306] The words σοφία/σοφός appear 29 times in 1 Corinthians (mostly in chs. 1–3) and seldom at all in the other undisputedly Pauline letters (5 times in Romans; once in 2 Corinthians). Cf. Fee 1987, 48 n. 7; Lampe 1990, 118; Schrage 1991, 129.

[307] See 1 Cor 1.29, 31; 3.21; 4.6f, 18f; 5.2, 6; 8.1.

[308] Dahl's main thesis is that 'the section 1 Cor 1:10–4:21 is ... to be characterised as an apology for Paul's apostolic ministry'. Thus 'the quarrels at Corinth were mainly due to the opposition against Paul'; 1967, 329, see further 321ff; cf. Fee 1987, 48–49.

[309] Cf. Welborn 1987, 89; Munck 1959, 142, 150; Mitchell 1991.

[310] Welborn 1987, 88. Cf. Héring 1962, 22: 'These schisms, centred around human beings, are the clearest sign of the unredeemed and purely human mentality of the members of the church.'

Welborn argues that 'it is a power struggle, not a theological controversy, which motivates the writing of 1 Corinthians 1–4'.[311] Welborn compares the slogans Paul quotes in 1.12 with declarations of personal allegiance in the realm of politics.[312] Similarly, Theissen refers to 'the conflict among followers of various apostles' as 'a struggle for position within the congregation'.[313] Given this background, we may understand why Paul particularly attacks '*worldly* wisdom' (1.19ff; 3.19ff etc.) and emphasises that the gospel itself is evidence of God's rejection of the wise and powerful in society (1.18ff). Boasting and pride in human figures are unnecessary and inappropriate: 'let the one who boasts, boast in the Lord' (1.31; cf. 3.21).

Theissen has adduced a number of arguments which suggest that the leading figures of the Corinthian parties were probably among the wealthier and more socially prominent members of the community.[314] First, those Paul names as having been baptised by him, probably important people in the 'Paul party', seem to have been people of relatively high social position.[315] Second, the missionaries in competition with Paul required provisions and money as well as lodging – 1 Cor 9.3–18 reveals that Paul's pattern of self-support may be contrasted with others of whom the Corinthians are aware[316] – and 'were [therefore] all the more dependent on these Christians who were economically well off'.[317] Third, the themes of 1 Cor 1–4, 'especially the transition from the theme of *schismata* (1:10–17) to that of the preaching of the cross (1:18ff)' are most understandable if the conflict within the congregation involves primarily those of higher social status.[318] Fourth, Paul seems to have been criticised by some, belonging to other parties, because of his lifestyle, specifically his manual labour. 'If the complaint that laboring with his own hands keeps him from being free (9:1) originates with them,

---

[311] Welborn 1987, 89.
[312] See Welborn 1987, 90–93; further Mitchell 1991, 68–99, with critique of Welborn on 83–86.
[313] Theissen 1982, 56.
[314] See Theissen 1982, 55–57. The fact that Paul does not name them should not surprise us: according to Marshall 1987, 341–48, in a certain rhetorical style, Paul never names an enemy (contrast 1 Tim 1.19f; 2 Tim 4.14). Instead, he applies the ideas 'figuratively' to himself and Apollos (4.6); see esp. Fiore 1985, 89–96.
[315] See §3.7. above and further Theissen 1982, 73–96; Welborn 1987, 98.
[316] See further §5.3.
[317] Theissen 1982, 55.
[318] Theissen 1982, 56; see further §4.2.1.

we can hardly imagine them to be a group of people who would thereby implicate themselves too.'[319] Fifth, Paul's information about the σχίσματα is brought by

> people who look at the problems of the Corinthian community from 'below'. In both 1 Cor.1:12ff. and 11:17–34 Paul obviously takes the side of those members of the community who come from the lower strata ... The party strife is apparently viewed negatively by these people, which is not surprising if it is an affair involving some of the more prominent members of the congregation who are competing for the most influence within the congregation.[320]

'All these observations together justify the assumption that the protagonists of the Corinthian parties were members of the upper classes (*Mitglieder höheren Schichten*).'[321] What the social level of these 'protagonists' within Corinthian urban society as a whole was, is impossible to tell with any precision. However, it seems reasonable to conclude that they were among the more socially prominent members of the congregation.

Whether the civil litigations of 6.1ff are in any way connected with the party strife is unprovable, but not unlikely.[322] And if Clarke and John Chow are right, then the man in whom some were proud (5.2) may also have been one of these leading figures.[323]

The origins of the factions may perhaps be sought in the support and hospitality offered to visiting missionaries, Paul, Apollos and others.[324] Such support clearly entailed a certain level of material giving, especially if the missionaries were 'helped on their way' when they moved on.[325]

Naturally, nobody wishes to spend money for a second-class missionary; for that reason all regard as the most important missionary the

---

[319] Theissen 1982, 56.

[320] Theissen 1982, 57.

[321] Theissen 1982, 57; German from 1979b, 229; cf. Fiore 1985, 95. On the translation of *Schicht* see above n. 189.

[322] On the 'connection between litigation and party strife' see Welborn 1987, 107; Winter 1991, 571.

[323] Clarke 1993, 73–88; Chow 1992, 130–41.

[324] 1 Thess 1.1 and 2 Cor 1.19 suggest that Silvanus and Timothy were with Paul on his mission to Corinth.

[325] Paul refers to such help, or to his hope of receiving it in Rom 15.24; 1 Cor 16.6; 2 Cor 1.16. 1 Cor 4.12 cannot be taken to imply that Paul received *no* material support while at Corinth, *contra* Schrage 1991, 151 n. 308 opposing Theissen's interpretation. See further §5.3.2.

one they have supported (and by whom they have surely been influenced theologically). What is more, if the missionary were important, so would his followers within the community be. Thus the disagreement among different parties may be a matter of scrapping for position within the pecking order. Paul sees its origin in the fact that the Corinthians are 'puffed up' in favor of one against another (1 Cor 4:6).[326]

Opposition to Paul might naturally be one aspect of such disagreement, as some expressed allegiance to other missionaries and apostles. Allegiance to particular leaders also seems to have been associated with baptism (1.13–16). Clearly this could happen in conjunction with the situation described above; missionaries were highly likely to baptise the members of the household where they were staying. Significantly Paul includes Gaius among those whom he baptised (1.14) and also refers to him as ὁ ξένος μου, 'my host' (Rom 16.23).

The baptism of households offers a further clue as to how divisions developed; the head of the household thereby had a ready-made group of supporters. This group could expand to include other 'slaves, freedmen, hired labourers, business associates – the whole *clientela*',[327] as the householder's patronage (expressed not least perhaps in offering hospitality for the Lord's Supper) encouraged or even required others to express allegiance to them. 'The existence of several house churches in one city goes far to explain the tendency to party strife.'[328] While theological disagreements may have caused some tensions, the divisions in the Corinthian community probably owe at least as much to social factors. Welborn argues that 'the power that enabled the protagonists of the Corinthian parties to create divisions in the community ... was based on material wealth and the dependence it induced'.[329] The hypothesis of social groups headed by certain prominent members of the congregation seems to make a good deal of sense as a background to 1 Cor 1–4.

3.8.5. Women and men in the community

One of the unique features of 1 Corinthians among the letters of the New Testament is the extent to which it addresses issues of sexuality and

---

[326] Theissen 1982, 55.
[327] Welborn 1987, 100.
[328] Filson 1939, 110.
[329] Welborn 1987, 100.

gender. Much has been written in recent years on this subject and I do not intend to cover the area in great detail.[330] It will be important, however, to consider how Paul responds to situations where the relationship of the sexes is at issue.

From 1 Cor 5.1ff we learn that the community was tolerating a case of incest in its midst. It is possible that such sexual licence was encouraged by an interpretation of the gospel message which stressed freedom ('all things are lawful')[331] and perhaps took the baptismal declaration that 'there is no longer male and female' to mean that bodily (sexual) actions were now morally irrelevant.[332] Such religious legitimation for the incestuous relationship may be hinted at in Paul's comment about 'the man who has done this in the name of the Lord Jesus' (5.3–4), if this is the correct way to construe the punctuation of the Greek.[333] It is also likely that at least some of the Corinthians were visiting prostitutes (6.12–20), although it has been argued that Paul is speaking hypothetically here, to illustrate his point.[334] Fee maintains, however, that Paul is dealing here with a 'specific expression of *porneia*': 'some men within the Christian community are going to prostitutes and are arguing for their right to do so.'[335]

On the other hand, some of the Corinthians, perhaps again inspired at least in part by the declaration that there is no male and female in Christ, considered that sexual activity belonged to a realm of fleshly behaviour which believers had now transcended:[336] 'it is good for a man not to touch a woman' (7.1).[337] Thus some abstained from sex within marriage (7.1–6), others contemplated divorce, especially if their partner was an unbeliever (7.10–16),[338] and marriage plans were delayed or abandoned in favour of an ascetic life (7.25ff).[339] The Corinthians were

---

[330] Examples include Fiorenza 1983, 205–41; Witherington 1988, 24–127; Byrne 1988; Keener 1992.

[331] 1 Cor 6.12; 10.23; generally regarded as a 'slogan' of the Corinthians, see Hurd 1965, 68, 86; Murphy O'Connor 1978a; Fee 1987, 251–52.

[332] Cf. Murphy O'Connor 1978a, 395.

[333] So Sanders 1991, 106–107; Murphy O'Connor 1977; Harris 1991, 15–16.

[334] Hurd 1965, 86–89.

[335] Fee 1987, 250.

[336] Cf. Murphy O'Connor 1980, 490; MacDonald 1987, 70; Radcliffe 1990, 63.

[337] Generally regarded as a citation of Corinthian opinion, probably from their letter; see Hurd 1965, 67–68, 163–64; Fee 1987, 276.

[338] Especially women, according to MacDonald 1990, 170.

[339] Cf. Byrne 1988, 16–20, etc, who gives considerable space to the possible influence of Gal 3.28 in creating such attitudes.

clearly concerned to seek Paul's guidance in these matters; assuming that Paul answered the Corinthians' written questions in order, their first two questions reflected concerns in this area (7.1,25).[340]

It is clear too that Paul is deeply concerned about the appearance of men and women in worship (11.2–16). For some reason he is concerned to modify the Corinthians' current practice, even though he praises them for maintaining the traditions he passed on to them (11.2f; see further §4.3.2. below). In this instance, however, there is no evidence that the Corinthians were concerned about the situation to which Paul refers. It is Paul who considers that further instruction is required (though he must presumably have learnt of the situation from those who brought news from the community to him).

It will be important to consider in the next chapter how Paul responds to these situations where the relationship between men and women is at issue, especially in 1 Cor 7, in relation to sex and marriage, and in 11.2–16, in the context of worship.[341] Without these areas being made a major focus, it is important that a discussion of the social ethos of Pauline Christianity at least takes account of the way in which Paul interprets the Christian symbolic order in the context of the relationships between men and women. Does Paul reinforce male dominance and demand the subordination of women?

3.9. The theology of Paul's Corinthian 'opponents'

Sociological and theological perspectives should not be viewed as mutually exclusive alternatives,[342] although their forms of analysis and priorities are very different. Giddens is explicit about his intention to formulate a 'hermeneutically informed social theory'[343] – by which he means a social theory that does not seek to 'explain' human behaviour solely on the basis of material or social causes but takes seriously the ways in which people's symbolic, interpretative, or 'theological' framework shapes their action and interaction (cf. §1.3. above). Furthermore, if theology is

---

[340] Cf. Hurd 1965, 65–74.
[341] I take 1 Cor 14.34f to be an interpolation; see excursus below pp. 184–95.
[342] Cf. Theissen 1982, 123: 'The sociological analysis of a theological quarrel does not, in my opinion, mean reducing it to social factors.'
[343] Giddens 1982a, vii.

profoundly contextual – arising from and acting within a particular social setting[344] – then we would expect particular forms of theology to be linked with particular social contexts. In this brief section I want to explore the possibility that there may be links between the theology of Paul's Corinthian 'opponents' and their social status. Indeed, I want to suggest that there may well be at least some significant overlap between the socially prominent members of the community whose activities have already been considered above and the proponents of a certain form of theology which Paul is concerned to oppose.

There is considerable agreement that the Corinthians' theology is characterised by an 'over-realised eschatology', in other words, by the belief that the future promises of God are fulfilled and experienced in the present.[345] So Barrett writes: 'The Corinthians are behaving as if the age to come were already consummated.'[346] Fee relates this particularly to their sense of 'experiencing the spirit in full measure' and prefers the term 'spiritualised eschatology':[347] 'Their outlook was that of having arrived (see 4:8) – not in an eschatological sense, but in a "spiritual" sense.'[348] The verse most frequently adduced as evidence for such a view is 1 Cor 4.8, linked perhaps with the Corinthians' denial of the resurrection in 15.12ff, a denial which may have been associated with the belief that life in the spirit was already present and that future resurrection from the dead was unnecessary and irrelevant.[349] Anthony Thiselton has developed these ideas further and argues that 'in every single section from the beginning of the epistle to xiv.40 there occurs evidence of *both* a realized eschatology *and* an enthusiastic theology of the Spirit on the part of the Corinthians'.[350] It is hard to say precisely how 'eschatologically' orientated the Corinthians' views were,[351] but clearly they regard themselves

---

[344] Cf. Milbank 1990, 2.

[345] See esp. Thiselton 1978, who defends and expounds this thesis in response to the criticisms of Ellis 1974; also Dahl 1967, 332; Watson 1992c, xxv–xxvii.

[346] Barrett 1971a, 109.

[347] Fee 1987, 12.

[348] Fee 1987, 339.

[349] It may have been the idea of the resurrection of the *body* which the Corinthians particularly rejected (so Hurd 1965, 199–200). Their denial of the resurrection should not be taken as reflecting a belief in a 'realised resurrection' (see above §3.5.1. with nn.121–123). Thiselton 1978, 523, concedes that there is no evidence for such a view.

[350] Thiselton 1978, 523.

[351] Litfin 1994, 168–69, argues that: 'The eschatological element in the verse [4.8] is purely the importation of the Apostle and it functions as a rebuke of their attempt to emulate such a worldly elite.' Cf. also Fee 1987, 339, quoted above.

with what Paul considers to be pride and self-satisfaction. We may perhaps, with Peter Marshall, characterise them as *hybrists*: those who consider themselves superior to others.[352] The Corinthians' self-understanding is surely linked with their belief that they are wise and have knowledge. They have 'arrived' on the basis of σοφία and γνῶσις. This much is clear from Paul's polemical attack upon 'wisdom' in 1 Cor 1–3, an emphasis unique in the Pauline epistles.[353] An emphasis upon 'knowledge' is also evident in the Corinthian letters,[354] particularly in 1 Cor 8.1–11, where Paul takes issue with those who act on the basis of their 'knowledge' without regard for others.

Whatever the source(s) of the Corinthians' view of wisdom – and in my view it is most likely to have come from their own socio-religious background stimulated perhaps by the preaching of Paul and Apollos[355] – Paul clearly attacks it as wisdom *of the world* (τοῦ κόσμου/ τοῦ αἰῶνος τούτου).[356] This is one hint that the people who Paul is engaged in polemic against are specifically those who regard themselves as 'wise' (and powerful and wellborn) in worldly terms (see further §3.8.4. and §4.2.1.).

The result of the Corinthians' false claims to wisdom and knowledge, in Paul's view, is that they are 'puffed up'. This, however, is a charge Paul applies to 'some' within the congregation (ἐφυσιώθησάν τινες; 4.18).[357] Again it may plausibly be suggested that it is a certain portion of the congregation who are puffed up; who regard themselves as full, rich, and living like kings (4.6–8). It is likely to be people of some social standing – those who possess a certain level of education and culture –

---

[352] Marshall 1984.
[353] Cf. above n. 306.
[354] See Moulton and Geden *s.v.* γινώσκω, γνωρίζω, γνῶσις; Gardner 1994, 23–27.
[355] Cf. Fee 1987, 13–14; Barclay 1992, 64–65 n. 29. Dahl 1967, 333: 'this type of enthusiasm … may have emerged spontaneously as a result of Paul's own activity. To some degree the tendencies may have been stimulated by the preaching of Apollos.' Works which explore the Corinthians' theology against the background of Jewish sapiential and Philonic theology include Pearson 1973; Horsley 1976; 1977; 1978a; 1978b; 1981; Davis 1984.
[356] See 1 Cor 1.20f; 2.6; 3.18f; and the fuller list of Paul's contrasts between worldly wisdom and Godly wisdom in Clarke 1993, 101–102. This is one of the many arguments, it seems to me, to be ranged against Goulder's (1991) interpretation of σοφία at Corinth. If the 'wisdom' which Paul attacks were a Jewish form of halakhic wisdom espoused by the Petrine party, I cannot see why Paul should specify it as the wisdom *of the world* and as what *Greeks* (and not Jews) seek (1.22).
[357] Cf. 4.19: γνώσομαι οὐ τὸν λόγον τῶν πεφυσιωμένων ἀλλὰ τὴν δύναμιν; 4.6; 5.2; 8.1; 13.4; 15.12.

who despise Paul's lack of rhetorical skills (1.17; 2.1–5; 2 Cor 10.10)[358] and whose self-congratulatory attitude may be contrasted with the weakness and dishonour of Paul and the other apostles (4.8–13).[359] 'Hybristic conduct', Marshall suggests, 'is about wealth and power, and the way Paul utilises the doctrines of *hybris* and *sōphrosynē* in Corinthians indicates that his opponents are of privilege and high status in their own environment.'[360]

Further evidence suggesting that the theology of wisdom and knowledge which Paul opposes is the theology of a particular group at Corinth, comprising, at least in part, some of the socially prominent members of the congregation[361] may be found in 1 Cor 8.1–11. Here Paul's attack on those who claim 'knowledge' is most clear. 'We all have knowledge' (8.1) is generally regarded as a quotation from the Corinthians' letter to Paul,[362] a letter reflecting the views of the so-called strong (see §3.8.2.). It is clear that the strong regarded their knowledge (specifically that 'there is no idol in the world and there is no god but one'; 8.4) as the basis on which to defend their freedom to eat idol-food (8.10f; note γνῶσις in v. 10 and v. 11). Paul asserts that knowledge 'puffs up' (φυσιόω again), whereas love builds up (8.1), developing the contrast between 'knowledge' and 'love' in such a way as to undermine the value of anyone's claim to 'know' anything (8.2f). Paul's emphasis upon what is beneficial and upbuilding is also clear in his qualification of the Corinthian slogan 'all things are lawful' (πάντα ἔξεστιν), quoted twice in 6.12 and twice in 10.23.[363] 'The phrase *panta exestin* not only

---

[358] See further §5.5., on 2 Cor 10–13.

[359] See further §4.2.1. and §5.2. below. Litfin, 1994, demonstrates well Paul's rejection of the values of Greco-Roman rhetoric in 1 Cor 1–4, in opposition to the 'status-conscious Corinthians' (163) who judged Paul's skills in proclamation negatively. However, he draws conclusions which generalise this passage into an expression of Paul's 'theory of preaching' (254); viewing Paul's method as an avoidance of persuasive technique (this, I think, is highly doubtful), a straightforward and simple proclamation of the cross (247). Thus: 'Each time Paul preached the Gospel he perceived himself to be introducing the *Constant,* the message of Christ crucified …' (250). This, it seems to me, fails to regard Paul's formulation of the word of the cross and its implications as a specific and contextual attempt to confront the *hybris* and competitive pride of the prominent Corinthians. Such a polemical passage cannot be taken to reflect Paul's constant 'theory of preaching'.

[360] Marshall 1984, 287.

[361] Some, but probably not all, for Stephanas (probably a household head) receives nothing but commendation from Paul (1.16; 16.15–17).

[362] Hurd 1965, 68, 279; Gardner 1994, 22–23, who argues that the οἴδαμεν ὅτι should be regarded as a part of the quotation.

[363] See n. 331 above.

characterises rulers obsessed with their power and rights but is a familiar catchcry of people of rank and status asserting their independence from those who would impinge upon their freedom.'[364]

One of the Corinthians' concerns, probably raised in their letter to Paul, was about 'spiritual matters' (or, 'spiritual people'; περὶ δὲ τῶν πνευματικῶν – 12.1ff).[365] However, it is difficult to say whether the Corinthian πνευματικοί should be regarded as coming exclusively, or even largely, from the group of socially prominent believers whose wisdom/knowledge theology reflected in part their social position. In his response Paul seems concerned to legitimate a diversity of gifts and functions within the 'body' – perhaps in opposition to what he saw as the superior attitude of some who despised the gifts of others – and to ensure the orderly use of the gift of tongues. His comments appear to be addressed to the congregation as a whole, as indeed is the epistle itself (1.2), and we should not assume in this case that it is only a particular group in view.

Nevertheless there are sufficient hints from which to gather that on the whole it is a particular section of the congregation who are 'puffed up' and whose theology and practice Paul opposes.[366] There is no indication, for example, that those who bring oral reports are implicated in the situations about which they bear news (1.10ff; 5.1ff; 11.17ff). And much of the rest of the epistle is concerned with points raised in the Corinthian letter to Paul, a letter which it seems likely reflected the viewpoint of a particular section of the congregation.

My suggestion is that the 'theological' interpretation of the Corinthian church's problems (viz. the 'theology' of wisdom, power and knowledge) and the 'sociological' interpretation (viz. a socially stratified congregation in which the behaviour of the socially prominent members is causing particular concern) may be brought together rather than separated as alternatives once it is recognised that Paul's 'theological' opponents are a particular group within the congregation comprising at least some of these higher status individuals.

---

[364] Marshall 1984, 278; citing Dio Chrysostom *Diss.* 62.3; 3.10.
[365] See further §4.3.3. below.
[366] Fee 1987, 8, speaks of anti-Pauline sentiment, initiated by a few but infecting nearly the whole. On the basis of the evidence we have, this is perhaps an exaggeration.

3.10. Conclusion

The main purpose of the sketch I have attempted above is to provide the context in which to consider Paul's teaching as we find it in 1 Corinthians. In the next chapter I shall seek to assess the ways in which Paul draws upon the rules and resources of the Christian symbolic order in response to these various situations, and to consider the 'social ethos' of his instruction – its impact upon social relationships within the community and its ideological potential.

It has not been my intention here, however, to claim that the disagreements and problems at Corinth are all primarily caused by 'social' factors, or by conflict between different social groups. Clearly there are also important theological and spiritual issues at stake (not least concerning the resurrection, for example; 15.12ff) and even where social factors are discernible, the theological dimensions of the disagreements should not be denied. The possibility that a certain theological perspective may be linked with those who inhabit a certain social position has briefly been explored. However, it does seem to be the case that a number of the 'problems' which Paul confronts in 1 Corinthians owe a good deal of their origin to sociological factors and to tensions between different social groups. The behaviour of the socially prominent members of the community seems particularly to have caused problems, at least in Paul's view. Paul's responses to these 'problems' should offer illuminating answers to the questions concerning the interests and ideology which his teaching may reflect.

The evidence surveyed above concerning the Corinthian community in its early years also presents a sharp challenge to socio-historical studies which describe the earliest Christian communities as radical or egalitarian communities standing in sharp contrast to their societal context,[367] or which characterise the movement as a 'discipleship of equals', into which patriarchalisation and social ordering gradually crept.[368] The assumption that these communities were egalitarian may owe more to a

---

[367] Lohfink 1985, 75–147, describes the early Christian communities as radical 'contrast' communities. A critique of the concept of 'Kontrastgesellschaft' in relation to the New Testament churches is offered by Kampling 1990. On the lack of social disjunction experienced by the Christians at Corinth, in contrast to the Thessalonians, see Barclay 1992.

[368] Cf. Fiorenza 1983, 250: 'The discipleship of equals was in the process of being transformed into a community of patriarchal submission.' (see further 160ff); Osiek 1984, 83.

sociological model based upon modern sects and millenarian movements than to historical reality.[369] The evidence from Corinth suggests that social distinctions and stratification were clearly evident among the believers and that struggles for power and position still took place. This is not to deny that Paul *may* have had a vision of the community as in some way 'egalitarian', but it certainly cannot simply be assumed that this ever or anywhere approximated to the reality encountered.[370]

Indeed, from his response to the Corinthians we shall learn something of what Paul expected or wanted the community to be like, and of his reactions to the reality. The necessity for ongoing interpretation and reformulation of the symbolic order is occasioned, at least in part, by the unintended and unanticipated consequences of what has preceded.

---

[369] Cf. §1.2. above. Allison 1988, 57 n. 22 refers to 'recent sociological analysis of the Pauline churches as a society in which countercultural, egalitarian values predominated'. Cf. also Scroggs 1975; 1974, 535–36.

[370] The weakness in Atkins' (1991) method is the lack of distinction between Paul's intention or vision, and the social realities. His results suggest that the 'bias' of the Pauline communities is towards low hierarchy and egalitarianism.

4

The social ethos of 1 Corinthians

4.1. Introduction: the issue of 'love-patriarchalism'

The theoretical discussions in chapter 1 stressed the importance of contextual understanding. The previous chapter therefore attempted to outline the context in which Paul's teaching in 1 Corinthians is given and to sketch the story of Paul's interaction with the Corinthian community. The research framework, outlined in §2.5. and built largely upon structuration theory, conceptualises Paul's instruction as part of the ongoing reformulation, or reconstruction, of the Christian symbolic order, occasioned by the demands of this context. The aim of this chapter is to explore the ways in which Paul draws upon and expounds the symbols, rules and resources of this symbolic order as he responds to the various situations and issues which have come to his attention; and to assess the social ethos of Paul's teaching and its (potential) impact upon different social groups. The functionalist focus upon what texts *do*, or attempt to do, will be evident, though approached from within an entirely non-functionalist framework (see §2.2. above). This approach views the text's impact as a range of consequences (both intended and unintended) which in turn form part of the context in which subsequent reformulation takes place. The assessment of this impact will include the critical questions concerning interests and ideology: Whose social interests does Paul's teaching reflect? Does it legitimate and sustain the relative positions of the socially strong and the socially weak?

As a part of this assessment I shall consider whether or not the social ethos of 1 Corinthians can accurately be termed 'love-patriarchalism'. This term, based upon Ernst Troeltsch's description of 'the Pauline Ethic',[1] has been coined by Theissen, who argues that it is an apposite

---

[1] Troeltsch 1931, 69–89, cited by Theissen 1982, 143 n. 26. See also §6.4.

summary of the ethos of Pauline Christianity, developed 'particularly in the deutero-Pauline and pastoral letters, but ... already evident in Paul (namely in 1 Cor 7:21ff; 11:3–16)'[2]. (Theissen also regards Paul's instruction in 1 Cor 8–10 and 11.17ff as 'characteristic' of 'the love-patriarchalism of the Pauline letters'.)[3]

Troeltsch described the Pauline ethic as a 'type of Christian patriarchalism' which 'receives its special colour from the warmth of the Christian idea of love'[4]. This ethic espoused an idea of equality in the religious sphere[5] but did not seek to carry this equality over into 'the sphere of secular relationships and institutions' nor to remove the inequalities of 'human life in ordinary affairs'.[6] However, these inequalities are made into 'the occasion and material for the activity of love':

> The mutual service of all to each other with the gifts which have been given to them by God,... the care of the strong for the weak, and the lifting up of the weak by the strong – all this causes a mutual give-and-take, in which the fundamentally Christian virtues of self-surrender and humility, of love and responsibility for others, are manifested ... As stewards of God the great must care for the small, and as servants of God the little ones must submit to those who bear authority.[7]

Theissen summarises the ethos in this way:

> This love-patriarchalism takes social differences for granted but ameliorates them through an obligation of respect and love, an obligation imposed upon those who are socially stronger. From the weaker are required subordination, fidelity and esteem.[8]

Theissen's reflections are particularly important because they explicitly suggest that Christianity's love-patriarchal ethos was a major factor contributing to its eventual success in the Roman world:[9] 'the society of late antiquity ... [adopted] a new pattern of integration which had been developed in small religious communities within the Roman Empire –

---

[2] Theissen 1982, 107.
[3] Theissen 1982, 139; cf. also 164.
[4] Troeltsch 1931, 78.
[5] Troeltsch 1931, 72.
[6] Troeltsch 1931, 75–76.
[7] Troeltsch 1931, 77–78.
[8] Theissen 1982, 107. Cf. also 1988b, 216.
[9] See Theissen 1982, esp. 107–10, also 138–40, 163–64.

Christian love-patriarchalism.'[10] Other scholars, moreover, accept 'love-patriarchalism' as an appropriate summary of Paul's social ethic, especially those whose main focus of study is upon later documents. Margaret MacDonald, for example, suggests that, as

> an overall description of the life patterns characteristic of the Pauline sect, Theissen's definition of 'love-patriarchalism' is very useful ... Despite the theological exposition of equality in Gal 3:28, it seems that with respect to the position of slaves and women, Paul felt it wiser to advise that the existing order of society be maintained.[11]

She argues, through a study of Colossians, Ephesians and then the Pastoral Epistles, 'that the ethos of love-patriarchalism became even more sharply pronounced in communities that continued to appeal to the authority of the Apostle after his death'.[12] There is, therefore, 'the thread of love-patriarchalism providing continuity between all these Pauline and deutero-Pauline writings. The ethos of love-patriarchalism which was born in the Pauline communities stretched far beyond the Apostle's own lifetime to shape the life of the second-century church.'[13]

Reggie Kidd, in a recent study of the Pastoral Epistles, also accepts the characterisation of Paul's ethic as one of 'love-patriarchalism' and therefore suggests that the supposed 'distance' between Paul and the Pastorals is less than is often thought.[14] He writes:

> Ernst Troeltsch got it basically right when early in this century he dubbed Paul's ethic one of mildly conservative 'patriarchalism'. According to this view, Paul's ethic does not challenge the inequities between people, but sees in those very differences the building blocks of a new type of human community.[15]

Theissen's definition and description of love-patriarchalism is also quoted with approval.[16]

A final example comes from Harry Maier's recent study of 'the social setting of the ministry as reflected in the writings of Hermas, Clement

---

[10] Theissen 1982, 109.
[11] MacDonald 1988, 43.
[12] MacDonald 1988, 44.
[13] MacDonald 1988, 202; cf. also 102–22.
[14] See Kidd 1990, 177–81.
[15] Kidd 1990, 177.
[16] Kidd 1990, 178–79.

and Ignatius'.[17] In a chapter on the Pauline epistles, Maier comments that 'Paul did not seek to upset existing household and patronage arrangements'. Maier offers examples from 1 Corinthians: Paul 'instructs slaves to remain in their servile state (7.21)';[18] 'elsewhere he tells women to cover their heads as a sign of their submission to men (11:2–13).'[19] Theissen's naming of Paul's 'community ethic "love-patriarchalism"' is quoted with approval, and, following Theissen, 1 Cor 8–10 and 11.17– 34 are offered as examples of this ethic in operation.[20]

Others, however, have reacted critically to Theissen's thesis. Elisabeth Schüssler Fiorenza suggests that Theissen 'superimposes this model on the text, especially on 1 Corinthians', and argues that his approach represents one way in which the 'patriarchalisation' of the early church is justified on the grounds of sociological necessity.[21] In a later article, however, she agrees that: 'It is Paul who introduces into the early Christian special missionary movement "Christian patriarchalism which receives its coloration from the warmth of the ideal of love".'[22]

Luise Schottroff observes that 'Theissen's characterisation of the structure of the Pauline and post-Pauline communities with the catch-word "love-patriarchalism" has been widely accepted'.[23] She, however, argues that the sociological implications of 1 Cor 1.26–31 are more radical than this catch-word would suggest. 'From the conversion/reversal (*Umkehrung*) which God's action effects, it can only be concluded that the members of the upper stratum gave up and lost all their privileges – power, position and regard – in the community (and in society).'[24] The Christian community was the place in which this reversal was experienced and lived.[25]

---

17 The title of Maier 1991.
18 Maier 1991, 35; on this latter point Maier (1991, 49 n. 43) wrongly refers to Bartchy 1973 'for detailed discussion and a similar conclusion'. See further excursus in §4.3.1.
19 Maier 1991, 35.
20 Maier 1991, 36.
21 Fiorenza 1983, 79–80.
22 Fiorenza 1987, 397, quoting Troeltsch and comparing also with Theissen.
23 Schottroff 1985, 248: 'Gerd Theißens Charakterisierung der Struktur der paulinischen und nachpaulinischen Gemeinden mit dem Schlüsselwort »Liebespatriarchalismus« ist breit akzeptiert worden.'
24 Schottroff 1985, 252: 'Aus der Umkehrung, die Gottes Handeln bewirkt, kann nur gefolgert werden, daß sie [sc. die Oberschichtsmitglieder in den Gemeinden] in der Gemeinde (und in der Gesellschaft) Macht, Wohlstand und Ansehen – alle ihre Privilegien – aufgeben und verlieren. '
25 See Schottroff 1985, 252–53, 255–56.

Troels Engberg-Pedersen has also sought 'to cast doubt on the view that the Pauline *ethos* is well captured in the concept of "love-patriarchalism"'.[26] He argues that Paul begins where people are by insisting on a form of behaviour which is within their immediate reach; yet he also shows what the implications of a radical understanding of the gospel would be. Paul's ' "allowances" (which are required by the gospel itself) are constantly overlaid by the alternative picture of an actual application of the gospel which is radical and which will destroy any social differences'.[27] Thus, 'although his [sc. Paul's] solutions are indeed realistic and practicable, they do not constitute a compromise. There is much more to them than that.'[28]

Dale Martin, while accepting much of Theissen's analysis of the Corinthian church's situation, rejects Theissen's view that 'love-patriarchalism' is an appropriate label for Paul's response to that situation. 'Benevolent patriarchalism' (as he prefers to term it) is more apposite as a description of the views of the 'strong' at Corinth. Paul's presentation of himself as a model, both in rhetoric (1 Cor 9) and in his actual lifestyle – choosing manual labour – represents a much more radical and disturbing challenge to the well-to-do members of the Corinthian community.[29]

My own reactions to Theissen's suggestions about the development of a love-patriarchal ethos in the Pauline and post-Pauline letters will be located within the wider theoretical framework which underpins this project. This framework allows, indeed requires, an assessment of both similarity and difference, both continuity and transformation. As with a language there is an essential continuity as rules and resources are produced and reproduced over time, yet, as Giddens maintains, in this reproduction there is the ever-present possibility of transformation (see §2.4. above). It is essential, I believe, to consider both the continuities in social ethos and the extent to which transformation occurs as the Christian symbolic order is reproduced over time. I shall argue that the idea that a love-patriarchal ethos runs continuously from Paul's Corinthian letters on to later documents, while not entirely without foundation, is in danger of obscuring the highly significant change in social ethos which

---

[26] Engberg-Pedersen 1987, 581.
[27] Engberg-Pedersen 1987, 580; cf. 576–77.
[28] Engberg-Pedersen 1987, 560; cf. 582.
[29] Martin 1990, 126–29. See further chapter 5 below.

is evident, at least in the case of the Corinthian correspondence, and, I would suggest, more widely too (see §7.1. and §7.2.).

4.2. Paul's reactions to social tensions at Corinth

4.2.1. Division and worldly wisdom: 1 Cor 1.10–4.21

The first major theme which Paul takes up in his letter concerns the σχίσματα, divisions, which Chloe's people have brought to his attention (1.11). I argued above that it was the divisions themselves that primarily troubled Paul more than the theology of any particular group. I also suggested, following Theissen and others, that the leaders of the factions were among the socially prominent members of the community. These were the people who had cause to consider themselves wise in the world's eyes and who sought to maintain and further their social standing.

Clearly Paul's attack on division (1.10–17) concerns the whole community, and he uses the 'fact' that there is only one Christ, the one crucified for them, to highlight the inappropriateness of division – 'Is Christ divided?' (1.13). However he seems to abandon this theme between 1.18 and 2.16, only to return to it with some force in 3.3f.[30] Thus Hans Conzelmann refers to the ' "circular" composition' of 1.18– 3.23: 'the section 3:18–23 leads back to the starting point'.[31] In rhetorical terms W. Wuellner sees 1.19–3.21 as a 'major digression'.[32]

However, if we take seriously the connection between party division and the competitive pride of the prominent 'ringleaders', then 1.18ff may seem less of a digression.[33] B. Fiore, for example, notes the 'double problem' which Paul addresses in these chapters; that of 'factionalism' and the deeper problem of which the divisions are a manifestation, namely, 'a far reaching failure in the community members' own self-estimation, with [their] exaggerated pretensions to knowledge (3:18–19) and faulty regard or denigration of others (4:6–7)'.[34]

---

[30] Cf. Lampe 1990, 118.
[31] Conzelmann 1975, 39. The German is 'die „ringförmige" Komposition' (Conzelmann 1969, 53).
[32] Wuellner 1979, 185, who also refers to the digression's appearance as a 'ring-composition'.
[33] Cf. Theissen 1982, 56.
[34] Fiore 1985, 86–87, 101.

Given such a situation, we may understand the considerable space Paul devotes to the contrast between *worldly* wisdom and the wisdom of God, which is displayed most clearly in the foolishness of the cross.[35] One of the central 'resources' of the Christian symbolic order – the crucified Christ – is brought to bear upon this particular situation. In 1.18–2.5, beginning with 'the word of the cross', Paul offers three demonstrations of the gospel's opposition to worldly wisdom.[36]

First, Paul declares that the word of the cross is the means whereby God has rendered foolish the wisdom of the world (v. 20b). Its action is a fulfilment of Isaiah's prophecy: 'I will destroy the wisdom of the wise, and I will bring to nothing the understanding of those who understand' (v. 19; Isa 29.14 LXX).[37] It is a word which can appear foolishness to the entire world, to both Jew and Greek, yet which is the power and wisdom of God (v. 23f). To those who consider themselves wise in the eyes of the world, Paul shows that the gospel, with the cross at its centre, is diametrically opposed to worldly power and wisdom.[38]

Secondly, in verses 26–31, Paul points to the Corinthians themselves as evidence of this truth. Verse 26, often the starting point for sociological analyses of the community,[39] describes a group comprised largely but not exclusively of the lower classes.[40] 'According to Paul, that provides an empirical proof that the strength and wisdom revered by human society are rejected and convicted by God. Through the proclamation of the word about the cross, God repudiated the ones who are considered strong

---

[35] The content of the section 1.18–3.23 concerns 'der λόγος τοῦ σταυροῦ versus σοφία τοῦ κόσμου'; Sänger 1985, 287. See the list of contrasts Paul draws in Clarke 1993, 101–102. Lampe 1990, 120–22, argues that in 1.18–2.16 Paul 'opposes the word about the cross to human *theological* wisdom' (my emphasis). However, to my mind this underestimates the divine/*worldly* contrast.

[36] Weiss 1910, 24, points to the three sections 1.18–25, 1.26–31 and 2.1–5, which show 'daß das Evangelium mit der Weisheit der Welt inkommensurabel ist'; similarly Schrage 1991, 166. Alternatively, the passage is sometimes seen as a basic theological point (1.18–25) followed by two illustrations, or empirical supports; cf. Lampe 1990, 128; Klauck 1984, 24–28. On the parallel construction of 1.18–2.5 and 2.6–3.23 see Theissen 1987, 345.

[37] Except that the LXX has κρύψω and not ἀθετήσω.

[38] Cf. Weiss 1910, 24: 'Das Wort vom Kreuz hat mit der Weisheit der Welt nichts gemeinsam.' This so-called digression, then, can hardly have 'pleased' all of its hearers, only to criticise them later, at 3.3, as Lampe 1990, 128, suggests! On the connection between wisdom and power, cf. Watson 1992a, 138, 141.

[39] Cf. Sänger 1985, 286; Schottroff 1985; see §3.7. above.

[40] Theissen 1982, 70–73; Sänger 1985, 286, 291 n. 39.

and wise by the world.'[41] For Paul, the divine *purpose* in the social composition of the community is of profound significance:

τὰ μωρὰ τοῦ κόσμου   ἐξελέξατο ὁ θεός,   ἵνα καταισχύνῃ
                                                                τοὺς σοφούς,
καὶ τὰ ἀσθενῆ τοῦ κόσμου   ἐξελέξατο ὁ θεός,   ἵνα καταισχύνῃ
                                                                  τὰ ἰσχυρά,
καὶ τὰ ἀγενῆ τοῦ κόσμου
καὶ τὰ ἐξουθενημένα   ἐξελέξατο ὁ θεός,
τὰ μὴ ὄντα,   ἵνα τὰ ὄντα
                                                                  καταργήσῃ

the foolish things of the world	God chose,	in order to shame the wise
and the weak things of the world	God chose,	in order to shame the strong
and the lowborn things of the world and the despised the nothings,	God chose,	in order to destroy the things that are. (1.27f)[42]

Paul's interpretation of the divine election could hardly be more forceful; the deliberate *purpose* (a purpose reiterated three times) of God's choosing of the foolish, weak, lowborn, despised nobodies is to shame and overthrow the powerful and prominent.[43]

---

[41] Lampe 1990, 126. Cf. Schrage 1991, 204 (also 217): 'Man kann den Abschnitt mit guten Gründen ein *exemplum* nennen.'

[42] Referring to 1.26–31, Klauck 1984, 26, notes: 'Die drei mittleren Sätze sind in strengem Parallelismus aufgebaut.' He also suggests that the use of the neuter plural τά ... in v. 27f has a definite significance, reflecting 'das verächtliche Urteil der oberen Klassen über die niedrigeren Schichten', noting that slaves were regarded as 'things'. However this is by no means certain; Paul does not seem to attach particular significance to the use of the neuter, using τὰ ἰσχυρά, τὰ ὄντα etc; cf. Schrage 1991, 210.

[43] Cf. Schottroff 1985, 255–56. Paul's thought here may be rooted in the theological idea of God's creation out of nothing (cf. Rom 4.17; Schrage 1991, 210ff), but the sociological dimensions should not therefore be denied; Paul chooses to bring these particular ideas in at this point.

The rhetorical nature of Paul's declaration should certainly make us wary of reading 1.26 simply as a piece of sociological information[44] (although it must broadly be true in order for Paul's point to be plausible). But it should make us even more aware of the impact of the text upon its readers. Its main aim is to deny all human grounds for boasting and to proclaim the Lord as the only one in whom boasting is appropriate.[45] To those all too conscious of their lowly status within Corinthian society and their inability to boast in their worldly position, Paul announces that God has *chosen* them, and chosen them for a purpose: to shame the powerful who place great value upon worldly status. And those who count themselves among the 'wise, powerful and well-born' of Corinthian society are shown quite bluntly that these signs of worldly privilege are precisely what God is destroying.[46] If they wish to count themselves among those called by God they must reject the valuation which society enables them to obtain.

Conzelmann refers to 1.27–29 as 'a Pauline way of taking up and working out Christologically the Jewish idea of the overthrow of the lofty and the exalting of the lowly by God'.[47] However, he then denies the specific social bias of the text and declares that 'Paul does not teach that "the" lowly will be exalted, but that *faith becomes the receiver of salvation regardless of its worldly standing*'.[48] While this idea may be theologically comfortable, it plainly contradicts the text itself, which clearly declares that God *chose* those with a *particular* worldly standing in order to shame and overthrow the wise and powerful. The symbolic order of the Pauline gospel expressed here stands in sharp contrast to the dominant symbolic order of Roman society. In the latter the poor are despised, and one's value is determined by education, wealth and breeding.[49] The cross, on the other hand, turns the world upside down and demonstrates God's rejection of the world's hierarchy. 'It is precisely the foolish, the weak, and the lowly who are the "wise" within the new frame of reference. They experience a total transformation of their evaluation.'[50]

---

[44] Cf. Judge 1960a, 59; Wuellner 1973.

[45] '…jeden menschlichen Selbstruhm unmöglich zu machen': Klauck 1984, 27.

[46] Note the use of καταργέω in 1.18 and 2.6 (also 6.13; 13.8, 10f; 15.24, 26); on which see Abbott-Smith 1936, 238; BAGD, 417. The German word 'vernichten' is used in the translations in Conzelmann 1969, 65, and Klauck 1984, 27.

[47] Conzelmann 1975, 50.

[48] Conzelmann 1975, 51, my emphasis; cf. Black 1984, 100.

[49] Cf. MacMullen 1974, 104–20, and for 'the lexicon of snobbery', 138–41; also §3.2. above.

[50] Theissen 1987, 387.

It should be remembered that Paul is likely to have introduced these ideas for a specific reason. He has heard about the way in which prominent members of the Corinthian community compete for position and status and lead rival factions, and is not afraid to attack this practice at its very core, to declare that such worldly valuations are entirely alien and worthless to God. He draws upon some of the central resources of the Christian faith, representing them in a particular way, in order to confront this particular context. Paul returns specifically and forcefully to the divisions in 3.3f, stressing that 'jealousy' (ζῆλος) and 'rivalry' (ἔρις) are evidence of 'fleshly' human conduct. In 3.18f he challenges anyone who reckons themselves 'wise in this age' to 'become a fool ... for the wisdom of this world is foolishness with God'.

Thus, thirdly, Paul describes his own preaching as characterised by 'weakness, fear and trembling' (ἀσθένεια, φόβος, τρόμος), insisting that it was not a message of human wisdom (2.1–5). The fact that Paul may indeed be a skilled rhetorician, as recent studies show, only confirms the observation that he is making a particular point here, and not simply repeating facts.[51] Any power in his words, Paul claims, comes through God's power (δυνάμει θεοῦ) not human wisdom (σοφίᾳ ἀνθρώπων; 2.5). The gospel message *is* wisdom, but not a wisdom 'of this age' (τοῦ αἰῶνος τούτου), nor (οὐδέ), Paul adds significantly, 'of the rulers of this age, who are being brought to nothing' (τῶν ἀρχόντων τοῦ αἰῶνος τούτου τῶν καταργουμένων; 2.6).[52] Hence also Paul insists that he and Apollos are only servants (3.5; 4.1), not figures who intend to be exalted as the heads of factions. Indeed, Paul's experience as an apostle is completely the opposite of success and honour (4.8–13).[53]

---

[51] Cf. the discussion by Lim 1987; also Judge 1968; Forbes 1986; Mitchell 1991. Studies of New Testament rhetoric have expanded in recent years; see for example the collection of essays in Watson 1991.

[52] Carr 1977 has shown that the rulers referred to here are earthly authorities and not demonic or supernatural powers, as has been frequently suggested (see also Fee 1987, 103–104, supporting Carr's view); though it is interesting that, in the context of a debate which revolved around the theological issues of Gnostic versus non-Gnostic influence, Carr concludes that 'the significance ... of these verses for the nature of the Corinthian error is negligible' (35). From the perspective of a sociological investigation into the character of the Corinthian church's problems and the nature of Paul's response to those problems it is a highly interesting reference.

[53] See further §5.2.

J. A. Gibbs suggests that the whole of 4.8–13 is cast in relation to the three motifs of 'wisdom, power and wellbeing' found in 1.26, pointing in particular to 4.10:

We are fools for Christ, but you are wise in Christ.– *Wisdom*
We are weak, but you are strong.– *Power*
You are held in honour, but we in disrepute.– *Wellbeing*[54]

However, the correspondence is much stronger if 1.27f is taken into account. The contrasts drawn there are strikingly similar to those drawn in 4.10:[55]

1.27f	(1.26)	4.10	
		ἡμεῖς ...	ὑμεῖς ...
τὰ μωρά /τοὺς σοφούς	(σοφοί)	μωροί	φρόνιμοι
τὰ ἀσθενῆ /τὰ ἰσχυρά	(δυνατοί)	ἀσθενεῖς	ἰσχυροί
τὰ ἀγενῆ			
τὰ ἐξουθενημένα /τὰ ὄντα	(εὐγενεῖς)	ἄτιμοι	ἔνδοξοι
τὰ μὴ ὄντα			
		we ...	you ...
the foolish/ the wise	(wise)	fools	wise
the weak/ the strong	(powerful)	weak	strong
the lowborn			
the despised/ the things that are	(well-born)	dishonoured	honoured
the nothings			

It therefore seems likely that the sarcastic criticism of the Corinthians in 4.8–13 is also directed primarily at the socially prominent members of the congregation. [56]

---

[54] Gibbs 1978, 133–34; cf. also Sänger 1985, 287–88. Gibbs 1978, 120, suggests that Jer 9.22f is in Paul's mind through the whole of 1.26–31. However, against this see Wuellner 1978, 166 and Schrage 1991, 205, who notes the similarity between 1.31 and 1 Sam 2.10 (LXX).

[55] Cf. Plank 1987, 47. Thus the 'ring' composition should be extended beyond 3.23 (cf. above p. 131 with nn. 31–32); Schrage 1991, 129–30, suggests that it should extend from 1.10 to 4.21 but warns against overemphasising the circular structure. The idea of τὰ ἐξουθενημένα in 1.28 may also be linked esp. with 4.13.

[56] See further §3.9. and §5.2.

While in 1.10–4.21 division as a whole is condemned, from 1.18ff it is those who pride themselves on their worldly status who face particular attack. Indeed, those who know themselves to be foolish, weak and despised, the nobodies, are specifically assured of their election by God. The symbolic order of the gospel, as Paul sees it, centred upon the cross of Christ, inverts the values of the dominant social order.[57] Anyone who wants to count themselves 'in' must cease to regard themselves as strong and wise 'in this age' and become weak and foolish in order to discover the power of God.

The way in which Paul uses central symbols of the Christian faith to attack the status and position of the socially prominent members of the congregation can hardly have been popular among such people. The impact of such rhetoric, intended or unintended, will emerge as the study proceeds.

4.2.2. Litigation among believers: 1 Cor 6.1–8

As the brief sketch in the previous chapter showed, the litigations to which Paul here refers were probably initiated by Christians of some wealth and social position. Unfortunately the text gives us no clues as to whether the cases involved clashes between people of roughly equal social status or were instigated by the powerful against the weaker members of the Christian community.[58] Paul's dismay arises primarily from the fact that there are such cases of litigation at all, and he does not specify their precise nature or name guilty parties. Since he is presumably dependant on an oral report concerning this situation he may not know much more than that cases of litigation are being pursued. However, his criticism is presumably directed primarily towards the litigants who initiate these cases (cf. v. 7).

Paul's sharp criticism of their practice is implicit in the very first word of verse 1; τολμᾷ. 'The word is an argument in itself; "How can you dare ...".'[59] Indeed, verse 1 summarises succinctly Paul's basic point in vv. 1–6: it is quite wrong for believers to take their disputes[60] to be judged[61]

---

57 For further reflections on this theme, see Watson 1992a, 139–49.
58 Mitchell 1993 argues that the latter is the case.
59 Robertson and Plummer 1914, 110.
60 On the translation of πρᾶγμα here (cf. v. 7; κρίματα), see BAGD, 697; cf. 450; Robertson and Plummer 1914, 110: 'a cause for trial', 'a case'; Dinkler 1952, 169; Vischer 1955, 9.
61 κρίνεσθαι: it is possible to draw some contrast between κρίνεσθαι as 'das egoistische Rechtssuchen' and διακρῖναι (v. 5) as 'die friedliche Schlichtung', although the contiguity of both verbs in 1 Cor 11.31 may warn against too strong a distinction; see Schrage 1991, 413–14.

ἐπὶ τῶν ἀδίκων ('before the unjust/unrighteous'). Paul's reference to secular judges as ἄδικος is generally taken to imply only that they are ἄπιστος ('unbelieving'; v. 6) and not to express moral criticism of their practices.[62] However, Bruce Winter has pointed to some of the reasons why Paul may have considered the civil courts to be unjust, including the frequent use of bribes and the advantages enjoyed by those with wealth and status.[63] While Paul's primary reason for the label ἄδικος may have been theological, based on the fact that the secular courts are composed of 'unbelievers', the criticism and rejection of the civil courts implied in the word ἄδικος may nevertheless have struck those who gained most from their operation.

Paul's basic argument in vv. 1–6 is theological, grounded fundamentally in the redemption which has separated the ἅγιοι from the ἄδικοι (vv. 9–11) and specifically in the eschatological conviction that the saints will one day judge both the world and angels. The fact that he is using these theological resources to make a particular point and to have an impact upon a particular situation is surely shown by the contrast between 5.12 and 6.2. In chapter 5 Paul is concerned with the purity of the community and with the expulsion of an offender. It is not his concern, he asserts, to judge 'those outside' (5.12). In chapter 6, however, where he is concerned to show why the Christians should not need to turn to the secular courts, he declares almost the opposite: 'the saints will judge the world' (6.2). The opening verses of chapter 6 build to a climax in vv. 5 and 6 through a series of rhetorical questions. Οὐκ οἴδατε ('Do you not know') may imply that Paul expects the Corinthians to be aware already of the ideas he conveys, but it may be a stylistic way of conveying new information which they ought now to know.[64] The eschatological ideas certainly have definite implications in the present and Paul draws two specific conclusions in vv. 2 and 3, in each case using an *a maiore ad minus* argument.[65] His first conclusion is based on

---

[62] E.g. Schrage 1991, 406–407; Orr and Walther 1976, 193–94; Barrett 1971a, 135; Conzelmann 1975, 104 n. 12; Fee 1987, 232.

[63] See Winter 1991 and §3.8.3. above. There is certainly a moral content to ἀδικία in vv. 9–11.

[64] Conzelmann 1975, 104 (cf. Fuller 1986, 104), suggests that 'Paul is in fact referring back to one of the teachings of the primitive Christian catechism', mentioning 1 Thess 5.1ff, although the saints' role in judgment is not mentioned there. On the possible implication of ἢ οὐκ οἴδατε cf. §3.5.1. n. 125. Schrage 1991, 409, sensibly suggests that the question as to whether this is new knowledge being passed on or not must 'offen bleiben'.

[65] Cf. Schrage 1991, 405, 410–11; Barrett 1971a, 136; Vischer 1955, 10; Dinkler 1952, 187; Fuller 1986, 99.

the belief that 'the saints will judge the world': if they are to do this, surely they must be competent to deal with minor cases (v. 2)?[66] The second conclusion derives from the idea that 'we will judge angels' (v. 3). If the saints are to execute judgments at this exalted level, surely they can make judgments concerning βιωτικά, everyday matters.

Verse 4 is notoriously difficult to interpret, yet is significant for an interpretation of Paul's response to the Corinthians' practices. It may be taken as another in the series of questions and thus translated, 'if then you have disputes about everyday matters, do you appoint (as judges) those who are despised by the church?' Alternatively, καθίζετε may be taken as a categorical indicative, making the verse a statement of what the Corinthians do in fact do. A third possibility is that καθίζετε is meant as an imperative, in which case a quite different meaning is implied: 'If then you have disputes about everyday matters, appoint those who are the despised in the church.'[67] Paul would then be 'instructing' the Corinthians, perhaps as an ironic way of shaming them for having such trials at all (v. 5), to appoint the lowliest members of the church as arbiters rather than go to the secular courts.[68] This interpretation, with its implied reversal of social roles and resonance with God's choice of τὰ ἐξουθενημένα ('the despised'; 1.28; cf. 4.8–13), is in some ways attractive but does not, I think, carry enough weight to be entirely convincing. The reference to τὰ ἐξουθενημένα in 1.28 is made when Paul is drawing an explicit contrast, and it seems unlikely that he would refer, without qualification, to certain Christians as τοὺς ἐξουθενημένους.[69] Moreover, the literary structure of the section suggests that a further question in the series of questions may be expected.[70] It is sometimes

---

[66] The translation of κριτήριον here is disputed; the question is whether the meaning 'lawsuit' or 'case' is justified, as opposed to the more common meaning 'tribunal' or 'law court'. BAGD, 453, Vischer 1955, 11, and Fee 1987, 233–34 suggest that the former is apposite here. Similarly, Büchsel TDNT 3, 943: 'the only possible sense [here] is "legal process".' Otherwise Robertson and Plummer 1914, 112. The general sense is clear enough, though the meaning of κριτήριον bears significantly upon the influence of this passage on the beginnings of ecclesiastical courts; on which see Conzelmann 1975, 104 and Schrage 1991, 419ff. On the history of interpretation see esp. Vischer 1955, 21–130.

[67] The options are discussed by Robertson and Plummer 1914, 113–14; Vischer 1955, 13–14; Schrage 1991, 411–12; Barrett 1971a, 137; Fuller 1986, 100; Fee 1987, 235–36.

[68] Derrett 1991, 28, takes καθίζετε as a command suggesting therefore that Paul means that such disputes 'should be brought before even the lowest-privileged "saint", provided he is "wise"' (32); cf. also Clarke 1993, 69–71.

[69] So Barrett 1971a, 137; Fee 1987, 235.

[70] Cf. Schrage 1991, 412.

objected that καθίζω means 'I appoint', and therefore is an inappropriate description of the Corinthians' relation to the secular judges, whom they did not appoint.[71] This might favour the imperative interpretation of καθίζετε, which relates it to the appointment of members of the church. However, it seems quite acceptable to take Paul as implying that the Corinthians appoint (in the sense of 'invoke' or 'endorse') the secular courts, simply by taking cases to them.[72] The following clause, πρὸς ἐντροπὴν ὑμῖν λέγω – 'I say this to shame you' (cf. 15.34; contrast 4.14), makes sense with either interpretation of καθίζετε.[73] Paul could mean that his suggestion that they appoint the lowliest believer to arbitrate is itself meant to shame their current practice (with its dependence upon wealth and status), or that a reference to the secular courts as 'despised by (ἐν) the church' is intended to portray the Corinthians' behaviour as shameful. Reading verse 4 as a question, however, seems the most plausible option. [74]

Paul's question in verse 5 may suggest that the idea of internal arbitration, by someone regarded as σοφός, would be an acceptable and preferable alternative to taking disputes to the secular courts (cf. v. 1). However, vv. 7–8 show that this could only be second best and is hardly Paul's preferred solution to the problem. Given too, that verse 5 comes in a context where Paul is explicitly seeking to bring shame upon them (v. 5a), the question is best taken as ironic, and relates to the discussion of 1.18ff above. Paul thus asks, 'With all your pretensions to being wise and educated people, can't you even find someone wise enough to decide matters among you?'[75] The fact that 'brother' goes to law with brother' is bad enough, but the fact that this is before unbelievers intensifies the scandal (v. 6).[76]

After the basic argument of vv. 1–6 – don't go to the secular courts with your petty grievances[77] – Paul strikes even more deeply in verses 7

---

[71] See Barrett 1971a, 137; Schrage 1991, 412; cf. also p. 110 n. 280 above.

[72] 'Wer einen heidnischen Richter in Anspruch nimmt, „anerkennt" ihn als für sich zuständig.' (Lang 1986, 77.)

[73] *Pace* Barrett 1971a, 137, who takes it as strong evidence against the 'appoint despised members of the church' interpretation.

[74] As, for example, Fuller 1986, 100; Fee 1987, 235–36.

[75] Cf. Schrage 1991, 413; Fee 1987, 237: 'This is biting sarcasm'. The irony in the question is not removed even if Paul uses σοφός here as a 'technical legal expression' like the Jewish *ḥākām*, *contra* Dinkler 1952, 171 (see also Barrett 1971a, 138).

[76] Cf. Schrage's comment on v. 6 (1991, 414).

[77] Of course, Paul's view that the cases are petty (ἐλαχίστων, v. 2) may not have been shared by the Corinthians.

and 8:[78] to have such grievances at all is a complete defeat, ὅλως ἥττημα (v. 7). The truly Christian way, Paul implies, without here offering any explicit theological foundation (but cf. 1 Cor 13.5), is to prefer to *be wronged* and *defrauded*, rather than to insist on exacting justice and recompense.[79] And, as what Wolfgang Schrage calls a 'paradoxical climax' (*paradoxe Zuspitzung*), Paul takes the same two verbs (v. 8) and puts them into the active voice, not to point now to those who actually commit the wrongs, but to maintain that 'calling on the courts and battling for supposed property rights *as such* are wronging and robbing'.[80] Clearly the conviction that fellow believers are brothers and sisters makes the act of dragging them before the courts profoundly wrong.

In this section, then, Paul has denied to the higher status members of the Corinthian church one of the important means by which they defended and promoted their prestige and status, at least if it involved another believer. The practice of civil litigation, intended as a way of upholding honour, is described as shameful for a believer.[81] The values of the dominant social order are reversed and opposed. And wanting to extract justice from a brother or sister is completely wrong to begin with. Not only has this practice been prohibited, but those who engage in it have been described themselves as people who wrong and defraud their brothers and sisters (v. 8). Such a description may well have annoyed those who saw civil litigation as a proper means of exacting justice and retribution. These people may also have been disturbed by the exhortation that they should 'opt out' of one of the primary secular avenues through which they were able to sustain their position and status and gain recompense from their opponents. As believers, Paul maintains, they should prefer instead to lose status, to suffer humiliation.[82] Paul's instruction on this matter hardly leaves untouched 'the sphere of secular relationships and institutions'[83] nor does it affirm or sustain the social position and practice of the socially strong.

---

[78] Cf. esp. Dinkler 1952, 172–86; Vischer 1955, 6: In vv. 7f, 'Paulus geht über die Lösung in v. 5, die er ja nur in Frageform hingestellt hat, hinaus'.

[79] Cf. Matt 5.38ff, a parallel mentioned, for example, by Vischer 1955, 16; Fuller 1986, 101.

[80] '… das Anrufen der Gerichte und der Kampf um angebliche Rechtstitel *als solche* Unrecht und Beraubung [sind]'; Schrage 1991, 417, my emphasis. Cf. Klauck 1984, 46; Wengst 1987, 77.

[81] On the significance of honour and shame in the New Testament world, see Malina 1981, 25–50.

[82] For reflections on the contemporary significance of 1 Cor 6.1–11, see Taylor 1986; Vischer 1955, 131–36.

[83] Troeltsch 1931, 75.

Paul has drawn on the theological resources of the Christian symbolic order in order to address this particular situation. He has insisted that the secular courts – embodiments of the Roman system of law and justice – are not the appropriate place for believers to take their disputes with one another. The Christian believers belong to an alternative community, one which rejects the values upon which 'worldly' judgments would be made, and should be more than capable of settling their own disputes. More than this, however, Paul shows that he expects the believers to inhabit a world with significantly different values and a significantly different ethos. Even to have disputes is a sign of complete defeat. The ethos of the Christian community is such that one should prefer to be wronged rather than to insist on exacting recompense from a brother or sister. The symbolic order which Paul, as a leader in a position of power, is seeking to construct and to see embodied in community living,[84] is one which stands in sharp contrast to the dominant social order.

4.2.3. Idol meat and the rights of the strong: 1 Cor 8.1–11.1

Alongside chapters 1–4, chapters 8–10 of 1 Corinthians have generated a considerable amount of discussion. It is these chapters above all which have led commentators to question the literary unity of the letter.[85] However, unconvinced by the arguments for partition, I consider that chapters 8–10 are best read as a unity.[86] Even chapter 9, while apparently digressive, plays a significant part in the argument of 8–10 and is clearly linked to its context.[87] While it might be suggested that a redactor spotted these links and thus assembled the various sections, I consider this less likely than that Paul composed the whole.[88] Commentators have also had enormous difficulty in deciding exactly what Paul's advice or instruction is.[89] The purpose of the following section, however, is

---

[84] Cf. pp. 53–55 above.
[85] E.g. Weiss 1910, xl–xliii, 210–13; Héring 1962, xiii–xiv, 75; Jewett 1978, 396–404; Sellin 1987, 2964–82. See Hurd 1965, 43–47, 131; Barrett 1971a, 16.
[86] Cf. p. 113 n. 302 above; also Gardner 1994; Mitchell 1991.
[87] Cf. Willis 1985b; Martin 1990, 77–80; Wuellner 1979, 186–87.
[88] Not least because the links and arguments are subtle and extended (cf. Brunt 1985, 121). See defences of the unity of these chapters by Hurd 1965, 131–42; Merklein 1984, 163–73. Conzelmann 1975, 137, points to the parallel in Rom 14.1–15.13 in support of literary unity here.
[89] Contrast, for example, Brunt 1985 with Tomson 1990, 185–220, and Fee 1980; 1987, 359–63, with Fisk 1989.

limited. I aim primarily to consider the social ethos conveyed by Paul's instruction on this subject, bearing in mind (with caution) the hypothesis outlined above, namely that it is the socially prominent members of the Corinthian church who claim the right to eat εἰδωλόθυτα, and the socially weak who consider such practice idolatrous.

Not surprisingly, if the sociological hypothesis is correct, the Corinthians' letter to Paul seems to have reflected the argument of the strong,[90] and it is the argument of their letter with which Paul deals first. Verses 1–6 and 8 of 1 Cor 8 are best read as Paul's interaction with the views directly expressed in the Corinthians' letter.[91] The 'strong' Corinthians, it seems, were assured of their γνῶσις, 'knowledge' (v. 1), presumably, in this context, that 'there is no idol in the world and there is no God but one' (v. 4). Such monotheistic γνῶσις Paul basically accepts, but stresses in response the importance of ἀγάπη and οἰκοδομή ('love builds up'; see vv. 1–3).[92] He is concerned because of those who do not share the γνῶσις concerning the non-existence of idols and still eat idol meat aware of its connection with an idol (τοῦ εἰδώλου ὡς εἰδωλόθυτον ἐσθίουσιν – v. 7).[93] The primary problem, in Paul's view, is the offence caused to these 'weak' brothers and sisters (8.7, 9–13). Thus the first reason Paul gives to the strong for changing their behaviour is that it causes problems for the weak;[94] causing such a person to stumble is reason enough never again to eat meat at all, as Paul says in the hyperbole of v. 13. Even the most insignificant member of the community is a 'brother or sister for whom Christ died' (v. 11). From a sociological point of view it is significant that this is the *first* reason Paul gives why the strong may need to cease the practice which gives offence to the weak. Regard for others, however weak, is the prime considera-

---

[90] See Hurd 1965, 117–25, although see pp. 106–107 above for criticism of Hurd's argument that there was no division of opinion on the matter at Corinth, only opposition to Paul, and that the 'weak' person is a hypothetical construction of Paul's.

[91] Cf. Fee 1980, 188; Hurd 1965, 119–123.

[92] Cf. Lang 1986, 108: 'Paulus kann dieser Parole grundsätzlich zustimmen, er verbindet sie aber sogleich mit dem Gesichtspunkt der Liebe.' Gardner 1994, 33–40, is right to stress that Paul 'corrects' their knowledge, but I think he underestimates the extent of Paul's agreement with the content of their γνῶσις. Cf. further Wright 1991, 120–36.

[93] Verse 7 is the main reason for not seeing the conflict primarily as a Jewish versus non–Jewish argument. The people mentioned in 8.7 are *accustomed* (συνηθείᾳ is the most likely textual reading; cf. Metzger 1971, 557) to eating idol meat as such; cf. Fee 1987, 14, 379–80; Lang 1986, 111.

[94] Cf. Lang 1986, 112: 'Die christliche Freiheit findet ihre Grenze an der Rücksichtnahme auf den schwachen Bruder.'

tion. Indeed, although other forms of warning are offered to the strong, it is this socially-orientated instruction which is particularly reiterated in 10.24 and 32f and which emerges as a fundamental motivation of Paul's exemplary conduct in 9.12 and 9.19ff.

Paul next uses his own apostolic lifestyle as an *example* of the setting aside of rights (9.1ff).[95] Having warned the Corinthians that their use of ἐξουσία may cause others to stumble (8.9), he now tells them how and why he has limited the exercise of his 'freedom' and apostolic ἐξουσία in order to remove potential barriers to the acceptance of the gospel (esp. 9.4ff, 12, 19ff). While this chapter is in part to be understood as a personal example of the conduct he is recommending to the Corinthians, it also reflects some criticism of Paul's conduct. Hence the sharp assertive questions of verses 1 and 2, and his description of what follows as ἡ ἐμὴ ἀπολογία τοῖς ἐμὲ ἀνακρίνουσιν ('my defence to those who judge me'; v. 3).[96]

The idea that even Paul himself may fail in his attempt to run the Christian race and might still be found ἀδόκιμος ('disqualified'; 9.24–27) perhaps forms the connecting link with 10.1–13, which some see as an already-formed midrashic passage utilised again by Paul in the context of this particular argument.[97] The main aim of the passage is to warn against the complacent assumption that through sharing in baptism and the Lord's Supper, people are irrevocably confirmed as God's people, a status which sinful behaviour is unable to affect. Sinful behaviour, Paul warns, can still lead to exclusion from the people who are saved.[98] In particular, the story of Israel's experiences in the desert is meant to warn against idolatry, as the forceful conclusion of verse 14 shows: 'flee from idolatry' (cf. v. 7). Thus, a second caution to the strong is offered, namely that temptation and sin are still real dangers, especially the sin of

---

[95] Cf. esp. Willis 1985b; Brunt 1985, 114; Lang 1986, 113.

[96] On chapter 9, and the debate over whether it is primarily example or defence, see §5.3. below.

[97] See, for example, Meeks 1982b.

[98] Cf. Fee 1980, 185. The references to baptism and 'spiritual food and drink' in vv. 2–4 are surely intended to oppose the view that partakers thereof are free from the dangers of sin and exclusion from the community (I am unconvinced by Gardner's (1994, 142–43) argument that an analogy with spiritual gifts is intended here). This does not necessarily confront a 'sacramentalism' (as is often assumed; e.g. Lang 1986, 122; Klauck 1982, 331; Lampe 1991, 199–200) so much as the social issue of one's membership of a community. See Willis 1985a, esp. 123–63. 10.1–13 is essentially an attack on complacency; cf. Gardner 1994, 115, 135, 149, 155.

idolatry. 'So whoever thinks they are standing, let them watch out lest they fall' (v. 12).[99] What Paul does *not* say clearly is when eating idol-food (εἰδωλόθυτα) is idol-worship (εἰδωλολατρία).[100] Paul's third warning to the strong centres around the concept of κοινωνία ('fellowship'; 10.15–22). W. L. Willis argues that κοινωνία here implies primarily a social or communal 'sharing', and not a mystical sacramentalism, a concept which he challenges throughout as an unlikely 'background' to 1 Cor 8 and 10.[101] Paul thus draws a contrast between the κοινωνία among those who share the bread and the cup of the Lord's Supper and those who share the cup and the table of demons.[102] Those who share κοινωνία in Christ are ἓν σῶμα ('one body'; v. 17). How can they therefore also share with those who are κοινωνοὺς τῶν δαιμονίων ('partners with demons'; v. 20)? Here again Paul does not specify the occasions at which eating εἰδωλόθυτα is 'partaking of the table of demons' (v. 21). Nor does he specifically say that eating εἰδωλόθυτα is unacceptable. Indeed, in 10.27, in the context of speaking about being invited to a dinner by an unbeliever, Paul advises 'eat everything which is set before you'.

There are those who suggest that 8.1–10.23 deal with a context ἐν εἰδωλείῳ ('in an idol's temple'; 8.10), where partaking by Christians is definitely wrong, whereas 10.24ff deal with meals in private homes, at which anything may be eaten without worry (given certain conditions).[103] However, if this is the case then Paul did not make himself clear, in what could surely have been a relatively simple argument. Furthermore, such a theory fails to consider the impossibility of drawing such a sharp and simple dividing line. Consider, for example, the following invitations:

Ἐρωτᾷ σε Σαραπίων γεγυμνασιαρχ(ηκὼς) δειπνῆσαι εἰς κλείνην τοῦ κυρίου Σαράπιδος ἐν τῇ ἰδίᾳ οἰκίᾳ αὔριον ἥτις ἐστὶν τε ἀπὸ ὥρ(ας) ἡ.

---

99 'The word Ὥστε shows the centrality of v 12 to Paul's argument': Gardner 1994, 152.

100 Therefore, *contra* Tomson 1990, 202–208, I cannot see that Paul clearly forbids the eating of all εἰδωλόθυτα, although he does plainly warn against εἰδωλολατρία; cf. Fisk 1989, 58, 63. Fee 1980, 193 states that 'εἰδωλολατρία of course means eating at the temples'. However, see below for the ambiguity that still remained. On the imprecision of Paul's advice, see Gooch 1993, 105–106.

101 See Willis 1985a, 167–222 and *passim*.

102 Cf. Fee 1980, 194: 'These are mutually exclusive options.'

103 Fee 1980, sees 'temple meals as the real problem Paul is addressing in all of 8,1–10,22' (187); cf. also 1987, 359–63; Wright 1991, 134–35; Gardner 1994, 176, 183. For a critical response to Fee's interpretation see Fisk 1989.

Sarapion, ex-gymnasiarch, requests you to dine at his house on the occasion of the *lectisternium* of the Lord Sarapis tomorrow, which is the 15th, at the 8th hour. (*P. Oslo* 157)

'Ερωτᾷ σε Διονύσιος δειπνῆσαι τῇ ϗᾱ εἰς κλείνην 'Ηλίου μεγάλου Σαράπιδος ἀπὸ ὥρας θ̄ ἐν τῆι πατρικῆι ἑαυτοῦ οἰκίᾳ.

Dionysios asks you to dine on the 21st at the *kline* of Helios, great Sarapis, at the 9th hour, in the house of his father. (*P. Yale* 85)[104]

'Idolatrous feasts' and meals in a private house can hardly be separated neatly; as well as 'religious' meals in the home, a variety of primarily social occasions were held in various temples, of which there were many at Corinth.[105] Peter Gooch makes a similar point, stressing the impossibility of dividing sacred and secular contexts.[106] Thus I prefer to regard 10.23–11.1 as Paul's summary and concluding advice. Indeed, Hurd sets out this view in some detail, showing, in his opinion, that: 'Closer comparison reveals that the whole of 1 Cor. 10.23–11.1 is a point by point restatement and summary of the argument of 1 Cor. 8 and 9.'[107] The summary begins by making a similar point to that made in 8.1ff, stressing the importance of συμφέρειν ('to benefit') and οἰκοδομεῖν ('to build up') over against the Corinthian slogan πάντα ἔξεστιν ('all things are lawful'; v. 23).[108] Paul then reiterates the most important point of chapters 8 and 9: μηδεὶς τὸ ἑαυτοῦ ζητείτω ἀλλὰ τὸ τοῦ ἑτέρου ('let no one seek their own [advantage], but that of the other'; v. 24). In terms of practical advice, then, everything sold in the market place may be eaten, μηδὲν ἀνακρίνοντες διὰ τὴν συνείδησιν ('without raising questions of consciousness'); invitations from unbelievers may be accepted if desired, and whatever is served, eaten (vv. 25–27). However, in the latter case, idol-food should be refused if anyone points out that it is such. Whether the person is a

---

[104] Translations cited from Papyrus collections; also cited by Willis 1985a, 40–41.
[105] Cf. Oates et al. 1967, 262–64; Oster 1992, 66–67; Willis 1985a, 42; Fisk 1989, 63; many such temples or shrines are mentioned by Pausanias (Book 2 [Corinth], 2–5). *P. Oxy.* 1484 refers to a coming of age celebration; 2791 to a birthday (cited by Willis 1985a, 41).
[106] See Gooch 1993, 1–46.
[107] Hurd 1965, 128; see 128–31.
[108] Cf. 1 Cor 6.12 and discussion by Murphy O'Connor 1978a. The phrase is generally accepted as a Corinthian slogan; see Hurd 1965, 68, and Fee 1987, 479 n. 13, 251–53.

believer or an unbeliever is hardly of central significance (though some considerations favour the former);[109] anyone can point this out and must be taken seriously. The principle is similar to that expressed in v. 25; it is the consciousness of the other which must be respected (v. 29a).[110] However, the Corinthians are given no help in discerning any dividing line between so-called 'private' dinners and 'temple' banquets, a line which seems anyway to have been difficult to draw. Certainly a distinction between social and religious occasions is not clear and cannot be based on a division between home and temple. Paul's concern, it would seem, is not to state that certain occasions and foods are idolatrous and therefore to be avoided, while others are acceptable; rather, his focus is upon the ways in which conduct must take account of others.[111]

Verses 29b and 30 are among the most enigmatic in these chapters: why does Paul cite opinions here which seem to oppose virtually all of his advice up to this point?[112] While they would seem to reflect the viewpoint of the strong, it is difficult to regard them as a quotation of the Corinthian letter because Paul makes no direct response to them. The best solution, though by no means wholly satisfactory, seems to be to read them as rhetorical questions which lead to the final conclusion.[113] They reiterate the points upon which the strong's argument is based and

[109] The concern for the συνείδησιν ... τοῦ ἑτέρου (v. 29a) may suggest that a Christian is in mind; so Barrett 1971a, 242; Fisk 1989, 67. Fee 1987, 483–85, argues that 'a pagan guest' is implied, on the basis particularly of the use of the term ἱερόθυτος, which, he suggests, reflects 'a pagan point of view' (cf. Watson 1992c, 107–108). However, Fisk 1989, 67 n. 74 argues that the term may be used to reflect the words of someone who wants 'to avoid offending the host', or who uses the term 'out of habit (cf. 8:7); or more probably Paul's lexical choice may be designed to reflect the informant's lingering pre-Christian perspective on things pagan'. 'Likely Paul chose this alternate form to stress that, *for the imaginary one using it*, there is real significance to the food's cultic past' (58 n. 36). Gardner 1994, 176–79, suggests that a 'strong' Christian is most likely.

[110] It is widely argued that συνείδησις here should not be translated 'conscience', implying the individual's moral sensibility: 'consciousness' or 'awareness' conveys a more appropriate sense. See discussion in Horsley 1978a; Tomson 1990, 195–96, 210–16; Maurer TDNT 7, 914–15; Gooch 1987; Gardner 1994, 42ff.

[111] Cf. Horsley 1978a, 586–87; Brunt 1985, 115.

[112] Fee 1980, 195 relates them to Paul's defence of his freedom to eat whatever is sold in the market. Gardner 1994, 179, argues that Paul's basic point is: 'The "strong" were not allowed to sit in judgment on anyone's freedom.' Klauck 1984, 76, takes them as indicating: 'Auch für den Schwachen gibt es eine Grenze.' Cf. Murphy O'Connor 1978b, 570–71; see also discussion by Barrett 1971a, 242–44.

[113] Fisk 1989, 68, suggests that in 10.31–11.1, Paul wants to 'reiterate and generalise'; cf. also Gardner 1994, 179. Lang 1986, 107, views 8.1–11.1 as a 'Ringkomposition'.

which Paul has been addressing: why should my (legitimate) freedom be compromised because of another, and why should I be criticised when I eat if I give appropriate thanks to God, recognising that the one God (and no idol) is the one to be thanked? The first part of Paul's conclusion takes up the issues raised by these rhetorical questions, and lays down the basic principle that the believer's primary responsibility is indeed not to please other people, but God (v. 31). But the qualifications which have dominated the three chapters are also strongly reiterated: do not give offence to anyone (including those in τῇ ἐκκλησίᾳ), and, as Paul does, seek not your own benefit but that of others (v. 32f). Thus 11.1 is a fitting conclusion to the whole section, echoing especially Paul's use of himself as example in chapter 9.

Few would claim that 8.1–11.1 forms one of Paul's clearer arguments. Murphy O'Connor suggests that this is because Paul opposes the stance both of the weak and of the strong and therefore treads a delicate line between them.[114] Part of Paul's problem doubtless lies in the fact that he agrees with the basic theological opinions cited by the strong in defence of their practice.[115] However, his personal lifestyle shows that he considers the relinquishment of rights to be profoundly right for the Christian, if any stumbling block to others will thereby be removed.

If the 'weak' are to be found among the humbler members of the congregation, then we have here another example of Paul's limitation of the social intercourse of the socially strong. While he does not deny the strong the right to eat whatever they want at dinners and banquets, he does insist that they must be prepared to give up this right if a weaker member of the community is troubled by the association of the food with idols. The opinion and consciousness of any brother or sister is not to be despised or ignored, however weak and foolish they may appear to the strong. We should note, moreover, that such instruction, if taken seriously, may require the strong to withdraw from some of their important social contacts. They may lose friends and position in the city if they refuse to attend celebrations and banquets to which they are personally invited.[116] And they may have to do this, according to Paul, merely because a weak nobody, a slave even, is troubled by their conduct!

---

[114] Murphy O'Connor 1978b, 556–74.
[115] Cf. Brunt 1985, 114–15.
[116] Cf. Theissen 1982, 130–32.

Even if the weak and the strong are not to be divided along social status lines, relevant comments may still be made about the social ethos which Paul's instruction conveys. Any member of the community may be required to give up their engagement in particular social circles if others are offended by their conduct. Any member of the community is a person whose consciousness about such matters must be respected. Paul's instruction, therefore, does not leave untouched the sphere of everyday secular life.[117] On the contrary, it indicates that the demands of membership in the Christian community may significantly and materially affect the wider social interaction and involvement of certain members of the community. If we take seriously the importance of the various gatherings from which people might have to withdraw – importance for sustaining social position, status, patron-client relationships, friendships etc. – then we will not underestimate the potential impact of Paul's instruction.

One of the most interesting things about this whole passage is that Paul seems to agree with the theological principles upon which the strong base their freedom to eat idol-food. He could, presumably, have developed and strengthened their point of view, drawing on precisely these theological fundamentals in order to respond to their questions. However, Paul emphasises a different value which must inform and direct the actions of the Corinthians: limitations of one's own rights and freedom in deference to the other. For Paul this seeking the benefit of others is the fundamental ethical maxim, demonstrated, he believes, in his own behaviour (9.1ff; 10.33), and most paradigmatically in the self-giving of Christ, who 'did not please himself' (Rom 15.3; cf. 1 Cor 11.1; 2 Cor 8.9; Phil 2.5–11).

Any member of the congregation – at least including the socially strong, and quite probably them in particular – must be prepared to amend their practices, to compromise their freedom, in response to the views of others. Rather than encouraging, or even allowing, the strong patriarchally to control the behaviour of the weak, Paul allows the consciousness of the weak to determine their behaviour.[118]

Paul gives the strong three reasons to be wary of their conduct in relation to εἰδλόθυτα: the consciousness of the weak, the danger of falling into sin, and the incompatibility of partaking in two opposing

---

[117] Cf. Troeltsch 1931, 75–76.
[118] Cf. Martin 1990, 141.

circles of fellowship. It is interesting that he begins and ends with the most socially-based concern: regard for others who take offence.

4.2.4. The Lord's Supper: 1 Cor 11.17–34

When Paul reacts to the reports of division at the Lord's Supper, his displeasure comes straight to the fore. In contrast to the praise he offers the Corinthians in 11.2, here he bluntly expresses his disapproval (vv. 17, 22b). Indeed, given the situation, their meal is no longer even worthy of the name 'Lord's Supper' (v. 20). It seems most likely that Paul's criticism is directed towards the wealthier members of the community; it is their behaviour which implies that they despise the church of God and shame τοὺς μὴ ἔχοντας, 'the have-nots' (v. 22).[119]

Verse 19 is generally taken to imply that Paul interpreted the divisions at the Lord's Supper as a sign of inevitable distinction in the community to show those who have God's approval.[120] The main enigma, of course, is why Paul should apparently accept or rationalise division so as to make it necessary (δεῖ), while seeming to oppose it so vigorously (11.17f, 20; 1.10ff).

R. A. Campbell has recently challenged the established interpretation of this verse. Campbell suggests that the verse may instead reflect the social situation Paul criticises here and elsewhere in 1 Corinthians, namely one in which the elite (οἱ δόκιμοι) act in such a way as to make themselves visible (φανεροί) and show their 'superiority'. He argues that αἱρέσεις should be translated 'discrimination', οἱ δόκιμοι as 'the elite'.[121] 'If this is right', he continues, 'then the δεῖ will refer not to some eschatological necessity of division, but to the requirement foisted on the Corinthian church by its well-to-do members.'[122] He therefore translates the whole verse as follows: 'For there actually has to be discrimination in your meetings, so that if you please the elite may stand out from the rest.'[123] Campbell's proposal is attractive but, in the end, I think, unconvincing.[124] As Campbell accepts, Paul elsewhere uses the terms

---

[119] See §3.8.1. above.
[120] See Campbell 1991, 62–63. Note the influence of the dominical saying recorded in Justin *Dialogue with Trypho* 35.3 (see Munck 1959, 136). Klauck 1982, 289, speaks of the 'eschatological δεῖ'; cf. also Barrett 1971a, 262; Fee 1987, 538–39.
[121] Campbell 1991, 65–69.
[122] Campbell 1991, 69.
[123] Campbell 1991, 70.
[124] In the original thesis I followed Campbell's suggestion (p. 105).

δόκιμος (and cognates) with the meaning 'genuine', 'acceptable', 'approved'.[125] It seems to me that the translation 'the [social] elite' is most unlikely. There is, I believe, a more plausible way to make sense of verse 19.[126] Paul is a little cautious about his acceptance of the oral reports: 'I hear there are divisions (σκίσματα) among you, and I partly believe it (μέρος τι πιστεύω)' (v. 18b). Why do I 'partly believe it'? 'Because there must be discrimination/ divisions (αἱρέσεις) among you, so that those who are genuine (οἱ δόκιμοι) may be clearly distinguished among you' (v. 19).[127] *Contra* Campbell, I think that the οὖν of verse 20 refers back to the report of verse 18: I hear there are divisions among you (and I partly believe it, because …) so the result is that when you meet together etc …[128] Campbell's argument that 'it is surely quite foreign to Paul's purpose in this letter to suggest that the church members should concern themselves with who is or is not a genuine Christian'[129] seems to take insufficient account of passages like 5.1ff, where Paul insists that the community must be concerned for its own purity, and must 'cast out the evil doer from among you' (5.13). Indeed Paul is concerned here precisely with those who are truly 'brothers and sisters': if anyone calls themselves an ἀδελφός but is guilty of certain sins, then the Corinthian Christians are not even to eat (note the choice of this specific term) with such a person (5.11). Certainly not all who regarded themselves as one of the company were accepted by Paul as 'genuine' or 'approved'.

Paul's response to the problem of division at the Lord's Supper, the problem he outlines in vv. 17–22, begins at v. 23, where he reminds the Corinthians of the narrative which is the foundation of the meal itself. The purpose of this citation is probably to remind the Corinthians that this is not merely a meal together (although it is that), it is a remembrance of the Lord Jesus, looking back to the night of his betrayal, and

---

[125] Rom 14.18; 16.10; 1 Cor 9.27; 2 Cor 10.18; 13.5–7; Campbell 1991, 67–68; cf. Engberg-Pedersen 1993, 120 n. 33.

[126] Note Campbell's useful analysis of the structure and flow of argument in 11.17–22 (1991, 63–65).

[127] There must be some reason why Paul uses αἱρέσεις and not σκίσματα in this verse (so Campbell 1991, 65). He must make some distinction between the σκίσματα which he attacks and the sort of division which he regards as inevitable. 'I partly believe that there are σκίσματα, because there will inevitably be some sort of αἱρέσεις to distinguish the true believers from others.'

[128] Cf. Campbell 1991, 63–65.

[129] Campbell 1991, 68.

instituted at his command.[130] The Pauline addition to the tradition, the explanatory gloss of v. 26, interprets the meal specifically as a proclamation of the Lord's *death*, ἄχρι οὗ ἔλθῃ, 'until he comes'. This fundamental focus, so central to the Christian symbolic order (at least for Paul), and so prominent in 1.18ff, serves here also as the basic foundation for the instructions which follow.[131] It is Christ's self-giving death which raises the convicting question concerning the Corinthians' own conduct: 'Does their conduct towards one another reflect the pattern of Christ's action in his death for others?'[132]

Paul presents his interpretation of the specific implications of the meal's character in vv. 27–34, although he also has further instruction in mind (v. 34). Because of the particular nature of the Lord's supper (ὥστε …), ὃς ἂν ἐσθίῃ τὸν ἄρτον ἢ πίνῃ τὸ ποτήριον τοῦ κυρίου ἀναξίως, ἔνοχος ἔσται τοῦ σώματος καὶ τοῦ αἵματος τοῦ κυρίου ('whoever eats the bread or drinks the cup of the Lord in an unworthy manner will be liable for the body and blood of the Lord'; v. 27). Stern words indeed, which have troubled many a Christian since, worried that they may be partaking ἀναξίως. However, given the situation he is addressing and the practical advice with which he ends, Paul can hardly be concerned with the internal problems of the individual's conscience.[133] His concern, rather, is that the way in which some people 'eat and drink' is completely inappropriate for the occasion of the Lord's Supper; they are *acting* in an unworthy manner.[134] Paul's stern words are addressed to those who turn the communal meal into an occasion characterised by a class-based division between the wealthy and τοὺς μὴ ἔχοντας. Such people, Paul insists, must test themselves and consider what they are doing, before they eat and drink (v. 28). For failure to 'discern the body' (v. 29), they are warned, leads to judgment, to sickness and even death (v. 30).

The phrase μὴ διακρίνων τὸ σῶμα, 'not discerning the body' (v. 29), is notoriously ambiguous; does it refer to the bread or the congre-

---

[130] Cf. Meeks 1983, 157–62; Klauck 1984, 82; Lampe 1991, 184.

[131] Cf. Engberg-Pedersen 1993, 115, who also points to the significance of v. 26b within this passage.

[132] 'Entspricht ihr Verhalten auf der zwischenmenschlichen Horizontalen dem, was Christus in seinem Tod für andere tat?' Lampe 1991, 211, see further 208–13.

[133] Cf. Fee 1987, 559–61 esp. n. 10; Klauck 1984, 83; Stendahl 1963.

[134] Klauck 1982, 324: 'Das Wort „unwürdig" … ist adverbial gebraucht, d.h., es bezeichnet nicht den sittlichen Zustand des Empfängers, sondern die Art und Weise seines Handelns.' See further Lampe 1991, 209ff.

gation?[135] Following the citation of the last supper narrative, it may certainly imply the need to realise what it means to eat *this* bread, as opposed to any everyday meal, but Paul's instruction also shows quite clearly that doing this properly, not ἀναξίως, means relating appropriately to the others who are gathered for the celebration. [136] It is significant that Paul does not write τὸ σῶμα καὶ τὸ αἷμα, 'the body and the blood', in spite of the fact that v. 29 contains both verbs ἐσθίω (to eat) and πίνω (to drink) twice and that the previous verses (27–29) have referred three times to both bread/body and cup/blood. This suggests that discerning what it means to be part of the congregation – the body of Christ – may be uppermost in his mind.[137] In 10.17 Paul has already stated his conviction that 'because there is one bread, we many are one body, for we all partake from the one bread' (ὅτι εἷς ἄρτος, ἓν σῶμα οἱ πολλοί ἐσμεν, οἱ γὰρ πάντες ἐκ τοῦ ἑνὸς ἄρτου μετέχομεν), and it is precisely this oneness that the behaviour of the more wealthy destroys.[138] The Lord's Supper is meant to be a meal when the believers celebrate and symbolically enact their oneness in Christ, but has become instead an occasion which highlights the difference between rich and poor.[139]

Paul's final advice in this matter is practical;[140] when you meet together to eat (εἰς τὸ φαγεῖν), ἀλλήλους ἐκδέχεσθε ('wait for one another'; v. 33). Whether ἐκδέχεσθε was intended to mean 'wait for', in a temporal sense, as Lampe argues,[141] or 'welcome', 'accept', referring to the character of the time together,[142] or both, it is the division and distinction between those who have plenty and the have-nots which must be overcome.

However, as Theissen points out, Paul is concerned only that the meeting ἐν ἐκκλησίᾳ should be a reflection of oneness and unity in

---

[135] Barrett 1971a, 273–75 discusses various possibilities.
[136] Cf. Lang 1986, 155; Klauck 1982, 327; 1984, 84.
[137] Cf. Fee 1987, 563–64, *contra* Barrett 1971a, 275. Engberg-Pedersen 1993, 121–22 argues that 'body' here refers to 'the bread and the wine' – the whole thing one eats and drinks. I find this interpretation more strained.
[138] Gardner 1994, 161, 167, 171, 183, is surely right to point out that in 10.16f Paul uses what is already known and accepted about the Lord's Supper as an illustration to illuminate the nature of worship in non-Christian cultic meals.
[139] This socially-based interpretation of Paul's instruction raises important questions for contemporary eucharistic practice; see Horrell 1995b.
[140] Klauck 1984, 84: 'In [33f] lenkt Paulus zu den praktischen Fragen aus [21f] zurück.'
[141] See Lampe 1991, 193, 203–205; Klauck 1982, 328.
[142] See Fee 1987, 540–43, 567–68; Theissen 1982, 151–55.

Christ. The wealthy may eat as they wish ἐν οἴκῳ, 'at home' (v. 34; cf. v. 22).[143] Moreover, Paul's recommendations, Theissen notes, are not dissimilar to Pliny's, who also refuses to draw class distinctions when offering food and wine to guests.[144] Paul does not make any critical comments about the fact that such social disparities exist and exhibits no revolutionary concern for social equality or the redistribution of wealth. His criticism here applies only to behaviour ἐν ἐκκλησία. Is Theissen therefore right to regard Paul's 'solution' to this problem as a 'compromise', an example of love-patriarchalism? Clearly Paul accepts that in the world believers have different levels of property and wealth, and experience inequalities in their ability to resource their material consumption. He does not require the termination of, or withdrawal from, these worldly positions, nor the communal sharing of all resources. To some extent, then, Theissen is right to suggest that Paul 'takes social differences for granted'.[145] However this is an acceptance of social difference and certainly not a religious or theological legitimation of it (this is important in regard to the question of ideology; see further below). Moreover, it is not true to suggest that Paul's concerns focus only upon the religious sphere, at least not if that is taken to mean a sphere which has no social impact or expression. It is the character of the meeting ἐν ἐκκλησία with which Paul is concerned, and this is a concrete and communal setting in which social conventions and class-based divisions must be overcome. The Lord's Supper must be a full meal,[146] a celebration in which food and drink are shared out equally[147] and in which the believers wait for one another. While Paul does not question (in this instance) the lifestyle of the relatively well-to-do outside the congregational gatherings, he does make real demands upon them in order to preserve what he believes to be the essential character of the Lord's Supper. His

---

[143] Theissen 1982, 163–64. However, this is not to suggest that the Lord's Supper should no longer be a satisfying meal; cf. Lampe 1991, 203–205.

[144] Theissen 1982, 157; Pliny *Ep.* 2.6, though the question about including '*even* the freedmen...' implies that slaves were not included in such banquets, as they surely were at the Corinthians' Lord's Supper celebrations.

[145] Theissen 1982, 107; cf. 163–64.

[146] Lampe 1991, 203–205; Engberg–Pedersen 1993, 110 n. 14.

[147] Engberg-Pedersen 1993, 110–11, argues that this is the implication to be drawn from Paul's criticism of the Corinthians in v. 21 and from v. 34: 'there may not in fact be enough food (and drink) present at the Eucharist to satisfy the rich people's appetite when the food is divided equally – and so they may make up at home for any deficiencies that they may feel' (111); against Theissen 1982, 164, who argues that Paul does not instruct or expect the rich to share their 'private meal'.

perception of this essential character is based upon fundamental Christian resources: the death of Christ, of which this celebration is to be a memorial and a proclamation, and the fact that the believers are one body in Christ. The ethos of Paul's instruction, I suggest, is not adequately encapsulated in the term 'love-patriarchalism', but neither is it a radical ethic of egalitarian redistribution. A continuing tension does remain between the character of life ἐν ἐκκλησίᾳ and the life which continues in the world. Moreover, from a structuration theory perspective it must be acknowledged that the formulation of instruction presented here by Paul offers resources which are certainly open to being taken up and developed in the direction of an ethos of love-patriarchalism.

4.2.5. Criticism of the socially strong

It is clear from the passages we have examined that Paul is quite prepared to direct blunt and stern criticism towards the socially strong. In each of the cases we have examined it is their behaviour which Paul regards as problematic and it is they who face the force of his criticism. It is equally clear that Paul does not promote a revolutionary social programme beyond the ἐκκλησία; he shows no explicit interest in changing what we might call 'the structures of society'. His primary concern is with the behaviour and relationships of members of the ἐκκλησία. No doubt this reflects his conviction that 'the world in its present form is passing away' (7.31) and 'the appointed time has grown short' (7.29). The word of the cross demonstrates that God is doing away with the rulers of this age and the things that now are (1.18–2.6), and it is ἐν Χριστῷ, in Christ, that the renewing work of God's Spirit is to be seen. However the consequences, as Paul sees them, of being one body in Christ – a new status enacted in baptism and the Lord's Supper – are social and communal as well as 'religious', and, moreover, extend into the sphere of everyday life and wider social interaction.

The extent to which Paul is prepared sharply to criticise the socially strong in a number of places in 1 Corinthians may lead us to suspect the appropriateness of the 'love-patriarchal' label. It would certainly be inaccurate to suggest that Paul's teaching reflected these people's social interests; he does not affirm or legitimate their social position. Indeed, on a wider level, Paul can hardly be said to be adding religious legitimation to the hierarchy or institutions of society. It is the central symbol of the Christian gospel, the cross of Christ, which opens 1 Corinthians, presented in a way that makes clear its opposition to worldly standards of wisdom and power. The rulers of this age are described as τῶν καταργουμένων – those who are being brought to nothing (2.6) – and God's choice of the nobodies (τὰ μὴ ὄντα) is a demonstration of God's desire to destroy the established things (ἵνα τὰ ὄντα καταργήσῃ; 1.28). On specific issues too, Paul is clearly prepared to instruct believers to withdraw from certain forms of social interaction, even though these may be established and accepted dimensions of the dominant social order. The discussion of 6.1–11 arises primarily out of concern about behaviour among believers but Paul prohibits the Corinthians from taking part in one of the institutions of civil life, at least if the dispute involves another believer. And Paul's teaching in chapters 8–10 also affects the normal social interaction of the strong, not merely their conduct ἐν ἐκκλησίᾳ. While Paul himself does not clearly instruct them to withdraw from any particular social occasions, he does argue that the troubled consciousness of even the weakest member of the community can require them to do just that. Paul's instruction concerning the Lord's Supper relates only to the character of the meeting ἐν ἐκκλησίᾳ, yet it is not insignificant to note that his vision of this meeting seems to reflect a concern precisely to transcend social distinctions.

If heeded, then, Paul's teaching would have a significant and negative impact upon the higher status members of the Corinthian congregation. It portrays their worldly status as worthless, requires them to withdraw from certain social institutions which are important for maintaining social position, and insists upon the value of the weakest members of the congregation. We certainly cannot suggest that Paul's teaching in 1 Corinthians is a religious expression of dominant class interests.

A considerable amount of 1 Corinthians is, in fact, addressed directly to the socially prominent members of the church, as it is often their behaviour which is the specific cause for Paul's concern. It might be suggested that this reflects the fact that such socially prominent people were also the leaders of the Christian community.[148] Indeed, due to their economic, social and political power, such people are likely to have been influential in the congregation. The people Paul *names* as having been baptised by him, Gaius, Crispus and Stephanas, Theissen points out, are

---

[148] Cf. Holmberg 1978, 104–107; Theissen 1982, 72–73, 102–106; Fiorenza 1987, 392–93, 399; Clarke 1993.

all likely to have been people of some wealth and position. [149] However, such a view must be balanced by other considerations. First, the socially dominant members of the congregation are likely to have been prominent in the commissioning and sending of the letter to Paul. [150] At least in relation to εἰδωλόθυτα their letter reflects the perspective of the strong. Paul's written response, then, is bound to be addressed to those who have sponsored this communication. Second, the oral reports Paul hears concerning division in the community and the shame brought on the have-nots at the Lord's Supper (1.11; 11.18) may well reflect the dissatisfaction of those 'from below', [151] among them perhaps some of Chloe's slaves or members of Stephanas' household. Hence again, Paul's critical response is directed towards the perpetrators of the divisions. Third, Paul nowhere refers only to socially prominent members of the community as leaders of the believers. [152] Although there is a hierarchy of leading functions (12.28), we are given no grounds for assuming that prophets and teachers came only, or even primarily, from a particular social group. [153] Noteworthy in this connection is 16.15ff, where Paul exhorts the Corinthians to recognise and submit to τὴν οἰκίαν Στεφανᾶ, 'the household of Stephanas' (v. 15). Paul does not name Stephanas alone as a leading figure, but his household, urging the Corinthians to submit – τοῖς τοιούτοις ('to such people' – plural!) καὶ παντὶ τῷ συνεργοῦντι καὶ κοπιῶντι ('and to every co-worker and labourer'; v. 16). He specifically mentions Stephanas, Fortunatus and Achaicus as people who should be recognised (v. 17); the latter two may well have been dependent members of Stephanas' household.

Thus, although Paul clearly benefited from the support of people like Gaius (Rom 16.23) and Stephanas (1 Cor 16.17f), who were prominent members of the congregation, it should not be assumed that the people he regarded as leaders came only from this social group, nor does it seem that his teaching reflected these people's social interests.

---

[149] Theissen 1982, 102; cf. §3.7. above.

[150] Theissen 1982, 57, 162.

[151] Cf. Theissen 1982, 57, 163.

[152] Clarke 1993, demonstrates the prominence of the wealthy within the Christian community, but assumes without argument that they may therefore be termed 'leaders'. His assumption that they are among the 'elite', the 'ruling class', of Corinth, may also be questioned; see §3.7. above.

[153] Though note the discussions of Wire 1990, 62–71; Holmberg 1978, 96–123.

4.3. Paul's attitude towards the weak

If Paul is by no means interested in sustaining or affirming the position of the socially strong, what is his attitude to the weak? Love-patriarchalism, according to Theissen, requires from the weak 'subordination, fidelity and esteem'.[154] There are three places in 1 Corinthians where it might be argued that Paul urges the subordination of weaker social groups: 1 Cor 7 (esp. 17–24); 11.2–16; 14.34f.[155] In the following sections I shall examine these important passages and also assess the social ethos of 1 Cor 12–14. I shall argue in an excursus that 1 Cor 14.34f is not authentically Pauline.

4.3.1. 'Remain in your calling': 1 Cor 7.1ff

Paul's primary concern in 1 Cor 7 is with answering questions the Corinthians have put to him about sexual relationships and marriage (7.1, 25). It seems that a number of the Corinthians, perhaps encouraged by the baptismal declaration that there is no male and female in Christ (Gal 3.28), considered that sexual activity belonged to a realm of fleshly behaviour which believers had now transcended (see §3.8.5. above). In the light of this apparent context it is understandable that Paul's thought throughout this chapter is focused upon the convictions that one's sexual status does not have to be altered in order to live in Christ, and that being a Christian believer does not necessitate an end to physical sexual relationships: 'the controlling motif of Paul's answer is; "Do not seek a change in status".'[156] However, Paul's own preference for the state of singleness and celibacy also emerges clearly.[157] Whenever he mentions the decision to marry it is allowed primarily on the grounds of lack of self-control and passion, and thus portrayed as a second-best option (vv. 8f, 28, 36, 38, 39f).[158]

However, while 1 Cor 7 may not offer a terribly positive view of sex and marriage, despite exegetical efforts to the contrary,[159] it does not

---

[154] Theissen 1982, 107.
[155] Theissen 1982, 107, suggests that love patriarchalism is evident in 1 Cor 7.21ff and 11.3–16.
[156] Fee 1987, 268.
[157] Cf. Sanders 1991, 107–108; Fiorenza 1983, 224.
[158] Cf. Pagels 1974, 542; Ste. Croix 1981, 104.
[159] Cf. Moiser 1983; Phipps 1982; Scroggs 1972, 295–96.

promote a patriarchal attitude to women and nowhere seeks to subordinate them to their husbands or to other men. Indeed, the chapter is notable for the considerable extent to which Paul throughout addresses *both* partners, through a number of almost 'monotonously parallel statements'.[160] Verse 4 is particularly remarkable in the context of a culture where the subordination of women was viewed (at least by a Roman elite) as an essential guard against disorder in both household, *polis*, and state:[161]

ἡ γυνὴ τοῦ ἰδίου σώματος οὐκ ἐξουσιάζει ἀλλὰ ὁ ἀνήρ,
ὁμοίως δὲ καὶ ὁ ἀνὴρ τοῦ ἰδίου σώματος οὐκ ἐξουσιάζει
ἀλλὰ ἡ γυνή.

the wife does not have authority over her own body, but the husband does, likewise the husband does not have authority over his own body, but the wife does (NRSV).

If the 'impulse for celibacy' came primarily from women at Corinth (and this is by no means certain), then this may explain in part why Paul chose to stress the responsibility of both men *and women* in particular connection with sexual relationships.[162] However, this contextual explanation does not remove the significance of Paul's formulation of advice in a way which addresses both men and women as partners with equal responsibility. Moreover, it is important to view Paul's preference for singleness in the light of its socio-historical context, which was one in which marriage was the norm, indeed, was for Roman citizens urged by imperial decree.[163] Given the patriarchal nature of marital and household institutions, Paul's teaching offered the possibility of a 'new and independent lifestyle for women by encouraging them to remain free from the bondage of marriage'.[164]

In his response to the Corinthians' question περὶ τῶν παρθένων ('concerning the virgins'), Paul's comments in vv. 36–38 may reflect a

---

[160] Meeks 1974, 199. Note the parallelism in vv. 2, 3, 4, 8 (esp. if the address is to widowers and widows), 10f, 12f, 14, 15 (explicit mention of 'brother or sister'), 16, 28, 32–34. Cf. Scroggs 1972, 294–95; Fee 1987, 270; Byrne 1988, 20, 23; Witherington 1988, 26–27.

[161] Cf. Stowers 1994, 51–53. Dio Cassius records Octavian's aim 'to conquer and rule all humankind, and to allow no woman to make herself equal to a man' (*HR* 50.28.3., quoted by Stowers 1994, 53). Cf. also Klassen 1984.

[162] MacDonald 1990, 172; cf. Fee 1987, 270.

[163] See Fiorenza 1983, 224–26; Pomeroy 1976, 164–70.

[164] Fiorenza 1983, 236; cf. Byrne 1988, 26–27.

situation where male authority is the norm, whether the person concerned is the husband to be or the father of the virgin,[165] – it is 'he' who is portrayed as the decision-maker regarding marriage – but they do nothing to promote or demand the man's authority in such a situation. If 'the virgins' were of both sexes, as Hurd argued, then even this point becomes largely irrelevant.[166] However, none of the references to males specifies them as 'virgins' and Hurd's suggestion seems somewhat unconvincing.

It is in this context that Paul illustrates his point by referring to circumcision and slavery (7.17–24),[167] illustrations which are associated with issues concerning 'male and female' due to the pattern of Gal 3.28.[168] The primary focus of the instruction to remain as you are (vv. 17, 20, 24) is upon sexual relationships. However, as is the case with sexual relationships, Paul maintains that a person's racial and social status does not have to be changed when they are called by God. The sign of circumcision should be neither removed nor sought (v. 18f). Slavery and freedom, similarly, are conditions which need not change, for the slave is ἀπελεύθερος κυρίου ('the Lord's freedperson') and the free person is δοῦλος Χριστοῦ ('slave of Christ'; v. 22). The social significance of these affirmations should not be underestimated. In the alternative symbolic order Paul is (re)constructing, the valuations are completely the reverse of those given to people in the dominant social order: the gospel *counterbalances* the differences in worldly status.[169] An ideologically aware analysis of structures of signification will be conscious of the importance of language and symbol in shaping people's perceptions, valuations and interaction with one another. Paul's language cannot be dismissed as merely an illusory compensation for worldly reality. If taken seriously it requires people to view one another differently. Paul makes a similar point in the letter to Philemon, insisting that Onesimos be received and regarded 'no longer as a slave, but more than a slave, a beloved brother ... receive him as me' (Phlm 16f).

---

[165] See discussion in Barrett 1971a, 182–84; Hurd 1965, 169ff (who argues that 'spiritual marriages' are in view).

[166] Hurd 1965, 68, who suggests reference to male virgins in 7.27, 28a, 32–34a, 36–38, and to females in 7.28b, 34b.

[167] On these verses as illustrations see Dawes 1990, 684ff; Trummer 1975, 344, 350ff.

[168] Bartchy 1973, 162–65; Witherington 1988, 26–27.

[169] Cf. Martin 1990, 65–66, who speaks of 'an actual reversal of normal status'.

However, other considerations must also be noted. Verses 17, 20 and 24 certainly encourage acquiescence in one's current situation, marital, racial or social, whatever it may be. Even if the primary reference of the words καλέω (to call) and κλῆσις (calling) is to the calling from God to live as a Christian,[170] and even though Paul does not quite take the step of equating a person's κλῆσις with their position in society,[171] this teaching certainly has the potential to be taken as a legitimation of social position as something ordained by God. This may easily become a form of ideology which 'naturalizes, reifies, the present social order (Giddens' third ideological form) so as to portray social position as something ordained by God, and thus to imply that the Christian's duty is to remain in that position'.[172] Moreover, Paul's insistence that one can be a Christian and a slave, that 'it doesn't matter' (v. 21), combined with the symbolic revaluation of such slaves as 'the Lord's freedpersons', can easily become an encouragement passively to accept whatever social state one finds oneself in.[173] Paul's text, therefore, which inevitably escapes the horizon of its creator and the context of its formulation,[174] may contribute to the formulation of a theological ideology which encourages slaves to retain their social position.

There are strong reasons evident in the text, however, for insisting that this was not Paul's intention. It is important to remember Paul's primary point; that men and women do not have to abandon their status as single or married simply by virtue of becoming believers. His comments on the positions of circumcised and uncircumcised, slave and free are primarily illustrative.[175] Moreover, it is hardly *social* conservatism to maintain in a similar way that Jews may remain Jews and Gentiles, Gentiles. Indeed, in the only instance where the socially conservative label might be appropriate, namely the illustration regarding slave and free, Paul specifically states the exception, that slaves may certainly seek and gain their freedom (v. 21b). Indeed, he encourages them, if they have the opportunity, to become free. P. Trummer insists: 'The Pauline

---

[170] So Bartchy 1973, 132–59; but see Fee 1987, 308 n. 8.
[171] Fee 1987, 309.
[172] Horrell 1995d, 229; see further there for reflections on the development of 'theological ideology' in Pauline Christianity.
[173] Cf. Ste. Croix 1975, 19–20; 1981, 416–41.
[174] Cf. Giddens 1979, 44; (quoted above in §2.4.).
[175] *Contra* Gayer 1976, 112ff, esp. 154–68, 210–12, who argues that Paul is combating emancipatory movements among slaves at Corinth. See further excursus on 1 Cor 7.21b below.

thesis of remaining in the divine calling must not therefore be misinterpreted as a fundamental conservation of structures of oppression'.[176] Verse 23 seems also to reiterate strongly Paul's view that slavery is not a desirable institution and should be avoided if possible: 'you were bought with a price, do not be/become (μὴ γίνεσθε) slaves to human beings'. I am of course aware that quite the opposite case could be made, based on a different understanding of v. 21b, namely that Paul instructs slaves to remain in slavery, even if the opportunity for freedom arises. However, I believe the arguments in favour of the 'take freedom' interpretation to be weighty and persuasive.

Excursus: 1 Cor 7.21b – freedom or slavery?

The basic problem with the Greek ἀλλ' εἰ καὶ δύνασαι ἐλεύθερος γενέσθαι, μᾶλλον χρῆσαι, is its ambiguity.[177] It allows two contradictory translations: either, 'but even if you are able to become free, make use of your present condition instead',[178] or, 'but if then you are able to become free, by all means make use of that opportunity'.[179]

The interpretation depends to some extent on three grammatical points: first, the force to be given to the words ἀλλ' εἰ καί; second, the sense intended by the word μᾶλλον; and third, the most crucial point, the implied object of the aorist imperative χρῆσαι – use which, τῇ δουλείᾳ or τῇ ἐλευθερίᾳ?[180]

The query about ἀλλ' εἰ καί is whether it should be translated 'but even if' (concessive), or 'but if indeed/then' (emphatic). Either translation must be granted as possible and the translation in favour of freedom certainly cannot be excluded.[181] It has the benefit of taking the ἀλλά with its more usual adversative force[182] and the translation of εἰ καί as emphatic rather than concessive can be supported from a number of

---

[176] 'Die paulinische These vom Verbleiben in der göttlichen Berufung darf also nicht als grundätzliche (sic) Konservierung von Unterdrückungsstrukturen mißdeutet werden.' Trummer 1975, 364.
[177] Cf. Lang 1986, 97; Klauck 1984, 54. Gayer 1976, 206–207, summarises the grammatical points on either side.
[178] Cf., for example, NRSV; NJB; Barrett 1971a, 170.
[179] Cf., for example, RSV; NIV; REB.
[180] Cf. Conzelmann 1975, 127; Gayer 1976, 206–207.
[181] *Contra* Weiss 1910, 188: 'Diese Deutung [sc. use freedom] wird aber auch durch εἰ καὶ verboten.'
[182] Cf. Bartchy 1973, 177, who notes the use of ἀλλά in 1 Cor 7.7, 10, 19, 35.

examples in 1 and 2 Corinthians.[183] 'Αλλά is linked with εἰ καί here, instead of the more usual δέ, according to Trummer, because the phrase stands in sharper opposition to what precedes.[184] The word μᾶλλον is also somewhat ambiguous. It can convey an adversative sense, implying 'use your position as a slave "instead of" (or, "rather than") taking your freedom', but may also have an elative sense (as it does in 1 Cor 9.12a and 14.1): ' "by all means" (or, "certainly") use the opportunity of freedom.'[185]

The most crucial question concerns the implied indirect object of χρῆσαι. It may be 'slavery',[186] but two considerations favour the choice of 'freedom'. The first is that 'in an elliptical sentence one would ordinarily supply a word from that sentence – in this case "freedom" – not a word from an earlier sentence'.[187] The second is that the aorist tense Paul uses is more appropriate if referring to the taking of a new opportunity rather than to the continuation in one's present state, which would really require the present tense.[188] This point is conceded by Barrett and Conzelmann, both of whom favour the 'remain a slave' interpretation.[189]

Although grammatical grounds seem to favour the 'freedom' interpretation they cannot in this case clearly decide the matter and the literary context must also be taken into account. It is on this basis that Barrett rejects the 'become free' translation: it 'does not make sense in the context'.[190] Indeed, this is often the reason given for preferring the 'remain a slave' option, as Paul's thought throughout 1 Cor 7 is based on

---

[183] Bartchy 1973, 178, lists 1 Cor 4.7; 7.11; 7.28; 2 Cor 4.2f; 7.8f; 11.5f; though I think some ambiguity remains in most cases, except 1 Cor 4.7. 2 Cor 4.16 does not solve the ambiguity either. See also Dawes 1990, 692; Trummer 1975, 355–56; Fee 1987, 316–17; Thrall 1962, 78–82; Llewelyn 1992, 69.

[184] Trummer 1975, 356.

[185] See Moulton 1979, 165 n. 1; Fee 1987, 316–317; BAGD, 489; Llewelyn 1992, 69–70 ('all the more'); cf. also Rom 5.9; Phil 3.4; Phlm 16.

[186] Weiss 1910, 188: 'Zu χρῆσαι kann ebenso gut τῇ δουλείᾳ ergänzt werden, wie τῇ ἐλευθερίᾳ.'

[187] Fee 1987, 317, followed by Dawes 1990, 690; and see esp. Llewelyn 1992, 67–69. Stuhlmacher 1975, 44–45, points to 2 Cor 13.10 as further evidence of an absolute ('objektlos') use of χράομαι, but relates the sense of χρῆσαι in 1 Cor 7.21 to 'Dienste des Christus'; cf. also Bartchy 1973, 156–57, 179. However this makes the implied object still more distant (relating it to κλῆσις; v. 20); see comments of Dawes 1990, 693–94, and Fee 1987, 317 n. 46.

[188] Robertson and Plummer 1914, 147–48: 'Still more decidedly does the aorist ... imply a new condition. ' Cf. Turner 1963, 76; Moule 1953, 21; Fee 1987, 317; Trummer 1975, 356–57; Lang 1986, 97.

[189] Barrett 1971a, 170; Conzelmann 1975, 127: 'in spite of the aorist ...'.

[190] Barrett 1971a, 170.

the principle 'stay as you are'.[191] However, this argument carries no weight, for throughout chapter 7 Paul has explictly mentioned permissible exceptions to the *general* advice to 'stay as you are'. An examination of verses 5 (εἰ μήτι ...), 9 (εἰ δὲ οὐκ ...), 11 (ἐὰν δέ ...), 15 (εἰ δέ ...), 28 (ἐὰν δέ ... καὶ ἐάν ...), 36 (εἰ δέ ...) and 39 (ἐὰν δέ ...) will reveal that in each of these cases Paul outlines acceptable exceptions to the general rule not to change one's sexual or marital status.[192]

Returning to v. 21b, we may expect it also to be an 'exception', particularly when we note that the *general* argument ('stay as you are'), and the text itself, would be entirely smooth and logical if the phrase in question were omitted:[193]

δοῦλος ἐκλήθης, μή σοι μελέτω· ὁ γὰρ ἐν κυρίῳ κληθεὶς
δοῦλος ἀπελεύθερος κυρίου ἐστίν

The γάρ with which v. 22 begins, then, does not refer to v. 21b but to 21a.[194] Paul must have added the specific advice to slaves (ἀλλ' εἰ καί ...) for a reason; there are two alternatives worth considering.

One possibility, which would support the 'remain a slave' interpretation, is that there was an emancipatory movement among Christian slaves at Corinth which was causing disruption and social disorder, inspired perhaps by the apparent transcendence of social divisions proclaimed at baptism (1 Cor 12.13; Gal 3.28).[195] However, *contra* R. Gayer, there is no evidence that *problems* were caused at Corinth by discontented Christian slaves demanding freedom, still less that Paul was concerned with such an issue. While the 'illustrations' regarding Jew and Gentile, slave and free must presumably have been relevant enough to make sense to the Corinthians,[196] 'the very lack of urgency in these matters indicates

---

[191] So Gayer 1976, 207; Crouch 1972, 125–26; Weiss 1910, 187–88; Lührmann 1975, 62. Bartchy 1973, 23, comments that 'most of those scholars who stress the grammatical considerations prefer the "take freedom" interpretation. . , and most of the scholars who stress the importance of the context prefer the "use slavery" interpretation'.

[192] Cf. Bartchy 1973, 9–10, 179; Fee 1987, 318; Dawes 1990, 689–99; Robertson and Plummer 1914, 148.

[193] Bartchy 1973, 177, suggests that the ἀλλά 'signals an interruption'.

[194] Cf. Dawes 1990, 692; Fee 1987, 318. *Contra* Barrett 1971a, 171, who sees the γάρ as supporting the 'remain a slave' argument.

[195] Gayer 1976, 112ff, esp. 154–68, 210–12; cf. also Crouch 1972, 120–51; Towner 1989, 38–45.

[196] Cf. Lührmann 1975, 61; Crouch 1972, 125.

that they are not at issue'.[197] Would Paul have written τιμῆς ἠγοράσθητε·
μὴ γίνεσθε δοῦλοι ἀνθρώπων (v. 23) if he was seriously confronting
such a situation and instructing slaves to remain in slavery?
The second, and far more likely reason for v. 21b is that Paul here
mentions another exception to the general advice to remain as you are:
you can be a Christian while remaining a slave, but if you are able to
become free, by all means take the opportunity.

Further support for such a conclusion might be drawn from Paul's
letter to Philemon, where it has been argued that Paul subtly requests
the manumission of Onesimos,[198] although if he does so his request is far
from direct.[199] 1 Cor 7.23 implies that Paul hardly found slavery an
especially attractive institution.[200]

Indeed, the manumission of slaves was so common that it is almost
impossible to see any reason why Paul should not have accepted it as a
normal and desirable feature of life.[201] 'The slave usually had the pros-
pect of manumission' and the chance of freedom was a 'carrot' used to
encourage good behaviour.[202] Given this historical context, Paul is surely
assuring slaves who hear 1 Cor 7 that seeking manumission is certainly
still acceptable.

Such a conclusion is strengthened still further by Scott Bartchy's main
argument; that a slave could neither refuse nor demand manumission.
There were many reasons why a slave-owner might benefit from
manumitting a slave and it is nonsense to tell a slave to refuse freedom;
they were not empowered to do so.[203] However, on this basis Bartchy

[197] Fee 1987, 307–308; conceded by Crouch 1972, 124, though he argues that emancipatory
desires were problematic among slaves and women at Corinth.
[198] Recently by Winter 1987.
[199] Cf. Barclay 1991, 172–75. Phlm 13f seems to suggest that Paul may like Onesimos to be
returned to him (cf. v. 11 also) but note v. 15f.
[200] Cf. Martin 1990, 199 n. 21.
[201] See Bartchy 1973, 82–91, 113; Alföldy 1985, 136, 140–41 and esp. Alföldy 1986, 286–
331. So widespread was manumission that in 2 BCE and 4 CE Augustus introduced legisla-
tion placing limits upon it; see Bartchy 1973, 83 n. 308; Alföldy 1985, 140.
[202] Alföldy 1985, 136; cf. Alföldy 1986, 309, 319, 329; Hopkins 1978, 126–32; Kyrtatas
1987, 50, 60–61; Bartchy 1973, 97, 111 etc. In a discussion of the behaviour of freedpersons
we find the comment that 'it would be no great burden to a manumitted slave to keep his
freedom by the same obedience which had earned it' (Tacitus Annals 13.26). 'Sticks' of
course were also common; Gaius Cassius commented that: 'You will never coerce such a
medley of humanity except by terror' (Tacitus Annals 14.44; see 42–45); cf. also Ste. Croix
1981, 409–11.
[203] Bartchy 1973, esp. 87–120, 175–77. Cf. Suetonius On Grammarians 21 (see Bartchy 1973,
107–109). See also Alföldy 1986, 310ff, 330, on the self-interest which motivated owners
to manumit their slaves.

also challenges the 'take your freedom' interpretation, maintaining that 'manumission was not an act which was "accepted" or "refused" by the slave. It happened to him.'[204] This leads Bartchy to translate ἀλλ' εἰ καὶ δύνασαι ἐλεύθερος γενέσθαι; 'But if, indeed, *you become manumitted*, . .'.[205] However, as Barrett points out, this 'omits to translate the word δύνασαι' in its attempt to convey the lack of choice which the slave had.[206] In fact Bartchy himself 'points out that there were many ways in which a slave could *contribute to* the possibility of his being freed'.[207] Good behaviour and hard work, or the saving up of an amount of money sufficient to buy freedom (though still at the owner's discretion) were all important factors.[208] So the socio-historical context seems to make the advice 'stay a slave' highly improbable, even nonsensical, whereas the advice to make use of the opportunity to become free is entirely unexceptional.[209]

The probability that 1 Cor 7.21b is intended as an exception to the general advice to stay as you are is suggested on the grounds of grammar, literary and socio-historical context. The cumulative arguments in favour of 'freedom' are overwhelming.[210] The phrase should therefore be translated: 'But if then you are able to become free, by all means use that opportunity.'

Is 1 Cor 7.17–24 then an example of Paul's love-patriarchalism? Certainly we must acknowledge that Paul accepts the continued existence of owner-slave relations; the social structures of his day are not repudiated. Even the encouragement to 'take your freedom' is hardly 'radical', given the widespread practice of manumission. Paul is perhaps mostly

---

[204] Bartchy 1973, 176; cf. also Klauck 1984, 54.
[205] Bartchy 1973, 183, my emphasis.
[206] Barrett 1975, 174; cf. Dawes 1990, 693; though note Bartchy 1973, 176–77.
[207] Dawes 1990, 694; cf. Trummer 1975, 368; see Bartchy 1973, 82ff, 97, 111, 176 etc.
[208] On the reasons for manumission, see Barclay 1991, 168–69; Hopkins 1978, 126–34. Both civil and sacral manumissions involved payment. Many examples of the latter are preserved at Delphi; see Barrett 1956, 52; Deissmann 1927, 319–30; Hopkins 1978, 133–71; see also *P. Oxy.* 722.
[209] The contrast between slave and free should not be allowed to hide the fact that freedpersons were often bound by certain obligations to their previous owners and may frequently have been quite poor; cf. Tacitus *Annals* 13.26; Ste. Croix 1981, 178–79; Hopkins 1978, 129–71; Bartchy 1973, 72–82; Barclay 1991, 169. However, manumission did bring significant freedoms and legal status, on which see Westermann 1943, 26–27.
[210] It is disappointing that the NRSV has moved in the opposite direction (cf. RSV).

concerned to assure slaves that the 'stay as you are' advice does not apply to them. Unlike the Essenes,[211] he does not reject slavery altogether or call for the abandonment of all such worldly relationships in favour of a completely alternative communal existence. However, he does nothing to affirm (theologically or otherwise) the position of slave-owners. Indeed, Paul insists that free people must regard themselves as slaves of Christ, while slaves are the Lord's freedpersons. He does not seem to regard slavery as a desirable institution (7.23) and encourages slaves to take the opportunity of freedom if they can (7.21). While the formulation 'let each one remain in the calling in which they were called' (7.20) certainly supports the general instruction to 'remain as you are', Paul makes a point of inserting the exceptional advice to slaves: you can be a Christian and a slave – μή σοι μελέτω, in other words, do not regard yourself as inferior on the basis of your social position – but use (imperative!) the opportunity of freedom if it is available. There is no sense here that Paul seeks (as Theissen's love-patriarchalism thesis suggests) to encourage 'subordination and fidelity' from the socially weak. It is not legitimate to use 1 Cor 7.21 as evidence of a socially conservative ethos which promotes continued and voluntary subordination from the weak. In the alternative symbolic order embodied ἐν ἐκκλησίᾳ it is the 'nobodies' who have been specifically chosen by God (1.26ff); the weakest members of the community have the right for their consciousness to affect the behaviour of even the strongest member (8.1–11.1); and the 'have-nots' must be full and equal sharers in the community meal (11.17–34). Moreover, as far as it is possible to tell, slaves as much as anyone else are able to take leading roles in the community. There is no hint in chapters 12–14 that the leading functions of teacher, prophet etc. are restricted to a particular social group. A concrete example of this, if we are right to assume that Fortunatus and Achaicus are subordinate members of Stephanas' household, is found in 16.15–17, where it is these leading figures (the household of Stephanas) who are to be recognised and submitted to. Paul does not reject the institution and structure of the household – he still refers to 'the household of Stephanas' – but this social hierarchy is not mirrored, legitimated or sustained ἐν ἐκκλησίᾳ. In the ἐκκλησία an alternative symbolic order shapes and patterns social relations.

---

[211] See Josephus, *Antiquities* 18.21.

4.3.2. 'Let a woman cover her head': 1 Cor 11.2–16

1 Cor 11.2–16 is a much discussed passage, partly because of its importance in relation to the question of Paul's attitude to women, and partly
because of its obscurity (at least to modern readers). Paul's imagery, logic
and instruction are all difficult to penetrate with much degree of certainty and have been much debated in the secondary literature.

One way of dealing with the passage is to argue that it is in fact
non-Pauline; that it was added to the text of 1 Corinthians by a later
redactor.[212] This case is argued on a number of grounds: 'the fact that it
so obviously breaks the context of the letter at this point';[213] the kind of
language used in these verses[214] and its similarity with the ethos of later
'pastoral' instruction;[215] and the apparently incompatible pericopae which
together comprise this passage.[216] Murphy O'Connor has offered forceful refutations of this proposal.[217] Decisions about what is unusual in
Paul are always somewhat suspect, since Paul's argument and
language vary so markedly depending upon the situation he is addressing. Unless there are other supporting reasons this is a weak basis on
which to argue that an interpolation has been added, as is the argument
that various sections of a passage seem incompatible with one another,
since Paul's extended and contorted arguments are often at least superficially in this form.[218] In particular, interpolation theories are always rather
hypothetical when the textual tradition itself shows no evidence of any
such activity. Certainly 11.2–16 stands as a distinct block in its present
epistolary context, but there is no textual evidence of its misplacement
or omission in any manuscripts. Kurt and Barbara Aland's first 'rule' of
textual criticism stands as an appropriate caution against such interpretative activity: 'Textual difficulties should not be solved by conjecture,
or by positing glosses or interpolations, etc., where the textual tradition
itself shows no break; such attempts amount to capitulation before the

---

[212] See Walker 1975; 1983; 1989; Cope 1978 (who suggests that it is vv. 3–16 which form the
interpolation); Trompf 1980; Munro 1983, 69–75.

[213] Walker 1975, 99; cf. Trompf 1980, 198–202.

[214] See esp. Walker 1989; Trompf 1980, 202–205.

[215] See esp. Munro 1983; Trompf 1980, 205–15; Walker 1975, 108; 1983.

[216] See esp. Walker 1975, 101–104: 'the passage actually consists of three originally separate
and distinct pericopae' (101), 'none of [which] ... is authentically Pauline' (104).

[217] Murphy O'Connor 1976 (against Walker 1975); 1980, 482–83; 1986, 87–90 (against
Trompf 1980).

[218] E.g. 1 Cor 8–10; Rom 9–11; and the apparent 'intrusion' of 1 Cor 13 between chapters 12
and 14.

difficulties and are themselves violations of the text.'[219] I shall argue in an excursus below that 1 Cor 14.34–35 should be regarded as a post-Pauline interpolation but the crucial difference between that passage and this is the textual evidence. Verses 2–16 of 1 Cor 11 should be regarded as a genuine and original part of Paul's letter.

The passage opens with Paul's praise of the Corinthians for their holding on to the traditions he passed to them (v. 2). In this context, it seems most likely that Paul is referring to the situation in which both men and women are free to pray and prophesy in worship (v. 5), a 'tradition' which was probably established during Paul's founding mission. [220] He may be referring more broadly to his original teaching which stressed the unity of man and woman in Christ (cf. Gal 3.27f), as L. A. Jervis has recently argued,[221] though it is significant that when Paul cites the same baptismal teaching in 1 Cor 12.13 he does not include 'no longer male and female'. It seems that Paul disagrees with what the Corinthians have made of this teaching. Indeed, here in 11.2–16, it is clear that Paul now wishes to modify their current practice through the introduction of new teaching (θέλω δὲ ὑμᾶς εἰδέναι ὅτι ... v. 3). He is clearly disturbed by certain aspects of their behaviour. Once again Paul must reformulate and develop the content of the symbolic order in response to a situation which owes at least something to his previous teaching (v. 2), but which now, in his view, requires correction.

There are two main possibilities which may explain Paul's concern over their practices in worship. The first is that the Corinthians' wild and ecstatic worship, in which many speak in tongues and in which the women unbind their hair in frenzied activity, may appear to outsiders like the ecstatic gatherings associated with various oriental cults: 'his instruction aims at playing down the impression of madness and frenzy so typical of orgiastic cultic worship.'[222]

The more dominant explanation of Paul's concern links it with the tendency of some of the Corinthians, possibly inspired by the baptismal declaration recorded in Gal 3.28, to act as though gender and sexuality

---

[219] Aland and Aland 1989, 280.
[220] Cf. Hurd 1965, 185, 281, 292, who argues that Paul had initially allowed women to go unveiled during worship, but then went back on this in his first letter. This seems unlikely to me.
[221] Jervis 1993, 234–35; cf. also §3.5.1. above.
[222] Fiorenza 1983, 230; see 227–30; cf. 1 Cor 14.23; Kroeger and Kroeger 1978. Against this interpretation see Theissen 1987, 163–65.

were no longer of significance.[223] Paul may be opposing the notion that through baptism, and perhaps especially in worship, Christians (re)attain a state of androgyny,[224] and he may be fearful that homosexuality would be tolerated or even encouraged within the congregation.[225] Paul's primary concern, on this view, is to establish the God-given (created) distinction between the sexes.

What is clear is that Paul's concern here is with appearance at worship, whereas in 1 Cor 7 it was the issues of sexual relations and marriage that were addressed. Paul's particular and practical aim, whether he is talking about veils or hairstyles (the former is in my view more likely),[226] is to ensure that the women are appropriately attired.[227] His main point is that it is shameful for a man to pray or prophesy with anything covering his head, and shameful for a woman to do the same without a head covering (vv. 4–6). His closing arguments focus on this major point (vv. 13–16); a woman should not pray ἀκατακάλυπτον, 'unveiled' (v. 13).

Paul surrounds his statements of this main point (vv. 4–6) with two theological legitimations (v. 3; vv. 7–9). The first, which provides the basis for the statements about shaming one's 'head', asserts the sexual difference between men and women by assigning them to different positions within a hierarchy. Whatever the precise meaning of κεφαλή (literally, 'head') – and this is much debated – woman's place is secondary to man's.[228] Some have argued that κεφαλή here means 'source',[229] thus

---

[223] See Murphy O'Connor 1980, 490; Fee 1987, 497–98; Jervis 1993, esp. 235–38.

[224] See esp. Meeks 1974; MacDonald 1987, 87–111.

[225] This potential fear was suggested by Scroggs 1972, 297; 1974, 534; cf. Barrett 1971a, 257; Murphy O'Connor 1980, 485–87, 490.

[226] Martin 1970, 233; Murphy O'Connor 1980, 484–90; Fiorenza 1983, 227; Padgett 1984, 70; and Radcliffe 1990, 68, have argued that Paul's concern here is with hairstyles and not, as traditionally assumed, veils. Against this see MacDonald 1987, 86–87; Byrne 1988, 39–40. Verse 15 is perhaps the strongest evidence in favour of the hairstyle interpretation, but, as Byrne 1988, 40, shows, Paul is using the argument from nature as an *analogy* to indicate that a headcovering is appropriate for women; cf. also Delobel 1986, 372–76 (*contra* Padgett 1994, who argues that there is no analogy between v. 15 and vv. 5–6, rather a contradiction; see further n. 252 below).

[227] So Byrne 1988, 39 with 54 n. 29; cf. Wire 1990, 118; Fee 1987, 495. Otherwise Oster 1988; Murphy O'Connor 1980, 483–90, who argue that Paul is equally concerned about men's appearance. The bulk of the passage is clearly concerned with women's appearance and attire; the references to men are primarily balancing illustrations: compare v. 4 (men), vv. 5–6 (women); v. 7a (men), vv. 7b–10 (women); v. 13 (women), v. 14 (men), v. 15 (women).

[228] Rightly emphasised by Delobel 1986.

[229] So Bedale 1954; Scroggs 1972, 298–99 n. 41; Fee 1987, 502–504; Byrne 1988, 42; Watson 1992c, 111–12; Jervis 1993, 240.

softening any sense of superiority or subordination, yet the implication is still that woman derives her being from man, whereas the man's is derived from Christ.[230] However, recent work has cast doubt on the appropriateness of 'source' as a translation of κεφαλή.[231] The other major proposal has come from Wayne Grudem and Joseph Fitzmyer, who argue that κεφαλή conveys the sense 'ruler' or 'authority over', thus implying a much stronger sense of hierarchy and subordination.[232] A. C. Perriman has, however, effectively argued against this translation (as well as against the rendering 'source'), and suggests that 'the most obvious metaphorical sense' is 'that which is most prominent, foremost, uppermost, pre-eminent'.[233] The κεφαλή hierarchy in particular, and the passage as a whole, 'has little or nothing to do with the issue of the man's authority over the woman'.[234] Paul uses the word κεφαλή in v. 3 not to talk about authority and subordination but *precisely because* he wants to talk about the way in which men and women must attire their κεφαλή in worship. [235] Nevertheless, the theological legitimation which the κεφαλή analogy provides clearly gives man priority over woman.

Woman's secondary place in the order of creation is underlined in vv. 7–9, where man is again set in closer relation to God, with the idea from Gen 1.27 of humankind[236] made in the image of God being applied here to the man (ἀνήρ); εἰκὼν καὶ δόξα θεοῦ ὑπάρχων – 'the image and glory of God' (v. 7a).[237] Woman, however, is δόξα ἀνδρός – 'the glory of man' (v. 7b).[238] This is grounded in the 'explanation' that woman was made from man, and not vice versa (v. 8f; cf. Gen 2.22f). 'In vv. 7–10 Paul makes clear that the creation stories are the warrant for his

---

230 Cf. Delobel 1986, 378–79.
231 Perriman 1994, 610–17; also n. 232 below.
232 Grudem 1985, 1990; Fitzmyer 1989, 1993; Ste. Croix 1981, 105–106.
233 Perriman 1994, 618; cf. Cervin 1989, who also argues effectively against the 'ruler', 'authority over', translation and suggests that 'pre-eminence' is the most appropriate meaning.
234 Perriman 1994, 620; and see further below.
235 Cf. Jervis 1993, 239; Perriman 1994, 619.
236 NRSV. Hebrew: hā'ādām (not hā'îš); LXX: τὸν ἄνθρωπον (not τὸν ἄνδρα). Cf. Gen 2.7, and see Trible 1993, 41–43; Watson 1992b, 87–89.
237 Cf. Wire 1990, 119. On the interpretation of Gen 1–3 in Pauline theology, see Watson 1992b, esp. 91–103.
238 On the sense of δόξα here, see Byrne 1988, 43–44; Watson 1992c, 113; Fee 1987, 516. Watson and Fee, in my opinion, are too concerned here to soften any sense of male dominance. 'Resistance', rather than 'recovery' may be a more appropriate hermeneutical strategy in such cases (see Watson 1992b).

injunctions.'[239] In his interpretative adaptation of these narratives Paul, Jervis suggests, 'is able to bring out what he considers to be the meaning of the stories: men and women are distinct and that distinction is good'.[240] This may well be Paul's primary intention but it must not be overlooked that he does this by interpreting the creation narratives in a way which differentiates men and women by assigning some form of (theologically legitimated) priority to the man. Paul has clearly presented to the Corinthians theological ideas which establish a woman's place in creation as secondary. As J. Delobel notes:

> [B]y determining man in his relation to God and woman (exclusively) in her relation to man, the very *nature* of the distinction is indicated. Paul again suggests that the distinction consists in priority of man and secondary place of woman. . . This rather obvious meaning of vv. 7–9 indirectly confirms the nuance of priority in the word κεφαλή.[241]

However, Paul's purpose here must be borne in mind, particularly in view of what follows in vv. 10–12. The basic point of the theological ideas presented in vv. 3, 7–9 is to explain why a man must have an uncovered head and a woman a covered one. Paul shows no concern here about authority or subordination. Indeed, he follows the assertion of woman's secondary place in the order of creation (v. 9) *not* with a command for her to be subordinate but with an insistence that she must ἐξουσίαν ἔχειν ἐπὶ τῆς κεφαλῆς – literally, 'have authority upon her head' (v. 10). Ἐξουσία used to be taken as a reference to authority *over* the woman, even though Paul's vocabulary therefore caused some surprise. 'Why does St. Paul say "authority" when he means "subjection"?', Robertson and Plummer wondered.[242] However, there is now widespread agreement that it cannot mean this and must refer to the woman's own possession of authority, even though the precise meaning of the verse remains somewhat enigmatic. The most likely interpretations are either that the head-covering is a sign or symbol of a woman's authority to pray or prophesy,[243] or that a woman should exercise con-

---

[239] Jervis 1993, 242, who however sees vv. 7–9 as an injunction to the Corinthian men.

[240] Jervis 1993, 243.

[241] Delobel 1986, 381.

[242] Robertson and Plummer 1914, 232; note Fee's comment, 1987, 519 n. 22.

[243] See esp. Hooker 1964, followed by Barrett 1971a, 254–55; Watson 1992c, 114; cf. also Byrne 1988, 44–45; Fee 1987, 519–21; also Jaubert 1972, 428, 430: 'En portant une coiffure, la femme a sur la tête le signe de sa capacité à participer à l'assemblée de prière.'

trol, power, or freedom over her head.[244] What seems clear is that there is no sense of subordination implied here. The equally enigmatic reference to 'the angels' may imply that 'the behaviour of women in worship has to respect the order of creation symbolised by the angels who are indeed present in worship and watching the observance of this order'.[245]

In the context of the present discussion we must note that, while the created order outlined in 1 Cor 11 is one in which a woman's place is secondary to man's, Paul's purpose seems clearly to be the establishment of 'proper' distinction between men and women and not superiority or authority. Women must pray and prophesy as women, and men as men.[246] This is surely confirmed by the note of 'correction' expressed in verses 11 and 12.[247] The conjunction πλήν (v. 11) is not generally used by Paul in a strongly adversative sense; he seems to use it when 'breaking off a discussion and emphasizing what is important'.[248] Nevertheless, 'the nuance of correction is not absent',[249] perhaps especially here. The translations 'only', 'in any case', 'however', 'but', or perhaps 'nevertheless', 'yet', may be appropriate.[250] Here in 1 Cor 11, 'the remark introduced by πλήν consists in a complement to the onesided emphasis in vv. 3–10 on woman's secondary place'.[251] The contrast between vv. 3–9 and 11– 12 is obvious, particularly from a comparison of vv. 8–9 and v. 12:[252]

> Indeed man was not made from woman, but woman from man. Neither was man created for the sake of woman, but woman for the sake of man. (vv. 8–9; NRSV)

> For just as woman came from man, so man comes through woman; but all things come from God. (v. 12; NRSV)

---

[244] Cf. Fee 1987, 520–21; Delobel 1986, 386–87.
[245] Delobel 1986, 386; cf. Hooker 1964.
[246] Cf. Meeks 1974, 201–203; Murphy O'Connor 1980, 491–500; MacDonald 1987, 102ff; Theissen 1987, 167–75; Allison 1988, 32–33; Watson 1992c, 110.
[247] Byrne 1988, 41, 47; cf. Kürzinger 1978, 270; Jaubert 1972, 429; Delobel 1986, 383–85.
[248] BAGD 669; see Phil 1.18 (if πλήν is original here); 3.16; 4.14; cf. Luke 22.22 for a more adversative use.
[249] Delobel 1986, 384 n. 54, citing Phil 4.13f as an example.
[250] Cf. BAGD, 669; NRSV, 'nevertheless'; REB, 'yet'.
[251] Delobel 1986, 384.
[252] Because of this tension (seen as a 'contradiction'), Padgett 1984, 76–84, has suggested that vv. 3–7 are a quotation of Corinthian, not Pauline opinion, refuted by Paul in v. 11f (similarly, Shoemaker 1987, 62–63; and cf. Padgett 1994). This is entirely unconvincing; see the sharp rebuttal by MacDonald 1987, 81–82 n. 54.

Verse 12 first reiterates the point made in vv. 8–9 and then counterbalances it, rounding the sentence off with the assertion that it is actually God who is the source of all things, including both men and women. Perhaps Paul sensed that, in seeking to stress the created differences between men and women, he had expressed a rather hierarchical picture of the relation between them. In view of what has preceeded, Paul therefore stresses that in any case (πλὴν...), οὔτε γυνὴ χωρὶς ἀνδρὸς οὔτε ἀνὴρ χωρὶς γυναικὸς ἐν κυρίῳ – 'woman is not independent of/ different from man, nor is man independent of/ different from woman in the Lord' (v. 11). The translation and interpretation of this verse depends to a considerable degree on the sense given to χωρίς. In this context, Josef Kürzinger argues that χωρίς must mean 'other than' or 'different from', and thus implies not only an interdependence between the sexes, but an *equality*.[253] This equality, Brendan Byrne stresses, is not merely eschatological, though it occurs 'in the Lord' (cf. Gal 3.28): 'it is an equality that goes back ultimately to the disposition of the Creator. That is why the statement of equality in v. 12a, resting upon the natural process of procreation, is bolstered by the addition that "all this is from God"' (v. 12b).[254] It would, however, be equally possible to render χωρίς here as 'without',[255] thus seeing the verse as implying interdependence rather than necessarily equality (cf. NRSV). Even Kürzinger does not see this expression of 'Gleichsein', equality, as contradicting Paul's '*demand for subordination* and veiling of the woman' in vv. 3–10.[256] However, *contra* Kürzinger, it must be pointed out that there *is* no 'demand for subordination' in vv. 3–10.

The arguments with which the passage closes clearly reveal and focus upon the main concern: attire in worship (vv. 13–16). Paul adds, to the theological and creational legitimations for his insistence on women covering their heads, arguments based on propriety, nature and church custom. The first argument is simply an appeal to what is 'proper' (πρέπον ἐστίν – v. 13). Indeed, Annie Jaubert argues that a woman's head-covering at that time was not a sign of subordination but precisely of

[253] 'Anders als' or 'verschieden von': Kürzinger 1978, esp. 273–75, followed by Fiorenza 1983, 229–30 and Byrne 1988, 47, 57 n. 59. Note esp. the use of χωρίς in Gen 26.1 (LXX).
[254] Byrne 1988, 48.
[255] So Delobel 1986, 383.
[256] '*Forderung nach Unterordnung* und Verschleierung der Frau': Kürzinger 1978, 275, my emphasis.

decency and honour.[257] The next argument – an appeal to nature – also focuses upon glory and shame: long hair is a shame/dishonour (ἀτιμία) for a man, whereas it is a woman's glory (δόξα). Nature thus demonstrates that a head-covering is appropriate for a woman but not for a man (vv. 14–15).[258] Finally Paul appeals to the general practice of the other churches, hoping that majority custom will perhaps convince the contentious Corinthians (v. 16).[259] The language of 'custom' (συνήθεια) here perhaps suggests that the Corinthian women's practice of worshipping with unveiled heads is regarded as a custom among the Corinthian believers, but it is clearly one Paul is unwilling to countenance.[260]

In this passage, then, it is clear that Paul's primary concern is not with authority or subordination, but with appearance, attire, in worship. His use of the word κεφαλή would not by itself have implied the sense of rulership or authority, and clearly the word is used because Paul's instruction relates to the appropriateness of covering or uncovering the κεφαλή in worship. Paul does not imply here that the appropriate attitude for women ἐν ἐκκλησίᾳ is one of 'subordination, fidelity and esteem'. Indeed, in 1 Cor 7, where his concern was with the marital relationship between man and woman, Paul apparently ascribed to each party equal rights and responsibilities and again showed no hint of an expectation that the woman should be subordinate. To this extent at least the description of Paul's ethos as one of love-patriarchalism must be considered somewhat wide of the mark. Nowhere in 1 Cor 7 or in 11.2–16 does Paul assert that women should be subordinate to men, or under their authority. Indeed, his 'corrective' comments in 11.11–12 imply that he explicitly opposed such an interpretation. The only place in 1 Corinthians where the subordination of a social group is explicitly demanded is 14.34f. However, like many scholars, I take this to be a post-Pauline interpolation, probably introduced as an early marginal note

---

[257] Jaubert 1972, 425–28: 'Or au cours de notre enquête sur l'obligation de la coiffure pour les femmes, nous n'avons jamais trouvé que c'était un signe de subordination à son mari, mais une nécessité culturelle, imposée par la décence selon la mentalité juive et qui fait l'honneur à son mari et à elle-même' (428).

[258] Cf. n. 226 above.

[259] I remain unconvinced by Engberg-Pedersen's proposal that the 'habit' Paul refers to is that of being contentious: thus, in his view, Paul is stating 'that the Corinthians must decide for themselves [cf. v. 13] since Paul as a matter of universal Christian principle does not have the habit of being contentious' (1991, 689).

[260] See Theissen 1987, 161–63, who shows that there did not seem to be a social *requirement* of veiling for women in Greece at this time.

(see excursus below). The only other place where ὑποτάσσω is used in relation to some people being subordinate to others is 16.16, which refers to the household of Stephanas and to every co-worker and labourer.[261]

It is clear that 1 Cor 11.2–16 reflects the specific circumstances of its production; Paul's concern, for whatever reasons, is with the appearance of women's heads in worship. However, despite some apologetic interpretations to the contrary, we must also consider the extent to which this text has ideological potential. It is clear that, in order to make his point on the practical issue of head covering, Paul draws on the rules and resources offered in the Genesis narratives, and apparently creates some new symbolic resources himself (the κεφαλή hierarchy),[262] and thereby builds into the Christian symbolic order the view that woman has a secondary place, below man, in the created order. Paul's primary concern may be with what he sees as the appropriate distinctions between the sexes, but the potential impact of his instruction is anti-emancipatory.[263] Although this theology is presented in a passage which relates to the context of worship, it may easily be taken to have wider implications; a social relationship of domination may be legitimised, 'reified', by rooting it in the fundamental and God-given pattern of creation. 1 Cor 11.2–16 appears to provide the earliest written Christian contribution to the formulation of a profoundly influential theological ideology which supports a hierarchical relationship between men and women. As Paul is engaged in reformulating and reshaping the content of the Christian symbolic order and thereby its social embodiment, so he also opens the way for further reinterpretation in a particular direction of the rules and resources which he himself develops.

4.3.3. Order in the Body: 1 Cor 12–14

At the beginning of 1 Cor 12, Paul turns to the subject of spiritual gifts (περὶ δὲ τῶν πνευματικῶν).[264] A particular concern in the chapters

---

[261] See §4.2.5. above. Cf. also 14.32; 15.27, 28 for other uses of ὑποτάσσω.

[262] Cf. Perriman 1994, 619 with n. 43.

[263] Especially if the removal of veils on the part of women is a symbolic emancipation from traditional roles; cf. Theissen 1987, 165.

[264] Another subject probably raised in the Corinthians' letter to Paul; so Hurd 1965, 71–73. Most commentators take this genitive plural as neuter ('spiritual things') rather than masculine/feminine ('spiritual people'); see Fee 1987, 575–76; otherwise Gardner 1994, 138–39.

which follow seems to be with the use of the gift of 'tongues'; a concern which emerges most clearly in chapter 14. More generally Paul seeks to legitimate diversity within the community. Unlike some of the other issues addressed in 1 Corinthians, there are few hints here on which to build a hypothesis concerning any impact which social tensions or divisions might have upon this situation, although Dale Martin has recently argued that the tongue-speakers are most likely to have been among the higher-status members of the community. On the basis of cross-cultural study, Martin concludes that:

> esoteric speech ... is usually considered a high status activity *except* in western, rationalistic societies where tongue-speaking is taken as evidence of ignorance, lowly origins, and a susceptability to "enthusiasm" ...
>
> [I]f glossalalia had any status significance at all in Greco-Roman society it would probably be construed as high status activity.[265]

If Martin is right then this situation may perhaps be tied in with the broader reconstruction of the social divisions and tensions outlined in chapter 3 above.[266] But even if we do not assume that the tongue-speakers were drawn from any particular social group, it is still relevant to consider the way in which Paul's teaching in these chapters – and especially his use of the 'body' analogy – might shape social relationships in the community.

Paul first affirms that there is one clear mark of the Spirit's activity: the confession of Jesus as Lord (Κύριος 'Ιησοῦς). This is the fundamental point of unity which distinguishes those who do speak by the Spirit from those who do not (12.3). However, from this point of unity Paul proceeds to develop his first major point: that there is nevertheless[267] a divinely given diversity within the community – unity does not imply uniformity. In a notably 'trinitarian' formulation Paul expresses this in three ways (12.4–6: 'the same Spirit ... the same Lord ... the same God').[268] And verse 7 makes the point that the purpose of every

---

[265] Martin 1991b, 556, 558.
[266] Martin 1991b, 576–80 and Fee 1987, 609, 612–13, both argue that the particular formulation of 1 Cor 12.21–26 reflects this social situation (see below).
[267] The δέ in verse 4a may be mildly adversative.
[268] On the trinitarian pattern here see Barrett 1971a, 284; Fee 1987, 586–88.

manifestation of the Spirit is for the common good (πρὸς τὸ συμφέρον). A range of examples follow, all of which serve to illustrate the diversity of the Spirit's manifestations[269] and culminating in an emphatic recapitulation of the point that it is the one and the same Spirit (τὸ ἓν καὶ τὸ αὐτὸ πνεῦμα) who is the source of all this diverse activity (12.11). The 'need for diversity within unity'[270] is further illustrated through the use of the analogy of the human body (12.12–26). The use of precisely this analogy was widespread in Greek and Latin literature, and since the analogy often functioned as a form of conservative political ideology[271] it will be important to consider carefully the way in which Paul uses it here.[272]

The paradigmatic story in ancient literature was that of Menenius Agrippa who in c. 494 BCE is said to have been sent as an ambassador to the Roman plebs in order to quell their anger and dissension against the ruling class (Livy *History* 2.32). Menenius uses the body analogy to convince the plebs that their sedition would be harmful to all – just as if the parts of the body resolved not to work because they objected to providing everything for the idle belly, the whole body would be reduced to weakness.[273] The analogy convinced the plebs (2.32.12) and 'steps were then taken towards harmony (*concordia*)' (2.33.1).

The same tale is recounted by Dionysius of Halicarnassus (*Roman Antiquities* 6.86). A similar point is made: the belly may be regarded by other parts of the body as a useless exploiter, living idly from the nourishment provided by the labour of other parts, but if the other parts asserted their freedom (ἐλευθερία) they would all die of starvation. The analogy is explicitly drawn with the *polis*, in which the senate is in fact a source of 'nourishment', 'even while it is itself nourished'.[274]

The other major use of the analogy was to demonstrate that the (social) whole is prior to the individual parts.[275] This is particularly stressed by Stoic writers such as Marcus Aurelius Antonius (2.1; 7.13), Seneca (*Ep.* 95.52: '*membra sumus corporis magni*' – we are the parts of one great body),[276] and Epictetus (*Diss* 2.10.3–4). Dio Chrysostom uses the body

---

[269] See further Fee 1987, 584–85, outlining the structure of this passage.
[270] Fee 1987, 600.
[271] Cf. Martin 1991b, 563ff.
[272] The analogy is also taken up in 1 Clement; see §6.4. below.
[273] Cf. also Xenophon *Memorabilia* 2.3.18; Cicero *De Officiis* 3.5.22.
[274] Cf. also 6.54; Josephus *War* 4.406–407.
[275] Aristotle *Pol.* 1.1.11 (1253a, 19ff); 2.1.4 (1261a, 18ff); 3.1.2 (1274b, 40–41).
[276] Cf. also *De Ira* 31.7; Cicero *De Officiis* 3.5.22; 3.6.26–28.

analogy frequently, especially in connection with the need to include all citizens in the *polis* (*Diss.* 34.22–23) and with the desire for ὁμόνοια and the avoidance of στάσις (*Diss.* 39.5–8; 41.1ff).[277] The body analogy provides him with the grounds on which to pity the δῆμος, the common people; for 'in the case of the body, it is always the ailing part we treat' (*Diss.* 50.3), though he stresses that the cause of any ailment is *not* that the plebs have been treated unfairly or illegally (50.4).

In 1 Cor 12 Paul therefore employs an analogy which was already widely used, and there are areas of similarity between his own and others' writing. The first point Paul makes with this analogy forms the basis from which the further illustrations and arguments proceed: the body is one but has many members (12.12–14).[278] Both assertions are made with force; Paul emphasises the oneness of the body, into which all have been baptised by the one Spirit,[279] but also stresses the fact that a body has not one member but many (τὸ σῶμα οὐκ ἔστιν ἓν μέλος ἀλλὰ πολλά – v. 14).

In 12.15–20 Paul elaborates the metaphor in order to stress still further his point about the inevitable diversity of members within the body. 'If the foot were to say "because I am not a hand I do not belong to the body" it would not for that reason cease to be part of the body' (v. 15). Both the foot and the ear 'speak' in a similar way and are declared nonetheless to be part of the body. Verses 17 and 19 spell out the impossibility of conceiving of a functioning body which was comprised of just one member. Verse 18 makes a theological point: it is God who has arranged the various members of the body, as he willed. The section closes by reiterating the assertion made in verse 14 (v. 20).

The fact that Paul choses as illustrations pairs of bodily parts which 'carry on comparable functions in the body' – foot and hand, ear and eye – suggests, as Gordon Fee rightly points out, that Paul is not here concerned with inferiority or superiority between parts of the body.[280] He does not talk here (but see below on 12.21–26) of the head and the feet, nor of the belly, as was common in the uses of the analogy cited above.

---

[277] Note 41.9, and cf. also 33.44.
[278] I follow Fee 1987, 600ff, here in dividing Paul's argument into three sections: vv. 12–14, 15–20, 21–26.
[279] Note the repetitive emphasis on the *one* Spirit in both 12.4–11 (esp. vv. 9 and 11) and here in v. 13; cf. Fee 1987, 606 n. 38.
[280] Fee 1987, 610–11.

His point, rather, is simply the need for diversity. Paul's insistence that the members are assigned to their position by divine appointment (ὁ θεὸς ἔθετο τὰ μέλη – v. 18) could form an element in a conservative ideology which legitimated a social hierarchy by appealing to divine ordering.[281] Yet it seems clear from Paul's choice of parts as illustrations that his concern here – whatever the potential of his language to be developed in particular ways[282] – is not to legitimate any kind of hierarchy within the body, but only to legitimate its diversity.

The following verses (12.21–26), however, are somewhat different. The parts of the body chosen for illustrative purposes in verse 21 relate differently: eye to hand, head to feet. 'Both the direction and content of what is said imply a view "from above".'[283] Fee regards this section of Paul's developed analogy as orientated towards the social divisions in the Corinthian church, 'where those who consider themselves at the top of the "hierarchy" of persons in the community suggest that they can get along without some others, who do not have their allegedly superior rank'.[284] We must therefore examine Paul's use of his analogy here with care. Does he use it to legitimate (ideologically) the social diversity which is undoubtedly present in the community. Does it serve to sustain a social hierarchy?

In fact Paul sharply contradicts the view expressed by the 'superior' parts – 'I have no need of you' (v. 21) – in the opening of verse 22: ἀλλὰ πολλῷ μᾶλλον ... ('on the contrary, by how much more ...').[285] Paul develops a contrasting perspective. Two features of Paul's argument are particularly notable. The first is Paul's insistence that the weak and dishonoured parts are only *apparently* so (τὰ δοκοῦντα μέλη ... ἀσθενέστερα ... ἃ δοκοῦμεν ἀτιμότερα – vv. 22–23): 'the normally conceived body hierarchy is actually only an apparent, surface hierarchy.'[286] The second is that these apparently weaker parts are deemed to be much *more* necessary (πολλῷ μᾶλλον ... ἀναγκαῖα ἐστιν), to be

---

[281] Cf. also the comments above on 7.17–24 (pp. 161) and in §6.4. below.

[282] Such observations will be relevant to the discussion of Clement's adaptation of this metaphor (see §6.4.).

[283] Fee 1987, 612.

[284] Fee 1987, 612; cf. 609, 613.

[285] The ἀλλά must be adversative (cf. NRSV; REB). NAB misses this completely by translating 'Indeed ...', which cannot be right here since the sentence does not follow logically from v. 21; it contrasts with it. Cf. Rom 5.15.

[286] Martin 1991b, 567. Martin 1991b, 568 n. 43, states that ' "weaker" is unambiguously a low status term, often referring in political rhetoric to the lower class'.

recipients of *greater* honour (τιμὴν περισσοτέραν), to be *more* respectable (εὐσχημοσύνην) than the respectable parts (τὰ εὐσχήμονα).[287] This cumulative emphasis reaches a climax in the theological assertion that this reversal of the apparent allocations of honour and status is the work of God (v. 24). Martin therefore summarises the 'end result' of Paul's argument in the following way:

[T]he usual, conventional attribution of status is more problematic than appears on the surface; the normal connection between status and honor should be questioned; and we must recognise that those who, on the surface, occupy positions of lower status are actually more essential than those of high status and therefore should be accorded more honor ... Paul's rhetoric pushes for an actual reversal of the normal, "this worldly" attribution of honor and status. The lower is made higher and the higher lower.[288]

Once again we see that the symbolic order embodied in the Christian community – specifically conceived of here as a body which is Christ – contrasts strongly with the dominant social order. Indeed it is to some extent its reverse, as Paul insists that it is precisely those who appear to be weak and without honour who are given most honour (by God!) within this new community (cf. 1.18–31 and §4.3.1. above).

Paul's use of the body analogy certainly does not legitimate the position or status of the socially prominent members of the community; quite the opposite. The language of divine ordering (ὁ θεὸς ἔθετο) is not used to legitimate theologically the dominant *social* hierarchy. Nor would it be fair to regard Paul's language as providing a merely illusory compensation to the socially weak.[289] Rather it represents a demand that an alternative pattern of values and relationships be embodied within the ἐκκλησία. Paul does not demand that members of this new community withdraw from or even abandon their position in the world; to this extent the dominant social order is accepted. But he does not theologically legitimate this social order; indeed the symbolic order by which the life of the Christian community is to be shaped stands in sharp contrast

---

[287] It is likely that Paul is allusively referring to the genitals in vv. 22–23; see Martin 1991b, 567–68; Fee 1987, 613.

[288] Martin 1991b, 568–69.

[289] Cf. Marx's comment: 'The abolition of religion as the *illusory* happiness of the people is required for their *real* happiness.' (Marx and Engels 1957, 42); cf. the discussion of 7.17–24 in §4.3.1. above; also Martin 1991b, 568–69.

to it. This may be regarded as 'compromise'[290] and indeed embodies a certain tension: believers continue to inhabit their various positions in the world yet are also to shape their interaction with one another by the contrasting symbolic order of the Pauline gospel.

The purpose of the 'redistribution of honour' in the body, according to Paul, is that there may not be division (ἵνα μὴ ᾖ σχίσμα ἐν τῷ σώματι) but rather that the members may show the same (τὸ αὐτό) care for one another (v. 25). The intended result of the reversal of the apparently 'normal' status hierarchy is a form of equality – at least an equality in the care and respect accorded to each and every member.[291] They must all both suffer and rejoice with one another (v. 26).

After a resumptive reiteration of the foundation for all this (v. 27), Paul does however proceed to outline a hierarchy of gifts/offices[292] which is explicitly the result of God's ordering (ἔθετο ὁ θεός – v. 28). This is a hierarchy ἐν τῇ ἐκκλησίᾳ and bears no relation to the social hierarchy embodied in the world (cf. §4.2.5.). Nevertheless, it is a theologically legitimated hierarchy in which Paul is (among others) at the top (πρῶτον ἀποστόλους) and the gift of tongues (γένη γλωσσῶν) is at the bottom.[293] The Corinthians are urged to seek the greater gifts (v. 31).

There is, however, something of more fundamental importance than any gift, and that is love, ἀγάπη, the subject of chapter 13, a chapter which may well have been 'inserted into 1 Corinthians as a ready-made piece'[294] but which fits perfectly into the pattern of Paul's argument here, set out in typical ABA' form.[295] All of the gifts – including those of which the Corinthians are most proud – are nothing without love (13.1–3). The qualities of love, Paul insists, are quite the opposite of those which characterise some of the Corinthians: jealousy, boasting, arrogance, rudeness, seeking one's own advantage (οὐ ζηλοῖ, οὐ περπερεύεται, οὐ φυσιοῦται, οὐκ ἀσχημονεῖ, οὐ ζητεῖ τὰ ἑαυτῆς κτλ. – see vv. 4–7). And, while prophecy, tongues and knowledge are temporary and provisional, love is ultimate and eternal (vv. 8–13). Clearly Paul shapes his

---

[290] Cf. Theissen 1982, 164, on Paul's response to the problems at the Lord's Supper (see §4.2.4. above).

[291] Cf. 2 Cor 8.13–15, on which see further Horrell 1995c, 76–78 and §5.6. below.

[292] Since the gifts which are listed are bestowed upon particular persons only (especially in the case, say, of apostleship), the hierarchy, whatever else it may be, is effectively a hierarchy of persons and not merely of gifts; see Martin 1991b, 569 n. 45; Fee 1987, 618–20.

[293] Fee 1987, 622, rejects this conclusion with regard to the 'position' of tongues here.

[294] Barrett 1971a, 297.

[295] Cf. also 1 Cor 8–10; and Fee 1987, 16 with n. 40.

presentation of love in the light of what he considers to be the false values and perceptions of some of the Corinthians.

In chapter 14 Paul returns to the topic of spiritual gifts, and specifically to prophecy and tongues. Prophecy is clearly preferable in the assembly (14.4f, 18f, 39), and tongues must be interpreted. The overriding aim is to build up the congregation (ἵνα ἡ ἐκκλησία οἰκοδομὴν λάβῃ – 14.5).[296] In the congregation prophecy is preferable since it gives a clear and understandable message (14.6–12), and facilitates communication through which both believers and outsiders (ἰδιῶται) may be encouraged and challenged (vv. 14–25). Tongues, if used ἐν ἐκκλησίᾳ, must be interpreted (vv. 5, 13). There is a danger that a group of believers speaking in tongues will appear to outsiders to be 'mad' (οὐκ ἐροῦσιν ὅτι μαίνεσθε; – v. 23).[297]

From 14.26 Paul begins to reiterate his conclusions (τί οὖν ἐστιν ἀδελφοί;) and to give practical instruction. Each person brings some gift to the worship gathering; the crucial point is that all must be done for the upbuilding of the community – πάντα πρὸς οἰκοδομὴν γινέσθω (v. 26). A limited number of tongue-speakers may speak in turn, as long as there is someone to interpret (v. 27). If there is not, they must remain silent in the assembly (σιγάτω ἐν ἐκκλησίᾳ – v. 28). The same numerical limitation – two or three (v. 27 and v. 29) – applies to prophets, and an interpretative responsibility rests upon the whole congregation (οἱ ἄλλοι διακρινέτωσαν – 'let the others discern [what is said]'; v. 29). The first prophet to speak must be silent (σιγάτω) if a revelation comes to another (v. 30). Paul is emphatic that this is a process in which *all* will have the opportunity to participate (δύνασθε γὰρ καθ' ἕνα πάντες προφητεύειν κτλ. – v. 31).[298] Order in the congregation's worship is possible because the spirits of prophets submit to prophets (προφήταις ὑποτάσσεται – v. 32); and God is, in all the churches, not a God of disorder (ἀκαταστασίας) but of peace (εἰρήνης – v. 33).[299]

---

[296] Note the frequent uses of οἰκοδομή/οἰκοδομέω in this chapter (14.3, 4, 5, 12, 17, 26; cf. 1 Cor 3.9; 8.1, 10; 10.23).

[297] Paul may be concerned that their assembly will appear like that of one of the ecstatic cults (see e.g. Fiorenza 1983, 227; Kroeger and Kroeger 1978). I shall not attempt here to sort out the apparent contradiction between v. 22 and vv. 23–25, on which see Theissen 1987, 74–80.

[298] Note the threefold repetition of 'all' (πάντες). This is one of the contextual arguments against vv. 34–35 being original to this chapter (see excursus below).

[299] See excursus below for arguments in favour of the bracketing and removal of vv. 34–35 and hence the linking of v. 33a with 33b.

Paul insists that what he has written is the Lord's command (κυρίου ἐντολή – v. 37) and summarises his practical instruction concisely: prophecy is to be eagerly sought, and tongues should not be forbidden (a cautious and guarded acceptance of their value ἐν ἐκκλησίᾳ). But everything must be done in a seemly way (εὐσχημόνως)[300] and 'in order' (κατὰ τάξιν – vv. 39–40).

Paul expresses clearly his desire for order in the congregation's worship (14.33, 40) but there is no sense in which this can be taken as legitimating or even relating to the social diversity present in the community. Indeed Paul is emphatic that all will be able to prophesy and learn and be encouraged (14.31). He clearly believes that there is a God-given hierarchy within the church (12.28–31), but there are no grounds from which to deduce that this ecclesiastical hierarchy is in any way connected with a hierarchy of 'worldly' social position.

In using the body analogy, Paul takes up a symbolic resource widely employed in his socio-cultural context, used particularly as a form of ideology by the social elite. Paul, it is clear, does not use the analogy to legitimate the social diversity which is encompassed ἐν ἐκκλησίᾳ. Rather, he demonstrates how in the Christian body God has reversed the normal attributions of status and honour. Rules and resources from a wider context are taken up, transformed, and used to convey a very different social ethos, one which Paul expects to see embodied in community life.

Excursus: 1 Cor 14.34–35

Of all the suggested interpolations in 1 Corinthians, this is the one most frequently accepted as such.[301] However, there is by no means a consensus on this, and scholars of a variety of theological persuasions argue for the authenticity of the text.[302] A number of feminist scholars, signifi-

---

[300] Cf. 1 Thess 4.12.

[301] See the review of proposed interpolations in 1 Cor by Murphy O'Connor 1986 and Sellin 1987, 2982–86. The extent of the insertion here is disputed, but interpolation is accepted, for example, by Fitzer 1963; Barrett 1971a, 330–33 (tentatively); Scroggs 1972, 284; 1974, 533; Conzelmann 1975, 246; Dautzenberg 1975, 257–73; Walker 1975, 109; Murphy O'Connor 1976, 615; 1986, 90–92; Munro 1983, 67–69; 1988, 28–29; Weiser 1983, 162 n. 6; Klauck 1984, 105–106; Lang 1986, 199–200 (cautiously); Fee 1987, 699–708; Sellin 1987, 2984–85; Wedderburn 1987, 238 n. 14; Watson 1992c, 153–54.

[302] Authenticity is accepted, for example, by Lietzmann 1949, 75; Héring 1962, 154; Grudem 1982, 239–55; Odell-Scott 1983; 1987; MacDonald 1988, 42; Witherington 1988, 90–104.

cantly, accept the text as Pauline and are wary of the possibility that decisions of interpolation may be favoured due to a desire to be apologetic for Paul.[303] Nevertheless, decisions concerning authenticity and authorship cannot be avoided, even if interpretative interests are inevitably involved (as, of course, they always are). A simple plea to read the text 'as it stands' is, as Fee points out, to read the text without engaging in textual criticism.[304] And, as Winsome Munro remarks, Fiorenza does not regard it as 'apologetic' to regard the Pastoral Epistles, for example, as non-Pauline.[305] But clearly the decision to regard 1 Cor 14.34f as a post-Pauline interpolation must be based on substantial grounds and not merely on their unpalatability.

The weight of evidence required to substantiate the interpolation theory will depend on how likely such interpolations are taken to be. Scholars such as John O'Neill, William Walker, and Winsome Munro have argued that interpolations and redactional activity are highly likely to have occurred as the Pauline corpus was assembled, and that since our earliest texts come from the early third or late second century, such redaction may be entirely invisible within our textual variants.[306] Walker insists that this general observation should reduce the 'burden of proof' placed upon the identification of interpolations; the acknowledgment that there are likely to be interpolations *somewhere* should warn against being over-cautious when a specific case is considered.[307] It is questionable, though, whether such an approach is legitimate in instances where there is no textual evidence to support the case for interpolation. Kurt and Barbara Aland's first 'rule' of textual criticism (cited above in §4.3.2.) is clearly a polemic against those who posit 'glosses or interpolations, etc., where the textual tradition itself shows no break', and it forms an appropriate critique, in my view, of those who enthusiastically excise

---

[303] See Munro 1988, 26–27. Prominent examples are Fiorenza 1983, 230–33; 1987, 403 n. 50; Wire 1990, 149–52, 229–32. Such apologetic might be suspected, for example, in the comments of Walker 1975, 109 and Scroggs 1972, 283 (see further 1974 and the response of Pagels 1974).

[304] Fee 1987, 702 n. 17. Grudem 1982, 241, Fiorenza 1983, 230, Hauke 1988, 365–67, and Keener 1992, 74–75, all dismiss the textual problems too easily. Hauke 1988, 390–94, later suggests that the textual dislocation may have occurred through the activity of Marcion.

[305] Munro 1988, 29.

[306] See O'Neill 1972, 1–12; 1975, 14–16; Munro 1990; Walker 1987; 1988.

[307] Walker 1987, 611, 615–16.

portions of the Pauline epistles and thus offer a reconstructed (more radical) Paul. However in the case of 14.34–35 the textual tradition clearly shows some sort of break and so allows that the case for interpolation should be carefully considered.

In this particular instance it should be remembered that *any* decision as to authenticity or interpolation is a hypothesis which should commend itself on the grounds of its plausibility; it is not only the interpolation case which needs to be demonstrated. Significant problems regarding the authenticity of 14.34f arise both from the textual dislocation of these verses, and from the apparent tension with 11.2–16 (esp. v. 5), where it is assumed that women are free to pray and prophesy. Every interpreter who accepts 14.34f as authentic must explain its content in such a way as to harmonise it with 11.2–16, and this leads to the qualification of 14.34f in ways which are not necessarily demanded by the text itself.[308] While some of the proposed solutions are more plausible than others, I consider that the interpolation theory offers the most coherent and satisfactory hypothesis.

The most plausible version of the interpolation hypothesis, in my opinion, must begin with textual criticism.[309] This means that the extent of the interpolation must be limited to verses 34 and 35, since it is only these verses which appear in a different location in the Western texts.[310] An initial question, therefore, is whether the text can make coherent sense without these two verses. This is a particularly crucial question since v. 33b, ὡς ἐν πάσαις ταῖς ἐκκλησίαις τῶν ἁγίων, is generally linked to v. 34.[311] However, the sentence as construed by joining v. 33b to v. 34 is unusually clumsy owing to the repetition of ταῖς ἐκκλησίαις.[312] This should at least make us suspicious of the link. Moreover, in other places in 1 Corinthians where Paul refers to general church

---

308 The argument that 11.2–16 is also an interpolation is, in my view, unconvincing; see §4.3.2. above.

309 Fee 1987, 699–702, argues strongly from the textual evidence.

310 The extent of the interpolation is disputed among those who hold the interpolation theory. Conzelmann 1975, 246, for example, argues for 33b–36. Dautzenberg 1975, 257–73, 297–98, includes 33b–36 and 37–38 acknowledging: 'Darum ist es nicht möglich, die Echtheitsfrage mit Hilfe der Textkritik zu lösen.' (271 n. 57). Wire 1990, 231, argues that disagreement over the length of the interpolation implies that the passage is closely welded to its textual context.

311 E.g. NA²⁷; UBS; RSV; NRSV; NIV; REB.

312 Cf. Fee 1987, 698; Fitzer 1963, 10; Allison 1988, 29. Ellis 1981, 214 suggests that '14:33b … presents problems whether it is joined to 14:33a or to 14:34' but favours the bracketing of vv. 34–35 as the textual evidence suggests.

practice, the phrase *concludes* the related comment rather than introducing it.[313] Fee argues that the clause which comprises the whole of v. 33 makes good sense as it stands, and maintains that the 'idea that v. 33b goes with v. 34 seems to be a modern phenomenon altogether'.[314] In many ancient manuscripts, vv. 34f appear as a distinct paragraph.[315] John Chrysostom (*Homily* 36.7) clearly connects v. 33b with 33a (though he adds διδάσκω to the end of v. 33).[316] Presumably the scribes who wrote the Western texts found that the link between v. 33 and v. 36 made reasonable sense. Indeed, v. 36 makes perfectly good sense as Paul's immediately succeeding comment after v. 33. Having appealed to the Corinthian prophets to discipline their prophetic activities, and maintained that God's way in all the churches is one of peace and not disorder, Paul sarcastically ridicules any rebellious independence which might resist such instruction: ἢ ἀφ' ὑμῶν ὁ λόγος τοῦ θεοῦ ἐξῆλθεν, ἢ εἰς ὑμᾶς μόνους κατήντησεν; – the wording seems particularly appropriate to those who claim to be prophets. G. Fitzer therefore concludes, 'daß keine Narbe oder Nahtstelle sichtbar wird, wenn die vv. 34f weggelassen werden'.[317] D. W. Odell-Scott's attempt to offer an 'egalitarian' interpretation of 14.33b–36 based on the contrary force of the particle ἢ (at the beginning of v. 36) is highly implausible in relation to vv. 34f (which must then be read as a statement of Corinthian, not Pauline, opinion);[318] the particle's 'contrary force' makes much better sense in connection with v. 33.[319] R. W. Allison makes a similar point about the force of the particle ἢ, thus also arguing that 'Paul's rhetorical questions are his sarcastic rebuttal to his opponents' position. . . *The decree that women should remain silent in Church, then, must have been the assertion of an opposing group within the Corinthian church.*'[320] However, Allison proposes a more complex editorial process, seeing v. 33b as an editorial insertion,[321] and suggesting that 11.2–16 and the *Taceat*

---

[313] 1 Cor 4.17; 7.17; 11.16; cf. Fee 1987, 698; Fitzer 1963, 9–10. Cf. Grudem 1982, 239 n. 13, who also mentions 1 Cor 16.1, but argues that 14.33b is linked with v. 34.
[314] Fee 1987, 697 n. 49; see 697–98.
[315] Payne 1993; 1995 (see n. 340 below).
[316] Cf. Codex Fuldensis, where *doceo* is the concluding word of v. 33. Cf. also Fee 1987, 701 n. 14; Hauke 1988, 367.
[317] Fitzer 1963, 10.
[318] Odell-Scott 1983, esp. 92; 1987; cf. also Flanagan and Snyder 1981.
[319] Cf. Fee 1987, 697–98; Grudem 1982, 251 n. 26.
[320] Allison 1988, 47, (italics original), and see 60 n. 45.
[321] Allison 1988, 48.

belonged to an earlier letter to the Corinthians, and that chapters 12–14 were originally written without the *Taceat*.[322] I find both aspects of the argument implausible, and the rejection of the interpolation theory unconvincing.[323] The point about the particle ἤ, as noted above, makes most sense when v. 36 is linked with v. 33. The text of 1 Cor 14, then, would make sense without vv. 34–35, the verses which are subject to an ambiguous textual location.

Next the textual evidence must be interpreted. No known manuscripts lack the verses in question, and the main evidence of critical interest is the displacement of the two verses to a position following v. 40 in the Western texts.[324] Antoinette Wire argues in some detail that this entire textual tradition may be 'traced back to one text' and 'originated from a single displacement'.[325] This Western tradition, she suggests, was also the source for the ordering within the Greek miniscule numbered 88, in which the verses appear after v. 40 but are also indicated as belonging by v. 33.[326] The scribe who wrote this text, she concludes, had 'both formats in hand' and knew 'once conscious of having followed one, that the other [was] correct'.[327]

Wire may well be right on this point; the question, of course, is how to explain the origin of this textual variation. Wire, rejecting the interpolation theory,[328] suggests three possibilities. Firstly, that the verses 'could have been omitted by haplography as the copyist's eye skipped from the word "churches" in 14:33 to the same word in 14:35'.[329] However, the number of lines needing to be skipped makes this unlikely.[330] Secondly, that a scribe moved the lines concerning women to a position which was deemed more appropriate, in the interests of clarity.[331] Grudem similarly suggests that 'some early scribes thought that vss. 34–35 were out of place and transposed them to follow vs. 40'.[332] Fee argues strongly against

---

[322] Allison 1988, 52–53.
[323] See Allison 1988, 42–44.
[324] D; F; G; 88*; it^{ar, d, e, f, g}; Ambrosiaster Sedulius-Scotus (UBS); cf. Metzger 1971, 565; Fee 1987, 699 n. 1.
[325] Wire 1990, 149–51; cf. Fee 1987, 700 n. 7.
[326] Wire 1990, 151.
[327] Wire 1990, 151.
[328] See Wire 1990, 149, 229–31.
[329] Wire 1990, 151.
[330] A point made by Payne 1993.
[331] Wire 1990, 152.
[332] Grudem 1982, 241.

this suggestion, questioning whether there is any evidence that anyone 'in the early church would have been troubled by the *placement* of these words in the text, since all who comment on it find the arrangement very logical'.[333] He continues:

> It is therefore most highly improbable that with this text before him it would ever have occurred to a copyist to take such an unprecedented step as to rearrange Paul's argument – especially so since in this case one can scarcely demonstrate that the 'displacement' makes better sense![334]

Wire's third possibility is that the passage was displaced 'due to the corrector's ideological point of view'; the lines were moved 'to make a point'.[335] But again one may question whether this is likely, and what point could possibly have been made through such a rearrangement. Wire's examples of 'corrections' in the Western texts are all small in scale and involve just one or two words. None offers a precedent for, or an example of, the moving of a whole block of text. Each of Wire's suggestions must remain a possibility, yet one may question the plausibility of any of them, not least on the basis of their infrequency elsewhere. It seems that Wire has been unable to do what Fee rightly requires: 'Those who wish to maintain the authenticity of these verses must at least offer an *adequate* answer as to how this arrangement came into existence if Paul wrote them originally as our vv. 34–35.'[336]

Earle Ellis's suggestion is that 1 Cor 14.34f was a marginal note added *by Paul* after reading through the draft of 1 Corinthians. Hence its 'rough edges' in its context. 'In transmitting the letter, the scribe or scribes behind the majority textual tradition incorporated the passage after 14:33; those behind the Western "displacement" thought 14:40 to be a more appropriate point to insert it, and a few others copied the letter and left 14:34–5 in its marginal position'.[337]

Ellis bases his conclusions in part on the evidence of Codex Fuldensis, a sixth-century Latin manuscript.[338] Following Bruce Metzger, Ellis notes that in this codex vv. 34f appear both after v. 40 and in the margin after

---

[333] Fee 1987, 700.
[334] Fee 1987, 700.
[335] Wire 1990, 152.
[336] Fee 1987, 700; see further there, with n. 11.
[337] Ellis 1981, 219–20; followed by Barton 1986, 229–30.
[338] See Metzger 1977, 20–21.

v. 33.[339] This, however, is incorrect. The codex contains the verses in their normal position after v. 33, but a textual sign directs the reader from the end of v. 33 to the marginal text at the foot of the page, where vv. 36–40 appear.[340] It seems likely, therefore, that bishop Victor ordered the rewriting of the text in the belief that verses 34–35 should be omitted.[341]

The most important point for the present discussion is that Ellis argues that a marginal note is the most likely origin of 1 Cor 14.34f. This indeed seems to be the most plausible interpretation of the textual evidence and offers an adequate answer as to how the dual location arose. However the crucial question then becomes whether the most likely originator of the note is Paul himself or a later interpolator. Against Ellis, the Codex Fuldensis evidence in fact points to an awareness of a textual tradition that omitted these verses rather than to an 'original' (Pauline) marginal note.

The interpolation hypothesis – that a marginal note was added to the text of 1 Corinthians – seems to offer the most plausible explanation of the textual evidence.[342] However, it cannot be sustained on text-critical grounds alone.[343] The literary content of the verses must also be compared with their context in 1 Corinthians. Literary considerations may also contribute to an assessment of whether the likely originator of the marginal note was Paul or a later editor.

There are certainly words which connect vv. 34f to their context, as is generally noted.[344] In a discussion orientated towards the community's worship meetings, three groups of people, tongue-speakers, prophets, and women, are told that they must (sometimes) be silent.[345] However such links could equally indicate why the place seemed an appropriate

[339] Metzger 1971, 565; Ellis 1981, 213, 219.

[340] I am indebted to Philip Payne for this information. He has obtained a copy of the codex and discussed the evidence with Prof. Metzger, who, apparently, confirmed the observations. Apart from our personal discussion, Dr. Payne presented these and other findings to the Cambridge NT Seminar on 11.5.93; now published as Payne 1995. The codex has been published by Ranke 1868.

[341] *Contra* Ranke 1868, 485, who suggests that the corrector (C; see p. 465) added the marginal passage in error. How could a corrector rewrite 5 verses of text at the foot of the page and indicate with a textual sign that these verses were to be read after v. 33, 'in error'?!

[342] Fee 1987, 699–702, argues that it is the most likely option given the textual evidence.

[343] Fitzer 1963, 8: 'Das textkritische Ergebnis führt zunächst nur auf einen Verdacht.'

[344] Σιγάω, λαλέω, ὑποτάσσω; see further Allison 1988, 37; Hauke 1988, 369–72.

[345] Cf. Grudem's structural analysis (1982, 245–51); on 242–44 he examines the NT uses of σιγάω and λαλέω, concluding that their implication is always contextual and not absolute.

location for the marginal note which now forms vv. 34f. Indeed, on closer examination, vv. 34f are quite incongruous and intrusive.[346] The tongue-speakers and prophets are told to be silent only in particular situations; when there is no-one to interpret (v. 28), or when a revelation comes to another prophet (v. 30). Notably, v. 30 is followed by the assurance that all (πάντες) will be able to prophesy, as long as it is orderly. By contrast, the women's silence is absolute, in the context of the ἐκκλησία.[347] The reasons given for the silences also vary markedly. Paul's concern in relation to prophecies and tongues is that they should be used for the upbuilding of the community: πάντα πρὸς οἰκοδομὴν γινέσθω (v. 26). But women are simply not permitted to speak, ἀλλὰ ὑποτασσέσθωσαν (v. 34). Αἰσχρὸν γάρ ἐστιν γυναικὶ λαλεῖν ἐν ἐκκλησίᾳ (v. 35). And the appeal to the law, καθὼς καὶ ὁ νόμος λέγει (v. 34), in this connection, is quite un-Pauline. Paul generally cites the passage in mind and uses it in his argumentation (e.g. 1 Cor 9.8f; 14.21).[348] Finally, in his summary of the whole of chapter 14 (14.37–40), Paul explicitly mentions προφῆται and πνευματικοί (v. 37) and concisely recapitulates his advice: ζηλοῦτε τὸ προφητεύειν καὶ τὸ λαλεῖν μὴ κωλύετε γλώσσαις (v. 39). But there is no mention of γυναῖκες. Indeed, in the whole of chapters 12–14 there is no hint that such a major restriction is to be introduced or observed.[349] And Paul's involved and extended attempt to argue his point in 11.2–16 is much more understandable *without* the forthcoming restriction commanded in 14.34f.

Most interpretations which do treat vv. 34f as original have to qualify the meaning of the text, not because of the content of the verses themselves, but in order to make sense of them in their immediate context and in the wider context of 1 Corinthians (especially 11.2–16).[350] One unlikely solution is to assign 11.2–16 and 14.34f to different letters.[351]

[346] In Byrne's words, they come as 'a bolt from the blue' (1988, 62). Allison 1988, 37, speaks of 'superficial verbal similarity' and 'thoroughgoing conceptual discontinuity'.

[347] Cf. Allison 1988, 38.

[348] Cf. Fee 1987, 707; Fitzer 1963, 11–12. Fitzer points to 1 Cor 15.3f where Paul uses γραφαί (not νόμος) when referring to the scriptures without citing them. However, Paul is probably dependent on tradition for this usage in 15.3ff.

[349] Cf. Grudem 1982, 247.

[350] Lietzmann 1949, 75, comments: 'Ohne den Rückblick auf c.11 würde niemand es anders aufgefaßt haben' (than as a comprehensive ban on women speaking). See the rebuttal of attempts to qualify the sense of 14.34f in Allison 1988, 35–42.

[351] Schmithals 1971, 243–45.

Allison regards this as 'an evasion of, rather than a solution to, the problem'.[352] Grudem argues that Paul is telling women to be silent 'during the evaluation of prophecies'.[353] Others suggest that the prayers and prophecies referred to in chapter 11 'may be hypothetical',[354] or may be silent (!),[355] or that Paul may have unwillingly conceded on the issue of women's praying and prophesying in chapter 11 and gives his real opinion here in 14.34f.[356] Still others propose that Paul faced a particular problem at Corinth, where certain women were engaging in unseemly ecstatic speaking, or were 'chattering', or disrupting proceedings by asking questions.[357] One of the more textually-based suggestions is that the instruction refers only to wives, whereas 11.2–16 refers to unmarried women.[358] This is the solution Ellis advocates, in order to support his proposal that Paul himself added the marginal note to 1 Corinthians. While the text may support such an interpretation with its mention of τοὺς ἰδίους ἄνδρας (v. 35) it remains a questionable solution. There is no hint in 11.2–16 that only single women are in view; indeed, 11.3 might equally well suggest that married women are referred to. Paul's preference for the single state (1 Cor 7.8, 28–35, 38) might support the argument, as Fiorenza suggests.[359] But 1 Cor 7 deals primarily with marriage and sexual relations and there is no direct indication that a single/married distinction plays any part in worship regulations in 11.2–16, or in 12–14. In 1 Cor 7, moreover, Paul portrays marriage as a relationship in which rights and duties are remarkably reciprocal (see 7.4 and further §4.3.1.). There is no hint there that Paul would have

---

[352] Allison 1988, 32.
[353] Grudem 1982, 249–255; similarly Hauke 1988, 376–77, who takes this as effectively a ban on teaching (380).
[354] Robertson and Plummer 1914, 325.
[355] Tomson 1990, 137, is convinced that: 'The silence of women in church (1 Cor 14:33–38) is emphasized by Paul according to ancient Jewish traditions.' He explains the conflict with 11.2–16 by suggesting that 'there is no reason to suppose that prayer and prophecy should always be aloud when practised in the community'. Cf. also Martin 1970, 240. Note the rejection by Grudem 1982, 240 n. 14: 'certainly the prophecy was audible'. How could prophecy be otherwise?
[356] Lietzmann 1949, 75: 'Anscheinend ist c. 11 das "Beten" und "Prophezeien" der Frau *ungern konzendiert*, aber der Schleier unbedingt gefordert. *Hier dagegen kommt die eigentliche Meinung des Apostels zutage:* Die Frau soll überhaupt schweigen.' (My emphasis.)
[357] Keener 1992, 80–88; Kroeger and Kroeger 1978, 333–36; Ellis 1981, 218. See the criticisms of Allison 1988, 36–37; cf. Hauke 1988, 379.
[358] Fiorenza 1983, 230–33; Ellis 1981, 216–18, who traces the 'wives' interpretation back to the 16th century Spanish reformer Juan de Valdez.
[359] Fiorenza 1983, 231. Against Fiorenza, see Dautzenberg 1983, 193–96.

considered it appropriate for married women in particular to be silent as a sign of submission to their husbands.[360] And is it likely that Paul 'would allow very young and immature girls to speak in church while denying that privilege to all married women, even those who were much older and wiser and thereby much more qualified to speak'?[361] The disqualification would apply, for example, to Prisca, whom Paul mentions before her husband and counts as a συνεργός (Rom 16.3).[362] Does 14.34f really imply that only a restricted group of women, the married, are in view, or is it more plausible to suggest either that the author assumes most women to be married (cf. 1 Tim 5.14), or that the instruction to ask τοὺς ἰδίους ἄνδρας is 'an example ... to cover most cases', implying that single women could ask their fathers or masters ἐν οἴκῳ?[363]

The proposed qualifications of 14.34f offer possible solutions, but given their conjectural nature it may well be that the interpolation theory offers the best interpretation of the text. A comprehensive Pauline ban on women speaking seems to be impossible due to the contrary evidence elsewhere. But such a ban is entirely in keeping with the ethos of the Pastoral Epistles. There are particularly close similarities between 1 Cor 14.34f and 1 Tim 2.11–15.[364] In both places women are told to be silent and submissive and both passages explicitly prohibit women from speaking (1 Cor 14.35) or teaching (1 Tim 2.12). Their learning must be done in silent submission (1 Tim 2.11) and any speaking or questioning reserved for ἐν οἴκῳ (1 Cor 14.35). Verse 34 of 1 Cor 14 contains a general reference to ὁ νόμος as the legitimation for the command and 1 Timothy explicitly draws on the Adam and Eve narratives for this purpose.[365]

---

[360] *Pace* Ellis 1981, 217, who sees Paul's instruction here in 14.34f as 'an ordering of the ministry of wives to accord with their obligations to their husbands ... The married couple ... are to be mutually subject to one another, and submission is an emphasized characteristic of the wife's marriage role' (citing 1 Cor 7.4; 11.3; Eph 5.21–24; Col 3.18). Leaving aside the Colossian and Ephesian *Haustafeln*, 1 Cor 7.4 in no way emphasises submission on the part of the wife, and 1 Cor 11.3 concerns neither marriage nor submission.

[361] Grudem 1982, 248 n. 24; cf. Byrne 1988, 64.

[362] Note also Andronicus and Junia (Rom 16.7; if Junia(s) is female) and Phoebe (Rom 16.1); see further Fiorenza 1986; Weiser 1983; Byrne 1988, 64. Ellis 1981, 218, notes Prisca's 'ministry of teaching' but still argues that the prohibition of 14.34f applies to *wives* on the basis of their relation to their husband.

[363] Grudem 1982, 248 n. 24; cf. Fee 1987, 706 n. 29.

[364] These similarities are often noted and explored; e.g. Fitzer 1963, 37–39; Dautzenberg 1975, 258–60; Ellis 1981, 214–16; MacDonald 1983, 87.

[365] Ellis 1981, 214, suggests a 'common allusion to Gen 3.16'.

Accepting these similarities, Ellis questions the assumption that both passages must reflect some chronological distance from Paul, suggesting that the material emanates from 'a common tradition or an existing regulation'.[366] But even if the instruction reflects elements of Jewish, Hellenistic or even early Christian tradition (though there is no evidence for any earlier Christian teaching like this), the crucial question is *when* such traditions were introduced to the Pauline churches. Three considerations point to a date for 1 Cor 14.34f somewhat later than 1 Corinthians. Firstly, its incongruity with the Pauline material in 1 Corinthians. Neither in 1 Cor 7.1ff nor in 11.2–16 does Paul use the verb ὑποτάσσω to describe the attitude required of women. Indeed, in 1 Cor 7 he portrays the marriage relationship as one involving equal and reciprocal rights and duties, and in 11.2–16 his clear assumption is that women are free to pray and prophesy in the worship meetings. A second consideration is the emergence of clearly stated rules of authority and subjection for husbands and wives in the *Haustafeln* of Colossians and Ephesians, letters which represent a more developed Pauline tradition;[367] and a third is the close similarities with the attitude expressed in 1 Timothy and in other documents dated some time after Paul's death.[368] However, the presence of the verses in all known manuscripts requires that the interpolation be an early one[369] (though the Codex Fuldensis evidence at least points to a textual tradition that omitted these verses).

In short, the hypothesis that 1 Cor 14.34f was added in the margin at a time very early in the textual history of 1 Corinthians, but some years after Paul wrote the letter, offers the most plausible explanation of all the available evidence. The textual evidence opens the possibility that a marginal note was added (and *requires* adequate explanation from those who argue for the authenticity of these verses to 1 Corinthians). The literary evidence strengthens the argument that the verses are intrusive and incongruous, though superficially appropriate in their present context.

---

[366] Ellis 1981, 214–16. Tomson 1990, 137–39, sees Paul as emphasising the silence of women in accordance with Jewish traditions.

[367] Col 3.18–4.1; Eph 5.22–6.9. Of course, the pseudonymity of Colossians and Ephesians is widely disputed, but one should at least be wary of making deductions about Paul's teaching on the basis of elements which appear only in these (and later) epistles.

[368] 1 Peter 3.1ff; 1 Clem 1.3; 21.6f; see further §6.4. below.

[369] Fitzer 1963, 39, suggests the first half of the second century. Klauck 1984, 105–106, suggests that the interpolation (of 33b–36!) was added 'bei der Zusammenarbeitung der korinthischen Korrespondenz zu den beiden kanonischen Korintherbriefen um 100 n. Chr'.

Their conflict with Paul's statements elsewhere in 1 Corinthians (7.4; 11.5, 11f) and with his descriptions of female co-workers (Rom 16.1, 3, 7) must also cast doubt upon their authenticity. Finally, the wider historical evidence suggests that these verses are most probably post-Pauline, reflecting an ethos similar to that found in the Pastoral Epistles, 1 Peter and 1 Clement. Given the weight of evidence it should be assumed that Paul did not write 1 Corinthians 14.34f.[370]

4.4. Conclusion

The aim of this chapter has been to explore and assess the ways in which Paul in 1 Corinthians draws upon the symbols, rules and resources of the Christian symbolic order to formulate his response to a specific context (insofar as he knows about it); and, in particular, to assess the social ethos of his teaching and its (potential) impact upon different social groups.

Throughout much of the letter, when Paul is addressing situations where some social conflict is evident, his instruction is notably radical, criticising and making strenuous demands upon the socially strong. It certainly cannot be claimed that Paul's teaching is an ideological legitimation of these people's position or social interests. Indeed, Paul confronts the situation of conflict and division at Corinth by presenting Christian symbolic resources in such a way as to invert the values and status-hierarchy of the dominant social order. It is, he asserts, specifically the weak, foolish, 'nobodies' who have been chosen by God (1.26–28) and to whom God has given the greatest honour in the body (12.22–25). Moreover, where he is critical of the behaviour of the socially prominent members of the community (6.1–8; 8.1–11.1; 11.17–34) it would not be true to suggest that his instruction has no impact upon normal social interaction, outside the ἐκκλησία. Paul instructs the socially 'strong' members of the community to abandon their use of the secular courts and to withdraw from social and religious gatherings in the city (under certain conditions). His criticism and exhortation, if heeded, would

---

[370] I do not think, however, that the hermeneutical problems can be shortcircuited as easily as Fee thinks, by the conclusion that the passage is an interpolation. 'If so', Fee states, 'then it is certainly not binding for Christians' (1987, 708). It is surely canonicity, rather than authorship, which gives scripture authority. Cf. on this passage, Hauke 1988, 368.

imply real changes in the social life of these members of the congregation. Even where his instruction does seem to reflect a willingness to leave untouched the social conditions which pertain outside the ἐκκλησία (11.34), it should not be thought that Paul's teaching applies only to a 'spiritual' realm 'in the sight of God'. For the ἐκκλησία is a social gathering, in which real social interaction takes place; it is the 'place' where the radical consequences of being 'one in Christ' are already to be lived.[371] The belief that all are one in Christ and that social distinctions have thus been transcended is to be embodied in the concrete act of the communal meal.

It must also be noted that nowhere in 1 Corinthians (excluding 14.34f) is there any explicit demand for the subordination of weaker social groups. There are two places where Paul's teaching certainly has the potential to be taken as requiring or legitimating a subordinate position for the socially weak – 1 Cor 7.17, 20, 24 and 11.3–9 – yet in both of these places it is notable that Paul explicitly opposes such an interpretation. In 1 Cor 7.21b he states a clear exception to the general advice that a change in status is unnecessary, encouraging slaves to take their freedom if they can. Being slaves to other people is by no means desirable (7.23). In 11.10–12 Paul specifically 'corrects' a subordinationist view of woman's place, highlighting the fact that his concern in the previous verses has been with appropriate attire and not with authority and submission.

Paul's criticism of the socially strong, coupled with the absence of any explicit demand for the subordination of weaker social groups, should surely lead us to question the appropriateness of the term love-patriarchalism as a summary of the social ethos of Paul's teaching in 1 Corinthians. It is not entirely inaccurate but does not convey the character of Paul's instruction. Certainly he does to a degree take 'social differences for granted' yet his instruction does have a significant impact on the social interaction of the socially strong; it does not leave untouched the sphere of secular relationships and institutions. Certainly Paul does accept the continued existence of owner-slave relations, and presents a theologically-legitimated hierarchy in which women have a secondary place; but he does not require from the weak 'subordination, fidelity and esteem'.

---

[371] Cf. Schottroff 1985, 255–56.

How then might we describe the social ethos of 1 Corinthians? Paul's multifaceted exhortation in 1 Corinthians is shaped and formed by the various situations and issues to which it responds and it is therefore difficult, and perhaps inappropriate, to suggest that a label could be applied to the whole. Nevertheless, the following observations may be made. Paul's focus is certainly upon life and relationships ἐν ἐκκλησία; even where his instruction will have an impact upon wider social interaction it arises from a concern about relationships between believers. (So in 1 Cor 6.1–11 it is lawsuits among believers which are prohibited and in 8.1–11.1 it is the concern of weaker brothers or sisters which is decisive.) Paul shows little if any concern about transforming 'the world', undoubtedly because this world and its rulers are being done away with. It is in Christ – a communal as well as 'spiritual' location – that the symbolic order of the gospel is to be embodied. Basic to the Christian symbolic order for Paul (and at least some of his predecessors) seems to be the idea of many people being made one in Christ. This is expressed in the two major Christian rituals: baptism and Lord's Supper. This fundamental perception about the nature of the Christian community leads Paul to attack division and disunity.[372] In 1 Corinthians he particularly attacks the socially prominent members of the community, requiring that their behaviour change, and demonstrating that God's way of achieving unity is to elect and honour the lowly and to call the strong to social self-lowering (see further chapter 5). Paul is nevertheless concerned with order in the church's life and worship. While it is true, I believe, that in 1 Corinthians Paul does not legitimate the dominant *social* order – on the contrary, he undermines and inverts it – he does legitimate an ecclesiastical hierarchy in which he is at the top (at least in relation to the Corinthians). He outlines a hierarchy of leading functions (12.28–30), calls for submission to particular leaders (16.16), and presents himself as the Corinthians' only father – a position from which he is able (and willing) to threaten them with punishment (4.14–21).[373]

The theoretical framework adopted in this study, derived from Giddens' structuration theory, views 1 Corinthians as a part of a process; a process in which the rules and resources of the Christian symbolic

---

[372] See esp. Mitchell 1991, who analyses 1 Cor as a piece of deliberative rhetoric the aim of which is to create unity and social concord. There are similarities here with the rhetorical aim of 1 Clement, which will be taken up below.
[373] Cf. Lassen 1991.

order are reproduced and transformed in relation to a particular context and have an impact within that context. This process structures, or shapes, the life of a particular community. The rules and resources, moreover, will be taken up again, like a language continually spoken and used, and will continue to shape the social embodiment of the symbolic order. From this perspective our response to the question of love-patriarchalism must be somewhat ambivalent. I have argued that it is inappropriate to characterise Paul's instruction in this way, yet it is clear that 1 Corinthians offers resources which can be taken up and developed in that direction. Indeed the various rules and resources which comprise the Christian symbolic order can and must be reproduced and transformed in a variety of directions, all of which retain some degree of continuity with the formulations which precede them. The symbolic order has no 'externalised' existence such that it could merely be preserved or protected; rather it must be continually reproduced in and through the actions of the human subjects who inhabit it.[374] This framework will provide the basis for a study of 1 Clement in chapter 6. Before that, however, I aim to gain some sense of how Paul's interaction with the Corinthian community continues. The next chapter considers the conflict which develops at Corinth, and Paul and the Corinthians' response to it. In part this will allow us to consider the impact of 1 Corinthians, the Corinthians' reactions to the letter and to Paul's self-presentation within it. This further investigation will add support to the hypothesis developed in this chapter, namely that 1 Corinthians represents, in many places, a stark attack on the status and position of the socially prominent members of the community and on the values of the dominant social order.

---

[374] Cf. the criticisms of Berger and Luckmann in §2.3. above.

5

Conflict at Corinth and apostolic lifestyle

5.1. Introduction

While much of 1 Corinthians contains reasoned argument in response
to Corinthian questions (7.1ff etc.), the letter also reveals significant
areas of conflict between Paul and some of the believers at Corinth. A
number of these have already been explored in the previous two chapters, such as the celebration of the Lord's Supper (11.17–34), or the
cases of litigation (6.1–8), where Paul deliberately writes to bring shame
on those who instigate such proceedings (6.5). Even Paul's stern judgment of the man who 'has his father's wife' (5.1) is not only a judgment
of this individual sinner, but also a criticism of the community which
tolerates such sin, yet is proud and boastful (5.1–13). Indeed, those who
are 'puffed up' are threatened with harsh treatment when Paul visits them
again (4.18–21).

In the previous chapter the social ethos of Paul's instruction was
investigated, as it is embodied in his responses to the particular situation
at Corinth. I argued that his instruction often contained harsh criticism
of the socially prominent members of the community and made significant demands upon them. The focus of this chapter is upon the conflict
which develops because of the ways in which Paul presents and practises
his apostleship. Two main areas of interest emerge in 1 Corinthians, and
play a significant part in the intensified conflict evidenced by 2 Cor
10–13. They concern the 'image' of the apostle – one of suffering and
weakness – and his lifestyle, particularly his manual work and rejection
of financial support. I shall argue that these issues, though they focus
much more upon Paul as an individual, are intimately related to the
wider analysis of the social ethos of his teaching. His self-portrayal and
self-understanding as apostle, I suggest, are a further reflection of the
ethos and conduct which he urges upon the Corinthian community;
and the conflict over his apostolic conduct is in part a reflection of the

wider social conflict between him and the socially prominent members of the Corinthian congregation. Paul's understanding and practice of his apostleship, I argue, in congruity with his more general instruction, demonstrate a conscious rejection of the values of the dominant social order and a degree of self-lowering and siding with the weak.[1] The opportunity to trace the conflict on through Paul's Corinthian correspondence, in the letters contained in 2 Corinthians, will enable us to see how the process of interaction continues between Paul and the Corinthian community, how Paul continues to reproduce and embody the symbolic order of Christianity, the way in which he therefore seeks to structure community life and to shape its ethos, and, I believe, to add further plausibility to the hypothesis developed in the preceding chapters.

5.2. The image of the apostles: 1 Cor 4.8–13

These verses contain one of a number of 'tribulation lists', or *peristasis* catalogues,[2] which are found not only in Paul's letters but in a wide variety of ancient literature.[3] In this particular passage, Paul is not simply listing hardships, as he does for example in 2 Cor 11.23–29, but drawing a sharp and ironic *contrast* between the Corinthians and the apostles.[4] The Corinthians are described in v. 8 as full, rich, and living like kings, whereas the apostles are displayed like people condemned to

---

[1] It will become clear that it is not my intention to explore in depth the possible parallels between Paul's self-understanding and lifestyle and that of other first-century preachers and philosophers, such as the Cynics. The fact that there are significant parallels, as has been demonstrated in much recent work, does not of course negate the thesis that Paul in some ways opposes the values and hierarchy of the dominant social order; it merely shows that he was not unique in this, nor unique in the manner in which he did this. See Malherbe 1989; Hock 1980; Betz 1972; also (though not focusing on Paul) Downing 1987, 51–125; 1992.

[2] On the term περίστασις in this context, see Fitzgerald 1988, 33–46.

[3] Hodgson 1983, 63, lists eight such lists in Paul's letters; Rom 8.35; 1 Cor 4.10–13a; 2 Cor 4.8–9; 6.4b–5; 6.8–10; 11.23b–29; 12.10; Phil 4.12. Hodgson also surveys a wide range of comparable ancient literature. On Paul's 'lists' and their ancient parallels see the recent book-length treatments by Fitzgerald 1988 and Ebner 1991.

[4] See esp. Fitzgerald 1988, 132–48. Hodgson 1983, 66–67, divides Paul's lists into 'simple' and 'antithetical' types. Ebner 1991, 391–92, prefers to classify taking function also into account.

die (v. 9).[5] The antitheses are stated starkly in v. 10, where the μωροί (foolish), ἀσθενεῖς (weak), ἄτιμοι (dishonourable) apostles are contrasted with the φρόνιμοι (wise), ἰσχυροί (strong), ἔνδοξοι (honourable) Corinthians.[6] Verses 11–13 mention only the apostles, cataloguing their deprivation and humiliation.

In the context of the whole section 1.10–4.21, these verses should be related to the themes explored above (see §3.8.4.; §4.2.1.). Paul is attacking the divisions within the community and specifically the social pride upon which they are based. The last thing he wants is for himself and Apollos to be exalted as the heads of competing factions (cf. 4.6).[7] He is also concerned to attack the worldly values which underpin such divisions and to overturn the conventional value given to wisdom and status. If the thesis is right that the powerful members of the Corinthian congregation were particularly involved as leading patrons of various factions, then it may be that these people are particularly in view here, as I have already suggested.[8] This is not to deny the 'spiritual' and metaphorical dimensions of 4.8–13, suggested not least by 'the spiritualizing phrase "in Christ"' in v. 10,[9] but neither should the text necessarily be entirely spiritualised and viewed only as a response to an over-realised eschatology.[10] Pace Fee, the irony of the text is not lost if it has sociological as well as spiritual implications,[11] for the Corinthians who place such importance on worldly status are being shown that their leaders, rather than mirroring these values, embody the complete opposite: 'What you powerful Corinthians see as success and prestige is hardly of any value at all – certainly it's the opposite of what your leaders are!' Indeed it seems here that Paul again subverts the ground upon which the prominent Corinthians have based their pride and status.

However, our main concern here is with Paul's presentation of his own experience as an apostle. Listing hardships experienced is not in itself unusual as a demonstration of worthiness for leadership, wisdom,

---

[5] On the nuances of the words used in v. 9 see Fee 1987, 174–75; Schrage 1991, 340–42.

[6] Cf. above p. 136.

[7] The 'covert' allusions Paul has made leading up to 4.6 are made explicit at this point; see further Fitzgerald 1988, 119–28; Fiore 1985.

[8] See above, p. 136.

[9] Fitzgerald 1988, 138 n. 68, opposing Theissen 1982, 72–73.

[10] On which see Thiselton 1978 and Fee 1987, 172–73; further §3.9. above.

[11] Fee 1987, 176 n. 57, also opposing Theissen 1982, 72–73. On the irony employed in this text see further Plank 1987.

or integrity,[12] but in contrast to the Corinthians' pride in their status and success, Paul describes his humiliation and degradation in such a way as to destroy any conception of him as a figure of social importance and prestige. From a worldly point of view, he is by no means a person to boast about (cf. 1 Cor 3.3ff). Indeed, his list of degrading experiences reaches a climax as it descends to the depths in the phrases with which v. 13 ends; ὡς περικαθάρματα τοῦ κόσμου ἐγενήθημεν, πάντων περίψημα ἕως ἄρτι.[13] Paul describes himself and the apostles as 'the scum of the earth', 'the muck scraped off'.[14] This is an extraordinary self-description. Paul's presentation of the position of the apostles is quite the opposite of what the socially prominent members of the Corinthian congregation would wish to hear: their leaders are right at the bottom of the social heap, nowhere near the top! The apostles will not fit into the role of exalted leader or appropriate head of any particular faction. Those who place great store on worldly status will find little value in their apostles. The apostles, rather, are like the despised nobodies, τὰ ἐξουθενημένα, τὰ μὴ ὄντα (1.28), whom God has chosen to shame and destroy the world's hierarchies.[15]

The 'self-lowering'[16] which Paul here describes is confirmed at another specific point in 4.8–13. After a conventional list of hardships (v. 11), Paul adds a further, less predictable item; κοπιῶμεν ἐργαζόμενοι ταῖς ἰδίαις χερσίν ('we labour, working with our own hands' – v.

---

[12] See further Fitzgerald 1988; e.g. Plutarch *Moralia* 326D–327E (about Alexander); Pliny *Natural History* 7.45.147–150 (about Augustus – contrast *Res Gestae*); cf. also Epictetus *Diss.* 2.19.24; *Testament of Joseph* 1.3–7; Ebner 1991, 161–72 (on the Heracles tradition).

[13] Cf. Lam 3.45, a parallel explored by Hanson 1982a. Fee 1987, 181 comments: 'Not a pretty picture, but with powerful imagery this catalogue carries the theme of the folly of God as wiser than merely human wisdom to a fitting conclusion.'

[14] Περικάθαρμα may also convey the idea of expiation; Hauck TDNT 3, 431: 'Three different strands meet in κάθαρμα, namely, the expiatory offering, that which is contemptible, and that which is to be thrown out. All three senses are apposite in 1 Cor 4:13.' On the translation of περικάθαρμα and περίψημα, see BAGD, 647, 653; Hauck TDNT 3, 430–31; Stählin TDNT 6, 90–91; Fee 1987, 180; Spicq TLNT 3, 93–95.

[15] This link is also suggested by Paul's description of his weakness in 1 Cor 2.1–5, which immediately follows 1.26–31. 'The juxtaposition of "scum" and "nobodies" in Dem., *Or.* 21.185 suggests ... that περικαθάρματα τοῦ κόσμου ... περίψημα is functionally equivalent to τὰ ἀγενῆ τοῦ κόσμου καὶ τὰ ἐξουθενημένα (1 Cor 1:28)' (Fitzgerald 1988, 142 n. 86; see further parallels cited there). The citation from Demosthenes' *Orations* refers to τοὺς μὲν πτωχούς, τοὺς δὲ καθάρματα, τοὺς δ' οὐδὲν ὑπολαμβάνων εἶναι. Priam's fifty offspring are described as περικαθάρματα in Epictetus *Diss.* 3.22.78.

[16] Cf. Martin 1990, 122–23; Judge 1972, 36; 1980, 214; 1984, 14.

12).[17] This is the only place where Paul specifically mentions 'that his work is actually *manual* labour' (*Hand*-arbeit), and in association with the verb κοπιῶμεν – 'we labour' – this may serve to stress that '*hard* physical work*' is in mind.[18] The fact that Paul views manual labour as degrading and humbling perhaps suggests that his view of it was essentially upper-class.[19] This may say something about Paul's own social level and about his 'stepping firmly down in the world',[20] but its mention here is of wider significance. Paul's self-presentation here and elsewhere in the Corinthian correspondence does not only reveal his personal views or experiences, but relates decisively to the conflict which develops between himself and some of the Corinthian congregation and to the pattern of Christian living to which he calls them. Paul's insistence on supporting himself in part through his own labour not only portrays him as someone of lower social status (and thus as a less worthy leader, to some) but also becomes a particular cause of conflict between him and some of the Corinthians. For his manual work is a part of a conscious decision to reject financial support from certain members of the Corinthian congregation. In what follows I will develop the argument, suggested already by others, that this rejection was a conscious decision to avoid becoming dependent upon particular wealthy patrons at Corinth and a means of identifying and siding with the weak.[21]

In 1 Cor 4.8–13, then, as in much of chapters 1–4, Paul deliberately opposes those who make much of their worldly position and who would like the apostles also to conform to such values. The word of the cross, on the contrary, has turned the world upside down; an eschatological act of God mirrored both in the calling of the converts (1.26–31) and now in the experience of the apostles (4.8–13; cf. 2.1–5). The insistence of Paul and his co-workers on working with their own hands is a particular and visible expression of their low social position, and one which indeed offends some of the Corinthian converts (see below). In other words, the social ethos which emerges from Paul's re-presentation of the Christian

[17] Fee 1987, 179: 'The sixth item, "we work with our own hands," seems out of place since it does not fit the same category of "hardship" as the others.'
[18] Ebner 1991, 69: 'daß es sich bei seiner Arbeit tatsächlich um eine *Hand*-arbeit handelt … *schwere* körperliche Arbeit.' Cf. Acts 18.3; 20.34; 1 Cor 9.6; 2 Cor 11.7–12; 12.13–18; 1 Thess 2.9; 2 Thess 3.8.
[19] Cf. Martin 1990, 123; Hock 1978, 558–64; MacMullen 1974, 114–20; Savage 1986, 102.
[20] Judge 1980, 214; see further Hock 1978; Malherbe 1987, 55–56.
[21] Of particular importance is the work of Hock 1980; Marshall 1987; Martin 1990; see also Chow 1992, 172, 188–89.

symbolic order also emerges from his self-presentation: the two are congruent with one another, and the latter is a specific embodiment and expression of the former. Paul presents the Christian symbolic order to the Corinthian congregation, in order to shape their social embodiment of it, both in his broad theological reflections (1 Cor 1.18ff) and in his own life.

It is important to note that the contrasts Paul draws in 4.8–13 are *not* meant only to portray the apostolic office in a particular way. On the contrary, their purpose is admonition, not shame (4.14);[22] Paul wants the Corinthians, or at least those who consider themselves to be living in kingly luxury, *to imitate him* (4.16). 1 Cor 4.8–13, then, like the further conflict in 2 Cor 10–13, does not reflect a merely personal battle concerning Paul's popularity or acceptability among the Corinthians, even though the conflict does indeed become focused upon him and his apostolic standing. It is more than this; it is a particular focus for the conflict over the social ethos which Paul presents to the Corinthians through his teaching and his practice. His challenge to the Corinthian strong, I suggest, is sociologically significant and reveals an ethos which challenges the strong to become like the weak and to accept a lowering of their own positions.[23] It is not irrelevant to note that the harsh warning of 4.18–21 follows almost immediately this call to imitation.[24] These themes emerge more clearly still in 1 Cor 9.

5.3. Apostolic lifestyle: 1 Cor 9.1–23

Even when 1 Cor 8–10 is accepted as a unity,[25] there is nevertheless debate concerning the purpose of chapter 9 within this larger section. Some see the passage as primarily an *example*: Paul establishes his rights (ἐξουσία) as an apostle in order to emphasise the fact that he has given them up, so as not to place any hindrance (ἐγκοπή) in the way of the gospel.[26] Others regard it as primarily a *defence*: Paul has been criticised,

---

[22] On the admonitory purpose of 1 Cor 1–4 see Fitzgerald 1988, 117–28.
[23] *Contra* Wengst 1988, 47. See further Martin 1990, 136–49.
[24] The theme of 'imitation' is explored by Castelli 1991, who is critical of Paul's use of power in this connection.
[25] See above p. 142 with nn. 85–88.
[26] E.g. Willis 1985b, 35: 'Paul has established his rights so strongly so that *he can make something* of his renunciation of them.' Mitchell 1991, 243–50; Gardner 1994, 67–69.

perhaps for his inconsistent conduct with regard to idol-meat, and certainly for his failure to accept material support from the Corinthians.[27]

The text demands, I believe, that both these dimensions of Paul's argument in chapter 9 be taken seriously.[28] Against Fee,[29] there is little direct evidence that Paul's conduct in connection with idol-meat had been inconsistent or criticised and there surely is evidence that Paul does appeal to the Corinthians to follow his example: apart from the strong verbal and thematic links between chapters 8, 9 and 10,[30] the first person singular forms of 8.13 provide a clear link with the personal example which follows,[31] and 9.24 turns again to exhortation. Moreover, if 8.1– 11.1 are a unity, then Paul's summarising advice is μιμηταί μου γίνεσθε καθὼς κἀγὼ Χριστοῦ ('be imitators of me, just as I am of Christ'; 11.1).[32] Where else in chapters 8–10 has Paul given them a personal example to follow?

However, against Willis, the 'vigor of the rhetoric'[33] in 9.1–14 seems to suggest that this is real defence against real criticism, and not merely the setting up of a personal example.[34] This seems especially clear from verse 3, which refers to ἡ ἐμὴ ἀπολογία τοῖς ἐμὲ ἀνακρίνουσιν – 'my defence to those who judge me'.[35] Margaret Mitchell argues against any element of defensiveness being present here, suggesting that 'Paul calls it "defense" to justify rhetorically his use of himself as the example for imitation'.[36] She cannot see any formal charge being presented and

---

[27] E.g. Fee 1987, 390 n. 71, 392–94, 402; Hurd 1965, 126–31.

[28] Cf. Hock 1980, 60–61; Dungan 1971, 5–6; Martin 1990, 80: 'Chapter 9, therefore, is both a defense and an example.' However, Martin suggests that the defence may at this time be merely hypothetical (77–80, 83).

[29] Fee 1987, 393.

[30] On which see Willis 1985b, 39–40.

[31] Cf. Willis 1985b, 34.

[32] Cf. Dautzenberg 1969, 225. On the recapitulatory nature of 10.31–11.1 see Fisk 1989, 68; Richardson 1980, 355–56.

[33] Fee 1987, 393.

[34] Cf. Barrett 1971a, 200; Hurd 1965, 126–27. Dungan 1971, 13–14, speaks of 'defensiveness', but stresses Paul's 'pedagogical' thrust here. Gardner 1994, 70, who regards the passage only as an example, states that 'Paul adamantly affirmed his freedom'.

[35] Willis 1985b, 34, suggests that the present participle ἀνακρίνουσιν 'could legitimately be understood as future' and thus proposes that 'Paul is anticipating criticism rather than answering a previous complaint'. Against this see Fee 1987, 401 n. 24. Barrett 1971a, 201–202 takes the participle as conative – 'those who would like to examine me' (cf. RSV). The grammar of the verse should surely make us at least consider the possibility of a genuine degree of defence against criticism here.

[36] Mitchell 1991, 246; see 243–50.

defended here (expecting perhaps too much rhetorical formalism in Paul's writing): 'the only possible charge which one can unearth is an historically implausible one: *that Paul did not take the Corinthians' money!*'[37] Yet there are reasons why the Corinthians should object to Paul's refusal of their money, and specifically to his insistence upon supporting himself through manual labour (see further below). Indeed, his personal example is precisely a challenging and (to some) offensive one. Clearly these matters do become a subject for criticism and defense by the time 2 Cor 10–13 is written. While Mitchell rightly warns against simply reading back the later situation onto the earlier,[38] the fact that the issues raised in 1 Cor 9 become a point of open conflict surely supports the view that there is at least some criticism of Paul on the issue of his manual work and refusal of financial support already evident at the time of writing 1 Corinthians. If 2 Cor 10–13 is to be dated before 2 Cor 1–9 and identified as the painful letter (as I argue in Appendix 1) then the close connections are even more clear.

We must, then, explore both the way in which Paul uses his own conduct as an example, and the nature of the criticism of him.

5.3.1. Paul's conduct as an example to the strong

In the context of chapters 8–10, the example which Paul presents must relate to the issue of idol-meat. The key words 'right' and 'offence'[39] suggest that it is the 'strong' who are being given an example; just as Paul has rights as an apostle but gives them up so as not to put any hindrance in the way of the gospel, so the 'strong' must be prepared to set aside their rights to avoid offending the weak.[40]

Much of the early part of chapter 9 is devoted to establishing and illustrating the 'right' of apostles to material support (vv. 4–14, on which more below). However, Paul does not use this right, so as to avoid hindering the gospel (v. 15). This decision is so important to him that he would rather die than give up the boast that he has used none of these

---

[37] Mitchell 1991, 246, italics original; also 244–45 n. 330.
[38] Mitchell 1991, 244 n. 328, 246 n. 332.
[39] Ἐξουσία ('right' or 'authority'): see 8.9; 9.4–6, 12, 18. Various words related to the idea of offence are used; πρόσκομμα (8.9), ἐγκοπή (9.12), ἀπρόσκοπος (10.32); cf. also the use of κερδαίνω (9.19–23).
[40] Cf. Dungan 1971, 21, 33; Dautzenberg 1969, 219.

rights.[41] But the *reason* given for this relinquishment of rights in vv. 16–18 is surprising. Paul has no choice about preaching the gospel; it is an ἀνάγκη, a necessity, laid upon him (v. 16).[42] If his labour were voluntary (ἑκών) he would be worthy of μισθός – pay, wage, fee or reward[43] – but it is not.[44] Paul has no choice in the matter, 'he is not a free agent', he acts ἄκων, 'unwillingly' or, perhaps, 'under complusion', as someone entrusted with an οἰκονομία (a stewardship; v. 17).[45] He asserts his freedom (v. 1) only to show that he has enslaved himself to all (v. 19).[46] This is a surprising argument in two ways. First, because 'Paul's argument that he preaches under compulsion and unwillingly would never have been made by first century moral philosophers', for whom freedom was an inner quality of those who were truly wise.[47] Second, because Paul's portrayal of himself as a servant acting under compulsion presents him not as a wise, free leader, but as a slave, even though his master is one of supreme power and status.[48] Thus, once more, Paul's self-description is potentially offensive at least to those who place great value on worldly wisdom, power and noble birth.[49] Although he has emphasised his freedom (9.1) and his rights (9.4ff), Paul explains his giving up of

---

[41] The Greek is broken off and does not complete the sentence 'I would rather die than …' but follows with the assertion that 'no one shall nullify my boast' (Fee 1987, 415). The train of thought is nevertheless clear. The textual variants are 'all attempts to clear up the grammar caused by Paul's breaking off his sentence'; Fee 1987, 414 n. 1; see further Metzger 1971, 558–59; Barrett 1971a, 208–209. Its hyperbole is not dissimilar to that of 8.13 (cf. Rom 9.1–3).

[42] Cf. Käsemann's memorable phrase: 'One can demand no reward from *ananke*, one can only bow to it or rebel against it.' (1969, 231; see further 228–33.)

[43] On the translation of μισθός see Martin 1990, 74–76; Fee 1987, 419 with n. 34; BAGD, 523; Spicq TLNT 2, 502–15.

[44] *Contra* Hock 1980, 100 n. 113, and others who suggest that 9.17a is the actual and 17b the hypothetical situation of Paul. Against this interpretation see Fee 1987, 419–20 with n. 35; Martin 1990, 71; Conzelmann 1975, 158; Käsemann 1969, 228–33.

[45] Käsemann 1969, 233; on the slave terminology here see Martin 1990, 74–77. Fee 1987, 419 n. 33 also believes that the terms ἑκών/ἄκων, linked with the reference to οἰκονομία, are intended to draw a contrast between 'free' and 'slave'.

[46] Thus 1 Cor 9 is not a defence of Paul's *freedom, contra* Hock 1980, 61.

[47] Martin 1990, 72; see 71–77. Cf. Epictetus *Diss.* 3.22.48. The Cynic-Stoic tradition generally taught that freedom lay in indifference to external conditions and relationships; see further Fitzgerald 1988, 59–65; Epictetus *Diss.* 2.19.24; 4.1.1–23, 128–31.

[48] See Martin 1990, 50–135, esp. 73–85. Martin argues that although being a slave made one contemptible in the eyes of the upper classes, to others a lot depended on whose slave one was and what position one held. Thus Paul's self-portrayal as a slave of Christ is one which gives him a certain power and status because of whose slave he is.

[49] On the different ways in which Paul's language may have been heard, depending on one's social position, see Martin 1990, 76.

these 'privileges' on the grounds that he is merely a slave. As an example to the Corinthian strong, this must have been deeply disturbing. Far from suggesting that the weak should be subordinate to the strong, the implication is that the strong should become as slaves, in order to gain the weak. The self-lowering of the apostle is a radical model for the strong at Corinth. However shocking, it is indeed such a suggestion which emerges more clearly still in 9.19–23. Although a new section seems to begin here, and a further step in the argument is taken, this section 'stands in close connection with what precedes. The introductory γάρ must be taken seriously; 9.19 seeks to give the reasons for v. 18 and to take it further.'⁵⁰ Indeed, to some extent the ἐλεύθερος γὰρ ὤν ... ('for being free ... '; v. 19) reaches back to the opening question οὐκ εἰμὶ ἐλεύθερος; ('Am I not free?' 9.1).⁵¹

Paul here makes explicit that, though 'free from all', he has not only become a servant of Christ, but also has enslaved himself to all (πᾶσιν ἐμαυτὸν ἐδούλωσα; v. 19).⁵² In the list which follows, in which Paul outlines his 'missionary stance', a certain climax is reached in the phrase ἐγενόμην τοῖς ἀσθενέσιν ἀσθενής, ἵνα τοὺς ἀσθενεῖς κερδήσω ('to the weak I became weak, in order that I might win the weak'; v. 22), the phrase which relates 'to the concrete problem of chaps. 8–10'.⁵³ This is the only phrase in the series without ὡς,⁵⁴ a word which elsewhere qualifies his becoming as becoming 'like' rather than actually being so. Indeed, in the references to those 'under the law' and those 'without the law', Paul explicitly declares that he is actually neither ὑπὸ νόμον nor

---

⁵⁰ Dautzenberg 1969, 228: ' ...steht in einem inneren Zusammenhang mit dem Vorherigen. Das einleitende γάρ muss ernst genommen werden; 9,19 will 18 begründen und weiterführen.'

⁵¹ Fee 1987, 425. Gardner 1994, 68: 'The first two questions of v. 1 are pursued in the rest of the chapter.'

⁵² See further Martin 1990, 117–35.

⁵³ Bornkamm 1966, 195; on Paul's missionary stance see 194–98. On the possible Jewish roots of Paul's missionary practice both of accommodation and of humility see Daube 1956, 336–50. For an interesting consideration of the apparent inconsistency of Paul's attitudes, comparing esp. 1 Cor 9.19–23 with Gal 2.11–14, see Richardson 1980. Chadwick 1955 also explores Paul's flexibility facing different situations.

⁵⁴ Noted by Fee 1987, 422 n. 5, 431; Conzelmann 1975, 161 n. 28; Gardner 1994, 103. Barrett 1971a, 215, thinks that the significance of this 'must not be pressed'. ὡς was added by a number of scribes and appears in א²;C;D;F;G;Ψ and became the Majority Text reading (see NA²⁷). But the insertion is more easily explained than an omission, and early witnesses like P⁴⁶ do not have ὡς (see NA²⁷).

ἄνομος (v. 20f). This leaves as unexpanded phrases the first and the last, referring to 'the Jews' and 'the weak'. That a Jew should write ἐγενόμην τοῖς Ἰουδαίοις ὡς Ἰουδαῖος ('to the Jews I became as a Jew') is at least surprising, as is shown by the texts which dropped the ὡς, presumably finding it an inappropriate way for Paul to express himself.[55] Thus we should realise the force of Paul's statement that ἐγενόμην τοῖς ἀσθενέσιν ἀσθενής.[56] The weak are the one group with which he fully identifies himself, even though the overall summary refers to becoming 'all things to all people' (v. 22).[57] There is no mention of the 'strong', the 'wise' or those with 'knowledge', probably because these are the people whom Paul is addressing and challenging to change their behaviour. 'Paul's main goal in 1 Corinthians 9 is to persuade the strong to modify their behaviour to avoid offending the weak.'[58] The social nature of the division between 'strong' and 'weak' proposed by Theissen thus offers a plausible background against which to read the apparently social concern of chapter 9. Paul's example is of one who has deliberately given up status and freedom, becoming a slave of all and becoming weak (cf. 2 Cor 11.7). Again, as in 1 Cor 4.8ff, the apostle's self-description is in conscious opposition to the values of the dominant symbolic order and expresses a degree of social lowering. One might expect that the strong and prominent members of the Corinthian congregation would indeed be highly reluctant to become imitators of the apostle who is the scum of the earth (4.13) and the slave of all (9.19), as they are instructed to in 4.16 and 11.1.[59] The (only) two clear calls to imitation in 1 Corinthians follow these two passages, each of which is directed particularly to the socially strong in the community and in which Paul speaks of his own social self-lowering and renunciation of privileges. In 4.8ff it is those who consider themselves to be 'full, rich and living like kings' who are challenged to be imitators of the apostle and his co-workers; in 8.1–11.1 it is the strong who are urged to set aside their rights in order to become like the weak, as Paul himself seeks to do.

---

55 The inclusion of ὡς is well attested (it is omitted only in (F);G*; 6*; 326; 1739 and a few others; see NA²⁷) and is clearly to be accepted as original; in addition to the stronger textual base, the omission is more easily explained than the insertion.
56 Martin 1990, 118–19: 'Paul ... makes his submission to the weak the rhetorical goal of the list.'
57 Cf. Gardner 1994, 104.
58 Martin 1990, 123.
59 Cf. also Gal 4.12; Phil 3.17; 4.9; 1 Thess 1.6; 2 Thess 3.7.

Through his presentation of himself and his practice as apostle, then, Paul continues to urge a particular pattern of behaviour and relationships upon the Corinthian community.

5.3.2. Criticism of Paul: the issue of support

But why does so much of 1 Cor 9 focus on the issue of material support, and why does Paul reject this support? Questions about the genuineness of Paul's apostleship seem to lie somewhere beneath the criticism to which Paul here responds (esp. v. 1f).[60] Thus Paul strenuously maintains that he and Barnabas have the same rights to support as the other apostles (vv. 4–6), rights which are illustrated with a wide range of images, from military, agricultural, Jewish and cultic contexts (vv. 7–13), and legitimated by a command of the Lord (v. 14).[61] The point of establishing these rights so emphatically may be twofold: firstly to show that Paul and Barnabas are by no means lesser apostles (cf. 2 Cor 11.11) – they possess the same ἐξουσία – and secondly to stress that they have indeed given up these rights, refusing to use them.[62] Certainly the point is not to encourage the community now to offer him support in view of these rights; this potential misunderstanding is explicitly opposed in verse 15.[63] Paul insists on supporting himself through his own labour, counting this as a hardship which is part of his apostolic experience (1 Cor 4.12).

Paul's rejection of material support is often taken as a sign of his desire to avoid being accused of preaching for personal gain and to offer the gospel freely.[64] 'He did not want anyone to think they had to pay to hear the "gospel". This would have denied the fundamental gospel concept of *grace*.'[65] This, however, is an inadequate explanation, for several reasons.

---

[60] Cf. Barrett 1971a, 200: 'Paul would hardly have spent so long on the question of apostolic rights if his own apostolic status had not been questioned in Corinth.'; Dungan 1971, 6–7; Dahl 1967, 321–29; Fee 1987, 399–400.

[61] On the use and development of this dominical saying see Dungan 1971, esp. 3–40; Harvey 1982. Cf. also Gal 6.6.

[62] So Willis 1985b, 35–36. It is of course profoundly interesting that Paul is prepared to turn a command of the Lord into a right which can be set aside; see further Dungan 1971, 20–40; Theissen 1982, 43–44.

[63] Cf. Dautzenberg 1969, 214. *Contra* Daube 1956, 395–96, who suggests that Paul is seeking to introduce and establish the right to support at Corinth (v. 12 also disproves this theory); against Daube see Dungan 1971, 5, 11, 13.

[64] Cf. Barrett 1971a, 207; Dautzenberg 1969, 218–32; Käsemann 1969, 233–34; Holmberg 1978, 92; Gardner 1994, 84.

[65] Gardner 1994, 84.

First, because Paul did accept material support from some churches at some times (see below). Second, because it is not clear why accepting support from churches, especially after they were well established, should be incompatible with the gospel of grace. Moreover, the Lord was known to have instructed his apostles 'to live from the gospel' (1 Cor 9.14): being utterly dependent upon the grace of God, expressed through the generosity of others, could equally express gospel theology. Indeed,

2 Corinthians ... reveals that at least some people at Corinth were offended not by a preacher accepting money but by Paul's refusal of their money ... If Paul took on manual labor in order not to offend these people, he blundered badly; they were offended by the very actions Paul undertook to avoid causing offense.[66]

Even in 1 Cor 9, Paul's defence surely suggests that this lifestyle *is* the subject of criticism. Why do he and Barnabas not live from the material support offered by the church? Are they not real apostles? Are they disobedient to the Lord's command?[67] Indeed, this lifestyle plays a significant part in the conflict evidenced by 2 Cor 10–13 (see 11.7–11; 12.13–18) and created a certain amount of enmity between Paul and some of the Corinthians.[68] It *was* an ἐγκοπή, a hindrance, to some. Yet the reason given for this rejection of support is to *avoid* any ἐγκοπή to the gospel.[69] Was this a mistake, an error of judgment?[70]

A number of possible explanations of Paul's behaviour must be rejected because of the direct evidence we have. Paul did not always refuse personal material support from his churches, and so a blanket rejection was clearly not his policy. He seems to have been happy to receive from the Philippian church on more than one occasion (Phil 4.15f)[71] and 'mentions specifically that he received assistance from other churches (presumably Philippa is intended) which was brought to him in Corinth by

---

66 Martin 1990, 120.
67 Cf. Theissen 1982, 44–46. Dungan 1971, 39, notes that Paul does not seem to have been specifically charged with this latter offence, though 1 Cor 9 lays him open to it; however, 2 Cor 11.7 may hint that some regarded his action as 'sinful'; see further Theissen 1982, 45–46.
68 The cause of this enmity is explored particularly by Marshall 1987. Cf. Judge 1984, 15.
69 On ἐγκοπή as a key word in the context of 1 Cor 9 see Dautzenberg 1969, 219.
70 Holmberg 1978, 95, for example, concludes that 'Paul's abstention [sc. from financial support] thus had the opposite effect to what he had intended'. Similarly, Dungan 1971, 36.
71 See further Marshall 1987, 165–66. On the phrase καὶ ἅπαξ καὶ δίς (v. 16) and the translation 'more than once', see Morris 1956; Spicq TLNT 1, 139–40.

brethren from Macedonia (2 Cor 11:8–9)'.[72] Phil 2.25–30 may also imply that Epaphroditus brought material service to Paul from the Philippians.[73] But at Thessalonica Paul insisted on working so as not to be a burden (1 Thess 2.9; cf. 2 Thess 3.7–9).[74]

The problem cannot be solved by suggesting, as Theissen does, that Paul rejected financial support only when engaged in initial evangelism, for he insists that he will *never* burden the Corinthians in such a way (2 Cor 11.9–12; 12.14), not to mention the fact that his initial visit was already some time past when 1 Corinthians was written.[75] Nor is Dungan's proposal plausible – that Paul was concerned not to burden the poorer churches[76] – for he 'accepted support from Macedonia (2 Cor 11:9; Phil 4:14–20), even though by his own testimony they knew "extreme poverty"; yet he rejected support from Corinth, a church that knew abundance (2 Cor 8:13–14)'.[77] Moreover, Paul had no compunction about initiating the collection in as many churches as possible, whether or not they were poor (2 Cor 8.2).[78] Neither would it be true even to imply that Paul rejected all material support from the Corinthians. One may or may not believe from Acts that Paul stayed with Prisc(ill)a[79] and Aquila (Acts 18.2) and Titius Justus (18.7) (though there seems little reason to doubt this), but Paul himself refers to Gaius as ὁ ξένος μου ('my host'; Rom 16.23) and must therefore have enjoyed some hospitality in Corinth (cf. also Phlm 22). A request for personal assistance is surely also implied in 1 Cor 16.6, where Paul outlines his plan to winter in Corinth, ἵνα ὑμεῖς με προπέμψητε οὗ ἐὰν πορεύωμαι – 'so that you

---

[72] Marshall 1987, 167; cf. also Dungan 1971, 29 with n. 3; Windisch 1924, 336.

[73] See Holmberg 1978, 91–92.

[74] There is no hint that this was a controversial practice at Thessalonica; perhaps the varied reactions (comparing Corinth and Thessalonica) were due to the different social composition of the Christian communities (cf. further Barclay 1992 and §3.7. above).

[75] Cf. Marshall 1987, 176. Theissen 1982, 40, suggests that Paul's 'renunciation [of material support at Corinth] arose from concrete conditions in order to make the pioneering mission as effective as possible in this new territory. Where these conditions are absent (as, for example, among congregations already founded) it can be revoked'.

[76] Dungan 1971, 15: 'In short, it seems that everything depended upon the financial strength of each particular congregation.'; cf. also 30–31. Dungan lists other suggestions on 14–15.

[77] Fee 1987, 400 n. 17.

[78] See 1 Cor 16.1–4; 2 Cor 8–9; Rom 15.25–31; also Gal 2.9f; Acts 11.29f. On the collection and its importance for Paul see, for example, Georgi 1965; Nickle 1966; Munck 1959, 282–308; Lüdemann 1984, 80–99; Watson 1986, 174–76; overview in Horrell 1995c, 74–76.

[79] See above p. 99 n. 214.

may send me on my way, wherever I may be going'.[80] The idea that Paul never accepted help when actually with any particular church – the suggestion of Hans Windisch – is disproved by this evidence.[81] Paul also refers to his being refreshed by Stephanas, Fortunatus and Achaicus, when they came to him at Ephesus (1 Cor 16.17f); this may imply material as well as spiritual support.[82]

So we are left with the puzzle that Paul insisted on rejecting a certain level of material support from the Corinthians in order not to place any ἐγκοπή in the way of the gospel. Yet this very decision did prove an ἐγκοπή to some at Corinth, at least in their relationship with Paul. If this was an error of judgment on Paul's part, as Bengt Holmberg suggests,[83] and if he was surprised by the offence which it caused, it is hard to see why he should insist upon continuing in this way, using words probably intended as a strong oath (2 Cor 11.9–12; 12.14).[84] It must be assumed that he considered this decision to be important, at least at Corinth, and that his refusal of support was a way of avoiding a certain ἐγκοπή.

There is, I believe, a twofold explanation which can do justice to the evidence and offer a coherent and satisfying interpretation of Paul's behaviour. One part of this explanation has been proposed by Ronald Hock, Peter Marshall, Dale Martin and John Chow; namely that Paul rejects the support and patronage of certain relatively wealthy members of the Corinthian congregation.[85] Hock suggests that to have accepted the patronage of a particular wealthy person would have cast Paul more closely into the role of *Hausphilosoph*, and would have obligated him

---

[80] Cf. 2 Cor 1.16, where a long journey (to Judaea) is specified; also 1 Cor 16.11, where the Corinthians are urged προπέμψατε δὲ αὐτὸν [sc. Timothy] ἐν εἰρήνῃ. On the term προπέμπω see Holmberg 1978, 89, who suggests that it acquired the content 'to equip somebody for the continuation of a journey'.

[81] Windisch 1924, 336: 'P. hat also mehrfach Unterstützung von auswärts angenommen, nur nicht von der Gemeinde, der er gerade diente.' Similarly Georgi 1987, 240; Martin 1986, 345.

[82] The phrase τὸ ὑμέτερον ὑστέρημα is closely paralleled in Phil 2.30, where material aid may be in view (see pp. 211–12 above). Conzelmann's comment (1975, 299 n. 13) – 'What cannot be meant is material support, because of chap. 9.' – wrongly takes 1 Cor 9 as proving that Paul accepted no material support from the Corinthians.

[83] See above n. 70.

[84] On the words ἔστιν ἀλήθεια Χριστοῦ (2 Cor 11.10) see below n. 128.

[85] Hock 1980, 50–65; Marshall 1987, 231, 233–51, 284 etc; Martin 1990, 138–39; Chow 1992, 172.

considerably.[86] On the other hand, to reject such an offer, regarded as an offer of friendship, was an offensive act which created a relationship of enmity between the parties.[87] But Paul may well have wished to resist becoming so closely tied to one particular household, not least to avoid the furtherance of party division (1 Cor 1.10ff).[88] The second part of the explanation concerns Paul's manual labour.[89] What was particularly offensive to some of the Corinthians was Paul's insistence upon working at a trade to support himself. It is interesting to note that one of the rights Paul mentions in 1 Cor 9.4–6 is 'the right not to work' (ἐξουσίαν μὴ ἐργάζεσθαι – 9.6). This is notable because somewhat unusual. It is a right negatively stated; the right not to do something. Clearly the apostles who do avail themselves of the support offered by congregations thereby have the 'right' not to work. Conversely, this is precisely one of the things Paul and Barnabas refuse to do – to give up their work. It is not that Paul and his co-workers refuse all material support – only a certain form and level of support – but rather that they refuse to give up their manual labour; Paul insists on working with his hands. This was not only a sign of continued independence, but also of lowly status which would hardly have made Paul seem an impressive leader to the well-to-do Corinthians.[90] Indeed,

the problem for the Corinthians is not simply that he [sc. Paul] took no support from them (i.e., that he refused to take patronage in the

---

[86] Hock 1980, 53–55, who refers to Lucian *On Salaried Posts in Great Houses*, 1–4 (esp. 3). Lucian stresses the slavery and lack of freedom that result from this way of seeking to escape poverty (see 4–5 etc). Note Hock's criticisms of Judge (Hock 1980, 37, 65; Judge 1960b, 128–34; 1972, 28), who argued that Paul was sponsored by a social elite, and Judge's acceptance of the criticism (Judge 1980, 213–14). On the various 'models' of support possible for the philosopher, see Hock 1980, 52–59; Ebner 1991, 71–73, both of whom list: charging fees (μισθοί), begging, entering a household, and labouring.

[87] See Marshall 1987, *passim*; Hock 1980, 62–63; Forbes 1986, 14.

[88] On Paul's desire to remain independent because of the party divisions, see Ebner 1991, 75–77.

[89] An issue upon which Martin 1990 focuses.

[90] Cf. Theissen 1982, 56. Savage 1986, 102–103, rejects the idea that the Corinthians despised Paul's manual labour, arguing that the inscriptions (in which pride in labour and trade are often revealed) give a better guide to the attitudes of common people than the elite literary sources. However, he suggests that it is Paul's humiliation and poverty which the Corinthians were troubled by (103–106). Against Savage, see Gardner 1994, 82–84, who questions the separation Savage draws between the 'Humble Handworker' and the 'Impoverished Leader'. We should also bear in mind that it is only *some* of the Corinthians who seem to despise Paul's lifestyle and self-presentation.

home of one of their wealthier members), but that he supported himself in the demeaning fashion of working at a trade. What kind of activity is this for one who would be an 'apostle of our Lord Jesus Christ'?[91]

It is possible that some of the Corinthians found his insistence on pursuing his trade personally embarrassing, seeming to imply that they lacked the means to support their apostles adequately.

Freedom and independence (*Unabhängigkeit*)[92] therefore cannot alone explain Paul's reasoning on the matter of financial support, although they are probably one aspect of it. For why should independence be a means of preventing ἐγκοπή? It might well be a matter of personal importance, but the argument of 1 Cor 9 suggests that this was not Paul's concern; he was quite prepared to become a slave to all if they might thereby be 'won' for the gospel (which also means, of course, 'won' for Paul and his understanding of the gospel, under his leadership and authority).[93]

From the evidence of 1 Cor 9, it seems that Paul's apostolic lifestyle, expressed particularly in his rejection of material support and of the right not to work (9.6), was seen as a means by which he could avoid placing an ἐγκοπή in the way of the weak. His manual labour both prevents him becoming dependent on and obligated to certain wealthy patrons and also enables him to become 'weak' like those he seeks to gain. If he seeks independence, then it is independence from a particular group or person within the congregation that Paul is concerned to maintain. *The ἐγκοπή Paul seeks to avoid relates to the weak and is important enough for his policy to be insisted upon even if this becomes an ἐγκοπή to the strong.* Thus:

The point of 1 Corinthians 9 is that Paul takes on manual labor *because* of (not in spite of) his view that it is demeaning; he takes it on in

---

91 Fee 1987, 404.
92 Stressed by Ebner 1991, 73–77; Hock 1980, 61.
93 Black 1983; 1984, 118–19, argues that κερδήσω probably has an evangelistic reference here in 1 Cor 9.19–22, on the basis that it is defined by σώσω (v. 22b), and this leads him to over-spiritualise the term 'weak' (see above p. 106 n. 254). Gardner is right, I think, to argue that 'κερδαίνω can be understood to refer *both* to initial entrance into the community (conversion), *and* to the continuing process of winning people from inadequate ideas (sic!) to a deeper Christian consciousness ... "salvation" for Paul was a much broader concept than conversion alone' (1994, 99); cf. Matt 18.15.

order to gain the weak. If *weak* here is understood in its social sense, Paul's argument throughout chapter 9 is coherent. He lowers himself in order to gain those who are themselves of lower status.[94]

Paul is determined to avoid the hindrance which would, in his view, result from his removal of himself from membership of the group he calls 'the weak' (ἐγενόμην τοῖς ἀσθενέσιν ἀσθενής). His solidarity with this social group is demonstrated in two ways: by his self-image as one who is the scum of the earth, and by his manual labour. What is more, he challenges the 'strong' members of the Corinthian congregation to imitate him.

The social ethos conveyed by Paul's style of leadership is a radical and challenging one, for far from being one in which the strong rule benevolently from above, it is one in which the leaders themselves are enslaved to those they lead and the lowest of all in worldly status.[95] However strongly Paul asserts his authority as their father in Christ (1 Cor 4.15–21), he does not use this authority to legitimate the position of the socially strong nor to demand subordination from the weak.[96] On the contrary, it seems that his stern criticism of those who are puffed up (ἐφυσιώθησάν τινες – 1 Cor 4.18) is an attack on the members of the community who consider themselves, in worldly terms, wise, powerful, and well-born.

If the hypothesis developed here is plausible, it is likely that some at Corinth (perhaps one household in particular) had been offended by Paul's rejection of their patronage, and by his apostolic lifestyle generally. Paul's self-description and justification of his ways in 1 Cor 4 and 9 would only have increased this offence, particularly as the 'strong' Corinthians are called upon to imitate him in his self-lowering and social degradation. The following investigation into the continued interaction and intensified conflict between Paul and the Corinthians will, I think, add further plausibility to this interpretative perspective.

---

[94] Martin 1990, 124. It is interesting to note the recording of Paul's policy in Acts 20.34f.

[95] See further Martin 1990, who explores two contemporary models of leadership, the 'benevolent patriarchal' and the 'populist' or 'demagogue' (86–116), arguing that Paul adopts the latter (see 117–135). Otherwise Fiorenza 1987, 397.

[96] These sociological dimensions to Paul's use of authority and his call to imitation are not taken adequately into account by Shaw 1983, 62–125, and Castelli 1991, both of whom are critical of Paul's use of power and position. Cf. Chow 1992, 187: 'Paul certainly sought to assert his authority in the church. The question is how and for what purpose that authority was exercised.'

5.4. Increased conflict

A structuration theory perspective encourages us to consider the ways in which the Corinthian Christian community is shaped through an ongoing process of structuration: formulations of Christian teaching arise from, and in reaction to, particular contexts, and they have a range of consequences, both intended and unintended, within that context and beyond it, structuring the life of the community. These consequences form part of the context within which further reformulations of the symbolic order take place. Having outlined in some detail the ways in which Paul responds to the Corinthian context, as he perceives it, both in his formulation of specific instruction and in his self-presentation, I now seek to consider how this process of interaction continued, and how Paul re-presented elements of the Christian symbolic order in the light of the consequences – whether intended or unintended – of his teaching and example in 1 Corinthians.

If Paul's teaching and personal example as presented in 1 Corinthians are as potentially radical as I have suggested, then increasing dissatisfaction with him is only to be expected, at least among an influential minority at Corinth. 1 Corinthians may only have exacerbated their discontent. Dissatisfaction over the particular issue of manual work and material support, moreover, is especially likely since the Corinthians are clearly aware of another 'model' of apostolic lifestyle practised by others, quite apart from Paul's informing them of the rights of an apostle (1 Cor 9.4–6).[97] In 1 Cor 9.12a Paul makes it clear that others do make use of these rights when among the Corinthians, while he and Barnabas[98] refuse to do so.[99]

The identity of these 'others' can scarcely be delimited precisely, since Paul refers to οἱ λοιποὶ ἀπόστολοι ('the rest of the apostles'; 9.5), but Jerusalem connections for at least some of them are clearly implied by the reference to 'the brothers of the Lord and Cephas' (9.5).[100] This is a

---

[97] On the tension and conflict between these two models of support, see esp. Theissen 1975c.

[98] The first person plurals in v. 12 seem to refer back to v. 6, whereas in vv. 15ff Paul focuses upon himself alone.

[99] Cf. Fee 1987, 409–10; Dungan 1971, 11, 13.

[100] These words do not necessarily imply that the brothers of the Lord or Cephas had visited Corinth, though they may have (so Dungan 1971, 37; cf. Barrett 1963), but they would seem to imply that the 'others' whom the Corinthians had supported had some connection with them, such that the Corinthians were aware of these examples.

not insignificant link with Paul's opponents in 2 Cor 10–13, who are apparently people with impeccable Jewish connections – they are 'Hebrews, Israelites, the seed of Abraham' (2 Cor 11.22) – even though it is often assumed that the problems to which 2 Corinthians responds are caused by 'new' intruders.[101] Whatever the precise identity of these opponents,[102] what is undisputable is that Paul's relationship with the Corinthians had indeed deteriorated badly by the time 2 Cor 10–13 was written, and that his status as the community's apostle had been largely usurped by others.[103] It would seem that 1 Corinthians had hardly served to secure the loyalty and obedience of the Corinthian believers. In part at least its consequence (surely unintended!) was a worsening of relations between Paul and certain of the community in Corinth. So Paul's reformulation of the rules and resources of the Christian symbolic order in 1 Corinthians, his response to the particular context to be addressed, led, in part, to increased rebellion against him. In view of the strength of his criticism of the socially prominent members of the community, his demands upon them, his insistence on engaging in manual labour, and of his challenge to them to imitate him in becoming like 'the scum of the earth', this is hardly surprising.

Increasing rebellion against Paul's apostolic authority may have come to Paul's attention and been the cause of the extra visit to Corinth which is revealed from a comparison of 1 Cor 16.5 and 2 Cor 1.15f.[104] In 1 Cor

---

[101] See Furnish 1984, 48–54; Martin 1986, 298; Barrett 1982, 14–15, 63–64. Dungan 1971, 37 suggests the opponents are the same; links between the problems confronted in both epistles are explored by Marshall 1984; Murphy O'Connor 1987; 1991a, 12–15.

[102] The subject of much debate: for major discussions see Georgi 1987; Sumney 1990; Barrett 1964; 1970b; 1971b. See overview by Lang 1986, 357–59; note the cautionary comments of Hickling 1975.

[103] Cf. Betz 1972, 9.

[104] Cf. Betz 1972, 11; Barrett 1973, 7; Taylor 1991, 85. Hyldahl 1973, 296–99, 303–305, (also 1986, 102–106) argues that no visit actually took place between 1 and 2 Cor; from the time of his founding visit Paul had not been in Corinth. Paul sends letters in place of visits and 2 Cor 12.14 and 13.1f refer to his third time of *preparing* to come to visit. 1 Cor is identified with the tearful letter (299–300); there was no 'Zwischenbrief', and the unity of 2 Cor is argued for (305–306). However, I find the argument unconvincing and consider it better to take 2 Cor 2.1 to refer to an actual visit, thus taking 2 Cor 12.14 and 13.1f as implying two visits and announcing a third. Hyldahl's argument falters especially on ὡς παρὼν τὸ δεύτερον (2 Cor 13.2; see 304–305). Hughes 1962, 51–52, suggests that the second visit took place before the writing of 1 Cor. Gilchrist (1988, 52–53) attempts, unsuccessfully I think, to argue that two visits took place between the founding visit and the writing of 2 Cor 10–13.

16.5f Paul's declared plan is to visit Corinth after Macedonia, presumably intending then to receive the collection, for in 1 Cor 16.3f the details concerning the appointment of those who are to take the gift to Jerusalem are discussed (cf. Acts 19.21). The bad news which precipitated the extra visit may have been brought by Timothy, who had been sent to Corinth around the time when 1 Corinthians was written (1 Cor 4.17; 16.10f).[105] But whatever the cause of Paul's visit, it was clearly a painful one which did nothing to restore relationships between Paul and the Corinthians and on which one person particularly took the lead in opposing and insulting Paul (2 Cor 1.23–2.11).[106]

Paul probably withdrew to Ephesus (perhaps via Macedonia,[107] though the sea route may be more likely), where he had written 1 Corinthians (1 Cor 16.8) and from where he later set out for Troas and thence to Macedonia (2 Cor 2.12f). Instead of fulfilling his original intention of visiting the Corinthians again (2 Cor 1.16, 23; 2.1) he wrote a 'painful' letter, mentioned in 2 Cor 2.4, 9 and 7.8, 12, and sent Titus (probably bearing the letter) to Corinth.[108]

If my argument is correct, that Paul's rejection of material support and his portrayal of his apostolic image were causes of offence to some of the Corinthians, and that his statements in 1 Corinthians were only likely to have exacerbated these problems, then we would expect these issues to feature significantly in the painful letter, the letter written when the conflict was at its worst. If this were to be the case, then, I suggest, as well as enabling us to see something of Paul's further response to this changing context, the content of this letter would lend some further support to the hypothesis that the conflict does indeed centre around the issues concerning the pattern of Christian living which Paul teaches and embodies and which he challenges the 'strong' Corinthians to imitate. I argue below that this is indeed the case, and that this letter, preserved more or less completely in 2 Cor 10–13, is tied in closely to the social conflicts which are already emerging in 1 Corinthians. This involves, of course, accepting not only the partition of 2 Corinthians, but also the

---

[105] So Murphy O'Connor, 1991a, 15; 1991b, 41; Furnish 1984, 54.
[106] Cf. Bruce 1971, 164; Barrett 1973, 7–8, 18–19, 85–86; 1982, 75; Furnish 1984, 140; Lang 1986, 261.
[107] So Murphy O'Connor 1991a, 16.
[108] Cf. the chronological reconstructions of Marshall 1987, 260–62; Betz 1972, 9–12; Barrett 1973, 7–9; Lüdemann 1984, 93–96. On Paul's later eager awaiting of news from Titus as to how things were in Corinth, see 2 Cor 2.12f; 7.5–16.

dating of chapters 10–13 before chapters 1–9 and the identification of 10–13 as the 'painful letter'. While the division of 2 Corinthians into at least two letters, with the most obvious division occuring between chapters 9 and 10, is widely accepted in New Testament scholarship, most recent commentators on the epistle prefer to date chapters 10–13 later than 1–9. In Appendix 1 I have therefore set out in some detail my reasons for adopting the opposite view. From this perspective, I suggest, a coherent reconstruction of the interaction between Paul and the Corinthians can be presented, once we see the prominence of the essentially social issues upon which I have focused. The relative dating of 2 Cor 1–9 and 10–13 must be decided on grounds other than the coherence thus offered to the hypothesis and perspective I am developing here – hence the detailed arguments in Appendix 1 – but having adopted the position I do, we find that the problems and opponents in 1 and 2 Corinthians are drawn much closer together than is often thought to be the case. Given the fact that this interaction between Paul and the Corinthians occured over a relatively short period of time, a reconstruction which demonstrates a continuity of issues of conflict and a coherence through the entire correspondence is to be preferred to those which must posit new outbreaks of opposition and short-lived reconciliations. The coherence of this reconstruction also adds further support to the epistolary hypothesis upon which it is based.

5.5. Paul's response to the conflict: 2 Cor 10–13

As we read 2 Cor 10–13 as Paul's response to the crisis at Corinth, it is notable that (as in 1 Cor 1–4) Paul scarcely makes anything of theological or 'doctrinal' disagreements, even though he is quite capable of arguing in this way when the dispute seems to require it (cf. Gal 2.11–5.24).[109] Paul's primary concern in these chapters is with the fact that some of the Corinthians have rejected *his* leadership and authority and have accepted and welcomed others in his place. And the struggle between Paul and the rival apostles, and the reasons for the Corinthians turning from one to the other, may be as much social as theological. Indeed it may be right

---

[109] The weight normally given to theological considerations is, I think, a reflection not of the balance of textual material but of the unbalanced interest of much New Testament scholarship. Cf. Scroggs 1980, 165–66; Elliott 1981, 3–4.

to focus upon the class-based interests which led the powerful Corinthians to favour one form of leadership over another – rejecting the one who labours and declares himself to be ὡς περικαθάρματα ('like scum') and who calls the strong to imitate him in service of the weak, and welcoming those who are happy to accept patronage rather than work, and who perhaps make less radical and disturbing challenges.

In contrast to the comparative lack of explicit doctrinal or theological argument, it is interesting to note how prominent in 2 Cor 10–13 are the subjects of the rejection of financial support and the image of the apostle, precisely the themes explored above. Indeed, an overview of the structure of 2 Cor 10–13 demonstrates the significance of the points at which this issue is raised. The broadly chiastic shape of the letter is noteworthy:[110]

The structure of 2 Cor 10–13

A	10.1–11	Watch out, I have power to be bold with you!
	(10.12–18)	The appropriate measurement of achievement.
B	11.1–4	I am concerned lest you turn from Christ.
C	11.5–12	Self-defence on the issue of financial support.
	(11.13–15)	Against the false apostles.
D	11.16–12.10	The boasting of a fool.
	(12.11–12)	Against the false apostles.
C'	12.13–18	Self-defence on the issue of financial support.
B'	12.19–21	I am concerned about how I will find you.
A'	13.1–10	Watch out, I have power to be bold with you!
	(13.11–14)	Final greeting.

The main purpose of 2 Cor 10.1–11 is to warn, indeed to threaten, the Corinthians with the assertion that Paul has the power of God on his side to destroy (v. 4), to avenge (v. 6) and to impose authority (v. 8). The background of these assertions is the criticism recently made of him by some (τινας – v. 2) at Corinth. For he has been accused of being humble

---

[110] Talbert 1987, 111, notes that '2 Cor 10–13 is a large thought unit which falls into an ABA pattern'. Talbert's section B encompasses 10.12–12.13. The classic study of chiasm in the NT is Lund 1942, though he does not examine 2 Corinthians.

(ταπεινός – v. 1), weak and despicable (v. 10) when with them. The language used seems to confirm precisely what we would expect from our reading of 1 Corinthians: that Paul's manner, teaching, and lifestyle are regarded with complete disdain by at least some of the Corinthians. The words the Corinthian critics apply to Paul are entirely in keeping with his self-portrayal (ταπεινός – v. 1; ἀσθενὴς καὶ ὁ λόγος ἐξουθενημένος – v. 10). Paul seems to point covertly to one particular opponent from whom this criticism stems and whose insulting view of Paul is quoted in 10.10 (using φησίν – third person singular; 's/he says').[111] This person has asserted confidently that he is 'of Christ' (v. 7) and has said that Paul's impressive letters are not matched by his personal presence (v. 10). It is this person – ὁ τοιοῦτος – who is particularly threatened that 'what we are when absent in word through letters, we shall also be when present in our actions' (v. 11). This person may, if my reasoning thus far is plausible, have been a prominent householder within the Corinthian congregation and thus a person with influence over others, perhaps a person whose support Paul had refused and who may have offered hospitality and aid to other visiting apostles.[112] However, rebellion against Paul seems to have involved a significant number within the congregation. A definite connection with the factions of 1 Cor 1.10ff (ἐγὼ Χριστοῦ κτλ. – cf. 2 Cor 10.7) can hardly be proved, but the divisiveness and assertiveness are of a similar nature, and the analysis of the party divisions offered above (§3.8.4.) suggests that similar foundations may have underlain both cases of rivalry and opposition to Paul.

In 10.12–18, Paul outlines his refusal to commend himself by comparison with others or according to their standards, referring now to the intruders who have come to Corinth. Rather, his vindication is dependent upon God's measure (μέτρον – v. 13; cf. v. 17f) and is demonstrated by his missionary labours and the faith of his converts (v. 15f; cf. 1 Cor 9.2; 2 Cor 3.1ff). This should have been sufficient commendation of Paul to the Corinthians; indeed, as the fruit of his apostolic labours they should have commended him (2 Cor 12.11; cf. 1.14). But instead they have welcomed those who commend themselves (cf. 10.12, 18; echoed in 3.1; 4.2; 5.12).[113]

---

[111] See further Appendix 1, pp. 308–309.
[112] Cf. Taylor 1991, 80, 86.
[113] On Paul's view of the bases on which apostleship is truly legitimated, see Käsemann 1942; Hafemann 1990.

At 11.1 Paul begins his own defence and self-commendation, announcing, though, that what follows will be foolishness (ἀφροσύνη). Verses 2–4, however, explain his concern, namely, that they, in rejecting him, will be diverted from their pure devotion to Christ and seduced by a different gospel.[114]

5.5.1. Paul's response to the criticism of his lifestyle

Paul's self-defence proper begins at 11.5, where he insists that he is not inferior to the ὑπερλίαν ἀποστόλων – the super-apostles.[115] He may be untrained (ἰδιώτης)[116] in speech (τῷ λόγῳ) – though there is some irony in the fact that the letter itself is a piece of skilled rhetoric[117] – but he is not lacking in knowledge and clarity (v. 6).[118] What is particularly significant is that the first specific defence Paul makes concerns his rejection of material support, an issue which occupies the whole of 11.7–12.[119] Was it a *sin*, he asks in provocative terms,[120] to adopt the stance outlined in detail in 1 Cor 9, 'humbling myself so that you might be lifted up' (ἐμαυτὸν ταπεινῶν ἵνα ὑμεῖς ὑψωθῆτε – v. 7a), so that the gospel might be preached δωρεάν, 'for nothing'?[121] Clearly this policy has been a major cause of offence to some at Corinth, and was presumably a significant difference between Paul and the other missionaries.[122] Paul's practice has been regarded as proving that he does not love the

---

[114] On the terms used in v. 4 see Murphy O'Connor 1990; Martin 1986, 334–42. The fact that Paul does not engage in argument about the nature of the gospel, as he does in Galatians, but focuses upon himself as a true apostle, shows that the primary danger is not acceptance of false doctrines, but of false apostles. To reject Paul as their apostle, is, by definition, to reject his (true) gospel and turn to another. *Contra* Murphy O'Connor 1990, 250–51.

[115] There is debate as to whether these are to be identified with, or distinguished from, the ψευδαπόστολοι (11.13); see Barrett 1971b; Thrall 1980; Barnett 1984.

[116] See BAGD, 370.

[117] On Paul's rhetorical training see Judge 1968; Forbes 1986, 22–24.

[118] See further Barrett 1973, 279–81.

[119] Cf. Martin 1986, 339: 'The starting point is the discussion over self-recommendation and boasting, but it comes to a practical matter which underlies much of chaps. 10–12, i.e., Paul's refusal to accept maintenance at Corinth'; see further 343–48.

[120] The term 'sin' may have come from the Corinthians, and may reflect an accusation in connection with Paul's apparent disobedience to the Lord's command (1 Cor 9.14); see Theissen 1982, 45–46.

[121] Plummer's translation of δωρεάν (1915, 303); cf. Gal 2.21.

[122] 11.20 may imply that the intruders 'take advantage' of the Corinthians in this way; cf. 2.17 with the reference to those who 'trade in' the word of God; i.e., take payment; also 1 Cor 9.12a. See further §5.3.2. above.

Corinthians, and that he favours other churches above them.[123] In order to try and win the Corinthians back, Paul offers the interpretation of financial support as a form of burden which he refrained from placing upon them (11.9).[124] The churches from which Paul did receive aid were hardly being favoured, but were *robbed*[125] to provide provisions[126] for Paul at Corinth. 'Paul's irony here', Barrett comments, 'is at its most bitter'.[127] But the policy itself is one which Paul swears he will not amend.[128]

Paul's 'foolish' boasting (on which see below), announced in 11.1, is announced again and properly commenced at 11.16,[129] finally concluding at 12.11 (γέγονα ἄφρων), at which point, insisting again that he is by no means a lesser apostle (12.11f), Paul once more raises the issue of financial support. Again he is ironic: 'for how were you treated worse than the other churches, except that I myself did not burden you? Forgive me this wrong!' (v. 13).[130] Paul stresses that on his forthcoming third visit 'I will not be a burden' (οὐ καταναρκήσω) 'for I do not seek your things, but you yourselves' (v. 14; cf. v. 16a). Another metaphor is offered to the Corinthians with which to view Paul's policy positively: he is acting like a good parent who saves up for their children rather than vice versa (v. 14). Indeed, Paul's spending himself for them is precisely a sign of love (v. 15; cf. 11.11).

Repeating his policy of not burdening them, Paul then responds (again with irony)[131] to a further accusation; that he cunningly deceived them

---

[123] See further Marshall 1987, 242–58.

[124] καταναρκάω implies 'imposing a burden' or even 'putting pressure' on (see Martin 1986, 347); used here and in 12.13f. Cf. καταβαρέω in 12.16 and ἐπιβαρέω in 1 Thess 2.9 (and 2 Thess 3.8), where not being a burden is the explicit rationale for Paul's lifestyle.

[125] συλάω may be rendered 'plunder', or 'pillage', (see Furnish 1984, 492; Hughes 1962, 385; Martin 1986, 346), or 'strip off' (especially the arms of a slain enemy; see LSJ, 1671). Spicq TLNT 3, 312–16, argues that the meaning here is based on a technical legal sense of the term; thus that Paul is authorised to 'seize' or 'recover' from other churches subsidies which are due to him from the Corinthians.

[126] For this translation of ὀψώνιον, and against the rendering 'salary' or 'wages', see Caragounis 1974; Spicq TLNT 2, 600–603.

[127] Barrett 1973, 281. On Paul's use of irony in the context of contemporary rhetorical practice, see Forbes 1986; also Betz 1972, 100ff.

[128] Note v. 9: ἐτήρησα καὶ τηρήσω.; v. 12: ὃ δὲ ποιῶ, καὶ ποιήσω, . . (cf.12.14). The words ἔστιν ἀλήθεια Χριστοῦ (v. 10; cf. Rom 9.1) are certainly a strong affirmation of truth; they may be an 'oath-formula', as Betz (1972, 102) and Bultmann (see 1985, 206) suggest (followed by Barrett 1973, 283; Martin 1986, 347).

[129] Cf. Talbert 1987, 119.

[130] This 'apology' must be ironic, because of his oath not to change his policy; see n. 128 above.

[131] Cf. Betz 1972, 104.

(v. 16b). Judging from the fact that Paul does not attempt to defend his personal conduct on this point, but turns immediately to 'those I sent to you', it would seem that this is a charge which concerns the way Paul's emissaries acted when in Corinth. The accusation of defrauding, whether it originated from the Corinthians or the ψευδαπόστολοι ('false-apostles'), is usually taken to relate to the money Paul is collecting for the saints in Jerusalem (1 Cor 16.1ff) and the suspicion that he 'has pocketed the proceeds himself'.[132] This seems plausible because of the specific mention of Titus, who had previously visited Corinth to initiate the collection (2 Cor 8.6).[133] However, the fact that Paul says nothing specific about the collection, nor about the destiny of the proceeds, may imply that the lifestyle of his co-workers is uppermost in his mind. Paul insists that their behaviour was just like his – 'did we not walk (περιεπατήσαμεν) in the same spirit, in the same steps?' – referring presumably to the policy of refusing material support (v. 18b; cf. 7.2).[134]

The issue of Paul's rejection of material support emerges, then, at crucial points in 2 Cor 10–13. In the main body of the letter it is both the opening and the closing issue on which Paul makes a defence.[135] It must be seen as a major cause of conflict between Paul and the Corinthians. This issue plays a fundamental role in the process whereby a significant number of the congregation rebel against Paul.

5.5.2. Paul's boasting: the self-image of the apostle

An overview of the structure of 2 Cor 10–13 (see §5.5. above) also shows that the central portion of this letter is taken up with what Paul calls foolish boasting (11.16–12.10).[136] He makes it clear at the outset that this is not really an appropriate way of speaking (οὐ κατὰ κύριον λαλῶ

---

[132] Barrett 1973, 324; cf. Georgi 1987, 242; Talbert 1987, 128–29.

[133] See Appendix 1, pp. 304–307.

[134] Cf. 1 Cor 9.4ff, where first person plural forms are used, though only Paul and Barnabas are named. How could the Corinthians have been deceived through the collection, when no money was yet received? This would be the case even if 2 Cor 10–13 postdated 1–9, as long as it preceded Paul's third visit, as it obviously does (13.1f), on which the collection was received (Rom 15.25f). It seems highly unlikely to me that Paul expected Titus to have *received* the collection on the 'painful visit' and brought it with him to Troas; Paul is unsure of the Corinthians' support for him, let alone for the collection, until he finds Titus in Macedonia (2 Cor 7.5ff; *contra* Barrett 1982, 131 n. 33).

[135] Martin 1986, 449: 'With the conclusion of 12:11–18 we see the ending of Paul's self-defense or *apologia* in 2 Corinthians.'

[136] Martin 1986, 356, entitles the section 11.16–12.10 'Paul's "Fool's Story"'.

– v. 17) and that he is doing so only in reaction to the boasting of others (v. 18). These others, Paul states, you bear with gladly, even though they abuse you thoroughly.[137] 'To our shame', he exclaims ironically, 'we were too weak to do that' (vv. 19–21)![138]

There follow two major sections of 'boasting', each of which begins with points on which genuine boasting could be based; presumably points on which Paul's opponents have specifically commended themselves.[139] In the first case (11.22f), Paul states that his Jewish credentials are as impressive as his opponents' and indeed that he is more of a servant of Christ than they. Yet instead of listing successes and achievements Paul does precisely the opposite, choosing 'for eulogy items that in the eyes of his opponents, at least, are to his discredit'.[140] In a self-derisory way, Paul glories in his humiliation and shame,[141] mentioning, again, his labour and toil (11.27).[142] Indeed, in a way which echoes the theme of 1 Cor 9.22, the climax of this catalogue is an assertion of Paul's weakness alongside all who are weak (τίς ἀσθενεῖ καὶ οὐκ ἀσθενῶ;) and of his deep concern for those who are caused to stumble (τίς σκανδαλίζεται καὶ οὐκ ἐγὼ πυροῦμαι; v. 29).[143] Thus:

> It is on the basis of his 'catalogue of humiliations' that Paul now formulates the principle which has shaped his 'boasting' to this point, and which animates and elucidates the entire passage. 'If I must boast, I will boast of the things which show my weakness' (v. 30). So far is Paul removing himself from the conventional attitudes of his opponents that, when 'forced' to boast, he will do so only ironically, in order to satirise precisely those kinds of achievements of which his opponents were most proud.[144]

---

[137] Perhaps a veiled reference to their willingness to accept material support (cf. Barrett 1973, 291; Martin 1986, 365). On the strong language used here see Martin 1986, 364–65.

[138] Forbes 1986, 18 explores Paul's 'deadly εἰρωνεία' at this point.

[139] Cf. Furnish 1984, 498, 532, 543; Georgi 1987, 40–60.

[140] Travis 1973, 529. Cf. Forbes 1986, 19; Judge 1966, 39; 1968, 47; 1972, 36; Marshall 1984, 285.

[141] Cf. Marshall 1987, 364; see 357–64 on Paul's 'self-derision'.

[142] Admittedly the specific reference to 'hands' (1 Cor 4.12) is missing, but it is hardly true to say that: 'Im Peristasenkatalog 2 Kor 11,23–29 wird der Bezug zur Handarbeit eliminiert.' (Ebner 1991, 152.)

[143] Cf. Furnish 1984, 520. Otherwise Barré 1975, who breaks the link with 1 Cor 9.22 (501 n. 6) and views 2 Cor 11.29 as referring to Paul's eschatological trials, in continued boasting against his opponents (517–18).

[144] Forbes 1986, 20.

Paul 'agrees', reluctantly, to play the rhetorical game, but at the same time radically opposes the conventional aims of the game itself.[145] His rejection of the conventional marks of honour and social standing may be further emphasised in the narrative of the Damascus incident which closes this section (v. 32f).[146] As Judge has suggested, this may be a conscious parody alluding to the Roman military award of the *corona muralis*, or 'wall crown', given to the first soldier up the wall and into an enemy city.[147] Thus Paul contrasts 'his frightened descent of the wall with the daring ascent of a wall for which a courageous soldier would be honored'.[148] 'Although the same story is presented in Acts as a sign of strength, Paul himself offers it here as further proof of his weakness ... Here in 2 Cor it is a story about Paul's humiliation, not about his heroism.'[149]

The second section of boasting also begins with a genuine topic of concern; ὀπτασίας καὶ ἀποκαλύψεις κυρίου ('visions and revelations of the Lord'; 12.1).[150] Paul recounts a profound visionary experience which he had 'fourteen years ago', though he actually reveals little about the content or significance of this episode.[151] Whatever the reasons and precedents for using third person singular forms to describe this experience,[152] this ingenious approach allows Paul to relate an experience worthy of boasting which is undoubtedly his own, yet at the same to refuse to boast in such things (v. 5)! Once more, Paul stresses that *he* will only boast ἐν ταῖς ἀσθενείαις, 'in weaknesses', pointing out again that he could boast in other things, but chooses to forbear (v. 6). He only wants to be credited with what is seen in or heard from him.[153]

---

[145] Cf. Judge 1984, 13–14; 1968, 40–48; Forbes 1986, 18–22; Marshall 1987, 357–64. Paul's skill and awareness of particular techniques may bespeak a certain educational level; cf. Forbes 1986, 22–24.

[146] Thus there is a reason for this short piece, *contra* Bultmann 1985, 218 (Windisch 1924, 364, suggested that Paul's amanuensis added the story), though whether v. 31 links primarily with what precedes or follows it is uncertain; see overview in Furnish 1984, 539–42.

[147] See Judge 1966, 44–45; Travis 1973, 530; Furnish 1984, 542; Forbes 1986, 20–21; Martin 1986, 384–85; Talbert 1987, 123.

[148] Furnish 1984, 542.

[149] Furnish 1984, 541–42; see Acts 9.23–25. Cf. Talbert 1987, 123; Barrett 1973, 303–304.

[150] Probably a topic arising from the claims of Paul's competitors at Corinth; so Furnish 1984, 543; Barrett 1973, 306.

[151] Cf. Furnish 1984, 545.

[152] On the possibilities see Furnish 1984, 543–44; note Plutarch, *On Praising Oneself Inoffensively*, 10.

[153] This is the thrust of v. 6b, whether v. 7a is to be included with it (so Furnish 1984, 528, 546; Martin 1986, 389; NA²⁷) or not (so Barrett 1973, 313–14; RSV; NIV).

Once again, Paul turns to focus not upon that which will demonstrate his power and eminence but upon weakness and humiliation.[154] He focuses on the 'thorn in the flesh, the messenger of Satan' (σκόλοψ τῇ σαρκί, ἄγγελος σατανᾶ – v. 7), which, irrespective of its precise identity,[155] attacked him (με κολαφίζῃ). The Lord refused to answer Paul's repeated prayer and remove it, but spoke instead the word which forms the foundation for so much of Paul's apostolic self-understanding:[156] ἀρκεῖ σοι ἡ χάρις μου, ἡ γὰρ δύναμις ἐν ἀσθενείᾳ τελεῖται ('my grace is sufficient for you, for power[157] is made perfect in weakness'; v. 9). Thus Paul explains and elaborates the *reason* why he is so prepared to boast and delight in weakness and hardship, for in this very weakness the power of Christ is displayed. Indeed it is a demonstration of the apostolic life as *imitatio Christi* (1 Cor 11.1); for just as Christ became humble, taking the form of a slave (Phil 2.7f; 2 Cor 8.9), so too the apostle 'humbled himself' (2 Cor 11.7; 6.10) and became a weak slave (1 Cor 9.19, 22) to serve others.[158] And just as Christ was 'crucified in weakness, but lives by the power of God', so also the apostles discover the power of God even in their weakness (2 Cor 13.4; cf. 12.9f).[159] One of the central symbolic resources of Pauline faith – the crucified Christ – clearly forms a pattern for Paul's own conduct and self-understanding, brought to bear here particularly against the so-called strong members of the Corinthian community.

Each of the major sections of 'foolish' boasting, then, begins with points of serious concern (11.22; 12.1) relating most probably to the claims of Paul's opponents. Yet in both, Paul insists on stressing his weaknesses and displaying his humiliation, playing the boasting game but inverting its conventional values. One might indeed refer to his 'pursuit of radical self-humiliation'.[160]

---

[154] Cf. Forbes 1986, 21.

[155] A much discussed but certainly unanswerable question; see overviews in Allo 1956, 313–23; Furnish 1984, 547–50; Martin 1986, 412–16; BAGD, 441.

[156] Hughes 1962, 451, calls it 'the summit of the epistle'.

[157] The textual evidence favours reading 'power', rather than 'my power' (μου, which was added in a number of texts; see Metzger 1971, 585–86) though the end of the verse specifies this as 'the power of Christ'.

[158] The link between apostle and Christ, and specifically between 2 Cor 11.7 and Phil 2.7f, is pointed out by Dautzenberg 1969, 222, 225 (cf. Mark 10.45); see further Hurtado 1984, 126; Stanley 1984; Wolff 1989.

[159] Those who preach 'another Jesus', according to Murphy O'Connor 1990, may have sought to avoid proclaiming a Jesus who suffers, is weak and humiliated.

[160] Judge 1972, 36.

So, the two particular themes which appear in 1 Cor 4 and 9 concerning the lifestyle and image of the apostle Paul certainly form a major focus in 2 Cor 10–13 too. Indeed these two issues seem to have become the central points of conflict, judging by the degree to which they dominate the 'painful' letter. In spite of the conflict and rejection which has developed after 1 Corinthians, Paul presents essentially the same picture and even intensifies it: he *swears* he will continue to reject the Corinthians' material support, and emphasises still more extensively his weakness and humiliation. The apostle refuses to alter his lifestyle or his self-presentation to accommodate or please his wealthier converts, even though they have turned away to other, more amenable apostles. His attempt to win the Corinthian congregation back does not involve a change in the social ethos which his apostleship expresses. It does, of course, involve quite specific threats about his power and authority which he promises to impose if necessary. Indeed, 2 Cor 10–13 both opens and closes with just such threats (10.1–11; 13.1–10). If my reconstruction of the nature of the interaction between Paul and the Corinthians is broadly correct then these threats, like much of the harsh criticism in 1 Corinthians, are directed particularly towards some of the socially prominent members of the community.

5.6. Reconciliation: 2 Cor 1–9

My comments on 2 Cor 1–9 will be brief, though it is important to note that there is nothing in these chapters (as far as I can see) which would require any reassessment of my observations concerning the social ethos of Paul's teaching and personal example in 1 Corinthians and 2 Cor 10–13. Paul does not address particular social groups or situations of social conflict here, but reflects upon the story of his painful interaction with the Corinthians and upon the nature of his apostolic ministry.[161]

We are able to learn only a little about the process by which the Corinthian church began to be reconciled to Paul, following the visit of Titus and the receipt of the painful letter, and less still about what in particular brought about the reconciliation.

One thing seems clear, the majority of the congregation turned against the ringleader of the opposition to Paul (2.6). This short reference may

---

[161] On the themes of 2 Cor 1–9, see Jones 1973, 23–48.

be significant. It is clear that the socially prominent members of the congregation are only a small minority – οὐ πολλοί (1 Cor 1.26) – so the majority of the congregation are drawn from those who cannot be proud of their worldly wisdom, power or noble birth, those regarded as nobodies by the world. I have argued that in 1 Corinthians Paul, as Theissen points out,[162] often takes a view 'from below'. He criticises the conduct and attitudes of the wealthier members of the community. Moreover, Paul has lowered himself socially by insisting on labouring with his hands and by presenting himself and his other co-workers as those at the bottom of the social heap (1 Cor 4.8–13). He then challenges the Corinthians to imitate him in this pattern of life and conduct. This presentation of Christian teaching and example has clearly led to conflict and rejection, at least by certain prominent members of the congregation. Its impact (presumably unintended) has been, in part, to foster criticism and antagonism against Paul. However, Paul's self-declared policy to become weak in order to win the weak, to avoid placing a hindrance between him and them, has perhaps also had a more intended impact. The majority have, in the end at least, sided with Paul and punished his opponent (ἡ ἐπιτιμία αὕτη ἡ ὑπὸ τῶν πλειόνων – 2.6), perhaps ostracising him (and his household?) from the congregation.

As far as Paul is concerned, the congregation's obedience (and power!) has been proved (2.9) and he urges the restoration and forgiveness of the offender (2.7ff). He is clearly heartened and relieved by the news which Titus brought concerning the Corinthians' repentance and renewed zeal (7.6–16). And, understandably, much of 2 Cor 1–7 is taken up with bold and thankful reflections concerning the apostolic ministry, the ministry of weakness, which has been vindicated. Paul is able to boast of his pure and sincere conduct (1.12), his innocence and honesty (7.2), and to reaffirm the mutual boasting which exists between apostle and community (1.14; 7.14–16; 8.24). In an extended comparison between his own ministry and that of Moses, drawing on Exod 34.29–35, he describes the glorious nature of the ministry of the καινῆς διαθήκης, the new covenant, a passage full of confidence (3.4–18). But the old themes and issues are still present, only presented now in a less confrontational context; Paul and his co-workers are still to be seen as δούλους

---

[162] Theissen 1982, 57, 163.

ὑμῶν διὰ Ἰησοῦν ('your slaves for Jesus' sake'; 4.5) and are still the suffering, humiliated ones who bear the death of Jesus with them always (4.8).[163] The treasure is kept in earthen vessels (4.7); the power is God's and human weakness is ever present. And in another extended *peristasis* catalogue (6.4–10), one of the conditions listed in which Paul and his associates 'commend themselves as God's servants (διάκονοι)' is ἐν κόποις ('in labours'; v. 5). Indeed, J. T. Fitzgerald suggests that the third triad of items – κόποις, ἀγρυπνίαις, νηστείαις ('labouring, sleepless, starving'; NJB) – are '*occupational hardships*, . . both as apostle and artisan', noting that the same three items occur, among others, in 2 Cor 11.27.[164] In this catalogue the extent to which Paul shapes and understands his own existence in terms similar to those he uses to describe Christ's self-giving is clear. There is a particularly close parallel between 6.10 and 8.9: Paul and his co-workers are ὡς πτωχοὶ πολλοὺς δὲ πλουτίζοντες ('as poor but making many rich'; 6.10) just as in his grace Christ, 'being rich, became poor', ἵνα ὑμεῖς τῇ ἐκείνου πτωχείᾳ πλουτήσητε ('so that you, by his poverty might become rich'; 8.9 – see further below).

Another feature of 2 Cor 1–9, reading it as a letter subsequent to 2 Cor 10–13, is that occasional digs at the now departed intruders occur. Paul mentions their apparent need for commendatory letters and the corrupting way in which they 'peddle', or 'trade in' the word of God, a thinly veiled reference to their policy with regard to the receipt of material support (2.17; 3.1; 4.2).[165]

A further result of the reconciliation between Paul and the Corinthians is that the collection project is rekindled. Paul writes to encourage the Corinthians to give generously, citing the Macedonians as an example to them (8.1–5), and expressing the wish that Titus should now complete what he began a year ago (8.6), when the Corinthians first willingly undertook the task (8.10; cf. 1 Cor 16.1ff). So Titus and two brothers are sent to Corinth (8.16–24). It is interesting to note that the pattern of Christ's self-giving, the inspiration for the reversal of conventional social values in the community (1 Cor 1.18ff) and for the lifestyle of the apostle himself, is cited here as the motivation for the redistribution which

---

[163] The unusual word νέκρωσις (4.10) suggests 'deadness', or 'putting to death' (BAGD, 535).
[164] Fitzgerald 1988, 193 with n. 205; on the structure and content of this *peristasis* catalogue, see 184–201.
[165] See further Appendix 1, p. 310–11.

the collection seeks to effect (8.9). This is the central symbolic resource with which Paul attempts to shape the community's life and ethos; once again he draws on this resource, presenting it here as the foundational motivation for giving to the collection project. Again it presents a challenge, to those who at present have abundance (8.14), to self-giving and self-lowering. The christological pattern is one of becoming poor, in order that others might become rich. But Paul also makes it clear that, in this material context, the intention of such self-giving is not to bring affliction and distress upon oneself. The aim, rather, is equality (8.13).[166] Chapter 9 continues to deal with the collection, most probably as an integral part of the same letter as chapter 8.[167] Here, Paul again encourages the Corinthian believers to complete their task, by telling them of his boasting about them to the Macedonians (9.2). He clearly remains concerned that his optimism may prove ill-founded, and warns the Corinthians of the embarrassment that will be his, if some of the Macedonians come with him to Achaia and find them *still* unprepared (9.4). He reminds them that the brethren were sent to them to make this gift ready (9.3, 5) and encourages them once more to generous giving (9.6ff).

We learn from Rom 15.25f that the task was successfully completed. Paul finally arrived in Corinth on his third visit, from where he wrote Romans[168] and prepared to travel to Jerusalem with the collection, as he had previously intended. The reconciliation enabled this practical goal to be attained.[169]

---

[166] See further Horrell 1995c, 76–79.

[167] See esp. Stowers 1990. On the range of opinion regarding the integrity or partition of 2 Cor 8–9 see Appendix 1, p. 297 with nn. 9–10.

[168] The evidence for this is: references to Phoebe (Rom 16.1f; διάκονος at the Corinthian port of Cenchreae); Gaius (Rom 16.23; 1 Cor 1.14); Erastus (Rom 16.23; cf. 2 Tim 4.20); and to Paul's travel plans (Rom 15.25f; 1 Cor 16.3f; 2 Cor 1.16; 9.1–4; Acts 19.21f; 20.1f). A Corinthian origin for Romans is generally accepted; see e.g. Sanday and Headlam 1896, xxxvi–xxxvii; Morris 1988, 5–6; Dunn 1988, xliv; Ziesler 1989, 18–19; Lüdemann 1984, 99; Jewett 1979, 165.

[169] In 1 Cor 16.3f Paul cautiously expresses the possibility that he may travel to Jerusalem with those appointed (and sent with commendatory letters!) by the Corinthians. Perhaps even at this time, he was wary of the accusation of deceit (cf. 2 Cor 12.16ff) which might result if the collection was taken away by him and his own co-workers.

5.7. Conclusion

In line with the theoretical perspectives outlined in chapters 1 and 2, my investigations into Paul's Corinthian correspondence have sought to assess his various writing in the light of the context which it addresses. I have conceived of this correspondence in terms of a process; an ongoing process of interaction in which Paul's presentations of Christian faith are formulated and reformulated in the light of the consequences (both intended and unintended) which have followed from previous interaction. Giddens' theoretical perspective is fundamentally based upon the conviction that social life must be viewed as an ongoing (diachronic) process.[170] Like a language, the rules and resources of the Christian symbolic order are written and rewritten, reproduced and transformed, changing with time, but also at the same time structuring and shaping the life of the communities in which this symbolic order is embodied. This process, in which the social life and ethos of a community are shaped and structured by a particular symbolic order, may, following Giddens, be termed a process of structuration.

The preceding three chapters can hardly claim to do justice to the whole of 1 and 2 Corinthians, still less to the mass of secondary literature which deals with one or both of the letters.[171] However, enough has been done to allow a number of significant sociological conclusions to be drawn. Because of the extent to which the behaviour and attitudes of the socially prominent members of the Corinthian congregation are problematic to Paul, 1 Corinthians draws on the symbols, rules and resources of the symbolic order in a way which presents the gospel as radically opposed to the dominant social order. Paul's Christianity, as presented to the congregation at Corinth, is often critical of and offensive to the socially prominent members of the community. It makes strenuous demands upon them, demands which will have an impact upon their worldly position and social interaction. On the other hand, nowhere in Paul's Corinthian correspondence do we find any demand for the subordination of the socially weak to the socially strong (see chapter 4). For these reasons the label 'love-patriarchalism' must be judged an inappropriate summary of the social ethos of 1 Corinthians.

---

[170] See esp. §1.5. and §2.4. above.
[171] Fee 1987, xxi, mentions 'several thousand items' relating to 1 Corinthians alone.

The social ethos which emerged from a study of Paul's instruction and response to various situations in 1 Corinthians is further embodied in Paul's presentation of his own lifestyle and self-understanding. Already in 1 Corinthians the social degradation of Paul and his co-workers and their insistence on manual labour, giving up their right to financial support, are presented as models which the Corinthian strong are instructed to imitate. Given both the way in which this personal model is set up as an example for imitation and the wider instruction and criticism contained in 1 Corinthians, it is unsurprising that relations between Paul and some of the Corinthians deteriorated badly after the sending of this letter. Judging from the issues which are prominent in the 'painful' letter (2 Cor 10–13), criticism of Paul was centred primarily around the 'weak' self-image which he presented and his rejection of the Corinthians' financial support.

Indeed, much of the conflict which develops between Paul and some of the Corinthian congregation stems precisely from the challenging social ethos which Paul's teaching and lifestyle express. His insistence on self-support by manual labour, contributing to a 'humble' and weak personal presence, is perhaps the major reason why some of the Corinthians turn against Paul in favour of alternative apostles whose lifestyle is different. The struggle between Paul and the 'false' apostles for the devotion of the Corinthian church, then, is as much a social as a theological struggle. Indeed, it is a struggle between a form of apostolic lifestyle which embodies social self-lowering and offends the would-be patrons, and another which does not. It is hard to say why this issue became so prominent at Corinth, and not elsewhere, and why Paul insisted so strongly on refusing support here, when he clearly accepted support from other churches (see esp. Phil 4.15ff; 2 Cor 11.8). Perhaps it had something to do with the fact that there were some influential and wealthy members of the church at Corinth who might easily have gained in influence, prestige and power, had Paul not resisted this level of dependence upon them. Was the presence of such a minority exceptional among the Pauline communities?[172] The particular character of

---

[172] Schöllgen 1988, 73–74, maintains that Corinth is the only Pauline community for which enough evidence exists to permit any kind of sustainable conclusion in this regard. We should at least be wary of over-generalising about the Pauline communities (a point made by Barclay 1992, 72–73) and be prepared to consider the way in which Paul's instruction and behaviour (and their impact – intended or otherwise) vary according to the context and make-up of a particular congregation.

Paul's Corinthian correspondence and the conflict which developed between Paul and some of the Corinthians may indeed be, at least in part, a reflection of the particular character of the Corinthian congregation. It seems, for example, that Paul accepted varying kinds of material support from most of his churches (including the Corinthian church), yet generally insisted also upon continuing his own labour. While this does not seem to have become a cause of conflict at Thessalonica, it clearly was at Corinth, because there some of the congregation found it an unacceptable and unattractive example to be set.

Paul, however, continues in the 'painful' letter to present the same model of apostolic lifestyle, threatening those who reject him with harsh treatment on his forthcoming visit. Reconciliation is achieved when the majority of the congregation reaffirm their loyalty to Paul and punish the particular offender who had been Paul's most prominent and vociferous opponent, such that Paul can subsequently call for this person's restoration and acceptance back into the community.

The sociological perspective developed here, combined with the epistolary hypothesis which dates 2 Cor 10–13 prior to 2 Cor 1–9, brings a good deal of coherence to Paul's Corinthian correspondence; and the nature of the conflict evidenced by 2 Corinthians adds plausibility to the analysis I offer of the context and impact of 1 Corinthians.

The theoretical perspectives derived from Giddens' structuration theory also lead us to ask the *critical* sociological questions concerning power, interests and ideology.[173] Our conclusions in this regard will be significant in relation to the sociological critique of religion, a critique which suggests that the function of religion is often to sustain and legitimate a particular social order. Paul's Corinthian letters, on the contrary, do not offer ideological support to the dominant social order. They do not reinforce or affirm the position of the dominant classes, nor do they demand the subordination of the socially weak. Neither, therefore, do they reflect the interests of dominant social groups. Rather, it seems that it is the interests of the socially weak which are more often represented. Paul's power is most often brought to bear against the socially stronger members of the community. However aggressively Paul uses, or attempts to use, his personal authority, it is not used to support the dominant social order or to promote the subordination of the weak.

---

[173] See pp. 55–59 above.

Nevertheless, other points must also be made. Paul certainly does use symbolic and theological resources in his attempts to legitimate his own position of domination: he is their father (1 Cor 4.14–21); the imitator of Christ whom they are to imitate (1 Cor 11.1); an apostle, among those whom God has placed at the top of the hierarchy in the church (1 Cor 12.28); one given authority and power by God (2 Cor 10.1–11). Moreover, submission to other leaders within the Christian community is explicitly demanded (1 Cor 16.15–17). While Paul's Corinthian letters do not ideologically legitimate the dominant social order – and this is a significant sociological conclusion – they do legitimate a hierarchy within the Christian community; they offer in places an ideology sustaining this particular pattern of domination.

It is also clear that there are places where Paul's formulations of Christian teaching have the potential to be taken as requiring or legitimating a subordinate position for the socially weak (1 Cor 7.17–24; 11.3–9). Although I have argued that, in their contexts, these passages do not seek to urge subordination, they certainly have ideological potential, a potential which may be developed as these texts 'escape' from the context of their creation.[174] In structuration theory terms, they become part of the set of rules and resources which comprise the Christian symbolic order and which may therefore be taken up and developed in a variety of directions, including the increasingly ideological and oppressive trajectory represented by the interpolation of 1 Cor 14.34f.

Indeed a structuration theory perspective encourages us to investigate precisely this question of reproduction and transformation; to consider how the Corinthian community continues to be shaped through a process of structuration. To what extent does the social ethos of Pauline Christianity change and develop in the time after the death of the apostle? As 'Pauline' teaching is reproduced in new contexts by new people, to what extent, if at all, does it become an ideology for the dominant social order, sustaining and legitimating the forms of domination on which society depended? To what extent does it come to express and sustain the interests of the socially strong? How does it shape and structure the life of the Christian community, both internally and in relation to the wider world?

---

[174] Cf. Giddens 1979, 44.

A comprehensive and widely documented investigation of these questions is beyond the scope of this study, which has only investigated the social ethos of Paul's Christianity as found in the Corinthian correspondence.[175] However, a limited but contextual answer may be sought by continuing the Corinthian focus and looking at 1 Clement, the next piece of extant ecclesiastical correspondence addressed to the Corinthian church. As Paul shaped the Corinthian community's life by his letters, so this role is later filled by 1 Clement.[176] The purpose of the next chapter will be to consider the ways in which 1 Clement takes up and reproduces the rules and resources of the Christian symbolic order in order to shape and structure the social life and relations of the Corinthian Christian community.

---

[175] For some preliminary thoughts on the Pastoral Epistles, see Horrell 1993, and, for a brief and exploratory trajectory through the Pauline corpus, Horrell 1995d; also §7.2. below.

[176] On the choice of 1 Clement as a focus of study, see Introduction above, p. 5.

6

The social ethos of 1 Clement

6.1. Introduction, date and authorship

The theoretical framework which underlies this project, outlined in chapters 1 and 2 and based largely on the work of Anthony Giddens, requires that texts be viewed as located, 'situated', productions which are embedded in the demands of a particular context. They arise from, and have an impact upon that context, and an ongoing process of structuration occurs in which the lives of communities are shaped, structured, by the rules and resources which, at the same time, are formulated within that particular context. In this chapter, I aim to consider the ways in which 1 Clement takes up and reproduces the rules and resources of the Christian symbolic order in order to shape and structure the social life and relations of the Corinthian Christian community. To do this, it is first necessary to 'locate' this letter within its socio-historical context, seeking, as I sought in relation to 1 and 2 Corinthians, to understand something of the situation within which this text seeks to act. Since the letter is not as well-known as Paul's letters, a more extended introduction and survey are appropriate. The first two sections of this chapter therefore deal with questions of date, authorship, and occasion.

The text known as 1 Clement is, from its own internal evidence, a letter sent from the church at Rome to the church at Corinth (prescript and subscription). Although 1 Clement was not included in the New Testament Canon it was, and is, an important and influential document.[1] Dionysius of Corinth, sometime around 170 CE, informed the church at Rome that the epistle sent to Corinth 'through Clement' (διὰ Κλήμεντος) was read out regularly for the instruction of the Corinthian

---

[1]   Cf. Jaubert 1971, 13. For 1 Clement's importance in ancient times, see Grant 1964, 13ff; Lightfoot 1890a, 148–200 (quotations and references up to the tenth century).

church.[2] Eusebius has occasion to mention the letter a number of times. He regards it as μεγάλη τε καὶ θαυμασία, 'great and wonderful', and mentions that it was 'publicly read in the common assembly in many churches both in the days of old and in our own time' (*HE* 3.16). There is some disagreement, however, as to whether 1 Clement was ever regarded as scripture.[3] Where Eusebius discusses which writings are canonical, he does not even mention 1 Clement (*HE* 3.3; 3.24–25) though he does include it among 'the disputed writings' (τῶν ἀντιλεγομένων γραφῶν) used by Clement of Alexandria in his *Stromateis*, a list which includes 'the Epistle to the Hebrews, and those of Barnabas, and Clement, and Jude' (*HE* 6.13.6). The 85th Apostolical Canon lists 1 Clement with the scriptural books.[4]

The prominence of 1 Clement in contemporary discussion, especially in Germany, owes a lot to Rudolf Sohm, who in his *Kirchenrecht* (1892) proclaimed 1 Clement as the letter which marked the fall from the charismatic and spiritual character of the early church, and the introduction of *Kirchenrecht* (ecclesiastial law).[5] 1 Clement has also been an important focus for discussion about ecclesiastical office.[6]

Although a precise and irrefutable dating of 1 Clement is impossible, there is widespread agreement that it was written in the last decade of the first century, perhaps around 95–96 CE.[7] Dissenting voices include G. Edmundson, who argues for a date of 70 CE and C. Eggenberger, who dates the epistle between 118 and 125, during the reign of Hadrian.[8]

---

[2] Letter of Dionysius to Soter, Bishop of Rome, cited by Eusebius, *HE* 4.23.11. Date of c. 170 given by Lightfoot 1890a, 154.

[3] Lake 1912, 6–7, thinks that 'l Clement appears to be treated by Clement of Alexandria as Scripture', but Lightfoot takes a different view; see 1890a, 366–78.

[4] See discussion of this evidence in Lightfoot 1890a, 368–78.

[5] See Mikat 1969, 7–9; cf. further von Campenhausen 1969, 294–301; Brent 1987. See the overview of the Sohm-Harnack debate in Fuellenbach 1980, 26–34. An overview of research since Harnack is given by Beyschlag 1966, 1–47.

[6] See esp. Fuellenbach 1980, whose book is devoted to a comparison of Protestant and Catholic approaches to the questions of ecclesiastical office and Roman primacy. Also Brown 1983, 162–66, 173–80.

[7] See for example: Lightfoot 1890a, 346–58 (95–96 CE); Knoch 1964, 31, cf. 28 (96–98 CE); Barnard 1966 (94–97 CE); Mikat 1969, 11–12 (late 90s); Jaubert 1971, 19–20 (95–98 CE); Fuellenbach 1980, 1–3, 147–50 nn. 1–16 (93–96 CE); Holmes 1989, 25 (95–96 CE); Jeffers 1991, 31, 90–94 (93–97 CE); Lindemann 1992, 12 (90s). Some are more cautious, e.g. Lake 1912, 4–5 (75–110 but probably 90s); Grant 1964, 38 (81–96 CE); Welborn 1984, 37 (80–140 CE).

[8] Edmundson 1913, 188–202, followed by Robinson 1976, 327–35. For a critique of Robinson's book see Sturdy 1979. Hooijbergh 1975, argues for 69 CE. Eggenberger 1951, 181–88; for a critique see von Campenhausen 1952.

239

A crucial question relating to the date of the epistle concerns the reference to τὰς αἰφνιδίους καὶ ἐπαλλήλους γενομένας ἡμῖν συμφορὰς καὶ περιπτώσεις ('the sudden and repeated misfortunes and calamaties which have happened to us'; 1.1; cf. 7.1). This phrase is generally taken to imply that the Roman church had recently suffered some form of persecution,[9] and thus to point either to the time of Nero (c. 64–68 CE) or to the end of Domitian's reign (c. 95 CE).[10] The deaths of Peter and Paul, while examples τῆς γενεᾶς ἡμῶν ('of our own generation'; 5.1), are portrayed as events in the past, seeming to imply that some years have passed since Nero's reign.[11] A date later than the 60s may also be suggested by the description of the Corinthian church as ἀρχαία ('ancient'; 47.6),[12] and by the reference to 'faithful and prudent men, who have lived among us without blame from youth to old age' (ἀπὸ νεότητος ... ἕως γήρους – 63.3; Lake).[13] On the other hand, the facts that Paul and Peter are 'examples of our own generation' (5.1; Lake) and that the apostolic appointment of leaders does not seem far distant (44.1–3), rule out a date much beyond the end of the first century.[14] The form of Church organisation revealed by 1 Clement (aware of ἐπίσκοποι, but not a monepiscopate, and in which bishops and presbyters are apparently undifferentiated – see 44.4f)[15] is also argued to imply a first century date.[16] The specific link with the end of Domitian's reign, however, has recently been questioned by L. L. Welborn, who stresses both the weakness of the evidence for any persecution of Christians under Domitian, and the weakness of the claim that persecution is implied by the wording of 1 Clem 1.1: 'the first sentence of the epistle is no more

---

[9] See e.g. Barnard 1966, 5–15, who argues against Milburn 1945 and the idea that Clement is referring to internal troubles of the Roman church.
[10] On Nero's persecution see Tacitus *Annals* 15.44. Roman evidence for persecution under Domitian is slight, and depends on the link with the Flavian household (see below pp. 242–44; note the caution of Grant 1964, 38 and esp. Welborn 1984), for which see Dio Cassius *HR* 67.14 and Suetonius, *Dom.* 15–17. The tradition of persecution under Domitian is rooted in early Christian tradition; see Eusebius *HE* 3.17–20; 4.26.9 (citing Melito), and evidence collected by Lightfoot 1890a, 104–15; also Barnard 1966, 12–15; Mikat 1969, 11–12.
[11] Cf. Lightfoot 1890a, 350–52; Grant 1964, 38; Holmes 1989, 25.
[12] Cf. Barnard 1966, 11 n. 1, though Lightfoot 1890a, 349–50, does not think weight should be put on this point.
[13] So Lightfoot 1890a, 349.
[14] Cf. Lake 1912, 4–5; Holmes 1989, 25.
[15] See further n. 38 below; and §6.2. below for reactions to the recent suggestion of Campbell 1994 in this regard.
[16] So Lightfoot 1890a, 352; Lindemann 1992, 12; cf. Brown 1983, 163.

than an apologetic formula like that which introduces numerous letters and speeches on concord.'[17] If the misfortunes mentioned existed at all, Welborn argues, they probably refer to internal problems of the Roman Christian community, and not to persecution. Nevertheless, Welborn accepts other evidence within the epistle and in tradition which dates 1 Clement not earlier than 80 CE, and he suggests 80–140 as the plausible range for a time of composition.[18] Even accepting Welborn's caution concerning the link with Domitianic persecution, it would still seem reasonable to assume that the letter was written towards the end of the first century, between 30 and 50 years after the writing of Paul's Corinthian letters. (Welborn does not assess the extent to which the form of church organisation reflected in 1 Clement leads many to posit a first-century date.)

External attestation is congruent with this dating, although it can hardly be said to confirm it beyond doubt. It is possible, though no more than this, that Ignatius (c. 110 CE) alludes to the letter from Rome to Corinth when he says of the Roman Christians, ἄλλους ἐδιδάξατε – 'you taught others'.[19] Another intriguing early reference in the Shepherd of Hermas (95–150 CE?), important because it constitutes the earliest evidence to connect the name of Clement with epistles sent from Rome, refers to a Clement whose duty it is to send communications εἰς τὰς ἔξω πόλεις ('to the cities abroad'; Vis. 2.4.3).[20] The numerous parallels between 1 Clement and Polycarp's Epistle to the Phillipians seemed to J. B. Lightfoot to 'furnish ample proof that Clement's Epistle was in the hands of Polycarp'.[21] Andreas Lindemann, however, is cautious, 'for in no cases do the parallels prove literary dependence'.[22]

---

[17] Welborn 1984, 48, see 35–48; cf. Milburn 1945; Brunner 1972, 101–102, who nevertheless accepts 96–98 as the most likely date (see 142–43 n. 1).

[18] Welborn 1984, 37; followed by Bowe 1988, 1–3 (see 2 n. 5; 8 n. 3).

[19] Ignatius Rom. 3.1. (Ignatius' time as bishop is dated to the reign of Trajan (98–117 CE) by Eusebius HE 3.21–22; 110 CE is estimated for the letter by Lightfoot 1890a, 149.) Harnack 1929, 10, thinks a reference to 1 Clement 'ist höchst wahrscheinlich'.

[20] The date of the Shepherd is much disputed, and the work may have been written in stages, perhaps by a number of authors. It is no later than 150 CE, and some would date portions, if not all of its material, considerably earlier. Jeffers argues that: 'The Visions almost certainly date to the time of Clement and the final portions of the work were done no later than 135' (1991, 112; see overview 106–12).

[21] Lightfoot 1890a, 149; see 149–52. He dates Polycarp's epistle to c. 110 CE. Mikat 1969, 10, suggests c. 135.

[22] 'denn die Parallelen verweisen in keinem Fall auf literarische Abhängigkeit': Lindemann 1992, 11.

241

If Eusebius is to be believed, then Hegesippus (c. 170 CE) made 'some remarks about the epistle of Clement to the Corinthians' (τῆς Κλήμεντος πρὸς Κορινθίους ἐπιστολῆς – *HE* 4.22.1), 'but [Eusebius] does not give any words of Hegesippus himself, testifying to Clement's authorship'.[23] Eusebius also tells us that Dionysius 'quotes the letter of Clement to the Corinthians', though here he actually cites the reference to the letter sent διὰ Κλήμεντος – (*HE* 4.23.11). Eusebius explicitly dates the epistle of Clement to the time of Domitian and ascribes it to Clement the third Bishop of Rome (*HE* 3.13–16; cf. also 3.21). He also makes clear that the epistle was written in the name of the Roman church (3.16), and notes the parallels with the epistle to the Hebrews (*HE* 3.38.1–3).[24] Irenaeus too mentions both the fact that Clement was the third Bishop of Rome, and that 'the church in Rome sent a most powerful letter to the Corinthians urging them to peace and renewing their faith and the tradition which they had recently received from the apostles'.[25] Clement of Alexandria also knows of Clement of Rome, author of the Epistle to the Corinthians.[26] He refers to him once as 'the Apostle Clement', attributing the letter to the Corinthians to him.[27] Once, however, he interestingly refers to 'the Epistle of the Romans to the Corinthians'.[28]

If the epistle sent from Rome to Corinth can be attributed to an author named Clement, and this must remain uncertain,[29] then the question of Clement's identity naturally arises. Eusebius, like Origen before him, identified him with the Clement mentioned by Paul in Phil 4.3, though this can hardly be granted plausibility.[30] More possible is a connection with the household of Titus Flavius Clemens, a consul and cousin of the emperor Domitian.[31] Dio Cassius records that Domitian had Flavius Clemens killed and his wife Domitilla banished on a charge of 'atheism' (ἀθεότητος), linking this with the condemnation of many

---

[23] Lightfoot 1890a, 358. For the date of 170, see Lightfoot 1890a, 153.

[24] The existence of a second letter ascribed to Clement is also here acknowledged (*HE* 3.38.4).

[25] Irenaeus *Adversus Haereses* 3.3.3 (c. 180 CE); cited by Eusebius *HE* 5.6.1–3. See Lightfoot 1890a, 156–57.

[26] *Strom.* 1.7 (p. 375); 4.17 (p. 187, 190); 4.18 (p. 190); 6.8 (p. 341).

[27] *Strom.* 4.17 (p. 187).

[28] *Strom.* 5.12 (p. 268). Cf. Lindemann 1992, 12 and further Lightfoot 1890a, 158–60; Grant and Graham 1965, 5–6.

[29] Note Lindemann's caution, 1992, 13 and 1979, 72–73. All manuscripts other than the Coptic version attribute the letter directly to 'Clement', but given their dates, this hardly proves the connection; see Lake 1912, 121 n. 1.

[30] Eusebius *HE* 3.15–16. See Lightfoot 1890a, 22–23.

[31] Suetonius *Dom.* 15.1; Dio Cassius *HR* 67.14.1.

others who had 'drifted into Jewish ways' (τὰ τῶν Ἰουδαίων ἤθη).[32] These hints have led to the hypothesis that Clemens and Domitilla may have been Christian sympathisers, if not actual converts.[33] To this limited literary evidence may be added the archaeological and inscriptional evidence relating to an apparently Christian burial ground on land which belonged to Domitilla.[34] The theory that the author of 1 Clement was Flavius Clemens himself has rightly been rejected,[35] but building on the evidence of the possible Christian connections of this household, Lightfoot, and more recently James Jeffers, have suggested that Clement, the author of our epistle, was 'a freedman or the son of a freedman belonging to the household of Flavius Clemens the emperor's cousin', from whom, as was customary, the name of Clemens came.[36] However, the limited nature of the evidence requires caution and the link between Clement and the Flavian household is hardly beyond dispute.

If a 'Clement' was responsible for writing the epistle on behalf of the church at Rome, it is still uncertain whether he was recognised in his own time as the third Bishop of Rome, as later lists designate him.[37] A conception of monepiscopacy is hardly explicit in 1 Clement: 'Only two orders are enumerated, and these are styled bishops and deacons respectively, where the term "bishop" is still a synonyme [sic] for "presbyter".'[38]

---

[32] Dio Cassius *HR* 67.14.2. Suetonius (*Dom.* 15.1) also mentions the putting to death of Flavius Clemens, but records only that the suspicion was slight (*ex tenuissima suspicione*) and that Clemens was a person of 'most contemptible laziness' (*contemptissimae inertiae*). The implied meaning of *inertiae* is disputed; see Jeffers 1991, 26 n. 34, who lists 'lack of energy/ activity/ reasonable ambition' as possibilities.

[33] See discussion in Lightfoot 1890a, 33–35; Jeffers 1991, 25–28; but against this hypothesis see Welborn 1984, 43.

[34] See esp. Lightfoot 1890a, 35–39; Jeffers 1991, 48–89, but note again the caution of Welborn 1984, 43–44.

[35] Lightfoot 1890a, 23: 'it is hardly conceivable that, if a person of the rank and position of Flavius Clemens had been head of the Roman Church, the fact would have escaped the notice of all contemporary and later writers, whether heathen or Christian.' Cf. Harnack 1929, 51.

[36] Lightfoot 1890a, 61; see further 14–63; Harnack 1929, 51 (freedman or slave of the Consul); Wong 1977, 87; Jeffers 1991, 31–34 (esp. 33). Lightfoot also argues that Claudius Ephebus and Valerius Vito (1 Clem 65.1) 'were brought up in the imperial household' (1890a, 29, see 27–29; also Jeffers 1991, 29–31). Paul's mention of Christians in Caesar's household in his time is noteworthy (Phil 4.22).

[37] Cf. Harnack 1929, 50. On the succession lists, see Lightfoot 1890a, 63–67, 201–345.

[38] Lightfoot 1890a, 69; cf. 352; Brown 1983, 163 n. 347; Jeffers 1991, 176; Lindemann 1992, 12. Note esp. 1 Clem 44.4f, where πρεσβύτερος and ἐπίσκοπος seem to be synonymous (cf. 42.4; 54.2). On the Protestant/ Catholic debate regarding ecclesiastical offices in 1 Clement, see Fuellenbach 1980.

In short, although the identification of the author as Clement seems likely, and his connection with the Flavian family quite possible, it is impossible to say much with certainty. But despite the uncertainty, I shall refer to 'Clement' as author of the letter, and to the letter as 1 Clement, since this seems the most concise and convenient way to refer to the letter which is so closely associated with this name.

6.2. Occasion: the situation at Corinth

'The occasion for the writing of 1 Clement may be determined fairly precisely.'[39] Right at the beginning of the letter a dispute at Corinth is named as the reason for the Roman church's concern. It is an occasion of μιαρᾶς καὶ ἀνοσίου στάσεως, 'abominable and unholy sedition', fomented by ὀλίγα πρόσωπα προπετῆ καὶ αὐθάδη ('a few rash and self-willed people'; 1.1). A concern about this sedition (στάσις) and a desire to see peace and harmony restored pervade the epistle.[40] In 47.6 the nature of the στάσις is revealed more precisely: the Corinthian church has been led δι' ἕν ἣ δύο πρόσωπα στασιάζειν πρὸς τοὺς πρεσβυτέρους ('through one or two people to rebel against the elders').[41] The particular problem is that the appointed elders have been ejected from their positions (44.3–6).[42]

This much is clear, unless one were to follow Eggenberger in his argument that this Corinthian 'occasion' is a complete fiction and that the entire letter is actually an *apologia* to the imperial regime assuring those in authority of the Church's loyalty and seeking to ensure their favour.[43]

---

[39] 'Der Anlaß für die Abfassung des 1 Clem ist einigermaßen genau zu bestimmen.' Lindemann 1992, 16; cf. Harnack 1929, 52.

[40] Note the frequent use of στασιάζω (4.12; 43.2; 46.7; 47.6; 49.5; 51.3; 55.1), στάσις (1.1; 2.6; 3.2; 14.2; 46.9; 51.1; 54.2; 57.1; 63.1), εἰρηνεύω (15.1; 54.2; 56.12f; 63.4), εἰρήνη (insc.; 2.2; 3.4; 15.1; 16.5; 19.2; 20.1,9ff; 21.1; 22.5; 60.3f; 61.1f; 62.2; 63.2; 64.1; 65.1), ὁμόνοια (9.4; 11.2; 20.3,10f; 21.1; 30.3; 34.7; 49.5; 50.5; 60.4; 61.1; 62.2 [ὁμονοέω]; 63.2; 65.1).

[41] See further 44.3ff, 47–57 (note 51.1; 54.1ff; 57.1f). In 54.1ff it is implied that the instigators of the στάσις should depart voluntarily from the community; see discussion in Mikat 1969, 32–35.

[42] On the centrality of 44.3–6, see Brunner 1972, 110, 120, 152ff.

[43] Eggenberger 1951, esp. 189–93.

Eggenberger, however, has convinced few, however valuable some of his comments on 1 Clement's political ethos might be.[44] Barbara Bowe claims that too much emphasis has been placed on 1 Clem 44.6 as the real point of the letter. She sees Clement as concerned both with the deposition of the presbyters and with the wider problem of division and strife: 'στάσις and the restoration of communal harmony, not the maintenance of ecclesiastical office, is the primary concern of *1 Clement*.'[45] But since the στάσις *is* the ejection of the presbyters, I do not see how Clement's concern can be divided in this way.

The precise cause of the στάσις in Corinth, however, and the identity of the instigators, are harder to assess. Anyone acquainted with the competing theories about the identity of Paul's opponents in 1 and 2 Corinthians will not be surprised to discover that the 'opponents' in 1 Clement have been variously designated as gnostics, pneumatic enthusiasts, libertines, ascetics, even 'ex-Essene Levites'.[46] Against all such theories it must simply be said that the text does not offer information sufficient to allow any convincing assessment of the theology or spirituality of the 'opponents'. 'Mirror-reading' from a number of the themes used by Clement is not only an unreliable guide to the stance of the rebels, but it leads, as can be seen from the number of suggestions, to a wide range of incompatible answers.[47] If there were doctrinal issues involved in the dispute at Corinth, then Clement does not confront them, nor does his letter imply that he knew anything of them. 'I Clement does not yield direct information concerning the position taken by the rebels.'[48]

---

[44] Most critical of all was von Campenhausen 1952; also Beyschlag 1966, 17–19: 'Man wird sagen müssen, daß Eggenbergers Arbeit als Ganze total verfehlt ist' (p. 19).

[45] Bowe 1988, 23; cf. 31, 153, 158 etc.

[46] See for example Bauer 1972, 98–104 (gnostics), cautiously followed by Vielhauer 1975a, 536–37; Aono 1979, 101–106, who gives an overview of discussion and sees the Corinthian rebels as 'pneumatische Enthusiasten'; Hooijbergh 1975, 280 and *passim* (ex-Essene Levites). Overview also in Maier 1991, 87–94, on whose suggestion see below.

[47] Cf. the methodological reflections of Barclay 1987; Hickling 1975. Jaubert 1971, 13 n. 1: 'L'obscurité qui entoure les événements de Corinthe a permis des suppositions diverses sur les motifs de la révolte.'

[48] Fisher 1974, 55; see further 57–62. Cf. Wong 1977, 81 n. 2; Lindemann 1979, 73; Countryman 1980, 156. Lightfoot 1890a, 82 agrees that no 'doctrinal question was directly involved, unless their old scepticism with respect to the Resurrection had revived' (it is prominent in 1 Clem 24ff). Campbell 1994, 216: 'that the problem is fundamentally social rather than doctrinal seems extremely likely.'

It may therefore be more plausible, as with 1 Cor 1–4, to see the problem, at least in Clement's view, as the division and rebellion itself.[49] It is possible (for Lindemann 'am wahrscheinlichsten'), 'that a group within the Corinthian church placed in question the (presbyter-)office as such'.[50] Lindemann points out that Clement does not state that the leaders of the sedition took up the presbyteral office. The idea that the office itself was being questioned was rejected by Adolf von Harnack, because only some of the presbyters had been removed (cf. 1 Clem 44.6).[51] The letter aims primarily not at justifying the existence of the presbyteral office, but at the restoration of order in the congregation and the reinstitution of the wrongly ejected elders.[52] Lindemann's observations may, however, be fruitfully combined with Campbell's argument that the elders were not those who held an office as such, but those who were in a position of honour at the head of their household.[53] If this is correct, then the rebels, who were probably not from this social group (see below for this argument), neither could nor would have pronounced themselves as 'elders'.

A potentially significant social analysis of the rebellion at Corinth has been proposed by L. W. Countryman, who argues that the schism 'was fomented by rich Christians'.[54] Countryman's main evidence for this hypothesis is 1 Clem 3.1–3 which he takes as implying 'that Clement blames the rebellion on the increased prosperity of the Corinthian church'.[55] However, since the terms which suggest this arise from the quotation of Deut 32.15 (LXX) in 1 Clem 3.1, it is surely unwise to assume that this is a 'veiled' reference to increased prosperity among the rebels. It seems more likely that Clement uses the LXX citation, from a story about Jacob's pride, simply to describe the 'fall' of the Corinthian church from its previously praiseworthy state (1.2–2.7), a fall perhaps attributed in a vague way to pride and complacency and interpreted in the light of the cautionary and paradigmatic stories from Israel's

---

[49]   Cf. Fisher 1974, 59; Wong 1977, 81 n. 2; Harnack 1929, 91–92. 1 Clem 47 explicitly makes the comparison with the factionalism confronted by Paul.

[50]   'daß eine Gruppe innerhalb der korinthischen Kirche das (Presbyter-)Amt als solches in Frage gestellt hat': Lindemann 1992, 135; cf. 16–17.

[51]   Harnack 1929, 91; though note Lindemann's comments (1992, 135).

[52]   Cf. 1 Clem 44.3–6; 45.3; 47.6; 57.1.

[53]   Campbell 1994; see further below, with n. 60.

[54]   Countryman 1980, 154.

[55]   Countryman 1980, 155.

history.[56] It is most probably an example of Clement's use of biblical citations and allusions wherever they seem to fit or illustrate his line of thought (cf. esp. 42.5). His description of the insurgents as οἱ ἄτιμοι, ἄδοξοι, ἄφρονες, νέοι ('those without honour and reputation, foolish, young'; 3.3) hardly sounds like the rich members of the congregation,[57] though some of this language too is drawn from the LXX (προσκόψει τὸ παιδίον πρὸς τὸν πρεσβύτην, ὁ ἄτιμος πρὸς τὸν ἔντιμον – Isa 3.5).[58] It is unlikely, moreover, if Clement saw the danger at Corinth coming specifically from the rich, that he would have contrasted the 'strong' and 'rich' with the 'weak' and 'poor' and urged the latter to reverence the former and thank God for them (38.2).

Roman Garrison also argues that tensions between rich and poor members of the congregation are likely to have played a significant part in causing the conflict to which 1 Clement refers, particularly given the earlier evidence (from Paul's time) for a degree of social diversity being contained within the community.[59] Garrison argues, however, that the rebels are much more likely to have been among the poorer members of the congregation – indeed this would surely be a more plausible inference to draw from 1 Clem 3.3. R. A. Campbell also maintains, against Countryman, that 'the elders who have been ousted are not the victims of the well-to-do; they *are* the well-to-do', since 'the elders' (not an office as such, but a position of honour at the head of the household, according to Campbell) were almost certainly prominent householders within the congregation.[60] However, Campbell suggests that the cause of the conflict at Corinth concerns

---

[56] Cf. Beyschlag 1966, 136ff, 330–31. On the widespread influence of the Song of Moses (Deut 32.1–43) in Jewish and Christian literature, see Bell 1994, 200–85.

[57] Countryman 1980, faces this difficulty on 155–56. The language used and the contrasts drawn are similar to those found in 1 Cor 1.26–28 and 4.8–13, though there Paul makes it clear that he (and God!) are on the side of the despised nobodies. Clement, by contrast, uses the language to designate those who have rebelled against the community and against God.

[58] Cf. Bowe 1988, 18–19, on the rhetorical use of Isaian language in 1 Clem 3.3. The assumption that the rebels were young (e.g. Jeffers 1991, 94; Wong 1977, 81) may also be questioned. This is only suggested in 1 Clem 3.3 and Bowe argues that 'the reference to νέοι cannot be taken out of its general rhetorical context and given a more concrete and historical interpretation' (1988, 19).

[59] Garrison 1993, 36–37, 84, 116–117; cf. also §3.7. above.

[60] Campbell 1994, 215; cf. also Maier 1991, 100. Campbell 1994, 246, summarises his thesis thus: 'the elders are those who bear a title of honour, not of office, a title that is imprecise, collective and representative, and rooted in the ancient family or household.'

an attempt to introduce monoepiscopacy in the manner recommended by the pastorals! The bishop has sought to be more than a chairman of the presbyters, and has sought to centralize the worship of the church under his own presidency in the way later to be advocated by Ignatius. The result is the *de facto* demotion of the other presbyters ...[61]

There is, however, little evidence to suggest that the dispute 'centres on one man', as Campbell argues. 1 Clem 54.1f might, as Campbell suggests, be an attempt to urge one particular 'trouble-maker' to leave the community, but it may just as well be an appeal to any number of rebels. Clement's comment that the apostles knew there would be 'strife for the title of bishop' (ἔρις ἔσται ἐπὶ τοῦ ὀνόματος τῆς ἐπισκοπῆς – 44.1) might reflect a 'dispute about how many people should bear the title of ἐπίσκοπος',[62] but it could equally well reflect the conflict over who should have oversight within the community; in Clement's view, the appointed and legitimate elders/overseers (cf. 44.4) have been wrongly deposed by a group of rebels. This more traditional reading of the evidence is, I think, confirmed at a number of points in the epistle. Clement's opening comment in the letter clearly accuses a few people (ὀλίγα πρόσωπα – 1.1) of causing the στάσις. The elders in the community, moreover, have not been 'demoted' but rather 'removed' (using ἀποβάλλω – see 44.3, 4). The weakness of Campbell's hypothesis becomes clear when we note that, having used the text of the epistle to reconstruct the situation to which it refers, he then suggests that the text actually misrepresents the situation (as he has reconstructed it). 'The Church at Corinth is represented as having risen up against its elders, when in reality it has demoted most of the elders in favour of the "monepiskopos".'[63] Valuable though many of Campbell's insights are, on this point I think his reconstruction is mistaken.

Another recent suggestion has been made by Harry Maier, for whom

the dispute which Clement describes as arising over the title of bishop [see 44.1ff] is best understood as referring to a division within one or two of the Corinthian house churches which has resulted in the creation of an alternative meeting place, the exodus of members who are

---

[61] Campbell 1994, 214; see 213–216.
[62] Campbell 1994, 214.
[63] Campbell 1994, 245.

sympathetic with these persons and, presumably, the exclusion of members who are opposed to them.[64]

This may be a plausible socio-historical background to the Corinthian dispute, and Maier is, I think, right to point to the prominence and leadership of (relatively) wealthy householders especially after the death of Paul.[65] However, it must be noted that Clement does not explicitly give us grounds for believing that house church division and 'the creation of an alternative meeting place' are at the root of the problem at Corinth. Indeed, Clement's advice that the instigators of the divisions should 'depart' and 'go away' (54.2) might not have been the most apposite instruction if such were the problem, since, on Maier's view, that is precisely what has already, in a sense, happened. Clement much more clearly implies that the elders of the church have been 'removed' (44.3, 4).[66] House church rivalry and inter-household strife may have played a part in the disruption at Corinth, but what little evidence there is suggests rather that the rebellion took place against those who were household heads, 'elders', and was led 'from below' by those of lower social position.

Given the difficulty of reconstructing with confidence the context and causes of the Corinthian dispute, it is hard to build a detailed theory concerning the intentions and character of the Corinthian rebellion. In Bowe's view:

> [T]he actual causes and motivation both for the deposition of the presbyters and for the general state of στάσις … in Corinth cannot be known. None of the attempts to identify the leaders of the dissenting group, either as a social subgroup or as an heretical faction, has proved convincing.[67]

Clement himself shows no interest in the particular grounds on which the discontent was based and reveals nothing about the substance of the disagreement at Corinth. What he may or may not have known is, of course, beyond our ability to recover. Nevertheless, Bowe's scepticism is too great. In my view, the Corinthian conflict may be described, with some confidence, in the following way.

---

[64] Maier 1991, 93; cf. Harnack 1929, 92.
[65] See Maier 1991, 100.
[66] Cf. the criticism of Campbell 1994, 213.
[67] Bowe 1988, 21, see further 18–21.

The basic outline of the conflict, as the letter reveals (though disputed by Campbell), is that a number of what Clement regards as rebels have risen up against at least some of the established leaders of the Corinthian congregation and have succeeded in throwing them out. Why they did so we cannot tell. It is most likely, and here Campbell is surely right, that the deposed elders were among the socially prominent members of the community, heads of households. It is probable that the rebels were those of lower social position who, for whatever reasons, rose up against these 'elders' and rejected their leadership. This last point is hard to substantiate (though 3.3 adds some textual support to it), but seems the most plausible assessment of the evidence, particularly in view of the character of Clement's response to the situation.

In the following exegesis and analysis, as we study Clement's reproduction and transformation of the rules and resources of the Christian symbolic order in this particular context, we shall search for evidence of 1 Clement's attitude to social relations and to particular social groups, and will assess its socio-political ethos. The issues and questions central to the theoretical framework adopted in this study lead us to investigate the intended social impact of Christian teaching upon communities and upon specific social groups within those communities. How does this document, this formulation of Christian teaching, shape people's social interaction, their interrelationships and their view of one another? Whose interests does it reflect, and in what sense(s) might it be described as ideological?

6.3. The main themes of 1 Clement

There is one word which summarises Clement's view of the dispute at Corinth: στάσις ('rebellion, discord').[68] This choice of vocabulary is of note, as we shall see. Those who have instigated the trouble are described at the outset as προπετῆ καὶ αὐθάδη, 'rash and self-willed' (1.1), and their actions are portrayed as the result of jealousy, envy and pride.[69] Clement describes the seditious people with words like ἀλαζονεία

---

[68] See 1.1; 2.6; 3.2; 14.2; 46.9; 51.1; 54.2; 57.1; 63.1. See further n. 40 above.
[69] See 3.2; 4.1–6.4; 9.1; 14.1; 46.5–9; 47.1ff; 63.2. Clement's negative portrayal of the Corinthian disturbance continues throughout the letter; cf. Brunner 1972, 101 with n. 14, who lists 2.6; 3.2; 14.2; 46.7,9; 47.6; 49.5; 51.1; 54.2; 57.1; 63.1.

('arrogance'), φιλόνεικος ('quarrelsome'), αὐθάδεια ('willfulness').[70]
While Clement uses terms such as σχίσμα ('division'; 46.5, 9; 54.2),
πρόσκλισις ('partiality'; 47.3f; cf. 21.7) and ἀκαταστασία ('disorder';
3.2; 14.1) to describe the Corinthian situation – language similar to that
used by Paul[71] – their troubles are fundamentally an instance of στάσις,
a word which does not appear in Paul's epistles. According to Bowe,
Clement's use of this word as the primary term to describe the Corinthian
rebellion roots his concern in a wider socio-political context: 'When Clement chooses to discuss "the questions disputed in Corinth" under the
term στάσις (1.1), he reveals his indebtedness to Hellenistic political
rhetoric. Such rhetoric deals at length with this, the greatest of all civil
maladies'.[72] By employing the term στάσις, Clement probably intends
to portray the situation at Corinth as a case comparable to the civil and
political rebellion against which writers like Aristotle warned.[73] This is,
however, not necessarily the case, since the word στάσις may be used
simply as a description for any kind of disorder or dissension, as, for
example, in Acts 15.2, 23.7 (though it has somewhat wider socio-political overtones in Acts 19.40, 23.10 and 24.5). Nevertheless, there is evidence to suggest that Clement's use of the term is related to the wider
socio-political context. Clement explicitly warns the Corinthians, rather
ominously, though perhaps realistically, that they are creating 'great danger' for themselves, especially since the report of their rebellion has reached
outsiders as well as Christians.[74] By labelling the Corinthian uprising
στάσις, Clement not only condemns it and its instigators, but also indicates that such action incurs the risk of intervention by state powers.[75]
For 'a στάσις is really nothing other than a sedition'[76] and as such would
be regarded as dangerous by the ruling authorities (cf. Acts 19.40; 23.10;
24.5).[77]

---

[70] Cf. Bowe 1988, 63. ἀλαζονεία (13.1; 14.1; 16.2; 21.5; 35.5; 57.2; cf. Rom 1.30); φιλόνεικος (45.1; cf. 1 Cor 11.16); αὐθάδεια (1.1 [αὐθάδης]; 30.8; 57.2).

[71] σχίσμα (1 Cor 1.10; 11.18; 12.25); ἀκαταστασία (1 Cor 14.33; 2 Cor 12.20; cf. 2 Cor 6.5).

[72] Bowe 1988, 62, further 61ff. See also Mikat 1969, 20–29; Delling TDNT 7, 568–71; Wengst 1987, 113 with 217 n. 52.

[73] Aristotle *Politics* 5.6.1; 5.7.5; Plutarch *Precepts of Statecraft* 825; Dio Chrysostom *Diss.* 39.4; Dio Cassius *HR* 44.24; Tacitus *Histories* 3.80.

[74] See 1 Clem 14.2; 47.7; 59.1. The reference to τοὺς ἑτεροκλινεῖς ὑπάρχοντας ἀφ' ἡμῶν (47.7) is taken to imply non Christians, i.e. outsiders, by Grant and Graham 1965, 79; Jaubert 1971, 178–79 ('Les païens et sans doute aussi les juifs'); Lindemann 1992, 139.

[75] See Mikat 1969, 28.

[76] 'eine stasis ist ja nichts anderes als eine seditio'; Mikat 1969, 23.

[77] Mikat 1969, 23–28, esp. 24; Peretto 1989, 104–105.

As a case of στάσις, the Corinthian disorder is for Clement a form of rebellion and uprising which is socially and politically dangerous and, moreover, is evil. The label στάσις is evaluative and condemnatory. It is notable that Clement shows no interest in the *reasons* for the rebellion, even though the deposition of some of the presbyters may well have been supported by a majority of the congregation.[78] This is not to say, however, that Clement necessarily saw the presbyters as simply beyond removal, for he devotes considerable energy to emphasising their blamelessness (44.3–6).[79] However, his lack of interest in the actual issues of conflict at Corinth and his failure to display any detailed knowledge regarding the behaviour of the presbyters or the rebels may lead us to suspect that his insistence that the presbyters are blameless and have been wrongly deposed arises more from conviction than from informed judgment.[80] Just as the labels ζῆλος (jealousy) and φθόνος (envy) 'are polemic and say nothing about the actual motives' of the rebels,[81] so the insistence that the presbyters have ministered 'blamelessly ... with humility, quietly and unselfishly', and with the approval of all (44.3) may be a highly perspectival judgment. When Bowe states that 'This much can be said with certainty: the "opponents" put their individual goals above the goal of peace and concord for the entire community',[82] it should be stressed that the only 'certainty' is that this is Clement's view of the situation.

The exact opposite of στάσις, for Clement, is εἰρήνη καὶ ὁμόνοια – 'peace and concord'.[83] He states that the Corinthian community once experienced εἰρήνη βαθεῖα καὶ λιπαρά ('a deep and rich peace'; 2.2) at a time when πᾶσα στάσις καὶ πᾶν σχίσμα βδελυκτὸν ἦν ὑμῖν ('all sedition and all schism was abominable to you'; 2.6, Lake). The result of rebellion is that righteousness and peace are now far away (3.4) and Clement's aim is that the goal of peace may be reattained (19.2;

---

[78] So Harnack 1929, 52; Lindemann 1992, 16.
[79] See further Mikat 1969, 19; Bowe 1988, 150.
[80] Brunner 1972, 147, suggests that because 1 Clement is a letter between two parties, the facts and background do not need to be mentioned. Nonetheless, it is significant that Clement does not seek to solve the crisis by showing the rebels why their cause is unjust, nor by arguing with their point of view.
[81] 'sind Polemik und sagen nichts über die tatsächlichen Motive ...': Lindemann 1992, 16.
[82] Bowe 1988, 21.
[83] Cf. Mikat 1969, 28. Cf. 1 Clem 20.11; 60.4; 61.1; 63.2; 65.1 and n. 40 above. On Clement's use of the term ὁμόνοια see Russell 1989.

22.5; 60.4; 65.1). Indeed, Clement's letter as a whole may be described as an 'entreaty for peace and concord' (63.2).[84] As with the negative terms associated with στάσις, so εἰρήνη and ὁμόνοια are terms often used in Greco-Roman political rhetoric.[85] The ideal of peace and concord for city and state is, for Clement, an appropriate ideal for the church.[86] Clement's concerns for peace over against disorder may certainly also be paralleled in 1 Corinthians. Paul too strongly attacks division in the congregation (1 Cor 1.10; 11.18; 12.25) and asserts that God's way in all the churches is one of peace and not disorder (1 Cor 14.33). In worship, everything must be done in a seemly and orderly way (1 Cor 14.40). To some extent, then, Clement may be regarded as taking up and reproducing Pauline concerns. Indeed, he explicitly makes the comparison between his own attempt to confront division in the church and Paul's earlier letter dealing with this matter (1 Clem 47). Both authors express a concern for unity and harmony.[87] Nevertheless, Clement's language (and social ethos, I shall argue) is significantly different (Paul never uses the words στάσις or ὁμόνοια); there is both continuity and transformation.

One clear example of Clement's taking up and shaping for his own purposes resources from 1 Corinthians is found in his version of the hymn to love, clearly based on 1 Cor 13, which Paul too may possibly have taken up from his predecessors. Few of Paul's words are precisely paralleled, though the dependence cannot be missed.[88] In the light of his own context and concerns, Clement insists that ἀγάπη σχίσμα οὐκ ἔχει, ἀγάπη οὐ στασιάζει, ἀγάπη πάντα ποιεῖ ἐν ὁμονοίᾳ – 'love admits no schism, love makes no sedition, love does all things in

---

[84] Cf. Peretto 1989, esp. 113–14.

[85] See Bowe 1988, 64–66; Brunner 1972, 134–41. Van Unnik 1970, esp. 278–79, criticises Beyschlag's attempt to root Clement's use of 'peace' in Jewish-Christian tradition and not in the political sphere. Note the response by Beyschlag 1972 and rejoinder by van Unnik 1972. Cf. Dio Chrysostom *Diss.* 39.2, 4; 40.26; 49.6; Dio Cassius *HR* 44.23–25; see further Bowe 1988, 65 n. 109.

[86] Thus Bowe 1988, 86–87, suggests that Clement 'considers as particularly appropriate the metaphor of the city-state as a model for the Christian church'.

[87] Cf. Mitchell 1991, 40 n. 95, 80 n. 88, 97 nn. 191, 195; 300 with n. 7.

[88] Bowe 1988, 143: 'the phrase ἀγάπη …πάντα μακροθυμεί (1 Cor 13.4 ≈ *1 Clem.* 49.5) is the only exact parallel between the two.' See also Brunner 1972, 139; Hagner 1973, 200. There are also less exact parallels, such as ἀνέχεται // στέγει, οὐδὲν ὑπερήφανον // οὐ φυσιοῦται; see further Sanders 1943, 93–95.

concord' (49.5; Lake). Each author portrays love as the embodiment of his own model for the community. But how does Clement believe that peace and harmony are to be restored and sustained? What precisely does 'love' demand?

The primary qualities required for such peaceful community life are stated early in the epistle, where Clement paints an ideal picture of what the Corinthian community is supposed to have been like in the past (1.2–2.8). These qualities are ὑποταγή, 'submission', and ταπεινοφροσύνη, 'humility'.[89] While ταπεινός ('humble') in classical and Hellenistic literature is generally a negative term, and appears with both positive and negative connotations in the LXX, for Clement it carries a positive sense.[90] His understanding of the term may owe a good deal to Paul, for whom imitating Christ meant humbling oneself (Phil 2.5ff; 2 Cor 11.7; cf. 1 Clem 16.1f, 17), although Paul also uses ταπεινός in a negative sense (2 Cor 10.1; Phil 3.21). Indeed, for Paul the 'negative' and 'positive' senses of the word can hardly be separated neatly, since following Christ (a positive thing!) involves the humiliations of suffering and hardship (see chapter 5 above). Bowe suggests that Phil 2.3f is 'the immediate source for the use of the term [ταπεινοφροσύνη] in *1 Clement*'.[91] The importance of the appeal to humble-mindedness for Clement is clear in the major section 13.1–19.1, and ταπεινοφροσύνη is clearly intended to be a characteristic of all within the community, including the leaders (2.1; 16.1; 44.3).[92]

Submission is also urged upon all, and is intended to have a degree of mutuality:[93] ὑποτασσέσθω ἕκαστος τῷ πλησίον αὐτοῦ – 'let each person submit to their neighbour' (38.1; cf. 2.1; 37.5). All are to submit, ultimately, to God (34.5; 56.1). The image of the body – another resource taken up at least in part from 1 Corinthians[94] – is used to illustrate the need for cooperation and interdependence (37.4f; 46.6f) with the focus again on God as the source of all things (38.4).

---

89 See 1.3 and esp. 2.1; also 21.8; 37.5. More frequently the verbs are used: ὑποτάσσω (1.3; 2.1; 34.5; 38.1; 57.1f; 61.1) and ταπεινοφρονέω (2.1; 13.1,3; 16.1f, 17; 30.3; 48.6; 62.2). See discussion in Bowe 1988, 107ff.

90 See Bowe 1988, 113–14; Wengst 1988, 4–35; Brunner 1972, 128–34; Grundmann TDNT 8, 1–26.

91 Bowe 1988, 114.

92 See further Bowe 1988, 115–20.

93 Cf. Jaubert 1964a, 78–79.

94 See further §6.4. below.

The qualities of ὑποταγή and ταπεινοφροσύνη, however, are required so that *order*, peace and concord may prevail. This is Clement's response to the rebellion. Again we may observe that this is, to at least some degree, a reproduction of the 'rules and resources' with which Paul attempted to shape the life of the Corinthian community. Order in worship, Paul insisted, must be preserved; the prophets must recognise that 'the spirits of prophets submit (ὑποτάσσεται) to prophets', and that silence may sometimes be required (1 Cor 14.26–40, without the interpolation in vv. 34–35). Paul also urged submission to the recognised leaders in the congregation (1 Cor 16.16). Paul's emphasis on οἰκοδομή, 'building up', is, however, not taken up by Clement, who develops a theology of 'order' to a much greater extent than Paul. Clement's primary aim is to restore proper order within the Corinthian church; to re-establish the position of the deposed presbyters and to end the στάσις.[95] This is the dominant concern of the letter: 'One need only note the frequent usage in *1 Clement* of words related to the verb τάσσω ("to order, arrange") to see how central is its concern for order and structure within the cosmic, political and social spheres as well as within the church.'[96]

In chapter 20, Clement points to the natural universe as a supreme example where all things move and co-exist as ordered by the creator. The whole universe has been ordained to be in peace and concord (20.11).[97] Clement's attention to the order of nature is reminiscent of Stoic writers, but, as W. C. van Unnik has shown, Clement focuses not merely on the natural order, but upon this universe as ordered by God the creator.[98] Hence his concept of order is theologically defined: 'in 1 Clement the order is established by the command of the Creator and reveals the *will* of God.'[99] Each element in the natural order knows its place and does not transgress its boundary (cf. 20.6). 'Clement's intention [in this section] is to show from examples that the established order in nature serves as an ideal pattern of God's perfect rule, a model for the

---

95 Cf. Wengst 1988, 54–57.
96 Bowe 1988, 107, who lists 42 occurrences in note 2.
97 'Of the forty-two occurrences of the ταγ- root in *1 Clement*, eight are clustered together in chapter 20.' (Bowe 1988, 108.)
98 See van Unnik 1950, 183–89, who stresses the extent to which Clement's thought here is also rooted in Jewish tradition (note 1 Enoch 2–5); Wong 1977, 83. On the Stoic parallels see Sanders 1943, 109–30; e.g. Cicero *De Natura Deorum* 2.73–153. Note also the judicious comments of Lindemann 1992, 76–77.
99 Van Unnik 1950, 184.

church to emulate.'[100] The fundamental lesson to be learned from the natural universe is the way in which God has ordained all things to exist in peace and harmony. Indeed, the following chapter opens with a warning of judgment upon those who do not conduct themselves worthily and do good deeds before God μεθ' ὁμονοίας, 'in concord' (21.1). Other examples which Clement uses as models of ordered and peaceful existence enable us to see more clearly what his concept of 'order' implies. Despite the apparent stress on mutual subordination and universal humility, Clement's picture of 'peace and concord' is not so much an egalitarian one as one in which each displays the obedience and submission appropriate to their rank and position. This is surely implied by the image of the army, which appears in 1 Clem 37.1–4. Certainly the army is an example of a body of people who are interdependent, but it is also one in which subordination is appropriate *according to one's rank*. According to Annie Jaubert, 'this is the first time in a Christian writing that the mutual subordination of the members of the community is attached to an ideal of military type'.[101] Whether Clement had the *Roman* army in mind or not,[102] the army image itself conveys the idea of a given hierarchy in which order and discipline are of primary importance. 'The aim of the statement is an emphasis upon order'.[103] Each level operates ἐν τῷ ἰδίῳ τάγματι, 'in its own order' (37.3),[104] and it becomes clear that obedience and submission according to one's rank or position are what Clement considers is required among Christians: "Εκαστος ἡμῶν ἀδελφοί, ἐν τῷ ἰδίῳ τάγματι εὐαριστείτω[105]

---

[100] Wong 1977, 81–82; cf. van Unnik 1950, 181–83.

[101] Jaubert 1964a, 79: 'c'est la première fois ... que dans un écrit chrétien elle [sc. la subordination mutuelle des membres de la communauté] est ratachée à un idéal de type militaire.'

[102] The uncertainty on this point arises because the Roman army did not have a rank 'in charge of fifty' (1 Clem 37.3) whereas this group size (followed usually, however, by 'groups of ten') is known in the LXX (Exod 18.21, 25; Deut 1.15; 4 Kings 1.9–14; Isa 3.3; 1 Macc 3.55) and at Qumran (1QS 2.21–22; CD 13.1–2); cf. also Mark 6.40 (with possibly military overtones? – note the reference to 5,000 *men*, ἄνδρες – 6.44). It is possible that Clement did have the Roman army in mind but drew his 'knowledge' of army structure from the LXX; so Wengst 1987, 108–109. See further Jaubert 1964a, esp. 80–81; Lindemann 1992, 115.

[103] 'Ziel der Aussage ist ... die Betonung der Ordnung.' Lindemann 1992, 115.

[104] Note the occurrence of this phrase in 1 Cor 15.23, though here referring to the proper order of events at the eschaton.

[105] Codex Alexandrinus (A) reads εὐχαριστείτω, which Lightfoot considered 'undoubtedly correct' suggesting that 'the allusion here is plainly to the public services of the Church, where order had been violated' (1890b, 124). Both Jaubert 1971, 166 and Lake 1912, 78 n. 2 choose εὐαριστείτω.

τῷ θεῷ – 'let each one of us, brothers and sisters, be pleasing to God in their own rank' (41.1; cf. 38.1). Submission to the elders is of course Clement's particular priority (57.1f; cf. 63.1): 'As the natural world obeys the command of the Creator, so the soldiers in military service obey their superior officers, so ought the Corinthians their church's established authority.'[106]

The theology of 1 Clement, with its emphasis upon order and appropriate submission, is at least potentially one which legitimates and sustains a dominant social order; it affirms that everything is ordered just as the master intended.[107] We may recall that for Giddens one of the principal forms of ideology was 'reification': 'the naturalisation of the present'. 'The interests of dominant groups are bound up with the preservation of the *status quo*.'[108] Clement insists that people should quietly and humbly remain in their place. Clearly this is primarily ecclesiastically orientated and relates to the particular concern of the letter. Both Paul and Clement, to some extent, offer an ideology which legitimates the hierarchy of leadership which is established within the congregation. Paul, like Clement, was concerned for order and submission within the congregation (1 Cor 4.18–21; 14.40; 16.15f), although this was hardly the dominant theme of his letter, and his appeal for unity has points of contact with Clement's. However, Paul's primary model for achieving unity was the self-giving of Christ. He made it clear that the 'order' of the world was opposed by the 'foolish' word of the cross and that this world and its leaders were in the process of being brought to nothing (1 Cor 1.18–2.6). In 1 Clement, by contrast, there is no sense of an evil or fallen world order being destroyed by God.[109] There is thus both continuity and change in relation to 1 Corinthians; the rules and resources of the Christian symbolic order are taken up and transformed (explicitly in part from 1 Corinthians), as a part of the process which shapes the social embodiment of that symbolic order within the Corinthian community.

[106] Wong 1977, 84.
[107] On the prominence and use of δεσπότης as a divine title in 1 Clement, see Brunner 1972, 121–28, who interestingly concludes: 'Dieser Begriff [i.e. δεσπότης] verkündigt dann, daß Christus und der Glaube ihre Bedeutung nicht verlieren, wo Herrschaft und Macht ausgeübt werden muß.' (128).
[108] See Giddens 1979, 195; and further above pp. 50–52.
[109] See further §7.3. below.

An important question, however, is whether Clement uses his theology explicitly to affirm or legitimate *social* distinctions within the dominant social order and within the Christian community. It was argued above that Paul, while attempting to sustain patterns of domination within the church, did nothing to sustain or ideologically legitimate the social position of members of the congregation. Paul's instruction to the Corinthian community cannot properly be summarised as 'love-patriarchalism', and in many places it is critical of, and opposed to, the values and hierarchy of the dominant social order. The theoretical framework which guides and informs this study requires an investigation of the social ethos expressed within the symbolic order as it is reproduced over time. To what extent is it transformed over time, and how does its social ethos and ideological character develop? We must therefore ask: Does Clement, like Paul, call only for order and appropriate submission to those in positions of leadership within the church, or does his theology also sustain and legitimate social relations of domination and subordination? Does it cement only an ecclesiastical hierarchy or also a social one? The questions that were asked of Paul's Christianity as revealed in 1 Corinthians may again be considered. How does 1 Clement portray the relative positions and responsibilities of the 'strong' and the 'weak'? Might it be accurate to describe Clement's ethos as one of 'love patriarchalism'?

6.4. 1 Clement's attitude to social distinctions: love patriarchalism in 1 Clement?

Clement's main concern is with disorder in the church and it is therefore ecclesiastical office upon which he focuses rather than social position or rank (see esp. 42.1–44.6). Nevertheless, we may look for evidence as to whether his theology of order, humility and appropriate submission should be taken to relate also to hierarchical social distinctions.

We may begin with Clement's use of the body analogy, one employed, of course, in 1 Corinthians, which is clearly the source for Clement at this point.[110] Clement uses the analogy to demonstrate why order should be preserved, and to show why division and sedition are so destructive; it

---

[110] See Hagner 1973, 197–200; 1 Cor 12.12–27; 10.17; cf. Rom 12.4f; Col 1.18; 3.15; Eph 1.23; 4.4ff.

is 'madness' when we rebel (στασιάζομεν) against our own body (τὸ σῶμα τὸ ἴδιον), madness 'to forget that we are members one of another' (46.7; Lake). The oneness of the body, of which all are a part, is stressed, as it was by Paul, though Paul put equal emphasis upon the need for diversity within the one body.[111] Clement concludes his comments on the lessons to be learned from the institution of the army (37.1–4) by asserting the necessity of both 'great' (οἱ μεγάλοι) and 'small' (οἱ μικροί): 'there is a certain mixture (σύγκρασις) among all, and herein lies the advantage' (καὶ ἐν τούτοις χρῆσις – 37.4; Lake). This point is then illustrated by speaking of the body:

ἡ κεφαλὴ δίχα τῶν ποδῶν οὐδέν ἐστιν, οὕτως οὐδὲ οἱ πόδες δίχα τῆς κεφαλῆς· τὰ δὲ ἐλάχιστα μέλη τοῦ σώματος ἡμῶν ἀναγκαῖα καὶ εὔχρηστά εἰσιν ὅλῳ τῷ σώματι· ἀλλὰ πάντα συνπνεῖ καὶ ὑποταγῇ μιᾷ χρῆται εἰς τὸ σώζεσθαι ὅλον τὸ σῶμα.

the head is nothing without the feet, in the same way neither are the feet anything without the head; the insignificant members of our body are necessary and valuable to the whole body, but all come together and in one subjection act to preserve the whole body. (1 Clem 37.5)

There is notable similarity here with 1 Cor 12.21f:

οὐ δύναται δὲ ὁ ὀφθαλμὸς εἰπεῖν τῇ χειρί· χρείαν σου οὐκ ἔχω, ἢ πάλιν ἡ κεφαλὴ τοῖς ποσίν· χρείαν ὑμῶν οὐκ ἔχω· ἀλλὰ πολλῷ μᾶλλον τὰ δοκοῦντα μέλη τοῦ σώματος ἀσθενέστερα ὑπάρχειν ἀναγκαῖά ἐστιν ...

the eye cannot say to the hand, 'I have no need of you', or again the head to the feet, 'I have no need of you'. On the contrary, the parts of the body which seem to be weaker are much more necessary ... (1 Cor 12.21–22)

Like Paul, Clement stresses the interdependence and importance of various parts of the body. However, unlike in 1 Cor 12.21–25, there is in 1 Clem 37.5 no questioning of the relative positions or honour of 'great' and 'small', of 'head' and 'feet'. Clement's point is simply that all parts

---

[111] See 1 Clem 46.5–7; cf. 1 Cor 1.10ff; 12.4–27; Eph 4.4–6; and see §4.3.3. above. Cf. also Seneca *Ep*. 95.52.

are necessary and valuable and work together for the benefit of the whole body (εἰς τὸ σῴζεσθαι ὅλον τὸ σῶμα). Their relative positions are taken for granted; and it is the wellbeing of the whole which is the greater good. The idea of a 'common subjection' (ὑποταγῇ μιᾷ – 37.5; cf. 38.1) to serve the greater good is foreign to 1 Corinthians,[112] although it is by no means unique to 1 Clement.[113] But the instruction to each to act 'according to the gift granted to them' – καθὼς ἐτέθη ἐν τῷ χαρίσματι αὐτοῦ (38.1) – sounds remarkably Pauline.[114]

What is particularly interesting, however, is the way in which Clement takes up Paul's language of χάρισμα, which is used so extensively in 1 Cor 12. Paul does apply the term χάρισμα to both 'spiritual' and 'practical' gifts,[115] and seems to view these gifts as forming some kind of hierarchy within the church (1 Cor 12.28), but what is striking in 1 Clem 38 is the use of the term χάρισμα to refer to the social 'position' in which people are placed (the aorist passive ἐτέθη probably implying divine ordering).[116] Social position is presented as divine gift.[117] The body analogy is used to legitimate *social* distinctions. Since this section of 1 Clement follows that in which the army is mentioned as a model to admire, Maier is no doubt right to point out that 'in the process of borrowing Paul's motif of the body ... Clement emphasizes God's sovereign dispensation of various gifts to support his argument that there is a certain order to be preserved in the community'.[118] But Maier does not draw attention to the fact that it is not only ecclesiastical 'order' that is portrayed as the result of God's dispensation (as is the case in 1 Cor 12.28), but social position too. The first 'χαρίσματα' mentioned are primarily 'gifts' of social location:

ὁ ἰσχυρὸς μὴ ἀτημελείτω[119] τὸν ἀσθενῆ, ὁ δὲ ἀσθενὴς ἐντρεπέσθω τὸν ἰσχυρόν·

---

[112] Cf. Bowe 1988, 130 n. 12.

[113] See Jaubert 1964a, 79, who cites Eph 5.21; 1 Pet 5.5; and Ignatius *Magn.* 13.2 (cf. also Gal 5.13).

[114] Cf. 1 Cor 12.4–31; Rom 12.6; 1 Cor 7.7; Jaubert 1971, 163 n. 4.

[115] Note ἀντιλήμψεις and κυβερνήσεις in 1 Cor 12.28; also Rom 12.6–13.

[116] Cf. 1 Cor 12.18, 28: ὁ θεὸς ἔθετο ... see further the comments in §4.3.3. above.

[117] It is hard to justify Lake's translation of χάρισμα as 'position' but this is indeed the implication of Clement's equating of social position with divine gift. Cf. the translations of Jaubert 1971, 163 (le don); Lindemann 1992, 114 (Gnadengabe); Grant and Graham 1965, 66 (spiritual gift).

[118] Maier 1991, 132; further comments on the body image on 107, 128.

[119] Lake has τημελείτω here (without the μη), as Jaubert 1971, 162 and many translations. A (Codex Alexandrinus) has μητμμελειτω (according to Lightfoot; μη τητμμελειτω ac-

ὁ πλούσιος ἐπιχορηγείτω τῷ πτωχῷ, ὁ δὲ πτωχὸς εὐχαριστείτω τῷ θεῷ, ὅτι ἔδωκεν αὐτῷ, δι' οὗ ἀναπληρωθῇ αὐτοῦ τὸ ὑστέρημα· let the strong person not neglect the weak, and let the weak person reverence the strong; let the rich person supply help to the poor, and let the poor person give thanks to God that he gave them someone through whom their need might be met; (1 Clem 38.2a)

The precise implications of the terms ἰσχυρός (strong) and ἀσθενής (weak) are hard to specify. Lindemann may be right to point out that 'it concerns not only the social position ... but also the spiritual'.[120] However, the more 'spiritual' qualities which follow in 38.2 – ὁ σοφός ('the wise person'), ὁ ταπεινοφρονῶν ('the humble person'), and ὁ ἁγνὸς ἐν τῇ σαρκί[121] ('the person who is pure in the flesh') – are not paired with any contrasting figures, as the strong and the weak, the rich and the poor, are. The parallel construction in relation to the two pairs strong/weak, rich/poor, may imply that the former as well as the latter has primarily a social reference. The instruction to the rich would then be a more specific formulation of that to the strong. The admonition 'not to neglect' (reading μὴ ἀτημελείτω) is similar to that to 'bestow help' and in each case the response expected from the weaker party is a passive one;[122] respect and gratitude to God. Both exhortations seem to refer to the care and material support of those most dependent on others.

However unsure we may be concerning the referents of the terms strong and weak, the following instruction undoubtedly refers to social groups: the rich and the poor.[123] The relative social positions of these two groups

cording to Lake), whereas C (Codex Constantinopolitanus) and S (Syriac version) read τημελείτω (without the preceeding μη). Lightfoot adopts μὴ ἀτημελείτω, suggesting that the α had accidentally been dropped from the texts followed by C and S, as it has in A, and that they therefore had to drop the μη 'in order to restore the sense' (1890b, 116; cf. 1890a, 143.). Lake agrees that μὴ ἀτημελείτω 'may be the true reading' (1912, 72 n. 3). Lightfoot's case seems more likely than that μη was added in A in a place where it would make no sense.

120 'es geht nicht nur um die soziale Stellung ... sondern auch um die geistliche': Lindemann 1992, 117, who notes Rom 15.1 in this connection.

121 The mention of the gift of ἐγκράτεια and the parallel in 1 Cor 7.34 suggests that celibacy may be in view here.

122 Cf. Wengst 1987, 109, 116.

123 Cf. Lindemann 1992, 117: 'Klar ist immerhin, daß von Angehörigen unterschiedlicher Schichten innerhalb der christlichen Gemeinde die Rede ist.'

are presented here as originating in the provision of God, thus forming a religious ideology which roots the social hierarchy in the will and purpose of the creator. Their common membership of the body of Christ obliges the rich to 'bestow help' on the poor,[124] and requires the poor to be grateful to God for such benefaction. The social distinctions themselves are in no way criticised, though their consequences are ameliorated through the obligations imposed upon the rich.[125] The parallel with Hermas *Sim.* 2 (esp. 5–7) is notable, although in Hermas there is a measure of counterbalance: the rich person is wealthy but is poor in relation to God, whereas the poor person is rich in intercession and confession (v. 5). The two groups therefore work together in a complementary way: ἀμφότεροι οὖν τὸ ἔργον τελοῦσιν ('both then complete the work'; v. 7). Particularly similar to 1 Clem 38.2 is the comment that 'the rich person therefore helps the poor in all things without hesitation, and the poor person, being helped by the rich, prays to God, thanking God for the one who has given to them' (vv. 5b–6). R. Grant and H. Graham therefore comment that this 'counsel ... is evidently characteristic of Roman Christian practice'.[126]

If we recall Theissen's summary of love patriarchalism, we may immediately be struck by the similarities with 1 Clem 38.2. Indeed, unlike anything to be found in 1 or 2 Corinthians, this short passage is almost a precise expression of the ethos outlined by Theissen and Troeltsch.[127] In 1 Clem 38.1–2 social differences do indeed seem to be 'taken for granted' yet ameliorated through the instruction to the strong and rich to care for and help the weak. Each is urged to submit in a way appropriate to their 'gift' (38.1), which means that the poor and weak are to respond to the rich with gratitude and respect.[128] We may indeed conclude in this case that the position of the socially strong within the

---

[124] Though, as Lindemann 1992, 117, comments: 'Allerdings bleibt (für uns) undeutlich, welche realen Handlungen hier gefordert werden (gehen sie über Almosen hinaus?).'

[125] Cf. Lindemann 1992, 117.

[126] Grant and Graham 1965, 66. Jeffers 1991, explores the differences in ethos between 1 Clement and the Shepherd of Hermas, arguing that the latter represents a protest within Roman Christianity against the ideology of a social elite within the church, represented by 1 Clement. However, he perhaps overstates the contrasts between the two documents. On the tensions relating to the role of rich Christians within the early Church see Countryman 1980.

[127] See §4.1. above. Note the prominence of ἀγάπη in 1 Clem 21.7f; 33.1; 49.1ff; 50.1ff; 51.2; 53.5; 62.2.

[128] ἐντρεπέσθω may also convey the sense 'reverence'; cf. 1 Clem 21.6.

Christian community is affirmed. Whereas Paul presented the body analogy in a way which subverted and upturned the dominant social hierarchy, Clement picks up the same symbolic resources but uses them as a form of ideology which legitimates the diversity of social position. I have argued that Paul did not seek to affirm the position of the socially strong, nor to demand from the weak 'subordination, fidelity and esteem'. The social ethos of 1 Clement, though drawing upon some of the rules and resources used by Paul in 1 Corinthians, seems to be rather different. Are there further indications that 1 Clement explicitly supports the subordination of weaker social groups?

Subordination, as we have already seen, is certainly a prominent theme in 1 Clement, much more prominent than it is in 1 and 2 Corinthians, though it is not entirely absent from these Pauline letters.[129] It is related, however, to a variety of relationships. Submission to God is a fundamental requirement (34.5), the virtue of which may be learnt from the natural universe (20.1ff). Indeed, all other submission may be said to derive ultimately from this (cf. 1 Cor 15.27f). Hence the Corinthians are urged to submit to the church leaders who are appointed by God (57.1f; cf. 1.3; 21.6; 1 Cor 16.16) and to the secular authorities, who likewise receive their position and authority from God (61.1; cf. 60.4; Rom 13.1). Clement can also speak of the virtue of mutual submission within the Christian community (2.1; 37.5; 38.1).

However, there is one place where the subordination of a social group is presented as the ideal. In 1 Clem 1.3 the women are said to have been taught to be ἐν τῷ κανόνι τῆς ὑποταγῆς – 'in the rule of submission'. This phrase occurs in one of two passages in 1 Clement which are similar in content to the so-called *Haustafeln*, codes of household ethics, found in the New Testament in Col 3.18–4.1, Eph 5.21–6.9, 1 Tim 2.1–6.2, Titus 2.1–10 and 1 Pet 2.13–3.7.[130] These codes of instruction stipulate the behaviour expected of various members of the household, demanding that the conventional relations of subordination be sustained.

---

[129] See §6.3. above; 1 Cor 14.32; 15.27, 28; 16.16.

[130] On which see esp. Crouch 1972 (Colossians); Verner 1983 (Pastorals); Balch 1981 (1 Peter); Lührmann 1981; Yoder 1972, 163–92 (though I find his approach somewhat ideologically naïve: there is nothing 'revolutionary' about a subordination which is willingly accepted. The consequence of ideology is precisely to present established relations of domination as 'natural' or desirable for all. Subordination is not generally maintained by brute force alone; see further Horrell 1995d, 232–33). On the 'household codes' in 1 Clement see Bowe 1988, 97–103; Jeffers 1991, 121–27.

The first block of such material in 1 Clement occurs at 1.3, where 'Rome presents its "ideal picture" of the perfect community'.[131] The second appears at 21.6–8, a passage of exhortation where 'the golden age' depicted in 1.3 'becomes the norm for future behaviour'.[132] The similarity in structure and content of these two passages may clearly be seen (see pages 266 and 267 below).

Both passages refer to the same groups in the same order (with the addition of children at the end of the list in 21.6–8) and convey essentially the same ideals: obedience to leaders,[133] honour for the elders,[134] appropriate instruction and behaviour for the young, and quiet meekness and purity for the wives.[135] The order itself is notably hierarchical: leaders, elders, the young, women, children.[136] As do the *Haustafeln* in

---

[131] Bowe 1988, 97–98.

[132] Grant and Graham 1965, 19.

[133] In 1 Clement ἡγούμενοι are often leaders *outside* the church – see 5.7; 32.2; 37.3; 51.5; 60.4 – but here most commentators take the references to ἡγουμένοις (1.3) and προηγουμένους (21.6) to mean church leaders; so Lindemann 1992, 28, 79; Grant and Graham 1965, 18–19; Lightfoot 1890b, 10 n. 6, 77 n. 9. Otherwise, Eggenberger 1951, 27ff. Cf. Hermas *Vis.* 2.2.6; 3.9.7 (τοῖς προηγουμένοις τῆς ἐκκλησίας) and Heb 13.7, 17, 24 (ἡγούμενοι). For Clement obedience to civil leaders is also praiseworthy; see 60.4–61.1 and §6.5. below.

[134] It is generally assumed that in 1 Clement a reference to πρεσβύτεροι is usually a reference to those who hold office in the church; see 44.5; 47.6; 54.2; 57.1. In 1.3 and 21.6, however, and in 3.3, due to the juxtaposition of πρεσβύτεροι and νέοι, and the preceding comment which has already given instruction regarding 'our leaders', commentators tend to argue that 'old' is meant; so Lindemann 1992, 28, 80; Jaubert 1971, 101 n. 4; Lightfoot 1890b, 11 n. 6, 77 n. 9. However, it seems that we should reckon with a degree of connection between seniority in faith and age, and position as a 'presbyter'. A blurred distinction between elder men and 'elders' is evident in a number of places: see 1 Pet 5.1–5; Polycarp *Phil.* 5.1–6.1; cf. Titus 1.5; 2.2–8. Thus Grant and Graham 1965, 18, comment: 'Here [in 1 Clem 1.3] ... the author is concerned not only with presbyters as such but with older men in general.' The prominence given to male heads of household as leaders within the communities makes this kind of connection between office and social standing entirely likely; see further below and Titus 1.5–9; 1 Tim 3.1–13. Young 1994, 97–121, argues that the Pastorals represent a transitional phase in the use of the term πρεσβύτεροι where it is used to refer both to a church office and to familial and age-related status. Campbell 1994, whose thesis represents a substantial and recent contribution to the understanding of the term 'elder', argues that the term πρεσβύτερος refers in early Christianity, as in Jewish and Greco-Roman contexts, not to an office but to those who have a position of honour and leadership in the community because of their seniority and social standing at the head of the household. This conclusion makes a good deal of sense of 1 Clement's use of the term here and elsewhere, though see above for my disagreement with Campbell's reconstruction of the situation which 1 Clement addresses.

[135] Both 1.3 and 21.7 seem to refer to wives rather than women in general, though this would appear to reflect an assumption that all women are married, except perhaps those who would be included under the category young/children.

[136] Cf. Bowe 1988, 102.

general, these passages essentially support and exhort the continuance of the traditional social order, particularly that within the household (women and children). Clement's primary concern is that the *church* should be a harmonious and peaceful community, but his instructions require that this be attained through the maintenance of the established hierarchical roles within the household (and within the state; see 60.2–61.2 and §6.5. below). It is significant that both of the codes of instruction in 1.3 and 21.6–8 are specifically linked with the ideal of peace: the result of the model behaviour outlined in 1.3 was εἰρήνη βαθεῖα καὶ λιπαρά, 'a deep and rich peace' (2.2), and the exhortations in 21.6–8 follow the passage which has shown the universe to be a model of peaceful and harmonious existence (20.1–11). 'The opening verse of chapter 21 calls for the same ὁμόνοια in living as "citizens worthy of God".'[137] Acceptance of the established social order is the declared way to 'peace'.

One of the interesting things about 1 Clem 1.3 is that it does not take the form of instruction or exhortation but of a historical report. This way of living, when all submitted to their leaders and when the women were appropriately submissive as ideal housewives, is presented as producing peace. However, it must be questioned whether Clement's picture of the Corinthian community in this regard has much basis in fact. To a large extent, of course, it is impossible for us to tell, but the assertions about what the women were taught and instructed by those within their own community are particularly open to question. There is evidence from 1 Corinthians that in its earlier years the Corinthian community was one in which the ideal of marital commitment was questioned and in which asceticism, perhaps especially among women, was popular.[138] Both women and men participated in worship in a manner which led Paul to be concerned that the created distinctions between them were being disregarded.[139] And 1 Cor 14.34f, especially when read in the context of the passage into which it was inserted (14.33–40), implies that the silence and subordination of women had to be imposed upon the Corinthian community and was not their already accepted norm.[140] Clement is not unaware of the earlier times of division in the

---

[137] Bowe 1988, 100.
[138] See 1 Cor 7.1ff; MacDonald 1990; Fiorenza 1983, 205–41; MacDonald 1987, 65–111; Murphy O'Connor 1978a; 1980.
[139] 1 Cor 11.2–16; see §4.3.2. above and esp. MacDonald 1987, 72–111; Byrne 1988, 49–52.
[140] On the prominence and leadership of women within the Corinthian community see Fiorenza 1983, 232–33; 1986 (on women's leadership generally); Wire 1990. For the argument that 1 Cor 14.34f is an interpolation see above pp. 184–95.

...ὑποτασσόμενοι τοῖς ἡγουμένοις ὑμῶν,

καὶ τιμὴν τὴν καθήκουσαν ἀπονέμοντες τοῖς παρ' ὑμῖν πρεσβυτέροις·

νέοις τε μέτρια καὶ σεμνὰ νοεῖν ἐπετρέπετε·

γυναιξίν τε ἐν ἀμώμῳ καὶ σεμνῇ καὶ ἁγνῇ συνειδήσει πάντα ἐπιτελεῖν παρηγγέλλετε, στεργούσας καθηκόντως τοὺς ἄνδρας ἑαυτῶν· ἔν τε τῷ κανόνι τῆς ὑποταγῆς ὑπαρχούσας τὰ κατὰ τὸν οἶκον σεμνῶς οἰκουργεῖν ἐδιδάσκετε, πάνυ σωφρονούσας.

(1 Clem 1.3)

τοὺς προηγουμένους ἡμῶν αἰδεσθῶμεν,

τοὺς πρεσβυτέρους τιμήσωμεν,

τοὺς νέους παιδεύσωμεν τὴν παιδείαν τοῦ φόβου τοῦ θεοῦ,

τὰς γυναῖκας ἡμῶν ἐπὶ τὸ ἀγαθὸν διορθωσώμεθα. τὸ ἀξιαγάπητον τῆς ἁγνείας ἦθος ἐνδειξάσθωσαν, τὸ ἀκέραιον τῆς πραΰτητος αὐτῶν βούλημα ἀποδειξάτωσαν, τὸ ἐπιεικὲς τῆς γλώσσης αὐτῶν διὰ τῆς σιγῆς φανερὸν ποιησάτωσαν, τὴν ἀγάπην αὐτῶν μὴ κατὰ προσκλίσεις, ἀλλὰ πᾶσιν τοῖς φοβουμένοις τὸν θεὸν ὁσίως ἴσην παρεχέτωσαν.

τὰ τέκνα ἡμῶν τῆς ἐν Χριστῷ παιδείας μεταλαμβανέτωσαν· μαθέτωσαν, τί ταπεινοφροσύνη παρὰ θεῷ ἰσχύει, τί ἀγάπη ἁγνὴ παρὰ θεῷ δύναται, πῶς ὁ φόβος αὐτοῦ καλὸς καὶ μέγας καὶ σώζων πάντας τοὺς ἐν αὐτῷ ὁσίως ἀναστρεφομένους ἐν καθαρᾷ διανοίᾳ.

(1 Clem 21.6–8)

Fig 2: Household codes in 1 Clement

submitting to your <u>rulers</u>,

and paying the fitting honour to the <u>elders</u> among you.

You instructed the <u>young</u>, too, to think in a moderate and seemly way

and you instructed the <u>women</u> to perform all things with a blameless and seemly and pure conscience, rendering the proper affection to their husbands. And you taught them to remain in the rule of submission and to work in the house in a seemly way, with all circumspection.

(1 Clem 1.3)

let us respect our <u>rulers</u>,

let us honour the <u>elders</u>,

let us instruct the <u>young</u> in the discipline of the fear of God,

let us direct our <u>women</u> to what is good. Let them show the lovely habit of purity, let them demonstrate the innocent will of their meekness, let them make clear the gentleness of their tongue through silence, and let them give their love not according to partiality, but equally and in holiness to all those who fear God.

Let our <u>children</u> share in the instruction which is in Christ, let them learn the strength of humility before God, the power of pure love before God, how good and great is the fear of him and how it saves all those who live in it with holiness and a pure understanding.

(1 Clem 21.6–8)

(Fig 2 continued)

Corinthian community (see 1 Clem 47) and it is possible that 1.3 refers to a time of 'deep peace' after Paul's final departure, when the hierarchy and subordination associated with traditional social roles had become the norm at Corinth, though it seems much more likely that Clement's presentation of the past merely represents his own view of what is desirable in the present. In any case we should, I think, label 1.3 *an ideological use of history.* Instead of simply exhorting the Corinthians to a certain pattern of behaviour (21.6–8), Clement also suggests that you *once* had a 'deep peace' *precisely because* you followed this pattern of ordered life. Clement's goal for the community is presented as a reattainment of a golden age in the past. The 'model' presented in 21.6–8 is thus legitimised by 'history' (1.3), or by a particular presentation of history;[141] it is the tried and tested way to peace. More specifically, the subordination of women in the present is legitimised through the assertion that this was taught in the past within the Corinthian community. This is ideological in that it legitimates a particular relation of domination in the present through a highly perspectival use of history and, in addition, represents the interests of particular (dominant) groups as universal ones;[142] the purpose of subordination is 'peace' for the whole community. It should be noted that nowhere in Paul's Corinthian correspondence do we find any form of household code, even though the Corinthian situation at the time of 1 Corinthians would have made its use entirely appropriate, if it were known and approved of by Paul.[143] This is another point of contrast between the social ethos of 1 Corinthians and of 1 Clement. On the other hand it must also be acknowledged both that there are certain elements in 1 Corinthians which could be developed in the direction of this type of material (1 Cor 7.17–24; 11.3–9) and that the household code clearly became a part of the rules and resources of the symbolic order of early Christianity before the time when 1 Clement was written (see further §7.2.).

Further observations about the material in 1 Clem 1.3 and 21.6–8 may be made. It is notable that the specific exhortation to be subordi-

---

[141] Any presentation of history 'tells the story' from a particular perspective and conveys its own values. But following the definition of ideology given above (pp. 50–52), a presentation of 'history' is 'ideological' if it becomes a means by which relations of domination are sustained in the present.

[142] Cf. Giddens 1979, 193.

[143] Cf. O'Brien 1982, 218; otherwise Ellis 1986, 485, 492.

nate (using ὑποτάσσω and cognates) is less prominent in 1 Clement's material than it is in the New Testament material of a similar kind.[144] Both ὑποταγή and ὑποτάσσω appear in 1.3 but neither is used in 21.6– 8, the passage of exhortation, though the reference to the silence of women here is a notable point of contact between this passage and 1 Tim 2.9– 15, the New Testament passage which perhaps most forcefully excludes women from leadership and authority in the Christian community.[145] The model for women's behaviour in 1 Clem 21.6–8 is one of silence and a meek will, clearly a model of subordination. The virtue of domesticity – working in the home – is also a point of contact between 1 Clem 1.3 (οἰκουργεῖν) and Titus 2.5 (οἰκουργός).

It appears to be only the male heads of households who are addressed directly by 1 Clement.[146] The group addressed as 'you' in 1.3 does not seem to include the young or the women. Rather, 'you' gave instruction to the young and to the women. The women themselves are 'not addressed as active subjects'.[147] Similarly in 21.6–8 it is clear that 'we' are the male heads of families: 'Let us instruct the young ... let us direct our wives ... Let our children ...'[148] Here too 'the women are seen as the objects of male activity'.[149] Thus Jeffers suggests that Clement 'sees the *paterfamilias* as ultimately responsible for the spiritual welfare of his entire household'.[150] It is not insignificant, then, that Clement uses the address ἄνδρες ἀδελφοί, even though it may have been widely used; it is the men of the community whom he addresses.[151] This is in contrast not only to the *Haustafeln* in Colossians and Ephesians, where each party is generally addressed directly,[152] but also to Pauline passages such as

---

[144] Cf. Bowe 1988, 102. Note the uses of ὑποτάσσω in Col 3.18; Eph 5.22; Titus 2.5, 9; 3.1; 1 Pet 2.13, 18; 3.1, 5; and of ὑποταγή in 1 Tim 2.11; 3.4.

[145] Cf. Lindemann 1992, 29. Note 1 Tim 2.12 (ἐν ἡσυχίᾳ); 1 Clem 21.7 (διὰ τῆς σιγῆς); 1 Cor 14.34 (σιγάτωσαν).

[146] Cf. Jeffers 1991, 123; Bowe 1988, 102; Fiorenza 1983, 292.

[147] '... nicht als handelnde Subjekte angesprochen': Lindemann 1992, 29 (a useful excursus on 'Frauen im 1 Clem').

[148] Cf. Polycarp *Phil.* 4.1–3.

[149] '... sind die Frauen als Objekte männlichen Handelns gesehen': Lindemann 1992, 29.

[150] Jeffers 1991, 123.

[151] See 14.1; 37.1; 62.1; cf. 16.17; 62.3; 63.3. Contrast Bowe 1988, 38 n. 20: 'The use of ἄνδρες contributes little to a discussion of gender issues in *1 Clement*. Ἄνδρες was the typical address for public speeches.' Cf. Acts 1.16; 2.29; 7.2; 13.15 etc. Paul uses ἀδελφοί alone; e.g. Rom 1.13; 7.1; 1 Cor 1.10; 2 Cor 1.8; 1 Thess 1.4 etc; cf. also 2 Clem 1.1; 5.1; 19.1; 20.2.

[152] See most clearly Col 3.18ff; Eph 6.1, 5.

1 Cor 7, where both men and women are clearly spoken to and addressed as responsible subjects.[153]

From the synopsis of the passages presented above it can clearly be seen that 1 Clement's 'household codes' give most space to the behaviour required of the women, without reciprocal elucidation of the responsibilities of husbands or fathers.[154] The men's responsibility, it would seem, is to submit to the leaders of the community and to ensure that other groups behave appropriately, as is shown by the repeated use of hortatory subjunctives in the first person plural in 21.6. The amount of space devoted to describing the behaviour which is required from the women is not surprising, given the extent to which a struggle over the role of women within the early Christian movement seems to have taken place.[155] What is perhaps more surprising is that 1 Clement does not provide any theological justification for the subordination of women, as is offered, for example, in 1 Tim 2.13–15, and is at least germinally present in 1 Cor 11.3–9.[156] On the contrary, it is notable 'that the subordination of women is nowhere justified, but is taken for granted'.[157] Clement's theological attention is much more directed to the overall theme of peace and concord and to the legitimation of the position of leaders in the church.[158]

'The great omissions in Clement's codes of household ethics, when compared to those in the New Testament, are instructions to slaves and masters.'[159] This omission is puzzling. Jeffers' observation that there were

---

[153] Note vv. 2, 3, 8, 10f, 16. See further §4.3.1. above.

[154] Note the reciprocality in Col 3.18–4.1; Eph 5.21–6.9 and 1 Pet 3.1–7 (though here the admonition is highly imbalanced; vv. 1–6 addressed to wives, only v. 7 to husbands). In the Pastorals and 1 Peter it is slaves who are addressed without reciprocal instruction to slave owners: 1 Tim 6.1f; Tit 2.9f; 1 Pet 2.18ff. Contrast *Did.* 4.10f; *Barn.* 19.7.

[155] Fiorenza 1983, 292–93, suggests that it also implies that women may have been among the rebels at Corinth; for caution on this see Bowe 1988, 19–20. On the conflict over the role of women, see Fiorenza 1983, 245–342; MacDonald 1983; MacDonald 1988, 176–83.

[156] Though I argued above (§4.3.2.) that Paul sought (explicitly; vv. 10–12) to use this theology primarily to maintain differentiation between the sexes and not a subordinate relationship; but the means of differentiation is to assign women a secondary place in a theological and creational order.

[157] '… daß die Unterordnung der Frauen durchweg nicht begründet wird, sondern als selbstverständlich gilt': Lindemann 1992, 29. Lindemann also points out that one must distinguish between Clement's presentation of particular women who achieved great things (πολλὰ ἀνδρεῖα – 55.3) and his view of women within the community.

[158] See §6.3. above.

[159] Jeffers 1991, 125; cf. Bowe 1988, 102.

probably no slave owners in Clement's congregation, though there were undoubtedly slaves,[160] even if correct, does not explicitly solve the puzzle, unless an absence of slave owners meant that there was no pressure from such people to expound teaching that would serve their particular social interests.

However the prominence of instruction to slaves in 1 Peter, probably written from Rome some years before 1 Clement,[161] and in the Pastoral Epistles,[162] makes the absence of such instruction from 1 Clement all the more notable. 1 Clement's only reference to slavery is an enigmatic one which refers to the radical action of 'many among ourselves' who 'have given themselves to bondage' or 'to slavery', 'that they might ransom' or provide 'food for others with the price they received for themselves' (55.2; Lake). Clement speaks positively of this action insofar as it is an example illustrating to the Corinthian rebels that they should pay the price of exile, so that the sedition might end (54.1–55.6).[163]

Despite the absence of explicit instructions to slaves, it would seem that the term 'love patriarchalism' offers an accurate description of the social ethos of 1 Clement, as it relates to relationships among Christians within the church. Relative social positions are sustained and legitimated. Obligations are imposed upon the rich and strong, though their behaviour and position are not criticised or challenged. The men have particular responsibility for instructing their households and the women are to be silent, submissive and domestic. The weaker members of the Chris-

---

[160] Jeffers 1991, 125.
[161] See 1 Pet 2.18ff. On the date and provenance of 1 Peter see, for example, Brown 1983, 128–30 (Rome, 80s CE); Balch 1981, 137–38 (65–90 CE); Elliott 1981, 84–87 (73–92 CE); Michaels 1988, lxii–lxvii (Rome, 70–80 CE).
[162] See 1 Tim 6.1f; Titus 2.9f. Dates for the Pastorals vary widely: Roloff 1988, 46, suggests, 'daß sie kaum sehr viel später als um das Jahr 100 entstanden sind'; Hanson 1982b, 13, suggests 96–110, probably 100–105. However, for a recent defence of Pauline authorship see Knight 1992, 4–54, whose suggested dates are therefore 61–67. On the similarities between 1 Clement and the Pastorals see Bernard 1899, xix; Hagner 1973, 230–36. The Pastorals' place of origin is usually thought to be Asia Minor (Hanson 1982b, 14) but the possibility of their originating in Rome is interesting: Lindemann 1992, 18, writes: 'Die auffallende Nähe des 1 Clem zu den Past, insbesondere beim Amtsverständnis und bei der Darstellung der Rolle der Frauen in der Gemeinde ... wäre leicht zu erklären, wenn die Past ungefähr gleichzeitig oder wenig später als 1 Clem ebenfalls in Rom verfaßt worden sein sollten.'
[163] It may be too strong to suggest that their actions are ones which 'the author praises', and thus 'that Clement is not wholly consistent in his conservative social views' (Bowe 1988, 102). It is rather a *reporting* of something that many have done, which illustrates Clement's advice at this point (cf. 1 Cor 15.29).

tian community are to be cared for, but in return are to offer humble respect and appropriate subordination.

One final question may be asked: to what extent does Clement's theology of order and subordination relate to the wider social setting: Is his model for the church and the household also his model for society?

6.5. 1 Clement's attitude to civil authority

1 Clement's primary orientation is not towards the wider socio-political sphere but towards the church.[164] However, Clement's 'political attitude' largely determines his response to the Corinthian στάσις, viewing dissension and rebellion as evil and dangerous, and contrasting them with the humble submissiveness by which 'order' is maintained.[165]

Explicit statements about the relationship of Christians to the state authorities appear in the lengthy prayer which is found towards the end of the letter (59.3–61.3), a prayer which makes extensive use of Jewish material and which may have been part of the established liturgy of the Roman church.[166] Noting the points of contact between the themes of the prayer and the problems dealt with in 1 Clement, Lindemann wisely and cautiously concludes: 'The author of 1 Clement has probably taken up a prayer used in the community, the same or similar in form, and reformulated it for his current purposes.'[167]

The prayer focuses throughout on God, emphasising at the opening not only the dependence of everything upon God, but particularly God's action in raising up the humble and weak and humbling the proud (59.3f; cf. 1 Cor 1.26ff). All who join in the prayer then pray, in words taken almost exactly from Deut 13.19 (LXX), for God's guidance in order that they may do τὰ καλὰ καὶ εὐάρεστα ἐνώπιόν σου – 'what is good and pleasing before you [God]'[168] – though Clement significantly adds

---

[164] Cf. Wengst 1987, 112 with 217 n. 47 against Eggenberger (see below n. 176)

[165] See §6.3. above and Wengst 1987, 113–15.

[166] See Lindemann 1992, 168; on the structure and content of the prayer, 165–68. Most commentators agree that civil rulers are in view here; see esp. 60.4; Grant and Graham 1965, 94; Jaubert 1971, 199; Lindemann 1992, 173–74.

[167] 'Wahrscheinlich hat der Vf des 1 Clem ein so oder ähnlich in der Gemeinde verwendetes Gebet aufgenommen und für seine aktuellen Zwecke umformuliert.' (Lindemann 1992, 168).

[168] Deut 13.19 LXX reads: ποιεῖν τὸ καλὸν καὶ τὸ ἀρεστὸν ἐναντίον κυρίου τοῦ θεοῦ σου. (Cf. Deut 12.25, 28; 21.9.)

καὶ ἐνώπιον τῶν ἀρχόντων ἡμῶν, 'and before our rulers'; a phrase not found in Deut 13.19 (1 Clem 60.2; cf. 61.2). Thus, in Clement's prayer here, 'what is well-pleasing to rulers runs parallel to what is well-pleasing to God'.[169] Clement's aim, characteristically, is for ὁμόνοιαν καὶ εἰρήνην,[170] 'concord and peace', not only within the church but for 'all those who dwell upon the earth' (60.4). The attainment of this goal is clearly linked with the prayer that 'we may be obedient to thy almighty and glorious name, and to our rulers and governors upon the earth' (60.4; Lake). Here again the parallel is explicit between obedience to God and obedience to rulers. The following verse asserts that the rulers' ἐξουσίαν τῆς βασιλείας ('authority of sovereignty') has been given to them by God, along with their 'glory and honour' (61.1). And an intimate connection is drawn, again in parallel, between submission to rulers and obedience to God's will: ὑποτάσσεσθαι αὐτοῖς, μηδὲν ἐναντιουμένους τῷ θελήματί σου – 'submitting to them, in nothing opposing your will' (61.1). 'Obedience to God and obedience to rulers correspond.'[171]

Clement proceeds in the verses which follow to pray for the rulers themselves (61.1f), asking that they may govern in a way which is pleasing to God.[172] Clement's prayer that Christians may be obedient, and his equation of civil obedience with conformity to the divine will, do not therefore represent an entirely uncritical acceptance of the state's use of its authority. Clement also prays that the rulers may govern ἀπροσκόπως ('without offence'; 61.1) and that God may 'direct their counsels according to that which is good and pleasing before thee ... etc.' (61.2; Lake). Klaus Wengst sees Clement 'dissociating himself from the prevalent ideology when he speaks of rulers and leaders as "sons of men" [61.2], whereas the emperor of the time is regarded as the "son of the deified"'.[173] However, this should not be seen, he urges, as evidence for a critical attitude towards existing rule: 'substantially the prayer was for the preservation of the empire.'[174] Indeed, 'Clement is a long way from ques-

---

[169] Wengst 1987, 107; note also 60.4 and 61.1.
[170] Note also the mention of peace in 60.3, though this is found in Num 6.26 (LXX); As backgrounds to 60.3, see also Num 6.25; Pss 66.2; 79.4, 8, 20 (LXX).
[171] Wengst 1987, 107.
[172] Cf. 1 Tim 2.1f. See the excursus on prayer for civil authorities in Lindemann 1992, 175–76; also Dibelius and Conzelmann 1972, 37–39.
[173] Wengst 1987, 108.
[174] Wengst 1987, 108.

tioning the rule of Rome in any way. On the contrary, the parallel between God and the ruler is an indication that he gives theological legitimation to this rule.'[175]

Eggenberger was thus right to point to 1 Clement's belief that the church should have an obedient attitude to the Roman state and should not be viewed as a threat by the authorities, but wrong to see this as the main concern of the whole letter, and wrong to view the Corinthian 'occasion' as a fiction.[176] It is rather the case that Clement's attitude to the state – encouraging humble submission and quiet obedience – is also his attitude to the church and the household. The main themes of his theology (see §6.3. above) – against στάσις and for τάγμα, εἰρήνη, ὁμόνοια, ταπεινοφροσύνη and ὑποταγή – are grounded in an interpretation of God's creative and 'masterful' action (e.g. 20.11), and are applied to every area of life. Hence Clement's closing and summarising advice is to 'bow the neck and take up the position of obedience', thus 'ceasing from vain sedition' (63.1; Lake). This is of course, *contra* Eggenberger, primarily ecclestiastically orientated, and relates to the principal purpose of the letter, but it is also the model of citizenship and social conduct which Clement advocates. 'What Clement is suggesting is, fundamentally, simply subjection to the already existing order';[177] ecclesiastical, social and political. This is the way to the attainment of peace (63.4; cf. 65.1).

A contrast may be drawn between 1 Clem 60.2–61.1 and 1 Cor 6.1–8, where Paul gave no support at all to an established civil institution and insisted that it was profoundly wrong for believers in disagreement to appeal to the courts as a means of obtaining justice.[178] Certainly there is nothing in Paul's Corinthian letters comparable in content or ethos to 1 Clem 60–61 and it may be true that 1 Clement's attitude to the state formed a noticeable contrast with what had previously been presented to

---

[175] Wengst 1987, 107; see further 106–18.
[176] Eggenberger 1951, 35: '*Unser ganzer Brief gewinnt den Charakter einer Kampfschrift um die rechte Einstellung zum Staat, d.h. zum römischen Imperium.*' 190–91: 'Wir möchten den 1. Klemensbrief in erster Linie als christliche Apologie bezeichnen, aber als *getarnte Apologie*. „*Der Brief*" *soll bei Hofe gelesen werden* und soll bei Hofe einen für das Christentum günstigen Eindruck erwecken.' Thus chapters 59ff are 'Ziel und Höhepunkt: die faktische restlose Unterwerfung im Fürbitte-Gebet' (203). For criticism see von Campenhausen 1952.
[177] Wengst 1987, 115.
[178] See §4.2.2. above.

the Corinthian church.[179] However, in 1 Cor 6 Paul deals with cases of civil litigation *between members of the Christian community.* Paul's primary concern there was for relationships among the believers. Ernst Käsemann is therefore right to point out that: 'From an apocalyptic standpoint secular courts, thus political authorities, are disparaged and rejected *when it is a matter of settling disputes within the community.*'[180] However, in Rom 13.1–7 Paul urges the Christian community at Rome to 'be subject to the governing authorities' (ἐξουσίαις ὑπερεχούσαις ὑποτασσέσθω – 13.1).[181] In this passage Paul insists that all authority is given and ordered by God (13.1),[182] drawing a parallel between opposing authority and opposing what God has ordered (13.2). Rulers are described as those who punish evil and approve good; they are διάκονοι and λειτουργοὶ θεοῦ ('servants and ministers of God'; 13.4, 6). The lack of caveat or qualification here means that Paul 'at least exposes himself to the danger of providing theological legitimation for *de facto* power no matter how it may have come into being and how it may be used'.[183]

The possible reasons why Paul wrote Rom 13.1–7 have been much discussed, for 'in many respects it is unique in Paul'.[184] Some have argued that the passage is an interpolation,[185] but most commentators agree that 'there is no reason to dispute the authenticity of the text ... on either external or internal grounds'.[186] J. Friedrich, W. Pöhlmann and P. Stuhlmacher have suggested that Paul's specific purpose was to urge the Christians in Rome to pay their taxes, in spite of the discontent over extortion and malpractice which led to public protests in 58 CE.[187] K. Beyschlag suggests that in his letter to the Romans, Paul may have

---

[179] We are simply not in a position to say how what the Corinthian church was taught developed during the years between the writing of 1 and 2 Corinthians and the sending of 1 Clement. The texts available only allow us to see how the Christianity presented to them first by Paul and then by the Roman church may differ. But for more general reflections on this trajectory within early (Pauline) Christianity, see §7.2. below.

[180] Käsemann 1980, 357, my italics.

[181] On the contrasts between 1 Cor 6 and Rom 13 see Winter 1991, 559–60.

[182] It is interesting to note that 'derivates of the stem ταγ- provide the leading idea in these verses' (Käsemann 1980, 351).

[183] Wengst 1987, 84.

[184] Käsemann 1980, 350; cf. Morris 1988, 457. For discussion see Käsemann 1980, 350–59 (bibliography on 350); Dunn 1986; 1988, 757–74 (bibliography on 757–58); Ziesler 1989, 307–15; Bammel 1984.

[185] E.g. Munro 1983, 56–67; Kallas 1965.

[186] Käsemann 1980, 351; cf. Dunn 1988, 758; Morris 1988, 458.

[187] Friedrich et al. 1976, 156–59; Tacitus *Annals* 13.50–51; cf. Bammel 1984, 371; also Dunn 1988, 766, 772, against Wengst 1987, 82 and Käsemann 1980, 359.

'accommodated' his views 'in relation to the theological presuppositions of a community ... which preserved a different, unpauline tradition, whose form is presented to us thirty years later in the Roman letter of Clement'.[188] This idea would also be compatible with Wengst's suggestion that Romans 13 may be viewed as a part of Paul's self apologia to the Roman Christians: as Paul was arrested several times 'on suspicion of disloyalty', they may have 'suspected Paul himself of having a problem over this question'.[189]

But whatever the reasons for Romans 13, the fact that it was addressed to Rome is probably not coincidental: 'If the apostle enters into the question in detail here, it must be connected with the fact that he is addressing the church in the capital city of the empire.'[190] Paul's exhortation to 'be subject to the governing authorities' (Rom 13.1) is reiterated in a later letter of Roman origin (1 Pet 2.13–17).[191] The prayers for the ruling authorities in 1 Clement mark a development not found in Romans or in 1 Peter (but cf. 1 Tim 2.1f), but the instruction to be loyal and obedient citizens is by no means an innovation.

What this illustrates is that, once again, Clement is taking up and at the same time developing and transforming rules and resources already introduced into the Christian symbolic order (in this case by Paul, though not in his Corinthian correspondence). Clearly in this particular instance traditions which become associated with the Roman church are especially important. As far as we can tell from the New Testament evidence, Paul's letter to the Roman church represents the first occasion on which the rule of obedience and submission to secular government is presented

---

[188] '... in bezug auf die theologische Voraussetzungen einer Gemeinde ... die eine andersartige, unpaulinische Tradition bewahrte, deren Abbild uns dreißig Jahre später der römische Clemensbrief präsentiert': Beyschlag 1966, 349. Brown 1983, 89–127, also argues that Christianity in Rome was from the outset strongly influenced by Judaism, and shaped by Jerusalem Christianity. However, note Fuellenbach 1980, 63 (with 209 n. 527): 'most of the sources which [Beyschlag] uses to prove his thesis are of much too late a date'. It is certainly methodologically dubious to reconstruct an earlier form of Roman Christianity (prior to Paul's letter to the Romans) on the basis of a letter (and other documents) written towards the end of the first century.

[189] Wengst 1987, 82. On Paul's concern in Romans to refute slanderous views of him (Rom 3.8) and to show his closeness to their form of Christianity, see Brown 1983, 105–27; and on Romans as an 'Ambassadorial Letter', Jewett 1982.

[190] Käsemann 1980, 350.

[191] On the date and origin of 1 Peter see n. 161 above. On obedience to civil authority as a theme shared by Romans, 1 Peter and 1 Clement, see Brown 1983, 171–73. Cf. also 1 Tim 2.1f; Titus 3.1f.

in textual form, undergirded by theological resources and legitimation. This Pauline formulation is taken up by 1 Peter, a letter from Rome, which presents this instruction to the scattered Christian communities in Asia Minor (1 Pet 1.1), and later by 1 Clement, also from Rome, which directs this teaching to the Corinthian Christian community. The theoretical framework derived from Giddens' structuration theory enables and requires us, unlike many other forms of sociological theory, to grasp the sense of both continuity and transformation here, and to consider the ongoing process of structuration which occured as the symbolic order was reproduced over time and embodied in the life of particular communities (see further §7.2.).

For whatever its precedents, the social ethos of Clement's instruction – the shape he seeks to give to social interaction and relationships both within and outside the Christian community – is significantly different from that found within Paul's Corinthian correspondence. We have seen that Clement's model for behaviour in the church and the household is also his model for society. Peaceful existence is ensured when all remain quietly and humbly in their place, submitting gladly to those who wield authority in whichever sphere.

One's evaluation of such a model of citizenship will depend, of course, on one's own political persuasions and context. Raymond Brown points out that the exhortations to obedient submission in Rom 13, 1 Pet 2 and 1 Clem 60–61 probably all emerged at times when abuses of civil power had recently been evident.[192] Assuming that Clement's 'prayer issued from the fiery furnace of persecution'[193] Lightfoot considered it to be 'truly sublime – sublime in its utterances, and still more sublime in its silence'. 'Who would have begrudged the Church of Rome her primacy', he continues, 'if she had always spoken thus?'[194] For L. W. Barnard too, Clement's political ethos is praiseworthy. Barnard makes his own sym-

---

[192] Brown 1983, 172: 'Caligula's madness and Claudius' expulsion of Jewish Christians' (*re* Rom 13); 'Nero's persecution' (*re* 1 Peter); 'misfortunes under Domitian' (1 Clem 1.1). Even if Domitian did not persecute Christians (see Welborn 1984, 40–44) his irrational and cruel actions against certain people would have been known (see Suetonius *Dom.* 10–17; Dio Cassius *HR* 67.1ff).

[193] An assumption which has been questioned; see above pp. 240–41 and Welborn 1984; Milburn 1945.

[194] Lightfoot 1890a, 384.

pathies clear, when he contrasts Clement's attitude with that of John of Patmos:

> For John of Patmos the present age was dying; the Roman State was anti-Christ which was doomed to terrible tortures through which Christians alone would be preserved for bliss. No greater contrast can be imagined than that between the seer of Patmos with his hatred of the Roman Power and his use of sub-Christian ideas of vengeance, and the gentle leader of the Roman Church with his sense of order, sobriety of temper, sweet reasonableness and forgiving spirit in a time of great difficulty. *We cannot doubt who is nearer to the mind of Christ.* [195]

It need hardly be said that Clement's model of citizenship might be assessed more critically, nor that the resources which John's apocalypse offers for a critical evaluation of secular authority may be more positively valued, especially by those with less conservative political commitments.[196]

6.6. Conclusion

There is clearly a good deal of continuity between Paul's Corinthian correspondence and 1 Clement, both in terms of purpose – to restore unity to the Corinthian congregation – and of content, for Clement takes up a number of the rules and resources which are used within 1 Corinthians.[197] More widely, Clement clearly takes up rules and resources from other Pauline and deutero-Pauline letters (Rom 13.1; household codes) as well as from other Jewish and Christian traditions.[198] We have conceptualised this continuity in terms suggested by Giddens' structuration theory, viewing the symbolic order of Pauline Christianity as a set of rules and resources which is produced and reproduced over time and which shapes the life of particular communities. Within this

---

[195] Barnard 1966, 18, my emphasis.

[196] See for example Wengst 1987, 105–35; Rowland 1988, 66–88; Rowland and Corner 1990, 131–55; Bauckham 1993a, 159–64; Fiorenza 1985.

[197] It is often doubted whether Clement knew of the letters contained within 2 Corinthians (cf. 1 Clem 47.1, where it is perhaps implied that Clement only knew of one epistle of Paul to the Corinthians). Hagner concedes that 'the evidence for Clement's knowledge of 2 Corinthians is rather slight', though he thinks that such knowledge 'remains a strong possibility' (1973, 211–13).

[198] Hence the debate over the sources of 1 Clement; see p. 5 n. 26 above.

theoretical framework we have sought to inquire as to the potential impact of successive formulations of the symbolic order upon the social life and relationships of those who inhabit this order; an impact summarised under the term 'social ethos'.

It is clear that, whatever the continuities, the social ethos of 1 Clement is notably different from that of 1 and 2 Corinthians (see §4.4. and §5.7. above). The symbolic order of 1 and 2 Corinthians often stood in stark opposition to the dominant social order, and did not sustain or legitimate that social order within the Christian community, though there was what must be termed an ideological legitimation of the ecclesiastical hierarchy which Paul supports. However, in contrast to the Christianity found in Paul's Corinthian letters, *1 Clement's form of Christianity is much more widely ideological: it legitimates and affirms the dominant social order, rooting the established social, domestic and ecclesiastical hierarchy in the ordering purposes of God the creator. It reinforces the position of the socially dominant within the Christian community, urging all to remain in their place. The subordination of women is assumed and presented as ideal. 'Love patriarchalism', as outlined by Theissen, accurately captures the ethos of Clement's Christianity.* If, as seems likely, the deposed elders were from among the socially prominent members of the community and the rebels from the lower strata, then there is a particular and contextual reason for the character and ethos of Clement's instruction. However Clement's reactions may nonetheless be contrasted with Paul's. Paul, it seems, reacted to the complaints of the weak by criticising the strong and presenting them with a radical and Christologically-based example of self-lowering. Clement, by contrast, against the rebels, supports the interests and position of the socially strong, insisting that the established order and hierarchy, political, domestic and ecclesiastical, must be sustained, and presenting such comprehensive order as originating in and reflecting the will of God. Paul stresses God's election of, and his own identification with, the dishonoured, foolish, nobodies (1 Cor 1.26–2.5; 4.8–13). Clement uses similar language to describe those who have rebelled against the community and against God (1 Clem 3.3).

It has not been my intention to investigate the range or variety of sources of 1 Clement's material, nor, therefore, to claim that it is a particularly 'Pauline' document. Whatever the extent of the continuity or discontinuity in terms of symbolic and theological resources, my investigations suggest that the social ethos which these resources are used to support is significantly different. Similar resources are in places used by both Paul and Clement – for example the analogy of the body – but are drawn upon in such a way as to convey a very different social ethos. The limitations of historical evidence prevent us saying a great deal about the actual impact of these texts upon the community to which they were sent (though the letters contained within 2 Corinthians offer some insight into the impact of 1 Corinthians). However, it is clear that the intended impact of the letters – the shape which they intend to give to social relationships within and outside the community – is very different. Similarities in ethos between 1 Clement, the Pastoral Epistles, and 1 Peter, all written after Paul's death, suggest that the chronological dimensions of this change should not be ignored. That is not to claim that other material, such as the *Haustafeln*, presented in these documents does not draw upon old and established traditions, be they Jewish or Greco-Roman. The relevant question in the context of this investigation is when (and why) it was introduced to, and urged as normative for, various Christian communities, in this case, the Corinthian one.

In a conclusion to the study as a whole, I shall draw together the threads of this investigation and present the main conclusions. I shall also sketch the wider picture into which the trajectory of change represented by the contrast between 1 Corinthians and 1 Clement must be located and consider some possible explanations of it. Some comments will also be offered on the importance of the sociological issues raised throughout this study for contemporary theological reflection.

7

Conclusion

7.1. Summary and conclusions

The methodological discussions in Part 1 of this study involved a careful consideration of what the theoretical bases for a sociological approach to the New Testament should be. Giddens' work was the major resource for the development of my own framework. I rejected the idea that a 'model' or a comparative approach must be used in a sociological study, though insisting that a theoretical basis must be carefully outlined. I rejected the idea that social-scientific research implied the search for the social determinants or typical 'laws' of human action, and, following Giddens, argued for a contextual and diachronic approach which effectively dissolves any sustainable methodological distinction between sociology and history. The theoretical framework I sought to develop derives certain of its perspectives from functionalism and from Berger and Luckmann's sociology of knowledge approach. However, significant criticisms of both of these prominent theoretical traditions required that their valuable insights be taken up within a theoretical framework which was decisively different from them both. My own research framework was primarily dependent upon theoretical resources derived from Giddens' structuration theory. This framework conceives of Pauline Christianity as a symbolic order comprising rules and resources which are embodied in the lives of particular communities and which are taken up, reproduced and transformed over time. In this ongoing process the social relationships within the community are shaped and structured – a process which may be labelled one of 'structuration'. Within this essentially diachronic framework, Giddens' work also offers a 'critical' perspective which focuses upon questions of power, interests and ideology.

The research framework adopted in this project has thus led to a careful consideration of the potential impact of the Corinthian correspondence upon the Christian community to which it was addressed. As the symbolic order of Pauline Christianity was reproduced over time, by those in positions of power, so I have sought to assess the extent to which each formulation of Christian teaching might support or legitimate the interests of dominant social groups and the hierarchical social order.

Part 2 of the study began by sketching the broad social context within which the history of the Corinthian Christian community is to be located. Then I outlined the methods adopted by Paul in his mission at Corinth, the basic elements of the symbolic order he conveyed to his converts, and the social composition of the congregation. After a brief outline of the interaction which took place between Paul and the Corinthian community before the writing of 1 Corinthians, I explored the evidence for social conflicts and tensions within the congregation, since these form the direct context to which 1 Corinthians is addressed (chapter 3).

I therefore studied 1 Corinthians as an example of Paul's taking up the rules and resources of the Christian symbolic order in order to address and confront a particular context. I sought to assess the social ethos conveyed by this letter, to consider whether it supports the interests of particular social groups and the senses in which it might be regarded as ideological, and to form a judgment as to whether its social ethos is accurately captured by the term 'love-patriarchalism'. I argued that Paul, while in places ideologically legitimating an ecclesiastical hierarchy, does not offer ideological support to the dominant social order. Although there are elements of his teaching which might be developed in this direction, on the whole he is notably critical of the behaviour and practices of the socially strong. He formulates the teaching about the cross in a way which completely inverts the values and positions of the dominant social order. Moreover, Paul shows no desire to demand from the weak 'subordination, fidelity, and esteem'. For these reasons, while acknowledging that there are some elements within Paul's instruction which might form a basis for an ethos of 'love-patriarchalism', the term 'love-patriarchalism' must be judged an inappropriate summary of the ethos of 1 Corinthians (chapter 4). Paul seems rather to use the central symbolic resources of his Christian faith – the self-giving of Christ, shown most fully in the cross, and the unity of believers in the one body of Christ – to undergird an ethos which builds community unity through the honouring of the weak and the self-giving and self-lowering of the socially strong. A symbolic order which contrasts strongly with the dominant social order is meant to be embodied in the Christian congregation.

This ethos is also conveyed in Paul's own self-presentation and apostolic lifestyle. His insistence upon portraying himself and the other leaders as 'the scum of the earth' and upon labouring with his own hands reflects this Christological pattern of self-lowering, and demonstrates a concern for solidarity with the weak and a rejection of the conventional social expectations imposed upon him by the strong. It is a pattern, moreover, which he calls the Corinthian strong to imitate. The conflict which develops between Paul and some of the congregation, in which these particular issues loom large, therefore, is more than a personal dispute; it is a clash of values in which the Christian ethos which Paul embodies and presents is rejected by certain of the congregation. In the ongoing interaction between Paul and the Corinthian community this conflict comes to a head in a painful visit, when Paul feels compelled to withdraw from the community. He follows this visit with a painful letter, in which he presents essentially the same self-image and insists upon the same pattern of life (2 Cor 10–13). Reconciliation begins when the majority of the congregation side with Paul and exclude his most prominent opponent from their number (chapter 5).

The reconstruction offered by this particular reading of Paul's Corinthian correspondence, I believe, reveals a good deal of coherence within this correspondence and, instead of positing different forms of opposition or conflict at different points in time, shows how certain issues run throughout and constitute the major focus for disagreement. The analysis of the ongoing interaction revealed by 2 Cor 10–13 and 2 Cor 1–9 (taken in that order) also adds plausibility to the hypothesis developed in connection with the social ethos of 1 Corinthians. It does indeed seem highly likely that Paul's teaching and self-presentation in 1 Corinthians, if they conveyed the radical social ethos and challenge to the position and status of the socially strong which I have suggested they do, would lead to antagonism and rejection from a particular section of the congregation. The clash between Paul and some of the more socially prominent members of the congregation does indeed come to a head and is resolved, to a degree at least, through the power of the majority, whose perspective Paul has sought to adopt and defend.

The structuration theory perspective upon which the study is based conceives of Pauline Christianity as a symbolic order comprising rules and resources which are embodied in the lives of particular communities and which are taken up, reproduced and transformed over time. In this ongoing process the social relationships within the community are shaped and structured. The study therefore proceeded with its diachronic perspective by considering the way in which 1 Clement, the next piece of extant ecclesiastical correspondence addressed to the church at Corinth, takes up the rules and resources of the Christian symbolic order, in response to a particular crisis at Corinth, in order to shape the life of this Christian community. As Giddens maintains, when these rules and resources are taken up, as with a language continually spoken and used, there will be both continuity and transformation. I have sought to illuminate the extent to which both occur in 1 Clement, and particularly to consider the social ethos which Clement's teaching conveys, whose interests his teaching supports and the ways in which it may be perceived as ideological.

Clement's response to division and strife in the Corinthian community, while taking up quite directly a number of the resources used by Paul, is notably different from Paul's. He seeks to re-establish order in the congregation by calling all to the humility and submission appropriate to their position. His call for order is based fundamentally upon a theology which affirms God as the master and the creator of established order. Clement's primary concern is with ecclesiastical order, but it is clear that he also uses this theology to legitimate ideologically the dominant social, political and domestic hierarchy; the basic consequence of God's activity as the creator of order is that all should quietly and humbly remain in their place. The *status quo* is theologically affirmed (chapter 6).

There is a major difference in social ethos between 1 Corinthians and 1 Clement; in 1 Corinthians the Christian symbolic order contrasts with and challenges the dominant social order, in 1 Clement it to some extent mirrors and legitimates it. Paul's teaching does not appear to support the interests of the socially strong and does, at least in places, express and defend the interests of the weak. Clement's teaching, on the other hand, largely sustains the interests of the socially strong. In terms of ideological analysis it seems clear that Paul's Corinthian letters do not offer ideological legitimation to the dominant social order, though there are places where an ecclesiastical hierarchy is ideologically sustained and where theological resources are presented which could form the basis of an ideology which legitimates the subordinate positions of both slaves and women. Clement's theology, by contrast, offers a strong and profound undergirding to the established order, ecclesiastical, domestic and political. It provides a theological ideology which legitimates the *status quo*; preserving this order is, for Clement, the way to peace and harmony.

7.2. A wider trajectory within Pauline Christianity?

This study has focused only upon the teaching sent to the Corinthian Christian community and has thus focused upon Paul's Corinthian letters and upon 1 Clement, comparing and contrasting the ethos conveyed by these two authors separated by time and space. A wider question, however, can hardly be ignored: To what extent does the reproduction of the Christian symbolic order found in 1 Clement represent a wider, more general, trajectory of change within Pauline Christianity of the first century? To explore this question in depth would take us well beyond the scope of the present study, but it is important nevertheless to offer some pointers concerning the wider picture.

First it must be stressed that the variety within the literature of early Christianity should certainly prevent us from positing any kind of unilinear development within early Christianity. Even within Pauline Christianity a variety of trajectories may be glimpsed, for example, in documents like the *Acts of Paul* [1] and the Gnostic literature,[2] and revealed also by the polemic in letters like the Pastoral Epistles, all of which clearly show that the interpretation of Paul's heritage was subject to variety and controversy.[3]

However, the particular trajectory represented by 1 Clement may be linked with the development apparent within the canonical Pauline epistles. A structuration theory perspective again offers a useful and illuminating way of viewing this process.[4] Within the epistles generally accepted as by Paul himself there is nowhere (excluding 1 Cor 14.34f) a direct instruction urging the submission of women or slaves, nor does

---

[1]   For an interesting exploration of the struggle between competing forms of Pauline Christianity, focusing especially upon the *Acts of Paul* and the Pastoral Epistles, see MacDonald 1983; on the *Acts of Paul* see also Bauckham 1993b, esp. 116–30, who disputes MacDonald's suggestion that the Pastorals are written in direct opposition to the oral legends eventually incorporated into the *Acts of Paul*, though he accepts that the 'contrast between the social attitude of the two bodies of literature is certainly real' (122).

[2]   See, for example, Pagels 1975.

[3]   See further Babcock 1990.

[4]   See also Horrell 1995d.

any form of 'household code' appear. (The extent to which the social ethos of 1 and 2 Corinthians is characteristic of Paul's other epistles is an interesting issue which cannot be explored here.) In Paul's letter to the Romans, however, there is a clear instruction to the Roman Christians to submit to the governing authorities (Rom 13.1), an instruction based upon the assertion that the government's position is granted to it by God. Whatever the reasons for Romans 13 Paul's formulation enters the rule-system of early Christianity and is taken up and developed by others. The geographical destination of Paul's instruction also affects the epistolary contexts in which it is later taken up.

The household codes, which urge upon the members of the household the behaviour and submission appropriate to their position, appear first in Colossians and Ephesians, two letters which clearly share some literary relationship and which are often taken to be the products of a post-Pauline group or author some years after the apostle's death.[5] The household codes in these two letters are very closely related in form and content and are the most formalised and clearly structured of any which appear in other (later) Christian literature. These letters (or, rather, whichever of them was the first to be written, in my view probably Colossians) are therefore responsible for introducing (as far as we can tell from the literary evidence) this ideology for the household into Pauline Christianity.[6]

Written from Rome not very long before 1 Clement, 1 Peter takes up these rules and resources and, interestingly, brings together Paul's instruction to be subject to governing authority (1 Pet 2.13–17) – an instruction sent initially to Rome – and the domestic-code form of teaching (1 Pet 2.18–3.7). Slaves and women are a particular focus of Peter's instruction. 1 Peter also combines rules and resources derived from Pauline Christianity with other strands of (Jewish-) Christian tradition, both presumably being influential within the life of the Roman congregations, a combination of traditions and resources which is also characteristic of 1 Clement.

The Pastoral Epistles also take up the rules concerning submission to governing authority (Titus 3.1), again in close proximity to rules concerning behaviour and submission within the household (Titus 2.2–10). 1 Timothy also urges prayers for the ruling authorities (1 Tim 2.1f;

---

[5] E.g. MacDonald 1988; Lincoln and Wedderburn 1993.
[6] See further Horrell 1995d, 230–33.

cf. 1 Clem 61.1f). Indeed in the Pastorals, especially in 1 Timothy, the ecclesiastical hierarchy becomes closely associated with the established domestic hierarchy, with the ideology for the household offered in the household codes becoming an ideology for the church, structured as 'the household of God' (1 Tim 3.15) with male heads of household as its ἐπίσκοποι.[7] The social, domestic and ecclesiastical hierarchies are together legitimated in a way not dissimilar to 1 Clement.

As an example of developing Roman Christianity then, 1 Clement may be located within this wider trajectory. The trajectory is one in which the rules and resources offered within Pauline Christianity are taken up in a way which is increasingly socially conservative, which supports the interests of the socially dominant, and which ideologically legitimates the established social, domestic and ecclesiastical order. The socially weak are urged to be submissive and obedient and the socially strong are urged to fulfil the responsibilities of leadership. From a structuration theory perspective we can give due attention to the continuity between these later letters and the resources found within earlier Pauline letters, but without claiming that essentially the same social ethos runs throughout, a claim which to my mind obscures the extremely important transformation which occurs and which is of considerable sociological significance.

As these rules and resources are taken up and developed, and are used to support this particular social ethos, so at the same time the geographical influence of this trajectory spreads. Reflecting an ethos developing within the Roman church, 1 Peter urges the pattern of behaviour congruent with this conservative social ethos upon the churches scattered in the provinces of Asia Minor. Also reflecting a Roman perspective, 1 Clement seeks to use a position of power to urge a pattern of conduct upon the Corinthian congregation.

If the observations concerning this trajectory are accepted – that a conservative ideology encapsulating a love-patriarchal ethos is present in literature like 1 Clement and the Pastoral Epistles, and that this represents a significant difference from the Christianity which Paul himself propagated – one important question concerns the reasons for such a development.

Some sociological studies of the New Testament have used sociological models of sect and institutionalisation as the basis for explanation,

---

[7] See further Horrell 1995d, 233–36; 1993, 93–103.

and view the process of change as one in which a sect moves closer towards the 'church' type.[8] A sect may typically be hostile towards the world, for example, and with progressing institutionalisation this hostility and opposition may soften. Through the process of institutionalisation patterns of leadership and hierarchy develop and greater attention is given to protecting and stabilising the life of the community. To a considerable extent the pattern of change I have discerned and outlined in the studies above does indeed fit within this 'developing sect' model. There are reasons, however, for questioning the value of such an approach as a starting point or basis for sociological study of the New Testament.

The model suggests that certain features are generally found in sects (though Bryan Wilson, for example, insists that sectarian typologies are useful only to summarise crucial elements in the empirical cases they are meant to epitomise)[9] and that certain forms of behaviour and attitude are typical. Using such a model as a starting point, however, may serve simply to obscure what is unusual and particular in this context,[10] or to squeeze the evidence into a particular mould. Moreover, with regard to the question of explanation, observations about what may or may not be typical (notwithstanding the problems of such an approach, outlined in §1.2. and §1.4. above) are of little or no help in understanding. For example, to explain the hostility to the dominant social order in 1 Corinthians on the grounds that 'sects are typically hostile to the outside world' is, of course, to offer no real explanation whatsoever. Even if there are such similarities between religious movements which may be termed sects, it cannot be assumed that the 'cause' of such similarity is in any sense the same from one case to another. Giddens, we may recall, insists that 'explanation is contextual' and maintains that 'most "why" questions do not need a generalization to answer them'.[11]

Similar problems attend the attempt to view the process of change we have described as one of 'institutionalisation'. While this approach clearly conveys something of the nature of the change which is observed it is

---

[8] E.g. MacDonald 1988.

[9] Wilson 1967, 2; quoted above p. 15.

[10] Wilson also expresses a concern not to obscure the rich diversity in the world (see previous note). Barton 1993, 158, makes the point that if all of early Christianity may be described as sectarian, then the model is too broad and general to 'make possible the discrimination ... which is necessary to do justice to the evidence'.

[11] Giddens 1984, xviii–xix.

based upon a model of what is typical as institutions develop. The danger is that the change will therefore be 'explained' as a typical process of sociological necessity – thereby legitimating and at the same time obscuring what is in fact a process of conflict in which the groups with most power ultimately come to dominate. This is not a sociological necessity except insofar as the powerful are indeed likely to 'win the day', a process which requires specific and critical sociological analysis and which must not be concealed as merely an inevitable change inherent in the nature of institutional development.[12]

Giddens' theoretical framework has led in this study both to a contextual focus upon a specific arena of human interaction as opposed to a model-based focus upon what is 'typical', and to an attempt critically to penetrate the interests and ideology which are conveyed by the instruction given by the powerful. So from this critical and contextual perspective, how might we seek to explain the trajectory of change which we have observed from 1 Corinthians to 1 Clement? There are to my mind two broad possibilities to be explored.

The first relates to what might be termed 'external' factors: suspicion and persecution. To what extent did the might of Rome (particularly perhaps in the capital city) create enormous pressure, whether actual or threatened, encouraging any religious movement to ensure as far as possible that it was not seen as a threat to the establishment? This pressure would naturally be felt with increasing force with the fading of the belief that the Lord's return was very imminent and that the form of this world would then pass away – an over-emphasised theological perspective whose significance should nevertheless not be too quickly dismissed. This must surely be a part of the picture, though there are a number of reasons for suggesting that it does not provide a complete answer. First, there is the early Christian literature (esp. James and Revelation) which refuses in any way to view the establishment positively; Revelation shows that the apocalyptic genre offered one way of continuing to express a longing for the downfall of the Empire in coded form. Second, it is striking that even within letters like the Pastoral Epistles there is no lack of bold

---

[12] Cf. further the critique of MacDonald 1988 in Horrell 1993, e.g.: 'The fact that the socially conservative side may have won the day and emerged as "orthodox" and canonical is not necessarily to be explained by the assertion that they were the ones "protecting" the community and its symbolic universe, but may connect in a more insidious way to differentials of power and influence' (98). Cf. also Castelli 1991, 21–33.

assertions about the position and uniqueness of Christ (1 Tim 2.3–7; 2 Tim 4.1; Titus 2.13), using terms often argued to be derived from the language of the imperial cult,[13] even though it was precisely such assertions and the refusal to participate in the imperial cult which led directly to the death of many Christians, at least some of whom, it seems, were quite willing to embrace martyrdom.[14] Moreover, there is little evidence for systematic persecution at this early stage in the history of the Christian church.[15]

A second possibility should therefore be considered alongside (not in place of) the 'external' factors, even though it may seem to imply a more cynical view of the early Christians. If there was a degree of social diversity within the Pauline congregations from the earliest days, a position now widely accepted within New Testament scholarship (see §3.7.), then we must at least consider the possibility that the prominent and powerful members of these congregations, particularly after the disappearance of the apostle Paul, may have used their positions of power to formulate teaching which reflected and sustained their social interests. One of the sociologically significant changes which took place after the death of Paul is that power and authority were transferred from itinerant leaders, especially the apostle and his co-workers, to resident leaders (and to particular places),[16] who may often have been among the socially prominent members of their communities (male householders; cf. 1 Tim 3.1–13).[17] As power within the churches is increasingly concentrated in the hands of this social group, so at the same time Christian teaching increasingly serves their social interests.[18] Is the patriarchal trajectory of Pauline Christianity due in part to this dynamic of internal sociology?

Whatever the answers to these questions, which require detailed research and consideration in themselves, the way in which the social ethos of Pauline Christianity developed among certain groups might be of significance for understanding the eventual adoption of Christianity as the religion of the empire. Theissen, we recall, suggested that the love-

---

[13] See Hanson 1982b, 186–88.
[14] See esp. Ignatius *Rom.* 4–8.
[15] Cf. Jeffers 1991, 18. Pliny seeks some precedent and clarification in c. 112 CE (*Ep.* 10.96).
[16] 1 Clement (as 1 Peter before) certainly demonstrates the increasing prominence of the Roman church as a centre of admonition and instruction, whether or not it constitutes a claim to 'primacy'. This is one of the areas of debate reviewed by Fuellenbach 1980.
[17] Cf. Maier 1991, 100; Holmberg 1978, 106–107.
[18] Cf. further Horrell 1995d, 235–36.

patriarchal ethos of Pauline Christianity was eventually found to offer a suitable social ethos for the wider society in which it had developed.[19] From a critical sociological perspective we might suggest that the development of a theological ideology within early Christianity was also of profound significance. Symbolic and theological resources were used in certain circles to legitimate the dominance of the ruling classes and to sustain the subordination of the weak. The particular form of Christianity reflected in 1 Clement, unlike that in 1 and 2 Corinthians, does indeed have the capacity to become 'a sheltering canopy over the institutional order', as Berger and Luckmann describe the function of a 'symbolic universe'.[20] Leonardo Boff makes a similar point: 'It [the Church] offered the empire an ideology that supported the existing order and even blessed the pagan cosmos.'[21] In such a form, Christianity would understandably be attractive to the ruling elite. Perhaps, as Walter Bauer suggested long ago, 'the Roman government finally came to recognise that the Christianity ecclesiastically organised from Rome was flesh of its flesh, came to unite with it, and thereby enabled it to achieve ultimate victory over unbelievers and heretics'.[22]

7.3. Contemporary reflections

An approach which employs a 'critical' conception of ideology and which speaks about the 'interests' of particular groups is clearly not a 'neutral' one (not that there is any such thing). Indeed, critical social theorists, from whom my theoretical resources are derived, are explicit about their commitment to human emancipation[23] and therefore seek to expose and criticise ideology, since it is a means by which oppression and domination are sustained and concealed. This is not to suppose, however, that domination or power could ever be transcended in some utopian future society; rather, as a critical discipline, sociology seeks to expose the ways in which power is used and domination legitimated, in order that

---

[19] Theissen 1982, 107–10, 138–40, 163–64.
[20] Berger and Luckmann 1966, 120.
[21] Boff 1985, 50.
[22] Bauer 1972, 232.
[23] Cf. for example Gregson 1989, 247; Craib 1992, 11; Giddens 1982a, 14; 1982b, 156–66.

uncritical acceptance may be replaced by critical awareness. According to Peter Berger, a sociological perspective entails 'the art of mistrust': a radical 'debunking', 'unmasking', of every 'taken-for granted' world view. A sociologist continually interjects the question, 'Says who?'.[24] Max Weber is reported as stating that 'the true function of social science is to render problematic that which is conventionally self-evident'.[25]

A theology which is committed to proclaiming a liberating gospel and to challenging forms of social injustice may find important points of contact with the agenda of critical social theory. Sociologically-orientated studies are, I consider, an important means by which theology may become aware of the impact which its formulations have upon human social relations.[26] The question of theological truth should not thereby be reduced to one of pragmatic impact,[27] but neither should any theology ignore its social dimensions, which are surely there, whether or not they are acknowledged. 'Beliefs' of various kinds inevitably shape social life.[28] The ease with which theological resources may be used to legitimate oppressive forms of social organisation should make us aware of the need to consider the sociological dimensions of every attempt to formulate the word of the gospel today and to remain alert to the question: Whose interests are reflected here and at what cost to whom? The reading of 1 and 2 Corinthians, I suggest, shows that the links with the interests of the socially powerful are by no means intrinsic to Pauline Christianity. These letters may therefore offer resources for a critical and liberating theology.

However, this is not to suggest that such a theology should simply affirm what one might call 'non-ideological' documents, letters like 1 Corinthians, which challenge rather than sustain a dominant social order, and reject those like 1 Clement. For documents from early Christianity like 1 Corinthians raise problems of their own. For a start it is clear that they do ideologically legitimate an ecclesiastical hierarchy, which may become another system of oppression and domination, not too

---

[24] See Berger 1963, 35, 41–43, 47, 51, 54–55, 78–80, etc.
[25] Corbridge 1993, 7.
[26] Cf. Gill 1987, 145–64.
[27] A pragmatic theory of 'truth' is famously elaborated by Marx (second thesis on Feuerbach; see Elster 1986, 21). Liberation theology's emphasis on the pragmatic assessment of gospel 'truth' is expressed by Charles Elliott: 'The liberation theologians will say very simply "the test for truth is the effect it has on people's lives. Is this proposition ... actually liberating people or enslaving them?"' (cited by Rowland and Corner 1990, 42).
[28] Cf. Gill 1987, 154–56; Milbank 1990, 139.

dissimilar from that deemed to be present in the world.[29] They may be seen to be anti-worldly, sectarian in the sense of drawing sharp boundaries between the insiders and the outsiders, and conditioned by an imminent eschatology; the rejection of the values of 'this age' is firmly rooted in the conviction that 'this age' is soon to end. The 'de-eschatologising' of the Christian message which is evident in 1 Clement[30] clearly reflects the view that the world as ordered by God the creator shows no signs of its imminent demise. The problems raised by both texts are apparent for a theology which seeks to affirm the world as the arena of God's activity without merely affirming the world as it is, or which sees the Christian community as an important embodiment of the reconciling work of God yet denies that this community is the sole or unique location where such activity is to be recognised. It might crudely be said that 1 Corinthians powerfully portrays the world (and thus the dominant social order) as evil and fallen, being brought to nothing by God, whose renewing work is to be seen in the new community called into being by the word of the cross. Yet as such it may inspire a theology which has little concern for the world and which views the Christian community as a unique location of light and renewal. On the other hand, 1 Clement powerfully portrays God as the creator of all things (including the dominant social order), which are ordered just as he willed. As such, and lacking a sense of the fallenness of the world, it offers a theology which sustains and affirms the world (and the dominant social order) as it is. So the theological task of formulating a liberating gospel proclamation demands much more than a simple selection of some texts and a rejection of others; repeating words from the past will certainly not be enough. The doctrines of both creation and fall must be held together in order to avoid, on the one hand, the danger of sectarianism, and, on the other, the danger of conformism.

As we engage in this hermeneutical task, there are reasons, I believe, for insisting that 'the word of the cross' must be at the heart of a Christian proclamation which is both rooted in the world yet critical of every worldly configuration of power and authority – a critique, rather than a form, of ideology.[31] It was 'the word of the cross' that Paul brought to

---

[29] Cf. Boff 1985, 47–64.
[30] See esp. Knoch 1964, 200, 202, 290–316, 349, 450–58; Chester 1992, 292–95.
[31] On the centrality of 'the word of the cross' for Christian theology, see Moltmann 1974, 1–7, 32–41, etc.

bear in polemical fashion against those in Corinth who were 'puffed up' because of their power, wisdom and noble birth. The cross raises critical questions about what passes for established wisdom (σοφία), unquestionable power (δύναμις) and inherited rights (εὐγένεια), and calls the church to constant criticism, of itself as much as of the world. For the cross not only roots the Christian faith in the world, but also embodies the gospel's critique of the powerful. The claim that the cross is a place of divine action cannot but be a critique of the regime which labels its victim a common criminal and subjects him to a slave's death.[32] It is not insignificant to note that the words σταυρός/σταυρόω (cross/crucify) are completely absent from 1 Clement.[33] The heresy of docetism, Francis Watson suggests, is not merely the denial of Jesus' humanity in general, but rather of 'the specific form of his humanity',[34] and, we might add, of the specific form of his death.[35]

Paul's declaration that the foolishness of the cross is mirrored by God's election of the weak and foolish nobodies is potentially discomforting to those who are Christians, yet who cannot realistically claim to be among that part of the world's population; just as it was perhaps discomforting for those members of the Corinthian community who would not willingly have attached such labels to themselves. But Paul's answer to such discomfort is perhaps still more disturbing; for he challenges his readers to conform in their own lives to the pattern of Christ's self-giving, 'who emptied himself, taking the form of a slave' (Phil 2.7).[36] It would be possible, as perhaps happens too often, to spiritualise this challenge, internalising and individualising such qualities as meekness and humility. However, a sociologically orientated study such as this one may present it in a different way; as a challenge to step down in the world, to give up material advantages and act in solidarity with the weak, in order that a just and equal distribution of wealth and opportunity may be enacted (cf. 2 Cor 8.13f).[37] A challenge of that nature may perhaps be unpalatable

---

[32] Cf. Hengel 1986, 143–55; Stambaugh and Balch 1986, 35–36.
[33] Cf. Russell 1989, 196; though they are also absent from Romans and 1 Thessalonians, as well as the Pastoral Epistles.
[34] Watson 1992a, 148–49.
[35] Cf. Hengel 1986, 107–13. Many discussions of the 'atonement' seem to focus on the death of Christ as a salvific event, but lose any sight of its specific form and context, and the implications of these.
[36] See further chapter 5 above.
[37] See further Horrell 1995c.

for those who have much in the way of material benefits, though it is undoubtedly of considerable relevance to the world in which we live. At least some of the 'strong' Corinthians, we have seen, rejected the apostle's challenge to 'become weak', though eventually Paul's foremost opponent was defeated by the power of the 'weak' majority. Some years later the established leadership of the Corinthian church, comprising in all probability the well-to-do heads of households known as 'elders', were challenged again 'from below'. This time the Christian teaching which the 'rebels' received insisted that obedience to God's will meant remaining quietly in their place and ceasing from 'vain sedition'. The interests of the socially strong and the theological resources of the Christian symbolic order had formed a close alliance in the form of a powerful religious ideology.

That may be a depressing conclusion to the story, but the preservation of the various texts that are our sources allows not only a historical reconstruction of the various conflicts and struggles that occurred but also that the subversive resource of the word of the cross may be reclaimed and reinterpreted by those who regard the Christian story as offering valuable resources for shaping our lives in the world today. Ernst Käsemann, whose high regard for Paul is based upon what he sees as Paul's theologically radical doctrine of 'the justification of the ungodly', believes that Paul has been generally misunderstood and domesticated within the church. However, the preservation of his letters in the canon of scripture means that he can be 'rediscovered' as a source of 'explosive power'. 'It is never long, to be sure', Käsemann suggests, 'until orthodoxy and enthusiasm again master this Paul and banish him once more to his letters. However, the Church continues to preserve his letters in her canon and thereby latently preserves her own permanent crisis.'[38] It seems to me that, on at least some points, Paul has some sociologically radical ideas too, which may also, if rediscovered, present a disturbing and uncomfortable challenge, especially to those who consider themselves wise, powerful and well-born.

---

[38] Käsemann 1969, 250–51.

Appendix 1

The painful letter and the chronological order of 2 Cor 1–9 and 10–13

1. Unity or partition of 2 Corinthians?

The unity of 2 Corinthians, initially attacked by J. S. Semler in 1776, is not frequently defended, and a range of partition theories require the interpreter's attention.[1] Indeed, it would be irresponsible to interpret 2 Corinthians without making explicit a hypothesis regarding its composition, since the transitions and interruptions in the text are so clear.[2]

In chapters 1–8 there are two passages – 2.14–7.4 and, within this, 6.14–7.1 – which seem to interrupt the flow of the text and could possibly be insertions.[3] The continuing enigma of 6.14–7.1 will not be addressed here, since its identity and date are not of relevance to the present argument.[4] The 'intricate linguistic links between 7:4 and 7:5–16' strongly suggest that these verses should not be separated,[5] and the digression which begins at 2.14 can be explained, as Francis Watson suggests, as a theological reflection on the 'contrast between the greatness of the gospel entrusted to the apostle and his own weakness',[6] which appropriately follows a description of Paul's missionary failure: a great opportunity had arisen in Troas (2.12) but 'Paul was so worried about Titus and the news he would bring from Corinth that he completely failed to take the opportunity'.[7] Even if 2.14–7.4 was originally separate

---

[1] On the history of debate and the current range of opinion see Betz 1972, 4–9; 1985, 3–36; Watson 1984, 324–31; Martin 1986, xl–lii; Taylor 1991, 67–69.

[2] Cf. Furnish 1984, 34–35.

[3] Hence the partition theories of Bornkamm 1961; 1962; Georgi 1987, 10–14; Bultmann 1985, 18; Taylor 1991 etc.

[4] For bibliography and discussion see above p. 89 with nn. 155–56.

[5] Thrall 1982, 110; see 109–11; Watson 1984, 338; Martin 1986, xliii, 216.

[6] Watson 1984, 337.

[7] Watson 1984, 336.

from 1–8, and this seems unlikely, it is possible to date both 'letters' after the painful letter which Paul mentions in 2 Cor 2.4–9; 7.8–12,[8] and it is this conclusion that is important here. Other breaks in the flow of 2 Corinthians occur at 8.1 and 9.1 and it has been suggested that both chapter 8 and chapter 9 were originally separate letters.[9] However, Stanley Stowers' careful study of the use of περὶ μὲν γάρ (9.1) in Greek literature offers strong grounds on which to argue that the two chapters are integrally linked as part of one letter. This short phrase indicates not the introduction of a previously unmentioned topic – one of the most prominent arguments among those favouring partition of the two chapters – but the introduction of further explanation and elaboration of the subject already under discussion.[10] Moreover, there are no strong grounds for separating chapter 8 from chapters 1–7; certainly a new topic is introduced, but this is insufficient evidence to suggest literary partition. Even if chapters 8 and 9 were originally separate letters, though this seems unlikely, they would be dated after the painful letter, since they are concerned with the recommencement and completion of the collection project.[11] This is undisputably the case; the important question here is whether 10–13 can be dated before 1–9 and identified as the painful letter.

The most obvious division in the text of 2 Corinthians occurs at 10.1, and most commentators agree that chapters 10–13 reflect a completely different mood and situation from those which precede. In Jean Héring's words: 'suddenly, at the beginning of 10, the storm breaks.'[12] Hans Lietzmann's notorious suggestion that the abrupt change can be explained with the 'assumption of a sleepless, wakeful night' is described by F. F. Bruce as 'incredibly frivolous'.[13] Such suggestions, of course, have simply abandoned the attempt to find serious and accessible historical explanations. Philip Hughes questions whether the change of tone is

---

[8]   Taylor 1991.
[9]   Betz 1985. For division between 8 and 9 see Héring 1967, xiii; Bultmann 1985, 18; Taylor 1991, 71, 81–83.
[10] See Stowers 1990; note Acts 28.22; also Jones 1973, 146 n. 68, making a similar point to Stowers concerning περὶ μὲν γάρ. For unity between 2 Cor 8 and 9 see also Bruce 1971, 225; Martin 1986, xliii (both of whom suggest a 'short break in dictation'); Furnish 1984, 429–33.
[11] Cf. Lüdemann 1984, 97–99.
[12] Héring 1967, xi.
[13] '... Annahme einer schlaflos durchwachten Nacht': Lietzmann 1949, 139; Bruce 1971, 166.

'really so abrupt'[14] and suggests that: 'In chapters 10 to 13 Paul is tying up the loose ends that remain.'[15] However, it is hard to miss the change of tone between chapters 1–9 and 10–13, and rather difficult to see how 10–13 can be regarded as 'tying up the loose ends that remain'. Indeed, such arguments for the unity of the canonical epistle have convinced few and are hardly sustainable.[16] The different tone of chapters 10–13 is striking enough, but when they follow the rhetoric of reconciliation in earlier chapters (2.5–11; 7.2–4; esp. 7.6–16) and a discussion of the organisation of the collection (chs 8–9), it is hard to see how they could possibly have been written as part of one and the same letter. Alfred Plummer makes the simple point: 'Is asking for money a good preparation for an incisive attack?'[17] Thus many commentators, conservatives included, support the hypothesis that chapters 10–13 belong to a separate letter.[18] The most significant debate about chapters 10–13 concerns whether they should be dated before or after chapters 1–9.

2. 2 Cor 10–13 as the painful letter?

In 1870, A. Hausrath argued that 2 Cor 10–13 should be identified as the 'painful letter' mentioned in 2 Cor 2.4, 9; 7.8, 12. He was followed in this by a number of scholars, including J. H. Kennedy and Plummer, though more recent English-speaking commentators have tended to reject this identification and to date 10–13 after 1–9.[19] Francis Watson, however, has eloquently restated the view that 2 Cor 10–13 precedes all of 2 Cor 1–9 and should be seen as the painful letter Paul refers to.[20]

---

14 Hughes 1962, xxiii, also xxx.
15 Hughes 1962, xxiv. Other defenders of the unity of the epistle include Kümmel 1975, 287–93; Stephenson 1964; 1965; Hyldahl 1973 (except 6.14–7.1; see 289).
16 Cf. Windisch 1924, 431: 'Es ist unmöglich, C [10–13] aus derselben Situation wie AB [1–9] herausgeboren zu denken.'; Murphy O'Connor 1991b, 32. Note also the comments of Betz 1972, 42, citing Windisch.
17 Plummer 1915, 269; see further xxix–xxx.
18 Plummer 1915, xxvii–xxxvi; Héring 1967, xi–xii; Bruce 1971, 166–70; Barrett 1973, 21, 23; Furnish 1984, 30–41; Martin 1986, xxxviii–lii; Talbert 1987, xviii–xxi; Watson 1993b, xx.
19 Bruce, Barrett, Furnish and Martin; references in previous note. Also, earlier, the influential German commentary of Windisch 1924, 17–18: 'C [10–13] ist die Reaktion des P. auf eine neue Verschärfung des Konflikts, die ihm nach Abfertigung von AB [1–9] gemeldet wurde'; followed by Betz 1972, 8, 13.
20 Watson 1984; he rejects any partition of chapters 1–9, except 6.14–7.1, which he views as an interpolation (see 331 esp. n. 57, 335); followed by Talbert 1987, xix–xxi, 112 and

(This hypothesis will be referred to hereafter as the 'identification hypothesis'.)

Given the decision that 10–13 is a separate letter from 1–9, and given that we know that Paul wrote a painful letter before he wrote 1–9, the identification hypothesis has a degree of *a priori* plausibility.

On a general level the following statements may be made about the letter to which 2 Cor 2.4 refers: it was a painful letter which it grieved Paul to write (2.4) and it was intended to test the Corinthians' obedience and loyalty (2.9; cf. 10.6[21]). It was a letter which could cause hurt and lead to repentance (7.8ff) and whose purpose was to make clear the Corinthians' zeal and devotion (7.12). Certainly, 2 Cor 10–13 may broadly be regarded as such a letter. It may be questioned whether 2 Cor 10–13 could be described as a letter written 'through many tears' (διὰ πολλῶν δακρύων – 2.4), though on this point the parallel in Phil 3.18 is illuminating: in the context there of a harsh attack on his Judaizing opponents and a warning to the community not to be led astray (Phil 3.2–21), Paul speaks 'even with tears' (νῦν δὲ καὶ κλαίων λέγω) of those who are enemies of the cross of Christ. If Paul can write in that polemical context of 'weeping' as he warns the Philippians, then 2 Cor 10–13 could also appropriately be said to have been written 'through many tears'.

The painful letter was also a letter which one might conceivably regret writing (7.8). Thus Paul can hardly be referring to 1 Corinthians, as some have suggested,[22] for although it is in places sharp and polemical and calls for the expulsion of a particular offender (see 1 Cor 4.8ff; 5.1ff; 6.1ff), much of it is a considered response to issues raised by the Corinthians themselves (1 Cor 7.1). On the other hand it is wholly conceivable that regret might have been felt in regard to 2 Cor 10–13, where Paul states that he feels driven to boast like a fool (11.1, 16, 21; 12.11), even though such boasting is not beneficial (12.1) and may be contrasted with the sort of speech which is appropriate κατὰ κύριον (11.17). Indeed, even as he writes, Paul is conscious of the 'madness' of his way of

Taylor 1991, 72 esp. n. 3 (supporting the view that 10–13 is the painful letter, but adopting a more complex partition theory). In response to Watson see Murphy O'Connor 1991b.

[21] A parallel pointed out by Kennedy 1900, 84–85 and Plummer 1915, xxxi.

[22] E.g. Hughes 1962, xxviii–xxx; Hyldahl 1973, 299–300; with the offender mentioned in 1 Cor 5 being the person referred to in 2 Cor 2.6–8; so Lampe 1967, 353–54; Hughes 1962, 63–64; Hyldahl 1991, 26. However, the identification is generally rejected; see Plummer 1915, xxviii; Barrett 1982, 111; Martin 1986, xlvii.

speaking (παραφρονῶν λαλῶ – 11.23);²³ a statement which finds an interesting echo in 5.13 – εἴτε γὰρ ἐξέστημεν, θεῷ· εἴτε σωφρονοῦμεν, ὑμῖν. We may also presume from 2 Cor 3.1 (ἀρχόμεθα πάλιν ἑαυτοὺς συνιστάνειν;) and 5.12 (οὐ πάλιν ἑαυτοὺς συνιστάνομεν) that Paul has previously attempted to commend himself. Does this refer back to 2 Cor 10–13? Paul is certainly not opposed to letters of commendation, for he writes one for Phoebe in Rom 16.1f (Συνίστημι δὲ ὑμῖν ... cf. also 1 Cor 16.3);²⁴ his point in 2 Cor 3.1 is that he and his co-workers, unlike others (a possible reference to the intruders who are attacked in 11.4ff), should not need them, for the Corinthian believers are themselves Paul's letter of commendation, proof of his apostolic ministry. Nevertheless in 2 Cor 10–13 we clearly witness Paul in a situation in which he feels compelled to defend and commend himself as a true apostle of Christ. Indeed he explicitly states that the Corinthians' failure to commend him necessitated his foolish boasting: Γέγονα ἄφρων, ὑμεῖς με ἠναγκάσατε. ἐγὼ γὰρ ὤφειλον ὑφ' ὑμῶν συνίστασθαι· (12.11).

Murphy O'Connor has suggested that 1 Corinthians could be the letter Paul refers to in which he 'speaks about himself in a way which could be considered self-praise'.²⁵ This, however, is far less likely than that 2 Cor 10–13 is in view; the verb συνίστημι is completely absent from 1 Corinthians but is used four times in 2 Cor 10–13.²⁶ Indeed, it is *only* in 2 Corinthians and in Rom 16.1 that Paul uses συνίστημι to refer to the commendation of people, including himself.²⁷ In 2 Cor 10–13 Paul is most reluctant explicitly to 'commend' himself – 'commending themselves' (τῶν ἑαυτούς συνιστανόντων) is clearly something he regards his opponents as doing (10.12) – because it is not, in his view, self-commendation but divine commendation which shows genuineness (οὐ γὰρ ὁ ἑαυτὸν συνιστάνων, ἐκεῖνός ἐστιν δόκιμος, ἀλλὰ ὃν ὁ κύριος συνίστησιν – 10.18). However, since the Corinthians have failed to recognise their own existence as Christians as proof of his apos-

---

²³ RSV: 'I am talking like a madman'; cf. BAGD, 623.
²⁴ See further Marshall 1987, 91–129.
²⁵ Murphy O'Connor 1991b, 35.
²⁶ 2 Cor 10.12; 10.18 (twice); 12.11.
²⁷ Rom 16.1 commends Phoebe; in 2 Cor 1–9 see 3.1 (note also συστατικός here); 4.2; 5.12; 6.4; 7.11; for other uses see Rom 3.5; 5.8; Gal 2.18; (Col 1.17). As can be seen, the Pauline use of the word is heavily concentrated in 2 Corinthians (9 out of 13 occurences).

tolic calling,[28] Paul is reluctantly forced to engage in some form of self-commendation (12.11). The evidence of 2 Cor 3.1 and 5.12 seems then to add weight to the identification hypothesis. In the chronological outline given in chapter 5 (§5.4.), it was mentioned that Paul most likely withdrew to Ephesus after his painful visit to Corinth and wrote the painful letter from there. Interestingly, an Ephesian origin for 2 Cor 10–13 may be hinted at in 10.16 where Paul refers to his desire to preach the gospel in the parts beyond them (τὰ ὑπερέκεινα ὑμῶν), presumably Rome and Spain (Rom 1.15; 15.23f, 28). If this were written from Macedonia, as 2 Cor 1–9 appears to be (7.5ff; 8.1ff; esp. 9.4), then the expression τὰ ὑπερέκεινα ὑμῶν would seem less geographically apposite.[29] It would be unwise to build much on this, but other aspects of 2 Cor 10–13 also locate these chapters plausibly within this episode of Paul's dealings with the church at Corinth.

In 1 Cor 4.18–21, Paul threatened that his power over 'the puffed up people' whom he opposed would be demonstrated when he visited, but it seems that his humiliating visit (2 Cor 2.1) had by no means been a demonstration of power. Thus at least one of the Corinthians observes that αἱ ἐπιστολαὶ μέν ... βαρεῖαι καὶ ἰσχυραί, ἡ δὲ παρουσία τοῦ σώματος ἀσθενὴς καὶ ὁ λόγος ἐξουθενημένος (2 Cor 10.10). Once more Paul warns that he will be as powerful in deed when present as he is through his letters when absent (10.11). In 2 Cor 13.2 Paul further warns that ἐὰν ἔλθω εἰς τὸ πάλιν οὐ φείσομαι, and this will be proof that Christ indeed speaks powerfully through him (see 13.3f). But the purpose of writing, according to 13.10, is so that when present he will not need to be severe in using the authority which the Lord gave him. These two verses are closely echoed in chapters 1–9, in ways which suggest the priority of 10–13. Having written 13.2 (ἐὰν ἔλθω ... οὐ φείσομαι), in the context of the threat of an imminent third visit (12.14; 13.1), 2 Cor 1.23 explains in the same terms that it was indeed to spare them (φειδόμενος) that Paul delayed this visit. And in a way most reminiscent of 13.10, 2 Cor 2.3 explains that the purpose of the painful letter was to avoid a further painful visit.[30]

---

[28] Cf. further Betz 1972, 132–37.

[29] A point made by Kennedy 1900, 92 (who cites Hausrath on this point) and Plummer 1915, xxxiii, but rejected by Hughes 1962, xxviii and Stephenson 1965, 91–92.

[30] These parallels, and others, are presented by Kennedy 1900, 79–94; Plummer 1915, xxix–xxxiii; see also Watson 1984, 326; Guthrie 1990, 447. Hughes 1962, xxiii–xxviii makes a detailed response to Plummer.

Murphy O'Connor, arguing against the identification hypothesis, and specifically against Watson (1984), sees a 'major difference between 2 Cor 10–13 and the Severe Letter. The former was written *in preparation for* a visit in the immediate future (2 Cor 12:14; 13:1–2, [sic] whereas the Severe Letter was written as *a substitute for* a visit which Paul had promised but now refused to make (2 Cor 2:1–4).'[31] There is, however, an equally plausible interpretation of the evidence. 2 Cor 12.14; 13.1f announce, indeed threaten, an imminent visit. However, Paul did not make this visit, in order to 'spare' the Corinthians (and himself) from pain and grief (2 Cor 1.23; 2.3). But the delay of the visit which seemed imminent in the painful letter led to the Corinthians' accusation that Paul vacillates; that he makes plans lightly and abandons them at will. It is precisely because the painful letter promised (or threatened) an imminent visit that Paul has to defend himself against the charge of vacillation and explain his movements, as he does in 2 Cor 1.15–2.13, 7.5–15. He mentions his initial confidence in planning an extra visit to them (1.15; based on 1.14), assuring them that he does not make plans lightly (1.17). He explains that the reason for delaying the third visit was to spare them (1.23) and to avoid another painful visit (2.1–3). The letter was written to test their obedience (2.9) and Titus was sent to ascertain how things were at Corinth. When Paul then left Ephesus his main concern was to find Titus and learn about the Corinthians' situation. Consequently he moved on from Troas, leaving an opportunity for missionary work, because Titus was not there (2.12f). When Paul finally arrived in Macedonia (7.5), he was comforted by the good news which Titus brought of the Corinthians' repentance and rekindled zeal towards Paul and his associates (7.6ff).

In many ways, then, the identification hypothesis is attractive and plausible. Not only do the chapters in question fit the kind of letter Paul reports having sent, but also specific references suggest that such an arrangement of the chapters of 2 Corinthians allows a coherent historical reconstruction of the interaction between Paul and the Corinthian church.

3. Problems with dating 2 Cor 10–13 after 1–9

While the identification hypothesis offers a coherent historical reconstruction of the interaction between Paul and the Corinthian church,

---

[31]   Murphy O'Connor 1991b, 43 n. 30.

there are, it seems to me, significant problems with the suggestion that 2 Cor 10–13 follows 2 Cor 1–9 as a later letter, as influential commentators like F. F. Bruce, C. K. Barrett, Victor Furnish and Ralph Martin argue. It requires that a similar historical sequence occur *twice*, yet suggests that the severe letter involved in the first crisis is lost (unless it is 1 Corinthians)[32] and only the second preserved. 'The hypothesis … requires that there were two crises in which the Corinthians showed disloyalty to Paul, two severe letters from Paul, and two reconciliations (the first illusory, the second suggested by the successful completion of the collection referred to in Rom xv.26).'[33] Chapters 8 and 9 of 2 Corinthians were clearly written near the time when Paul visited Corinth to receive the collection, a visit confirmed by Rom 15.26, and so there is little time for a fresh outbreak of trouble, another severe letter and another reconciliation. 8.1–5 and 9.4f suggest that the Macedonians' contribution is all but ready and that Paul's preparations to come to Corinth, perhaps with some of the Macedonians, may very soon be implemented. Moreover, the hypothesis which dates 10–13 after 1–9 requires that Paul wrote 2 Cor 10–13 without giving any indication of the bitterness he must have felt when the reconciliation he had gratefully spoken of in 2 Cor 7.2–4, 6–16 turned out to be so ephemeral.[34] It also requires that Titus was mistaken in his optimistic reporting to Paul.[35] Indeed Barrett suggests that 'Titus had misjudged and misrepresented the situation in Corinth'.[36] 'A new outbreak of opposition to Paul's apostolic authority', caused by 'the arrival and influence of the anti-Pauline teachers of 11:4–18', is a possible explanation for the renewed polemic of 10–13,[37] but, given the short time available for such developments, and the extent to which the issues of conflict are already present in 1 Corinthians (see chapter 5 above), this is initially at least less attractive than the hypothesis that the conflict which 2 Cor 10–13 addresses precedes 2 Cor 1–9.

Barrett sees an advantage of the hypothesis that chapters 10–13 follow 1–9 in the fact that 'it does not require us to suppose that a situation

---

32 Cf. above p. 299 with n. 22.
33 Watson 1984, 332.
34 Cf. Watson 1984, 332; Lang 1986, 327.
35 Cf. Watson 1984, 332.
36 Barrett 1973, 9.
37 Martin 1986, li, 298.

Paul could not control was finally reduced to order by Titus. Titus was doubtless a good man, but ... it was Paul who in the end established discipline and order'.[38] But apart from the unwarranted *assumption* of Paul's superiority in such matters, Barrett's argument also fails to consider that it was *Paul's* severe letter, along with Titus' visit (probably bearing the letter), which produced the Corinthians' repentance (cf. 2 Cor 10.10!; 2.9; 7.8–12).

However, for many, it is the specific objections to the identification hypothesis which count decisively against it. Do these objections outweigh the positive evidence favouring the identification hypothesis and the problems with the theory that 1–9 precedes 10–13?

4. Problems with the identification hypothesis

4.1. Titus

One apparent problem with the identification hypothesis concerns the visits of Titus to Corinth. In 2 Cor 7.14 Paul reports his boast to Titus about the Corinthians, and this has been taken to imply that Titus had not been to Corinth prior to the visit which led to the reconciliation (and on which he probably delivered the painful letter).[39] If this is the case, then 2 Cor 12.17f cannot have been written before this, since it asks the Corinthians whether Titus took advantage of them. Moreover, 12.17f is generally taken to relate to the charge that the collection was a means by which the Corinthians were defrauded. If this were so, then it seems likely that it was written after 8.16–24 and 9.3.[40] However, these points are by no means persuasive.

First it is not at all clear that 2 Cor 7.14 necessarily means that Titus had not previously been to Corinth.[41] The verse simply implies that Paul expressed his confidence in the Corinthians to Titus, presumably before his departure with the painful letter.[42] Indeed, 2 Cor 8.6 confirms the likelihood of an earlier visit of Titus to Corinth:

---

[38] Barrett 1973, 21; cf. 1982, 131 n. 35.
[39] See Stephenson 1965, 93–95; Bruce 1971, 168; Murphy O'Connor 1991b, 38.
[40] See Barrett 1982, 127; Stephenson 1965, 95–96 (defending the unity of the epistle); Murphy O'Connor 1991b, 38–39.
[41] So Bornkamm 1971a, 187. See further Watson 1984, 332–34.
[42] Cf. Martin 1986, 242. Note Paul's boasting of them in 1.14; 7.4; 9.2.

The zeal of the Macedonian churches for the collection (viii.1–5) has led Paul to send Titus ἵνα καθὼς προενήρξατο οὕτως καὶ ἐπιτελέσῃ εἰς ὑμᾶς καὶ τὴν χάριν ταύτην (viii.6). The verbs 'begin' and 'complete' must balance each other, and the meaning of viii.6 is thus that Titus had been responsible for the initiation of the collection at Corinth.[43]

This initiation may have taken place when Paul's first letter to Corinth was sent (1 Cor 5.9), if Hurd is right to argue that the collection was one of the topics in this letter about which the Corinthians asked in their letter to Paul (1 Cor 7.1).[44] Other possibilities are that Titus delivered 1 Corinthians (1 Cor 16.12 mentions 'brothers' visiting the Corinthians) and thus set in motion the collection process outlined in 1 Cor 16.1f, or that he visited Corinth after 1 Corinthians was delivered and implemented Paul's instructions. Certainly one cannot use the absence of greetings from Titus, or his non-appearance in 1 Corinthians, to prove that he had not been to Corinth prior to the visit to which 2 Cor 7.5ff refers.[45] Titus may not have been mentioned because he was not with Paul when 1 Corinthians was written; if he did deliver the letter then Paul would not necessarily have mentioned him in it. Titus appears in 2 Corinthians, as in Gal 2.1, 3, where he is of particular significance. He is neither named at the beginning of 2 Corinthians, nor does he send greetings at the end, though he is clearly by this time known to the community. Arguments from silence are always uncertain and the evidence of 2 Cor 8.6 should outweigh the assumption that Titus had not previously been to Corinth. The reference to the Corinthians' beginning ἀπὸ πέρυσι (8.10), using the same verb as in 8.6 (προενάρχομαι), strongly suggests that 'Titus had initiated the collection in Corinth a year ago',[46] a time which would probably be roughly contemporary with 1 Corinthians.[47]

It is unlikely that 2 Cor 12.18 refers to the visit of Titus announced in 2 Cor 8.6, 16ff, as some who date 10–13 later argue, for the further reason that in 12.17f only one brother is mentioned along with Titus,

---

[43] Watson 1984, 334; cf. Martin 1986, 447. Martin dates this visit of Titus before the visit to deliver the painful letter, thus *allowing* the conclusion that 12.18 was written before 2 Cor 8, though this is *not* Martin's own position.

[44] Hurd 1965, 73–74. The connection with Titus is tentatively suggested by Plummer 1915, xviii.

[45] As Barrett 1982, 123 does.

[46] Watson 1984, 334.

[47] Cf. Lüdemann 1984, 97–99.

whereas 8.16–23 explicitly announces the sending of *two* companions with Titus.[48] No convincing reasons can be offered as to why Paul did not mention the second companion in 12.18, if the same occasion is in view. It seems unlikely, despite some linguistic similarities (on which see below), that the two passages refer to the same visit. Titus and 'the brother' may have been the people who initiated the collection at Corinth, just as Titus and two brothers are sent to complete the task. We can hardly know why Paul does not name the brother of 12.18 – presumably the Corinthians knew who he was – but the fact that Paul does not name the two brothers sent with Titus to complete the task (8.6, 18, 22) hardly proves that 12.17f refers to the same visit.[49]

A. M. G. Stephenson has argued that the linguistic links between 2 Cor 8 and 2 Cor 12 offer strong evidence for the view that chapter 12 follows chapter 8, as part of one and the same letter.[50] However, the use of the verbs συνπέμπω (8.18, 22) and συναποστέλλω (12.18), which appear only here in the New Testament, does not confirm either that the two passages refer to the same visit, or that 12.17f must follow chapters 8–9.[51] Verbal similarities do not mean that the same occasion is being referred to, still less do they prove the order of the accounts. Moreover, Paul uses πέμπω and ἀποστέλλω elsewhere (1 Cor 1.17; 4.17; 16.3) and his tendency to add συν- to verbs where appropriate is obvious and widespread.[52]

The use of παρεκάλεσα 'on its own' in 12.18, without ἵνα ἔλθῃ or similar (cf. 1 Cor 16.12), though it seems to mean 'urged him to come to you', is certainly terse, but it is not so obvious that this is because it is 'an abbreviated account of what is written at greater length in chapter 8', as Stephenson argues, defending the unity of the epistle.[53] Firstly

---

[48] Cf. Watson 1984, 333; see further Jones 1973, 136–38 n. 30. Barrett's attempt to overcome this difficulty is possible but hardly convincing – only one of the two brothers needed Paul's defence (1982, 127). Stephenson suggests that 'the second brother is left out of account because his presence would not necessarily guarantee Titus' honesty' (1964, 645). Jones 1973, 137, makes just the opposite point: if 2 Cor 12 followed chs 8–9 then 'having prepared his defence in 2 Cor. 8:6 [referring to the sending of the threefold delegation] Paul dispenses with most of it when he came under fire in 2 Cor. 12:18. A curious procedure!'

[49] *Contra* Murphy O'Connor 1991b, 39.

[50] Stephenson 1964; 1965; similarly Barrett 1982, 127 (dating 10–13 after 1–9 and not defending the unity of the epistle).

[51] *Contra* Stephenson 1964, 643–44.

[52] E.g. Rom 6.4, 6, 8; 1 Cor 4.8; 2 Cor 7.3; Gal 2.19.

[53] Stephenson 1964, 642–43.

because there too παρακαλέω is used first without a verb of motion (8.6), though ἵνα προέλθωσιν amplifies it in 9.5; secondly because, as Stephenson himself points out, 'Paul is obviously writing or dictating rather quickly in chapter 12, as is shewn [sic] by the faulty syntax of verse 17'.[54] The anacolouthon in 12.17 seems as likely to have arisen simply in the context of a terse, aggressive and impassioned letter (or possibly through Semitic influence)[55] as through an awareness that it formed an abbreviation of what is stated more fully in chapters 8–9.[56]

The evidence concerning Titus, therefore, does not undermine the identification hypothesis. There is evidence to support the view that Titus paid three visits to Corinth; the first to initiate the collection (referred to in 2 Cor 8.6 and 12.17f), the second to deliver the painful letter when the crisis had occurred (2 Cor 7.5ff), and the third to complete the collection (2 Cor 8.6, 16ff).[57] This analysis of the history of Titus' visits to Corinth is accepted by Ralph Martin, though he prefers to date 10–13 later than 1–9.[58]

4.2. The offender

A second major objection to the identification hypothesis concerns the specific 'offender' mentioned in 2.5ff and 7.12. These passages seem to imply that the painful letter was one which accused a particular offender and called for his punishment, yet there seems little, if any, reference to such a person in 2 Cor 10–13.[59] To answer this objection by arguing that the relevant part of the painful letter is now missing, but that 2 Cor 10–13 constitutes another part of it, is weak and unconvincing.[60]

The relevant passages, 2 Cor 2.1–11 and 7.12, certainly do not suggest that Paul's 'painful' letter addressed only one individual. Its purpose was to test the Corinthians' obedience to Paul (2.9) and to make clear their devotion to him and his co-workers (7.12). Indeed, 7.12 specifically states that the purpose of the letter was *not* to focus on the person who had done wrong or on the one who was wronged.

---

[54] Stephenson 1964, 643.
[55] Cf. Moule 1953, 176.
[56] On the anacolouthon in v. 17 see Barrett 1973, 325; Martin 1986, 446.
[57] Cf. Watson 1984, 335.
[58] Martin 1986, 447.
[59] Munck 1959, 170; see also Lang 1986, 326; Watson 1984, 339–40.
[60] Cf. Martin 1986, xlix.

The offence Paul refers to in 2.5ff is unlikely to have been a case of sin such as that reported in 1 Cor 5.1ff; the exhortation to forgive and restore the person and the indications that Paul himself was personally hurt (2.1ff) suggest rather that the offence was against the apostle.[61] 'We should probably think', Barrett suggests, 'of an occasion during the second visit ... when Paul was insulted and his authority flouted'.[62] Paul's failure to be as powerful in person as he had threatened to be (1 Cor 4.18–21), especially when compared with the other impressive missionaries who had come to Corinth (2 Cor 11.5ff), had led some at Corinth to turn against him and question his apostleship.[63] Nevertheless the crucial point is that 2 Cor 2.5–10 strongly implies that one particular person (ὁ τοιοῦτος) has been singled out for punishment and ostracism. Can 2 Cor 10–13 possibly have led to this?

Considering this point it is important to remember that in 2 Cor 10–13 Paul is concerned primarily with his relationship with the Corinthian believers and with their acceptance of his apostleship. His attack on the false apostles and his personal boasting arise because the Corinthians have turned to them and away from him, in spite of the fact that they are the fruit of *his* labour (cf. 2 Cor 10.13ff; 12.11–13 etc). The punishment Paul threatens in 10.1–6 and 13.1–4 is directed towards members of the Corinthian congregation.[64]

A somewhat more specific focus is implied in 10.2, where *some* (τινας) of the congregation are said to regard Paul in a particular way. In 10.7–11 the references to τις (v.7) and ὁ τοιοῦτος (v.11) not only correspond to 2.5 and 2.6 but also suggest that a particular person may be in mind.[65] This person's insulting view of Paul is quoted in 10.10, where we should note the use of φησίν – third person singular.[66] Interestingly Barrett, who dates 2 Cor 10–13 after 1–9, proposes this interpretation

---

61 Cf. Martin 1986, 32, 37, 327–39; Bruce 1971, 164; Betz 1972, 12; Watson 1993b, xviii; Barrett 1982, 109, 111, 128; 1973, 7, 89. *Contra* Lampe 1967, 353–54; Hyldahl 1991, 26.
62 Barrett 1982, 89.
63 This point is made particularly by Watson 1984, 342–46.
64 Cf. Watson 1984, 343; Travis 1973, 531.
65 Cf. Watson 1984, 345.
66 Bultmann 1985, 190: 'φησίν is the customary quotation formula, used especially of an opponent's objection.' The reading φασίν is surely a 'simplification'; so Barrett 1973, 260; 1982, 117 n. 35. But the variant reading may show that later scribes, taking v. 10 as reporting the view of a number of Corinthians, found φησίν an inappropriate way of expressing this. This may strengthen the view that Paul was actually covertly quoting one prominent opponent.

of 10.10: 'This view, that Paul is quoting the words of a specific person, receives a good deal of confirmation from verses 7, 11. No one is named; the words used are capable of generalization; but the multiplication of references ... adds to the probability that Paul has in mind a leader of the opposition.'[67] While Barrett considers this opponent to be one of the intruders,[68] it is at least as plausible that this individual was the leader of a group opposed to Paul within the congregation (cf. τινας, 10.2),[69] quite possibly 'the householder who offered hospitality and patronage to Paul's opponents, and against whom the Corinthians had ... turned when they resumed their loyalty to Paul'.[70] However, the severe tone of chapters 10 to 13 makes it clear that a wider group is implicated in the rebellion.[71] Thus, in the letter of reconciliation, Paul emphasises the repentance and renewed zeal of the congregation as a whole, and urges the forgiveness and restoration of the particular offender (2.5–11, esp. v. 9; 7.7–15).

The conflict between Paul and ὁ ἀδικήσας (7.12) occurred during Paul's painful visit; thus the Corinthians were well aware of the confrontation that had taken place. This confrontation and the individual involved are referred to somewhat obliquely in 2 Cor 10–13, but Paul's main concern in this letter is to restore the congregation's loyalty to him as their true apostle. The restoration of loyalty which did indeed occur led, unsurprisingly, to the ostracism of the one who had particularly confronted and offended Paul. This reconstruction of events accounts for the relevant literary evidence and the identification hypothesis remains plausible on this matter.[72]

---

[67] Barrett 1973, 260; cf. 256, 261; 1982, 115, 117 n. 35. Similarly Martin 1986, 307, 311, 313. Otherwise Furnish 1984, 466, 468–69. Marshall 1987, 341–48 points out that Paul never *names* an enemy (cf. 1 Cor 5.1, 5).

[68] See Barrett 1982, 113–15 and 1973, 260, where 10.12f and 11.12–15 are associated with the group this person belongs to; also Martin 1986, 313. Barrett 1982, 112ff focuses on the phrase in 7.11 which concludes ... ἁγνοὺς εἶναι τῷ πράγματι and argues that the Corinthians 'were innocent in the affair that had caused so much pain' (113). Hence his conclusion that ὁ ἀδικήσας was an intruder and not a Corinthian. However, this surely underestimates the nature of the Corinthians' repentance (ἐλυπήθητε εἰς μετάνοιαν; 7.9). Against Barrett's interpretation see Martin 1986, 238. Note also Barrett's comments elsewhere (1982, 76–77) where he stresses the guilt of some of the Corinthians.

[69] Cf. Watson 1984, 345–46; Bornkamm 1971a, 174–75; Talbert 1987, 112.

[70] Taylor 1991, 86; cf. 80.

[71] Cf. Watson 1984, 346, though it may not be the 'whole congregation' who are involved, as he suggests.

[72] See further Watson 1984, 342–46.

4.3. The rival missionaries

Another point made against the identification hypothesis is that the rival missionaries, who are so prominent in 2 Cor 10–13, do not feature in 1–9. If Paul had already faced these opponents and engaged in such strong polemic, would he not have referred to them also in his subsequent letter?[73]

The apparent lack of attention to the rival missionaries in chapters 1 to 9, however, can be explained on the grounds that they were not directly Paul's concern. Even in chapters 10 to 13, Paul's concern is not with the opponents' doctrine or message, but primarily with the fact that the Corinthians have rejected *his* leadership and apostolic authority, though he founded their community, and have accepted and welcomed others in his place.[74] Paul's main aim is to win the Corinthians back to him, to prove the validity of his apostleship (12.12f), and to restore the mutual boasting and commendation which exist between apostle and community (10.12–18; 11.16ff esp. 12.11). Thus, in 1–9, Paul focuses upon the reconciliation between himself and the Corinthians (2.5–11, 7.2–16), the nature of his apostolic ministry (2.14–5.21), and his gratitude for their zealous repentance (7.8–16).

This is not to say, however, that occasional digs at the intruders do not occur in 2 Cor 1–9.[75] At 3.1, for example, Paul contrasts himself with others, perhaps the intruders of 10–13, who 'need' commendatory letters to or from the Corinthians. In Paul's case, the Corinthians themselves are his commendatory letter, his apostolic work (cf. 10.12–18). Other slights at the rival missionaries include 2.17, where Paul contrasts himself with οἱ πολλοὶ καπηλεύοντες τὸν λόγον τοῦ θεοῦ. The reference to those who 'trade in'[76] the word of God may well be intended to contrast Paul and his associates, who refuse to be a financial burden, with those who gladly take advantage of such offers (cf. 2 Cor 11.7ff; 12.14–18; 1 Cor 9.3ff; see chapter 5). Similarly in 4.2 Paul stresses that he and his associates renounce shameful and cunning ways and refuse to

---

[73] An objection listed by Lang 1986, 326, who nevertheless cautiously concludes that 10–13 may precede 1–9.

[74] Cf. Betz 1972, 19: 'Sie [die paulinische Apologie 2 Kor 10–13] wendet sich ... gegen die Gegner im Hintergrund, ist aber an die korinthische Gemeinde und nur an sie gerichtet.'

[75] Cf. Watson 1993b, xxxii.

[76] BAGD, 403. See further on καπηλεύω Barrett 1982, 93; Windisch TDNT 3, 603–605; Georgi 1987, 234–35.

falsify the word of God, possibly another thinly-veiled reference to those whose conduct and preaching Paul has opposed (cf. 11.3f).[77] Again it seems that the apparent problems for the identification hypothesis are by no means insurmountable, and, indeed, that reading 2 Cor 1–9 as subsequent to 10–13 makes a good deal of sense.

4.4. Redaction and composition

A final challenge to any redactional and compositional theory is to offer a plausible way in which the text could have come to be in its present form. Although G. Bornkamm, for example, devotes considerable attention to this very issue, this always remains a problem for those who propose complex compositional theories.[78] However, the assumption that 10–13 predates 1–9 hardly demands implausible redactional activity any more than the theory that 1–9 and 10–13 are separate letters but in their correct chronological order. Bornkamm suggested that the redactor in this case followed an established pattern, placing the warning against false teachers at the end of the letter.[79]

However, pragmatic considerations may offer more convincing possibilities. The redactor may simply have followed the general principle of placing a shorter letter after the longer,[80] or perhaps either 10–13 had lost their opening or 1–9 had lost their closing greetings[81] (if the greeting of 13.11–13 was originally part of 10–13).[82] Perhaps the painful letter had always opened so bluntly that 1.1ff seemed a much more suitable letter opening. The placing of chapter 9, if originally separate from 1–8, would be entirely understandable given the subject matter of chapters 8 and 9, though the evidence seems to favour the literary integrity of 8–9. Once it is assumed that 1–9 and 10–13 were originally separate letters, then their position in the canonical text can hardly be decisive with regard to their relative dating.[83] It is just as possible that a compiler

---

[77] Note the use of πανουργία in 11.3. Cf. Barrett 1982, 93–94.
[78] Bornkamm 1962, 261–63; 1971a, 179–90.
[79] Bornkamm 1962, 261; cf. 1971a, 180.
[80] Cf. Lang 1986, 327; Furnish 1984, 40.
[81] Cf. Furnish 1984, 40; Bruce 1971, 167; Kennedy 1900, 154, 159.
[82] Betz 1985, 142, detaches it from 10–13.
[83] Betz 1972, 5: 'Ist der Abschnitt 10–13 erst einmal vom Rest des Briefes abgetrennt, ist dessen zeitliche Ansetzung eine völlig offene Frage.' Betz, however, prefers to date 10–13 later than 1–9.

(perhaps unknowingly) placed the earlier letter after the later as that they were kept in chronological order.

5. Conclusion

The identification hypothesis, then, seems to offer the most satisfactory solution to the problems raised by the contrast between 2 Cor 1–9 and 10–13. Given what we know of the interaction between Paul and the Corinthian congregation and of the kind of painful letter Paul reports having written, the identification hypothesis offers at least an initially attractive proposal. There are, moreover, significant problems with the hypothesis which dates 10–13 later than 1–9; and the objections generally raised against the identification hypothesis have been shown not to be decisive. The evidence is not such as to allow either hypothesis to be incontrovertibly verified; the decision must be taken on the grounds of probability and plausibility. The evidence, I believe, favours the identification hypothesis. 2 Cor 10–13 may with reasonable confidence be dated before 1–9 and identified as the painful letter.[84]

---

[84] A conclusion also supported now by Welborn 1995, though this article appeared too late to be taken account of here.

Bibliographical Appendix
Giddens' work on selected topics

1. Introductions to structuration theory

    The most clear and brief, in my opinion, is 1982a, 28–39 (see also 1–17 in same).
    Other brief introductions to this theoretical perspective include 1976, 126–29, 155–62; 1977, 121–34; 1979, 49–95; 1981, 26–29; 1984, xiii–xxxvii, 1–40.
    The works in which Giddens develops the theory most fully are 1979 and 1984.

2. Giddens' approach to sociology as a discipline

    Most concise are 1987, 1–51, and 1979, 234–59.
    See also 1982b and 1989a for introductions to the discipline as a whole. (1989a in particular offers a huge but readable initiation into sociology.)

3. Approach to ideology

    See 1979, 165–97 (especially 193–96).

4. Conceptualisation of power

    Condensed discussions are found in 1976, 110–13; 1979, 88–94; 1984, 256–62.

5. Critique of functionalism

    The most extended is 1977, 96–129. Concise statements of points of criticism may also be found in 1981, 15–19 and 1984, 293–97.

Abbreviations used in bibliography

ABR	*Australian Biblical Review*
ANRW	*Aufstieg und Niedergang der römischen Welt,* H. Temporini & W. Haase (eds.); Walter de Gruyter: Berlin; New York.
BNTC	Black's New Testament Commentaries
BTB	*Biblical Theology Bulletin*
CBQ	*Catholic Biblical Quarterly*
EKKNT	Evangelisch-katholischer Kommentar zum Neuen Testament
ExpTim	*Expository Times*
HTR	*Harvard Theological Review*
ICC	The International Critical Commentary
IESS	International Encyclopedia of the Social Sciences, D. L. Sills (ed.)
Int	*Interpretation*
JAAR	*Journal of the American Academy of Religion*
JBL	*Journal of Biblical Literature*
JRH	*Journal of Religious History*
JSNT	*Journal for the Study of the New Testament*
JSNTSup	Journal for the Study of the New Testament, Supplement Series
JTS	*Journal of Theological Studies*
LCL	The Loeb Classical Library; Harvard University Press: Cambridge, Massachusetts; William Heinemann: London
NICNT	The New International Commentary on the New Testament
NovT	*Novum Testamentum*
NovTSup	Novum Testamentum, Supplement Series
NTS	*New Testament Studies*
RB	*Revue Biblique*

SBLDS	Society of Biblical Literature, Dissertation Series
SBLSP	Society of Biblical Literature, Seminar Papers
SNTSMS	Society for New Testament Studies, Monograph Series
SJT	*Scottish Journal of Theology*
ThLz	*Theologische Literaturzeitung*
TJ	*Trinity Journal*
TU	Texte und Untersuchungen zur Geschichte der altchristlichen Literatur; Akademie-Verlag: Berlin
TynBul	*Tyndale Bulletin*
VC	*Vigiliae Christianae*
WBC	Word Biblical Commentary
WUNT	Wissenschaftliche Untersuchungen zum Neuen Testament
ZNW	*Zeitschrift für die neutestamentliche Wissenschaft*

Bibliography of works cited in the text

1. Primary sources

(a) Jewish and Christian

The Apostolic Fathers, vol. 1: *1 & 2 Clement; the Epistles of Ignatius; Polycarp's Epistle to the Philippians; the Didache; the Epistle of Barnabas*, translated by K. Lake; LCL, 1912.

The Apostolic Fathers, vol. 2: *the Shepherd of Hermas; the Martyrdom of Polycarp; the Epistle to Diognetus*, translated by K. Lake; LCL, 1913.

The Apostolical Canons, in: The Nicene and Post-Nicene Fathers, vol. 14; *The Seven Ecumenical Councils of the Undivided Church*, H. R. Percival (ed.); James Parker & Co.: Oxford; The Christian Literature Co.: New York, 1900.

John Chrysostom, *Homilies on the Epistles of Paul to the Corinthians*; The Nicene and Post-Nicene Fathers, vol. 12; Wm. B. Eerdmans: Grand Rapids, Michigan, 1979.

The Writings of Clement of Alexandria, translated by W. Wilson, in: The Ante-Nicene Christian Library, A. Roberts & J. Donaldson (eds.); T. & T. Clark: Edinburgh, 1867 & 1869.

Codex Fuldensis: Novum Testamentum Latine interprete Hieronymo ex manuscripto Victoris Capuani, E. Ranke (ed.); N. G. Elwert: Marburg & Leipzig, 1868.

The Dead Sea Scrolls in English, G. Vermes (ed.), 3rd edn; Pelican Books; Penguin: London & Harmondsworth, 1987.

Eusebius, *The Ecclesiastical History*, 2 vols, translated by K. Lake & J. E. L. Oulton; LCL, 1926, 1932.

Josephus, *Jewish Antiquities*, 7 vols, translated by H. St. J. Thackeray, R. Markus, A. Wikgren and L. H. Feldman, LCL, 1930–1965.

Josephus, *The Jewish War*, 2 vols, translated by H. St. J. Thackeray, LCL, 1927, 1928.

Justin Martyr, *Dialogue with Trypho*, Corpus Apologetarum Christianorum, vol. 1, Iustinius Philosophus et Martyr; I. C. T. Otto (ed.); F. Mauke: Ienae, 1847.

The Mishnah, translated from the Hebrew with Introduction and Brief Explanatory Notes by H. Danby, Clarendon Press: Oxford, 1933.

The Greek New Testament, K. Aland et al. (eds.); 3rd edn (corrected); United Bible Societies, 1983.

Novum Testamentum Graece, E. Nestle, K. Aland et al. (eds.); 27th edn; Deutsche Bibelgesellschaft: Stuttgart, 1993.

The Old Testament Pseudipigrapha, vol. 1, *Apocalyptic Literature and Testaments*, J. H. Charlesworth (ed.); Darton, Longman & Todd: London, 1983.

Origen, *Contra Celsum*, translated with an introduction and notes by H. Chadwick; Cambridge University Press: Cambridge, 1965.

Septuaginta, A. Rahlfs (ed.); Deutsche Bibelgesellschaft: Stuttgart, 1979.

Die Texte aus Qumran, Hebräisch und Deutsch, E. Lohse (ed.), 4th edn; Wissenschaftliche Buchgesellschaft: Darmstadt, 1986.

(b) Other

Appian, *Roman History*, 4 vols, translated by H. White; LCL, 1912–1913.

Aelius Aristides, *Die Romrede des Aelius Aristides*, herausgegeben, übersetzt und mit Erläuterungen versehen von Richard Klein, Texte und Forschung 45; Wissenschaftliche Buchgesellschaft: Darmstadt, 1983.

Aristotle, *Politics*, translated by H. Rackham; LCL, 1932.

Augustus, *Res Gestae Divi Augusti* (with Velleius Paterculus, *Compendium of Roman History*), translated by F. W. Shipley; LCL, 1924.

Marcus Aurelius Antonius, translated by C. R. Haines; LCL, 1916.

Dio Cassius, *Roman History*, 9 vols, translated by E. Cary; LCL, 1914–1927.

Dio Chrysostom, *Discourses*, 5 vols, translated by J. W. Cohoon & H. L. Crosby; LCL, 1932–1951.

Cicero, *De Natura Deorum*, vol. 19 of 28, translated by H. Rackham; LCL, 1933.

Cicero, *De Officiis*, vol. 21 of 28, translated by W Miller; LCL, 1913.

Corinth: The Inscriptions, 1926–1950, Results of Excavations carried out by the American School of Classical Studies at Athens, vol. 8, pt. 3; The American School of Classical Studies at Athens: Princeton, New Jersey, 1966.

Demosthenes, *Orations*, 7 vols, translated by J. H. Vince et al.; LCL, 1930–1949.

Dionysius of Halicarnassus, *Roman Antiquities*, vol. 4 of 70, translated by E. Cary; LCL, 1943.

Epictetus, *Discourses*, 2 vols, translated by W. A. Oldfather; LCL, 1925, 1928.

Justinian, *The Digest of Justinian*, T. Mommsen, P. Kruger & A. Watson (eds.), vol. 1; University of Pennsylvania Press: Philadephia, Pennsylvania, 1985.

Juvenal, *The Satires*, translated by G. G. Ramsay; LCL, 1918.

Livy, vol. 1 of 14, translated by B. O. Foster; LCL, 1919.

Lucian, 8 vols, translated by A. M. Harmon, K. Kilburn & M. D. Macleod; LCL, 1913–1967.

Martial, *Epigrams*, 2 vols, translated by W. C. A. Ker; LCL, 1919, 1920.

Papyri Osloenses, 3 vols, S. Eitrem & L. Amundsen (eds.); Det Norske Videnskaps-Akademi i Oslo: Oslo, 1925–1936.

The Oxyrynchus Papyri, B. P. Grenfell, A. S. Hunt et al. (eds.), 59 vols; The Egypt Exploration Society: London, 1898–1992.

Pausanias, *Description of Greece*, 4 vols, translated by W. H. S. Jones; LCL, 1918–1935.

Pliny, *Natural History*, 10 vols, translated by H. Rackham, W. H. S. Jones, and D. E. Eichholz; LCL, 1938–1962.

Pliny, *Letters and Panegyricus*, 2 vols, translated by B. Radice; LCL, 1969.

Plutarch, *Moralia*, 15 vols, various translators; LCL, 1927–1969.

Plutarch, *Lives*, 11 vols, translated by B. Perrin; LCL, 1914–1926.

Seneca (the Elder), *Controversiae*, 2 vols, translated by M. Winterbottom; LCL, 1974.

Seneca, *Epistulae Morales* and *Moral Essays*, 6 vols, translated by R. H. Gummere and J. W. Basore; LCL, 1917–1935.

Strabo, *The Geography of Strabo*, 8 vols, translated by H. L. Jones; LCL, 1917–1932.

Suetonius, *The Lives of the Caesars and The Lives of Illustrious Men*, 2 vols, translated by J. C. Rolfe; LCL, 1913, 1914.

Tacitus, *The Histories and The Annals*, 4 vols, translated by C. H. Moore & J. Jackson; LCL, 1925–1937.

Tacitus, *Agricola*, translated by M. Hutton and revised by R. M. Ogilvie; LCL, 1970.

Vitruvius, *On Architecture*, 2 vols, translated by F. Granger; LCL, 1931, 1934.

Xenophon, *Memorabilia and Oeconomicus*, translated by E. C. Marchant; LCL, 1923.

Yale Papyri, American Studies in Papyrology, vol. 2, no. 1, J. F. Oates, A. E. Samuel & C. F. Welles (eds.); The American Society of Papyrologists: New Haven & Toronto, 1967.

2. Secondary literature

Abbott-Smith, G. 1936 *A Manual Greek Lexicon of the New Testament*, T. & T. Clark: Edinburgh, 1936; 3rd edn, 1981.

Abercrombie, N., Hill, S. & Turner, B. S. 1984 *The Penguin Dictionary of Sociology*, Penguin: Harmondsworth, 1984.

Abrahamson, M. 1978 *Functionalism*, Prentice-Hall Methods and Theories in the Social Sciences Series, Prentice-Hall: Englewood Cliffs, New Jersey; London, 1978.

Abrams, P. 1980 'History, Sociology, Historical Sociology', *Past and Present* 87 (1980) 3–16.

Abrams, P. 1982 *Historical Sociology*, Open Books: Shepton Mallet, 1982.

Aland, K. and Aland, B. 1989 *The Text of the New Testament: An Introduction to the Critical Editions and to the Theory and Practice of Modern Textual Criticism*, translated by E. F. Rhodes, 2nd edn; Wm. B. Eerdmans: Grand Rapids, Michigan, 1989.

Alexander, J. C. 1987 'The Centrality of the Classics', 11–57 in Giddens and Turner (eds.) 1987.

Alföldy, G. 1984 *Römische Sozialgeschichte*, 3., völlig überarbeitete Auflage; Franz Steiner Verlag: Wiesbaden, 1984.

Alföldy, G. 1985 *The Social History of Rome*, translated by D. Braund and F. Pollock (ET of Alföldy 1984); Croom Helm: London and Sydney, 1985.

Alföldy, G. 1986 *Die römische Gesellschaft: Ausgewählte Beiträge*, Franz Steiner Verlag: Wiesbaden, 1986.

Allison, R. W. 1988 'Let Women be Silent in the Churches (1 Cor. 14.33b–36): What did Paul Really Say, and What did it Mean?', *JSNT* 32 (1988) 27–60.

Allo, E. B. 1956 *Saint Paul: Seconde Épître aux Corinthiens*, Études Bibliques; J. Gabalda: Paris, 1956.

Aono, T. 1979 *Die Entwicklung des paulinischen Gerichtsgedankens bei den Apostolischen Vätern*, Europäische Hochschulschriften, Reihe 23, Theologie, Band 137; Peter Lang: Bern; Frankfurt; Las Vegas, 1979.

Archer, M. 1990 'Human Agency and Social Structure: A Critique of Giddens', 73–84, 86–88 in Clark, Modgil & Modgil (eds.) 1990.

Atkins, R. A. Jr. 1991 *Egalitarian Community: ethnography and exegesis*, University of Alabama Press: Tuscaloosa and London, 1991.

Babcock, W. S. (ed) 1990 *Paul and the Legacies of Paul*, Southern Methodist University Press: Dallas, Texas, 1990.

Balch, D. L. 1981 *Let Wives Be Submissive: The Domestic Code in 1 Peter*, SBL Monograph Series 26, Scholars Press: Chico, California, 1981.

Bammel, E. 1984 'Romans 13', 365–83 in *Jesus and the Politics of His Day*, E. Bammel & C. F. D. Moule (eds.), Cambridge University Press: Cambridge, 1984.

Banks, R. 1980 *Paul's Idea of Community: The Early House Churches in their Historical Setting*, Paternoster: Exeter, 1980.

Barbour, I. G. 1990 *Religion in an Age of Science*, The Gifford Lectures 1989–1991, vol. 1; SCM Press: London, 1990.

Barclay, J. M. G. 1987 'Mirror-Reading a Polemical Letter: Galatians as a Test Case', *JSNT* 31 (1987) 73–93.

Barclay, J. M. G. 1991 'Paul, Philemon and the dilemma of Christian slave-ownership', *NTS* 37 (1991) 161–186.

Barclay, J. M. G. 1992 'Thessalonica and Corinth: Social Contrasts in Pauline Christianity', *JSNT* 47 (1992) 49–74.

Barnard, L. W. 1966 'St. Clement of Rome and the Persecution of Domitian', 5–18 in *Studies in the Apostolic Fathers and their Background*, Basil Blackwell: Oxford, 1966.

Barnard, L. W. 1967 'The Early Roman Church, Judaism, and Jewish Christianity', *Anglican Theological Review* 49 (1967) 371–384.

Barnard, L. W. 1969 'Review of Beyschlag, *Clemens Romanus*', *VC* 23 (1969) 63–65.

Barnett, P. W. 1984 'Opposition in Corinth', *JSNT* 22 (1984) 3–17.

Barré, M. L. 1975 'Paul as "Eschatologic Person": A New Look at 2 Cor 11:29', *CBQ* 37 (1975) 500–526.

Barrett, C. K. 1956 *The New Testament Background: Selected Documents*, SPCK: London, 1956 (revised edn, 1987).

Barrett, C. K. 1963 'Cephas and Corinth', 1–12 in *Abraham Unser Vater*, Festschrift für Otto Michel; O. Betz, M. Hengel & P. Schmidt (eds.); E. J. Brill: Leiden, 1963; cited from reprint in Barrett 1982, 28–39.

Barrett, C. K. 1964 'Christianity at Corinth', *Bulletin of the John Rylands Library* 46 (1964) 269–297; cited from reprint in Barrett 1982, 1–27.

Barrett, C. K. 1965 'Things Sacrificed to Idols', *NTS* 11 (1965) 138–153; cited from reprint in Barrett 1982, 40–59.

Barrett, C. K. 1969 'Titus', 1–14 in *Neotestamentica et Semitica:* Studies in Honour of Matthew Black, E. E. Ellis & M. Wilcox (eds.); T. & T. Clark: Edinburgh, 1969; cited from reprint in Barrett 1982, 118–131.

Barrett, C. K. 1970a "Ο 'ΑΔΙΚΗΣΑΣ (2.Cor 7,12)', 149–157 in *Verborum Veritas:* Festschrift für Gustav Stählin, O. Böcher & K. Haacker (eds.); Theologische Verlag Rolf Brockhaus: Wuppertal, 1970; cited from reprint in Barrett 1982, 108–117.

Barrett, C. K. 1970b 'ΨΕΥΔΑΠΟΣΤΟΛΟΙ', 377–96 in *Mélanges Bibliques en Hommage au R. P. Béda Rigaux*, A. Deschamps & A. de. Halleux (eds.); Éditions J. Duculot: Gembloux, 1970; cited from reprint in Barrett 1982, 87–107.

Barrett, C. K. 1971a *The First Epistle to the Corinthians*, 2nd edn; BNTC; A. & C. Black: London, 1971.

Barrett, C. K. 1971b 'Paul's Opponents in 2 Corinthians', *NTS* 17 (1971) 233–254, cited from reprint in Barrett 1982, 60–86.

Barrett, C. K. 1973 *The Second Epistle to the Corinthians*, BNTC; A. & C. Black: London, 1973.

Barrett, C. K. 1975 'Review of S. S. Bartchy, ΜΑΛΛΟΝ ΧΡΗΣΑΙ', *JTS* 26 (1975) 173–174.

Barrett, C. K. 1982 *Essays on Paul*, SPCK: London, 1982.

Bartchy, S. S. 1973 *ΜΑΛΛΟΝ ΧΡΗΣΑΙ : First-Century Slavery and the Interpretation of 1.Cor.7.21*, SBLDS 11; University of Montana: Missoula, Montana, 1973.

Bartlett, D. L. 1978 'John Gager's *"Kingdom and Community"*: A Summary and Response', *Zygon* 13 (1978) 109–122.

Barton, S. C. 1982 'Paul and the Cross: A Sociological Approach', *Theology* 85 (1982) 13–19.

Barton, S. C. 1984 'Paul and the Resurrection: A Sociological Approach', *Religion* 14 (1984) 67–75.

Barton, S. C. 1986 'Paul's Sense of Place: An Anthropological Approach to Community Formation in Corinth', *NTS* 32 (1986) 225–246.

Barton, S. C. 1992 'The Communal Dimension of Earliest Christianity: A Critical Survey of the Field', *JTS* 43 (1992) 399–427.

Barton, S. C. 1993 'Early Christianity and the Sociology of the Sect', 140–162 in Watson (ed.) 1993a.

Batomsky, S. J. 1990 'Rich and Poor: The Great Divide in Ancient Rome and Victorian England', *Greece and Rome* 37 (1990) 37–43.

Bauckham, R. 1993a *The Theology of the Book of Revelation*, New Testament Theology; Cambridge University Press: Cambridge, 1993.

Bauckham, R. 1993b 'The *Acts of Paul* As A Sequel to Acts', 105–152 in B. W. Winter and A. D. Clarke (eds), *The Book of Acts in Its Ancient Literary Setting*, Wm. B. Eerdmans: Grand Rapids, Michigan; Paternoster Press: Carlisle, 1993.

Bauer, W. 1972 *Orthodoxy and Heresy in Earliest Christianity*, SCM Press: London, 1972 (ET of 2nd German edn, 1964).

Bauer, W., Arndt, W. F., Gingrich, F. W. & Danker, F. W. 1979 *A Greek-English Lexicon of the New Testament and Other Early Christian Literature*, 2nd edn; from Bauer's 5th edn; The University of Chicago Press: Chicago and London, 1979.

Baur, F. C. 1831 'Die Christuspartei in der korinthischen Gemeinde, der Gegensatz den petrinischen und paulinischen Christentums in der ältesten Kirche', *Tübinger Zeitschrift* 4 (1831) 61–206.

Bedale, S. 1954 'The Meaning of κεφαλή in the Pauline Epistles', *JTS* 5 (1954) 211–15.

Beker, J. C. 1980 *Paul the Apostle: The Triumph of God in Life and Thought*, T. & T. Clark: Edinburgh, 1980.

Beker, J. C. 1991 'Recasting Pauline Theology: The Coherence-Contingency Scheme as Interpretive Model', 15–24 in J. M. Bassler (ed.), *Pauline Theology, vol. 1: Thessalonians, Philippians, Galatians, Philemon*, Fortress Press: Minneapolis, 1991.

Bell, R. H. 1994 *Provoked to Jealousy: The Origin and Purpose of the Jealousy Motif in Romans 9–11*, WUNT 2nd series, 63; J. C. B. Mohr (Paul Siebeck): Tübingen, 1994.

Berger, K. 1977 'Wissensoziologie und Exegese des Neuen Testaments', *Kairos* 19 (1977) 124–133.

Berger, P. L. 1963 *Invitation to Sociology: A Humanistic Perspective*, Penguin Books: Harmondsworth, 1963.

Berger, P. L. 1967 *The Social Reality of Religion*, Faber & Faber: London, 1969 (USA title: *The Sacred Canopy*). N. B. also published by Penguin: Harmondsworth, with different pagination.

Berger, P. L. 1969 *A Rumour of Angels*, Penguin: Harmondsworth, 1970.

Berger, P. L. & Luckmann, T. 1966 *The Social Construction of Reality: A Treatise in the Sociology of Knowledge*, Penguin: Harmondsworth, 1967; N. B. pagination differs in American original; Doubleday: New York, 1966.

Berger, P. L. & Pullberg, S. 1966 'Reification and the Sociological Critique of Consciousness', *New Left Review* 35 (1966) 56–71.

Bernard, J. H. 1899 *The Pastoral Epistles*, Cambridge Greek Testament for Schools and Colleges; Cambridge University Press: Cambridge, 1899.

Best, E. 1972 *The First and Second Epistles to the Thessalonians*, BNTC; A. & C. Black: London, 1972.

Best, T. F. 1983 'The Sociological Study of the New Testament: Promise and Peril of a New Discipline', *SJT* 36 (1983) 181–194.

Betz, H. D. 1972 *Der Apostel Paulus und die sokratische Tradition. Eine exegetische Untersuchung zu seiner ,,Apologie" 2 Korinther 10–13*, Beiträge zur historischen Theologie 45; J. C. B. Mohr (Paul Siebeck): Tübingen, 1972.

Betz, H. D. 1979 *Galatians*, Hermenia series; Fortress Press: Philadelphia, 1979.

Betz, H. D. 1985 *2 Corinthians 8 and 9: A Commentary on Two Administrative Letters of the Apostle Paul*, Hermeneia; Fortress Press: Philadelphia, 1985.

Beyschlag, K. 1966 *Clemens Romanus und der Frühkatholismus: Untersuchungen zu I Clemens 1–7*, Beiträge zur historischen Theologie 35; J. C. B. Mohr (Paul Siebeck): Tübingen, 1966.

Beyschlag, K. 1972 'Zur ΕΙΡΗΝΗ ΒΑΘΕΙΑ (1 Clem 2,2)', *VC* 26 (1972) 18–23.

Bhaskar, R. 1979 *The Possibility of Naturalism: A Philosophical Critique of the Contemporary Human Sciences*, Harvester: Brighton, 1979.

Bilton, T., Bonnett, K., Jones, P. , Sheard, K., Stanworth, M. & Webster, A. 1981 *Introductory Sociology*, Macmillan: London & Basingstoke, 1981

Black, D. A. 1983 'A Note on "the Weak" in 1 Corinthians 9,22', *Biblica* 64 (1983) 240–242.

Black, D. A. 1984 *Paul, Apostle of Weakness: Astheneia and its Cognates in the Pauline Literature*, American University Studies, Series 3, Theology and Religion, vol. 3; Peter Lang: New York; Berne; Frankfurt; Nancy, 1984.

Bloch, M. 1947 'Comment et pourquoi finit l'esclavage antique', 204–228 in Finley (ed.) 1960.

Boer, M. C. de 1990 'Comment: Which Paul?', response to A. Lindemann, 45–54 in Babcock (ed.) 1990.

Boff, L. 1985 *Church, Charism and Power: Liberation Theology and the Institutional Church*, SCM Press: London, 1985.

Bornkamm, G. 1961 'Die Vorgeschichte des sogenannten Zweiten Korintherbriefes', first published 1961, part ET in Bornkamm 1962, cited from reprint in Bornkamm 1971a.

Bornkamm, G. 1962 'The History of the Origin of the so-called Second Letter to the Corinthians', *NTS* 8 (1961/62) 258–264.

Bornkamm, G. 1966 'The Missionary Stance of Paul in I Corinthians 9 and Acts', 194–207 in *Studies in Luke-Acts*, L. E. Keck & J. L. Martyn (eds.), Abingdon Press: Nashville, New York, 1966; SPCK: London, 1968.

Bornkamm, G. 1969 *Early Christian Experience*, SCM Press: London, 1969.

Bornkamm, G. 1971a *Geschichte und Glaube*, vol. 2, Beiträge zur evangelischen Theologie Band 53; Chr. Kaiser Verlag: München, 1971.

Bornkamm, G. 1971b *Paul*, Hodder and Stoughton: London, Sydney, Auckland, Toronto, 1971.

Bowe, B.E. 1988 *A Church in Crisis: Ecclesiology and Paraenesis in Clement of Rome*, Harvard Dissertations in Religion 23; Fortress Press: Minneapolis, 1988.

Brent, A. 1987 'Pseudonymity and Charisma in the Ministry of the Early Church', *Augustinianum* 27 (1987) 347–76.

Brown, R. E. & Meier, J. P. 1983 *Antioch and Rome: New Testament Cradles of Catholic Christianity*, Geoffrey Chapman: London, 1983.

Bruce, F. F. 1971 *1 and 2 Corinthians*, New Century Bible; Oliphants; Marshall, Morgan & Scott: London, 1971.

Bruce, F. F. 1982 *The Epistle of Paul to the Galatians: A Commentary on the Greek Text*, The New International Greek Testament Commentary; Paternoster: Exeter, 1982.

Brunner, G. 1972 *Die theologische Mitte des Ersten Klemensbriefes: Ein Beitrag zur Hermeneutik frühchristlicher Texte*, Frankfurter theologische Studien 11; Verlag Josef Knecht: Frankfurt am Main, 1972.

Brunt, J. 1985 'Rejected, Ignored or Misunderstood? The Fate of Paul's Approach to the Problem of Food Offered to Idols in Early Christianity', *NTS* 31 (1985) 113–24.

Bryant, C. G. A. & Jary, D. 1991 *Giddens' Theory of Structuration: A Critical Appreciation*, Routledge: London and New York, 1991.

Bultmann, R. 1960 *Jesus Christ and Mythology*, SCM Press: London, 1960.

Bultmann, R. 1969 *Faith and Understanding*, vol. 1; SCM Press: London 1969.

Bultmann, R. 1985 *The Second Letter to the Corinthians*, (ET from German of 1976); Augsburg Publishing House: Minneapolis, 1985.

Burke, P. 1980 *Sociology and History*, Controversies in Sociology 10; Allen and Unwin; London, 1980.

Burke, P. 1985 'Review Essay: Historical Sociology', *American Journal of Sociology* 90 (1985) 905–908.

Bush, R. R., Luce, R. D. & Suppes, P. 1968 'Mathematical Models', IESS, vol. 10, 378–386.

Byrne, B. 1988 *Paul and the Christian Woman*, St. Paul Publications: Homebush, NSW, Australia, 1988.

Cadbury, H. J. 1931 'Erastus of Corinth', *JBL* 50 (1931) 42–58.

Caird, G. B. 1980 *The Language and Imagery of the Bible*, Duckworth Studies in Theology; Duckworth: London, 1980.

Cairns, D. 1974 'The Thought of Peter Berger', *SJT* 27 (1974) 181–197.

Callinicos, A. 1985 'Anthony Giddens: A Contemporary Critique', Theory and Society 14 (1985) 133–166.

Campbell, R. A. 1991 'Does Paul Acquiesce in Divisions at the Lord's Supper?', *NovT* 33 (1991) 61–70.

Campbell, R. A. 1994 *The Elders: Seniority within Earliest Christianity*, Studies of the New Testament and Its World; T. & T. Clark: Edinburgh, 1994.

Campbell, W. S. 1989 'Did Paul advocate separation from the synagogue? A reaction to Francis Watson: *Paul, Judaism and the Gentiles: A Sociological Approach*', *SJT* 42 (1989) 457–467.

Campenhausen, H. von 1952 'Review of Eggenberger, *Die Quellen der politischen Ethik des 1. Klemensbriefes*', *ThLz* 1 (1952) 38–39.

Campenhausen, H. von 1969 *Ecclesiastical Authority and Spiritual Power in the Church of the First Three Centuries*, A. & C. Black: London, 1969.

Caragounis, C. C. 1974 ' Ὀψώνιον: A Reconsideration of its Meaning', *NovT* 16 (1974) 35–57.

Carney, T. F. 1975 *The Shape of the Past: Models and Antiquity*, Coronado Press; Lawrence, Kansas, 1975.

Carr, W. 1977 'The Rulers of This Age – I Corinthians II.6–8', *NTS* 23 (1976–77) 20–35.

Carrington, P. 1940 *The Primitive Christian Catechism: A study in the epistles*, Cambridge University Press: Cambridge, 1940.

Castelli, E. A. 1991 *Imitating Paul: A Discourse of Power*, Literary Currents in Biblical Interpretation; Westminster/ John Knox Press: Louisville, Kentucky,1991.

Cervin, R. S. 1989 'Does Κεφαλή Mean "Source" or "Authority Over" in Greek Literature? A Rebuttal', *TJ* 10 (1989) 85–112.

Chadwick, H. 1955 '"All things to All Men" (1 Cor. ix.22)', *NTS* 1 (1954/55) 261–275.

Chester, A. 1992 'The Parting of the Ways: Eschatology and Messianic Hope' 239–313 in *Jews and Christians: The Parting of the Ways A.D.70 to 135*, J. D. G. Dunn (ed.), WUNT 66; J. C. B. Mohr (Paul Siebeck): Tübingen, 1992.

Chow, J. K. 1992 *Patronage and Power: A Study of Social Networks in Corinth*, JSNTSup 75; JSOT Press: Sheffield, 1992.

Clark, J. 1990 'Anthony Giddens, Sociology and Modern Social Theory', 21–27 in Clark, Modgil & Modgil 1990.

Clark, J., Modgil, C. & Modgil, S. (eds) 1990 *Anthony Giddens: Consensus and Controversy*, The Falmer Press; London, New York, Philadelphia, 1990.

Clarke, A. D. 1991 'Another Corinthian Erastus Inscription', *TynBul* 42 (1991) 146–151.

Clarke, A. D. 1993 *Secular and Christian Leadership in Corinth: A Socio-Historical and Exegetical Study of 1 Corinthians 1–6*, Arbeiten zur Geschichte des antiken Judentums und des Urchristentums 18; E. J. Brill: Leiden; New York; Köln, 1993.

Cohen, I. J. 1987 'Structuration Theory and Social Praxis', 273–308 in Giddens & Turner (eds.) 1987.

Cohen, I. J. 1989 *Structuration Theory: Anthony Giddens and the Constitution of Social Life*, Macmillan: Basingstoke and London, 1989.

Conzelmann, H. 1969 *Der erste Brief an die Korinther*, Meyers Kommentar V; Vandenhoeck & Ruprecht: Göttingen, 1969.

Conzelmann, H. 1975 *A Commentary on the First Epistle to the Corinthians*, Hermeneia; Fortress Press: Philadelphia, 1975.

Cope, L. 1978 '1 Cor 11:2–16: One Step Further', *JBL* 97 (1978) 435–436.

Corbridge, S. 1993 *Debt and Development*, The Institute of British Geographers, Studies in Geography; Blackwell: Oxford, 1993.

Corley, B. (ed.) 1983 *Colloquy on New Testament Studies: A Time for Reappraisal and Fresh Approaches*, Mercer University Press: Macon, Georgia, 1983.

Coulson, M. A. & Riddell, C. 1980 *Approaching Sociology*, revised edn, Routledge and Kegan Paul: London and Boston, 1980.

Countryman, L. W. 1980 *The Rich Christian in the Church of the Early Empire: Contradictions and Accommodations*, Texts and Studies in Religion 7; The Edwin Mellen Press: New York and Toronto, 1980.

Craffert, P. 1991 'Towards an Interdisciplinary Definition of the Social-Scientific Interpretation of the New Testament', *Neotestamentica* 25 (1991) 123–144.

Craffert, P. 1992 'More on Models and Muddles in the Social-Scientific Interpretation of the New Testament: the Sociological Fallacy Reconsidered', *Neotestamentica* 26 (1992) 217–239.

Craib, I. 1992 *Anthony Giddens*, Routledge: London and New York, 1992.

Crouch, J. E. 1972 *The Origin and Intention of the Colossian Haustafel*, Forschungen zur Religion und Literatur des Alten und Neuen Testaments 109; Vandenhoeck & Ruprecht: Göttingen, 1972.

Dahl, N. A. 1967 'Paul and the Church at Corinth according to 1 Corinthians 1:10–4:21', 313–335 in Farmer, Moule & Niebuhr (eds.) 1967.

Daube, D. 1956 *The New Testament and Rabbinic Judaism*, The Athlone Press: London, 1956.

Dautzenberg, G. 1969 'Der Verzicht auf das apostolische Unterhaltsrecht: Eine exegetische Untersuchung zu 1 Kor 9', *Biblica* 50 (1969) 212–232.

Dautzenberg, G. 1975 *Urchristliche Prophetie: Ihre Forschung, ihre Voraussetzungen im Judentum und ihre Struktur im ersten Korintherbrief*, Beiträge zur Wissenschaft vom Alten und Neuen Testament, 6te Folge, Heft 4; Verlag W. Kohlhammer: Stuttgart, Berlin, Köln, Mainz, 1975.

Dautzenberg, G. 1983 'Zur Stellung der Frauen in den paulinischen Gemeinden', 182–224 in Dautzenberg, Merklein & Müller (eds.) 1983.

Dautzenberg, G., Merklein, H. & Müller, K (eds.) 1983 *Die Frau im Urchristentum*, Quaestiones Disputatae 95; Herder; Freiburg, 1983.

Davis, J. A. 1984 *Wisdom and Spirit: An Investigation of 1 Corinthians 1.18 – 3.20 Against the Background of Jewish Sapiential Traditions in the Greco-Roman Period*, University Press of America: Lanham; New York; London, 1984.

Dawes, G. 1990 '"But if you can gain your freedom" (1 Corinthians 7: 17–24)', *CBQ* 52 (1990) 681–697.

Deissmann, A. 1927 *Light from the Ancient East: The New Testament Illustrated by Recently Discovered Texts of the Graeco-Roman World,* Hodder & Stoughton: London, 1927.

Delobel, J. 1986 '1 Cor 11,2–16: Towards a Coherent Interpretation', 369–389 in *L'Apôtre Paul: Personnalité, Style et Conception du Ministère,* A. Vanhoye (ed.), Bibliotheca Epheridum Theologicarum Louvaniensium 73; Leuven University Press: Leuven, 1986.

Derrett, J. D. M. 1991 'Judgement and 1 Corinthians 6', *NTS* 37 (1991) 22–36.

Dibelius, M. & Conzelmann, H. 1972 *A Commentary on the Pastoral Epistles,* Hermeneia; Fortress Press: Philadelphia, 1972.

Dinkler, E. 1952 'Zum Problem der Ethik bei Paulus: Rechtsnahme und Rechtsverzicht (1.Kor.6,1–11)', *Zeitschrift für Theologie und Kirche* 49 (1952) 167–200.

Dodd, C. H. 1933 'The Mind of Paul: I', 67–82 in *New Testament Studies,* Manchester University Press: Manchester, 1953.

Dodd, C. H. 1934 'The Mind of Paul: II', 83–128 in *New Testament Studies,* Manchester University Press: Manchester, 1953.

Dodd, C. H. 1953 '῎Εννομος Χριστοῦ', 134–148 in *More New Testament Studies,* Manchester University Press: Manchester, 1968.

Domeris, W. R. 1991 'Sociological and Social Historical Investigations', 215–233 in *Text and Interpretation: New Approaches in the Criticism of the New Testament,* P. J. Hartin and J. H. Petzer (eds.), E. J. Brill: Leiden, New York, København, Köln, 1991.

Donfried, K. P. (ed.) 1991 *The Romans Debate: Revised and Expanded Edition,* T. & T. Clark: Edinburgh, 1991.

Downing, F. G. 1987 *Jesus and the Threat of Freedom,* SCM Press: London, 1987.

Downing, F. G. 1992 *Cynics and Christian Origins,* T. & T. Clark: Edinburgh, 1992.

Dungan, D. L. 1971 *The Sayings of Jesus in the Churches of Paul: The Use of the Synoptic Tradition in the Regulation of Early Church Life,* Basil Blackwell: Oxford, 1971.

Dunn, J. D. G. 1970 *Baptism in the Holy Spirit,* SCM Press: London, 1970.

Dunn, J. D. G. 1975 *Jesus and the Spirit: A Study of the Religious and Charismatic Experience of Jesus and the First Christians as Reflected in the New Testament,* SCM Press: London, 1975.

Dunn, J. D. G. 1986 'Romans 13.1–7 – A Charter for Political Quietism?', *Ex Auditu* 2 (1986) 55–68.

Dunn, J. D. G. 1988 *Romans,* 2 vols, WBC 38A and 38B; Word Books: Dallas, Texas, 1988.

Dunn, J. D. G. 1990a *Jesus, Paul and the Law: Studies in Mark and Galatians,* SPCK: London, 1990.

Dunn, J. D. G. 1990b *Unity and Diversity in the New Testament: An Inquiry into the Character of Earliest Christianity,* 2nd edn; SCM Press: London; TPI: Philadelphia, 1977, ²1990.

Dunn, J. D. G. 1993 *The Epistle to the Galatians,* BNTC; A. & C. Black: London, 1993.

Eagleton, T. 1991 *Ideology: An Introduction,* Verso: London; New York, 1991.

Ebner, M. 1991 *Leidenslisten und Apostelbrief: Untersuchungen zu Form, Motivik und Funktion der Peristasenkatalogue bei Paulus,* Forschung zur Bibel, Band 66; Echter Verlag: Würzburg, 1991.

Edmundson, G. 1913 *The Church at Rome in the First Century: An Examination of Various Controverted Questions Relating to Its History, Chronology, Literature and Traditions,* Longmans, Green and Co.: London, 1913.

Edwards, O. C. Jr. 1983 'Sociology as a Tool for Interpreting the New Testament', *Anglican Theological Review* 65 (1983) 431–448.

Eggenberger, C. 1951 *Die Quellen der politischen Ethik des 1. Klemensbriefes,* Zwingli-Verlag: Zürich, 1951.

Eldridge, J. E. T. (ed.) 1971 *Max Weber: The Interpretation of Social Reality,* Thomas Nelson and Sons Ltd, London, 1971.

Elliott, J. H. 1981 *A Home for the Homeless: A sociological exegesis of 1 Peter, its situation and strategy,* SCM Press: London, 1982.

Elliott, J. H. 1985 'Review of W. Meeks, *The First Urban Christians*', *Religious Studies Review* 11 (1985) 329–335.

Elliott, J. H. 1986 'Social-Scientific Criticism of the New Testament and its Social World: More on Method and Models', *Semeia* 35 (1986) 1–33.

Elliott, J. H. 1993 *What Is Social-Scientific Criticism?* Fortress Press: Minneapolis, 1993.

Ellis, E. E. 1974 '"Christ Crucified"', 69–75 in R. J. Banks (ed.), *Reconcilation and Hope: New Testament Essays on Atonement and Eschatology Presented to L. L. Morris on his 60th Birthday,* Paternoster Press: Exeter, 1974.

Ellis, E. E. 1981 'The Silenced Wives of Corinth (1 Cor. 14:34–5)', 213–220 in *New Testament Textual Criticism: Its Significance for Exegesis,* Essays in Honour of Bruce Metzger, E. J. Epp & G. D. Fee (eds.), Clarendon Press: Oxford, 1981.

Ellis, E. E. 1986 'Traditions in 1 Corinthians', *NTS* 32 (1986) 481–502.

Elster, J. 1986 *Karl Marx: A Reader*, Cambridge University Press: Cambridge, 1986.

Engberg-Petersen, T. 1987 'The Gospel and Social Practice according to 1 Corinthians', *NTS* 33 (1987) 557–584.

Engberg-Pedersen, T. 1991 '1 Corinthians 11:16 and the Character of Pauline Exhortation', *JBL* 110 (1991) 679–689.

Engberg-Pedersen, T. 1993 'Proclaiming the Lord's Death: 1 Corinthians 11:17–34 and the Forms of Paul's Theological Argument', 103–132 in D. M. Hay (ed.), *Pauline Theology. vol II: 1 and 2 Corinthians*, Fortress Press: Minneapolis, 1993.

Engels, D. 1990 *Roman Corinth: An Alternative Model for the Classical City*, The University of Chicago Press: Chicago and London, 1990.

Esler, P. F. 1987 *Community and Gospel in Luke-Acts: The Social and Political Motivations of Lucan Theology*, SNTSMS 57; Cambridge University Press: Cambridge, 1987.

Esler, P. F. 1994 *The First Christians in their Social Worlds: Social-Scientific Approaches to New Testament Interpretation*, Routledge: London, 1994.

Farmer, W. R, Moule, C. F. D & Niebuhr, R. R. (eds.) 1967 *Christian History and Interpretation:* Studies Presented to John Knox, Cambridge University Press: Cambridge, 1967.

Fee, G. D. 1980 'Εἰδωλόθυτα Once Again: An Interpretation of 1 Corinthians 8–10', *Biblica* 61 (1980) 172–197.

Fee, G. D. 1987 *The First Epistle to the Corinthians*, NICNT; Wm. B. Eerdmans: Grand Rapids, Michigan, 1987.

Filson, F. V. 1939 'The Significance of the Early House Churches', *JBL* 58 (1939) 105–112.

Findlay, G. 1900 'The letter of the Corinthian Church to St. Paul', *The Expositor*, 6th series, vol. 1, (1900) 401–407.

Finley, M. I. 1970 'Slavery', 994–996 in *The Oxford Classical Dictionary*, N. G. L. Hammond & H. C. Scullard (eds.).

Finley, M. I. 1973 *The Ancient Economy*, Chatto and Windus: London, 1973.

Finley, M. I. (ed.) 1960 *Slavery in Classical Antiquity: Views and Controversies*, W. Heffer & Sons: Cambridge, 1960.

Finn, T. M. 1985 'The God-fearers Reconsidered', *CBQ* 47 (1985) 75–84.

Fiore, B. 1985 '"Covert Allusion" in 1 Corinthians 1–4', *CBQ* 47 (1985) 85–102.

Fiorenza, E. S. 1979 '"You Are Not to Be Called Father": Early Christian History in a Feminist Perspective', 394–417 in *The Bible and Liberation*, N. K. Gottwald (ed.); Orbis Books: Maryknoll, New York, 1983, reprinted from *Cross Currents* 29 (1979) 301–323.

Fiorenza, E. S. 1983 *In Memory of Her: A Feminist Theological Reconstruction of Christian Origins*, SCM Press: London, 1983.

Fiorenza, E. S. 1985 *The Book of Revelation: Justice and Judgment*, Fortress Press: Philadelphia, 1985.

Fiorenza, E. S. 1986 'Missionaries, Apostles, Co-Workers: Romans 16 and the Reconstruction of Women's Early Christian History', 57–71 in A. Loades (ed.) *Feminist Theology: A Reader*, SPCK: London, 1990.

Fiorenza, E. S. 1987 'Rhetorical Situation and Historical Reconstruction in 1 Corinthians', *NTS* 33 (1987) 386–403.

Fisher, E. 1974 *Soteriology in First Clement*, Claremont Graduate School PhD, 1974; University Microfilms International; Ann Arbor: Michigan USA; London, England, 1981.

Fisk, B. N. 1989 'Eating Meat Offered to Idols: Corinthian Behaviour and Pauline Response in 1 Corinthians 8–10 (A Response to Gordon Fee)', *TJ* 10 (1989) 49–70.

Fitzer, G. 1963 *„Das Weib schweige in der Gemeinde", über den unpaulinischen Charakter der mulier-taceat-Verse in 1. Korinther 14*, Theologische Existenz Heute, Neue Folge 110; Chr. Kaiser Verlag: München, 1963.

Fitzgerald, J. T. 1988 *Cracks in an Earthen Vessel: An Examination of the Catalogues of Hardships in the Corinthian Correspondence*, SBLDS 99; Scholars Press: Atlanta, Georgia, 1988.

Fitzmyer, J. 1989 'Another Look at ΚΕΦΑΛΗ in 1 Corinthians 11:3', *NTS* 35 (1989) 503–511.

Fitzmyer, J. A. 1993 'Kephalē in I Corinthians 11:3', *Int* 47 (1993) 52–59.

Flanagan, N. M. & Snyder, E. H. 1981 'Did Paul Put Down Women in 1 Cor 14:34–36?', *BTB* 11 (1981) 10–12.

Forbes, C. 1986 'Comparison, Self-Praise and Irony: Paul's Boasting and the Conventions of Hellenistic Rhetoric', *NTS* 32 (1986) 1–30.

Ford, J. M. 1966 'Review of *The Origin of 1 Corinthians*, by J. C. Hurd', *JTS* 17 (1966) 442–444.

Friedrich, J., Pöhlmann, W. & Stuhlmacher, P. 1976 'Zur historischen Situation und Intention von Röm 13,1–7', *Zeitschrift für Theologie und Kirche* 73 (1976) 131–66.

Fuellenbach, J. 1980 *Ecclesiastical Office and the Primacy of Rome: An Evaluation of Recent Theological Discussion of First Clement*, The Catholic University of America Studies in Christian Antiquity 20; The Catholic University of America Press: Washington DC, 1980.

Fuller, R. H. 1986 'First Corinthians 6:1–11. An Exegetical Paper', *Ex Auditu* 2 (1986) 96–104.

Fung, R. Y. K. 1988 *The Epistle to the Galatians*, NICNT; Wm.B. Eerdmans: Grand Rapids, Michigan, 1988.

Furnish, V. P. 1968 *Theology and Ethics in Paul*, Abingdon Press: Nashville, Tennessee, 1968.

Furnish, V. P. 1984 *II Corinthians: A new translation with introduction and commentary*, Anchor Bible vol. 32A; Doubleday: Garden City, New York, 1984.

Furnish, V. P. 1985 'Review of J. Murphy O'Connor, *St. Paul's Corinth: Texts and Archaeology*', *JBL* 104 (1985) 351–352.

Gager, J. G. 1975 *Kingdom and Community: The Social World of Early Christianity*, Prentice-Hall: Englewood Cliffs, New Jersey, 1975.

Gager, J. G. 1979 'Review of Grant, Malherbe and Theissen', *Religious Studies Review* 5 (1979) 174–180.

Gager, J. G. 1982 'Shall We Marry Our Enemies? Sociology and New Testament Interpretation', *Int* 36 (1982) 256–265.

Gallagher, E. V. 1984 'The Social World of St. Paul', *Religion* 14 (1984) 91–99.

Gamble, H. Jr. 1977 *The Textual History of the Letter to the Romans: A Study in Textual and Literary Criticism*, Studies and Documents, vol. 42; Wm. B. Eerdmans: Grand Rapids, Michigan, 1977.

Gardner, P. D. 1994 *The Gifts of God and the Authentication of a Christian: An Exegetical Study of 1 Corinthians 8–11.1*, University Press of America: Lanham; New York; London, 1994.

Garnsey, P. 1970 *Social Status and Legal Privilege in the Roman Empire*, The Clarendon Press: Oxford, 1970.

Garnsey, P. and Saller, R. 1987 *The Roman Empire: Economy, Society and Culture*, Duckworth: London, 1987.

Garrett, S. R. 1992 'Sociology of Early Christianity' *The Anchor Bible Dictionary* (6 vols), vol. 6, 89–99; D. N. Freedman (ed.); Doubleday: New York, 1992.

Garrison, R. 1993 *Redemptive Almsgiving in Early Christianity*, JSNTSup 77; JSOT Press; Sheffield Academic Press: Sheffield, 1993.

Gayer, R. 1976 *Die Stellung des Sklaven in den paulinischen Gemeinden und bei Paulus*, Europäische Hochschulschriften, series 23, Theology, vol. 78; Herbert Lang: Bern; Peter Lang: Frankfurt, 1976.

Geertz, C. 1957 'Ethos, World-View and the Analysis of Sacred Symbols', *Antioch Review* 17 (1957) 421–437.

Geertz, C. 1966 'Religion as a Cultural System', 1–46 in *Anthropological Approaches to the Study of Religion*, M. Banton (ed.), Tavistock Publications: London, 1966.

Gellner, E. 1962 'Concepts and Society', 115–149 in *Sociological Theory and Philosophical Analysis*, D. Emmett & A. MacIntyre (eds.), Macmillan: London and New York, 1970.

Georgi, D. 1965 *Die Geschichte der Kollekte des Paulus für Jerusalem*, Theologische Forschung 38; Herbert Reich; Evangelischer Verlag: Hamburg-Bergstedt, 1965 (ET now 1992).

Georgi, D. 1987 *The Opponents of Paul in Second Corinthians*, T. & T. Clark: Edinburgh, 1987 (ET, German original 1964).

Georgi, D. 1992 *Remembering the Poor: The History of Paul's Collection for Jerusalem*, Abingdon Press: Nashville, 1992.

Gibbs, J. A. 1978 'Wisdom, Power and Wellbeing', 119–55 in *Studia Biblica* 3 (1978), E. A. Livingstone (ed.), JSNTSup 3; JSOT Press: Sheffield, 1980.

Giddens, A. 1971 *Capitalism and Modern Social Theory: An analysis of the writings of Marx, Durkheim and Max Weber*, Cambridge University Press: Cambridge, 1971.

Giddens, A. 1973 *The Class Structure of the Advanced Societies*, Hutchinson: London, 1973.

Giddens, A. 1976 *New Rules of Sociological Method: a positive critique of interpretative sociologies*, Hutchinson: London, 1976.

Giddens, A. 1977 *Studies in Social and Political Theory*, Hutchinson: London, 1977.

Giddens, A. 1979 *Central Problems in Social Theory*, Macmillan: London and Basingstoke, 1979.

Giddens, A. 1981 *A Contemporary Critique of Historical Materialism: Vol. 1. Power, property and the state*, Macmillan: London and Basingstoke, 1981.

Giddens, A. 1982a *Profiles and Critiques in Social Theory*, Macmillan: London and Basingstoke, 1982.

Giddens, A. 1982b *Sociology: A Brief but Critical Introduction*, Macmillan: London and Basingstoke, 1982, 1986 (2nd edn).

Giddens, A. 1984 *The Constitution of Society: Outline of the Theory of Structuration*, Polity Press: Cambridge, 1984.

Giddens, A. 1985 'Marx's correct views on everything', *Theory and Society* 14 (1985) 167–174.

Giddens, A. 1987 *Social Theory and Modern Sociology*, Polity Press: Cambridge, 1987.

Giddens, A. 1989a *Sociology*, Polity Press: Cambridge, 1989.

Giddens, A. 1989b 'A reply to my critics', 249–301 in Held and Thompson (eds.) 1989.

Giddens, A. 1990 'Structuration Theory and Sociological Analysis', 297–315 in Clark, Modgil & Modgil (eds.) 1990.

Giddens, A. 1991 'Structuration theory: past, present and future', 201–221 in Bryant and Jary (eds.) 1991.

Giddens, A. & Turner, J. H. (eds.) 1987 *Social Theory Today*, Polity Press: Cambridge, 1987.

Gilchrist, J. M. 1988 'Paul and the Corinthians – The Sequence of Letters and Visits', *JSNT* 34 (1988) 47–69.

Gill, D. W. J. 1989 'Erastus the Aedile', *TynBul* 40 (1989) 293–300.

Gill, D. W. J. 1992 'The Meat-Market at Corinth (1 Corinthians 10:25)', *TynBul* 43 (1992) 389–393.

Gill, D. W. J. 1993 'In Search of the Social Élite in the Corinthian Church', *TynBul* 44 (1993) 323–337.

Gill, D. W. J. 1994 'Review of A. D. Clarke, *Secular and Christian Leadership in Corinth*', *JTS* 45 (1994) 676–679.

Gill, R. 1974 'Berger's Plausibility Structures: A Response to Professor Cairns', *SJT* 27 (1974) 198–207.

Gill, R. 1975 *The Social Context of Theology*, Mowbrays: London and Oxford, 1975.

Gill, R. 1977 *Theology and Social Structure*, Mowbrays: London and Oxford, 1977.

Gill, R. (ed.) 1987 *Theology and Sociology: A Reader*, Geoffrey Chapman: London; Paulist Press: New York/ Mahwah, 1987.

Gooch, Peter D. 1993 *Dangerous Food: 1 Corinthians 8–10 in Its Context*, Studies in Christianity and Judaism 5; published for the Canadian Corporation for Studies in Religion by Wilfred Laurier University Press: Waterloo, Ontario, Canada, 1993.

Gooch, P. W. 1987 '"Conscience" in 1 Corinthians 8 and 10', *NTS* 33 (1987) 244–254.

Goulder, M. D. 1991 'ΣΟΦΙΑ in 1 Corinthians', *NTS* 37 (1991) 516–534.

Grant, R. M. 1964 *The Apostolic Fathers: A New Translation and Commentary, Vol. 1: An Introduction*, Thomas Nelson and Sons: New York; London; Toronto, 1964.

Grant, R. M. and Graham, H. H. 1965 *The Apostolic Fathers: A New Translation and Commentary, Vol. 2: First and Second Clement*, Thomas Nelson and Sons: New York; London; Toronto, 1965.

Grayston, K. 1990 *Dying, We Live: A New Enquiry into the Death of Christ in the New Testament*, Darton, Longman and Todd: London, 1990.

Gregory, D. 1980 'The Ideology of Control: Systems Theory and Geography', *Tijdschrift voor economic en sociale geografie* 71 (1980) 327–342.

Gregory, D. 1981 'Human Agency and Human Geography', *Transactions of the Institute of British Geographers*, new series 6 (1981) 1–18.

Gregory, D. 1986 *The Dictionary of Human Geography*, 2nd edn, R. J. Johnston, D. Gregory & D. M. Smith (eds.); See articles on Functionalism; Ideology; Models; Structuration Theory; Blackwell Reference: Oxford, 1986.

Gregson, N. 1989 'On the (ir)relevance of structuration theory to empirical research', 235–248 in Held and Thompson (eds.) 1989.

Grudem, W. 1982 *The Gift of Prophecy in 1 Corinthians*, University Press of America: Lanham; New York; London, 1982.

Grudem, W. 1985 'Does κεφαλή Mean "Source" or "Authority Over" in Greek Literature? A Survey of 2,336 Examples', *TJ* 6 (1985) 38–59.

Grudem, W. 1990 'The Meaning of κεφαλή ("Head"): A Response to Recent Studies', *TJ* 11 (1990) 3–72.

Guthrie, D. 1990 *New Testament Introduction*, Apollos; Inter-Varsity Press: Leicester, 1990.

Haenchen, E. 1971 *The Acts of the Apostles: A Commentary*, Basil Blackwell: Oxford, 1971.

Hafemann, S. 1990 '"Self-Commendation" and Apostolic Legitimacy in 2 Corinthians: A Pauline Dialectic?', *NTS* 36 (1990) 66–88.

Hagner, D. A. 1973 *The Use of the Old and New Testaments in Clement of Rome*, NovTSup 34; E. J. Brill: Leiden, 1973.

Hammond, N. G. L. & Scullard, H. C. (eds.) 1970 *The Oxford Classical Dictionary*, 2nd edn; Clarendon Press: Oxford, 1970.

Haney, C., Banks, C. & Zimbardo, P. 1973 'A study of prisoners and guards in a simulated prison', reprinted as 226–239 in Potter (ed.) 1981.

Hanson, A. T. 1982a '1 Corinthians 4.13b and Lamentations 3.45', *ExpTim* 93 (1982) 214–215.

Hanson, A. T. 1982b *The Pastoral Epistles*, New Century Bible Commentary; Marshall, Morgan & Scott: London; Wm. B. Eerdmans: Grand Rapids, 1982.

Harnack, A. von 1929 *Einführung in die alte Kirchengeschichte: Das Schreiben der römischen Kirche an die korinthische aus der Zeit Domitians (1. Clemensbrief)*, J. C. Hinrichs'sche Buchhandlung: Leipzig, 1929.

Harrington, D. J. 1980 'Sociological Concepts and the Early Church: A Decade of Research', *Theological Studies* 41 (1980) 181–190.

Harrington, D. J. 1988 'Second Testament Exegesis and the Social Sciences: A Bibliography', *BTB* 18 (1988) 77–85.

Harris, G. 1991 'The Beginnings of Church Discipline: 1 Cor. 5', *NTS* 37 (1991) 1–21.

Harris, W. V. 1989 *Ancient Literacy*, Harvard University Press: Cambridge, Massachusetts; London, 1989.

Harvey, A. E. 1982 '"The Workman is Worthy of His Hire": Fortunes of a Proverb in the Early Church', *NovT* 24 (1982) 209–221.

Hauke, M. 1988 *Women in the Priesthood?: a systematic analysis in the light of the order of creation and redemption*, Ignatius Press: San Francisco, 1988.

Hausrath, A. 1870 *Der Vier-Capitelbrief des Paulus an die Korinther*, Bassermann: Heidelberg, 1870.

Held, D. & Thompson, J. B. (eds.) 1989 *Social Theory of Modern Societies: Anthony Giddens and his critics*, Cambridge University Press: Cambridge, 1989.

Hengel, M. 1986 *The Cross of the Son of God*, containing, *The Son of God, Crucifixion, The Atonement*, SCM Press: London, 1986.

Héring, J. 1962 *The First Epistle of Saint Paul to the Corinthians*, Epworth Press: London, 1962.

Héring, J. 1967 *The Second Epistle of Saint Paul to the Corinthians*, Epworth Press: London, 1967.

Hickling, C. J. A. 1975 'Is the Second Epistle to the Corinthians a Source for Early Church History?', *ZNW* 66 (1975) 284–287.

Hock, R. F. 1978 'Paul's Tentmaking and the Problem of his Social Class', *JBL* 97 (1978) 555–564.

Hock, R. F. 1979 'The Workshop as a Social Setting for Paul's Missionary Preaching', *CBQ* 41 (1979) 438–450.

Hock, R. F. 1980 *The Social Context of Paul's Ministry: Tentmaking and Apostleship*, Fortress Press: Philadelphia, 1980.

Hodgson, R. 1983 'Paul the Apostle and First Century Tribulation Lists', *ZNW* 74 (1983) 59–80.

Holmberg, B. 1978 *Paul and Power: The Structure of Authority in the Primitive Church as reflected in the Pauline Epistles*, Coniectanea Biblica, NT Series 11; CWK Gleerup: Lund, 1978.

Holmberg, B. 1980 'Sociological versus Theological Analysis of the Question concerning a Pauline Church Order' 187–200 in *Die Paulinische Literatur und Theologie*, S. Petersen (ed), Forlaget Aros: Arhus; Vandenhoeck und Ruprecht: Göttingen, 1980.

Holmberg, B. 1990 *Sociology and the New Testament: An Appraisal*, Fortress Press: Minneapolis, 1990.

Holmes, M. W. 1989 *The Apostolic Fathers, Second Edition*, translated by J. B. Lightfoot and J. R. Harmer, edited and revised by M. W. Holmes, Baker Book House: Grand Rapids, Michigan, 1989.

Holtz, T. 1986 *Der erste Brief an die Thessalonicher*, EKKNT; Benziger: Zürich, Einsiedeln, Köln; Neukirchener: Neukirchen-Vluyn, 1986.

Hooijbergh, A. E. W. 1975 'A Different View of Clemens Romanus', *Heythrop Journal* 16 (1975) 266–288.

Hooker, M. D. 1964 'Authority On Her Head: An Examination of 1 Cor. XI.10', *NTS* 10 (1964) 410–416.

Hopkins, K. 1978 *Conquerors and Slaves: Sociological Studies in Roman History*, vol.1, Cambridge University Press: Cambridge, 1978.

Horrell, D. G. 1993 'Converging Ideologies: Berger and Luckmann and the Pastoral Epistles', *JSNT* 50 (1993) 85–103.

Horrell, D. G. 1994 *The Social Ethos of Pauline Christianity: Interests and Ideology in the Corinthian Correspondence from 1 Corinthians to 1 Clement*, PhD thesis; Cambridge University, 1994.

Horrell, D. G. 1995a 'Review of Peter D. Gooch, *Dangerous Food: 1 Corinthians 8–10 in Its Context*', *JTS* 46 (1995) 279–282.

Horrell, D. G. 1995b 'The Lord's Supper at Corinth and in the Church Today', *Theology* 98 (1995) 196–202.

Horrell, D. G. 1995c 'Paul's Collection: Resources for a Materialist Theology', *Epworth Review* 22/2 (1995) 74–83.

Horrell, D. G. 1995d 'The Development of Theological Ideology in Pauline Christianity: A Structuration Theory Perspective', 224–236 in P. F. Esler (ed.), *Modelling Early Christianity*, Routledge: London, 1995.

Horrell, D. G. 1995e 'Review of Paul D. Gardner, *The Gifts of God and the Authentication of a Christian: An Exegetical Study of 1 Corinthians 8–11.1*', *JTS* 46 (1995) 651–654.

Horsley, R. A. 1976 'Pneumatikos vs. Psychikos: Distinctions of Spiritual Status among the Corinthians', *HTR* 69 (1976) 269–288.

Horsley, R. A. 1977 'Wisdom of Word and Words of Wisdom in Corinth', *CBQ* 39 (1977) 224–239.

Horsley, R. A. 1978a 'Consciousness and Freedom among the Corinthians: 1 Corinthians 8–10', *CBQ* 40 (1978) 574–589.

Horsley, R. A. 1978b '"How can some of you say that there is no resurrection of the dead?" Spiritual Elitism in Corinth', *NovT* 20 (1978) 203–231.

Horsley, R. A. 1981 'Gnosis in Corinth: 1 Corinthians 8.1–6', *NTS* 27 (1981) 32–51.

Horsley, R. A. 1989 *Sociology and the Jesus Movement*, Crossroad: New York, 1989.

Hughes, P. E. 1962 *Paul's Second Epistle to the Corinthians*, The New London Commentary on the New Testament; Marshall, Morgan & Scott: London and Edinburgh, 1962.

Hunter, A. M. 1961 *Paul and his Predecessors*, SCM Press: London, [2]1961.

Hurd, J. C. 1965 *The Origin of 1 Corinthians*, SPCK: London, 1965.

Hurd, J. C. & Richardson, P. (eds.) 1984 *From Jesus to Paul: Studies in Honour of Francis Wright Beare*, Wilfrid Laurier University Press: Ontario, 1984.

Hurtado, L. 1984 'Jesus as Lordly Example in Philippians 2:5–11', 113–126 in Hurd and Richardson (eds.) 1984.

Hyldahl, N. 1973 'Die Frage nach der literarischen Einheit des Zweiten Korintherbriefes', *ZNW* 64 (1973) 289–306.

Hyldahl, N. 1986 *Die paulinische Chronologie*, E. J. Brill: Leiden, 1986.

Hyldahl, N. 1991 'The Corinthian "Parties" and the Corinthian Crisis', *Studia Theologica* 45 (1991) 19–32.

Jaubert, A. 1964a 'Les sources de la conception militaire de l'eglise en 1 Clément 37', *VC* 18 (1964) 74–84.

Jaubert, A. 1964b 'Thèmes lévitiques dans la Prima Clementis', *VC* 18 (1964) 193–203.

Jaubert, A. 1971 *Clément de Rome. Épître aux Corinthiens: Introduction, Texte, Traduction, Notes et Index*, Sources Chrétiennes 167; Les Éditions du Cerf: Paris, 1971.

Jaubert, A. 1972 'Le voile des femmes (I Cor. XI.2–16)', *NTS* 18 (1971–72) 419–30.

Jeffers, J. S. 1991 *Conflict at Rome: Social Order and Hierarchy in Early Christianity*, Fortress Press: Minneapolis, 1991.

Jervis, L. A. 1993 ' "But I Want You To Know ...": Paul's Midrashic Intertextual Response to the Corinthian Worshipers (1 Cor 11:2–16)', *JBL* 112 (1993) 231–246.

Jewett, R. 1978 'The Redaction of 1 Corinthians and the Trajectory of the Pauline School', *JAAR* 44/4 Supplement B, (1978) 389–444.

Jewett, R. 1979 *Dating Paul's Life*, SCM Press: London, 1979.

Jewett, R. 1982 'Romans as an Ambassadorial Letter', *Int* 36 (1982) 5–20.

Joas, H. 1990 'Giddens's Critique of Functionalism', 91–102, 111–112 in Clark, Modgil & Modgil (eds.) 1990.

Jones, A. H. M. 1956 'Slavery in the Ancient World', *The Economic History Review* 9 (1956) 185–199, cited from reprint in Finley (ed.) 1960, 1–16.

Jones, G. 1991 *Bultmann: Towards a critical theology*, Polity Press: Cambridge, 1991.

Jones, G. S. 1976 'From historical sociology to theoretical history', *British Journal of Sociology* 27 (1976) 295–305.

Jones, I. H. 1973 *The Contemporary Cross: A Study for Passiontide – a theme and four biblical variations*, Epworth Press: London, 1973.

Judge, E. A. 1960a *The Social Pattern of Christian Groups in the First Century: Some Prologomena to the Study of New Testament Ideas of Social Obligation*, The Tyndale Press: London, 1960.

Judge, E. A. 1960b 'The Early Christians as a Scholastic Community', Part I; *JRH* 1 (1960) 4–15; Part II, *JRH* 1 (1960) 125–137.

Judge, E. A. 1966 'The Conflict of Educational Aims in New Testament Thought', *Journal of Christian Education* 9 (1966) 32–45.

Judge, E. A. 1968 'Paul's Boasting in relation to Contemporary Professional Practice', *ABR* 16 (1968) 37–50.

Judge, E. A. 1972 'St. Paul and Classical Society', *Jahrbuch für Antike und Christentum* 15 (1972) 19–36.

Judge, E. A. 1980 'The Social Identity of the First Christians: A Question of Method in Religious History', *JRH* 11 (1980) 201–217.

Judge, E. A. 1984 'Cultural Conformity and Innovation in Paul: Some Clues from Contemporary Documents', *TynBul* 35 (1984) 3–24.

Kallas, J. 1965 'Romans XIII.1–7: An Interpolation', *NTS* 11 (1964/65) 365–74.

Kampling, R. 1990 'Kontrastgesellschaft. Zur Brauchbarkeit eines Begriffes für die neutestamentliche Wissenschaft', *Biblische Notizen* 52 (1990) 13–18.

Karlsaune, E. (ed.) 1988 *Religion as a Social Phenomenon: Theologians and Sociologists sharing research interests,* 'Relieff' series no. 25; Tapir Publishers: Trondheim, Norway, 1988.

Karris, R. J. 1973 'Romans 14:1–15:13 and the Occasion of Romans', *CBQ* 25 (1973) 155–78; 65–84 in Donfried (ed.) 1991.

Käsemann, E. 1942 'Die Legitimät des Apostels. Eine Untersuchung zu II Korinther 10–13', *ZNW* 41 (1942) 33–71. Reprinted by Wissenschaftliche Buchgesellschaft: Darmstadt, 1956.

Käsemann, E. 1969 *New Testament Questions of Today,* SCM Press: London, 1969.

Käsemann, E. 1980 *Commentary on Romans,* SCM Press: London, 1980.

Keck, L. E. 1974 'On the Ethos of Early Christians', *JAAR* 42 (1974) 435–452.

Kee, H. C. 1980 *Christian Origins in Sociological Perspective,* SCM Press: London, 1980.

Kee, H. C. 1989 *Knowing the Truth: A Sociological Approach to New Testament Interpretation,* Fortress Press: Minneapolis, 1989.

Keener, C. S. 1992 *Paul, Women and Wives: Marriage and Women's Ministry in the Letters of Paul,* Hendrickson Publishers: Peabody, Massachusetts, 1992.

Kelly, J. M. 1966 *Roman Litigation,* Clarendon Press: Oxford, 1966.

Kennedy, J. H. 1900 *The Second and Third Epistles of St. Paul to the Corinthians,* Methuen and Co.: London, 1900.

Kent, J. H. 1966 *Corinth: Results of Excavations conducted by the American School of Classical Studies at Athens, vol. 8, part 3; The Inscriptions, 1926–1950,* The American School of Classical Studies at Athens: Princeton, New Jersey, 1966.

Kidd, R. M. 1990 *Wealth and Beneficience in the Pastoral Epistles. A "Bourgeois" Form of Early Christianity?,* SBLDS 122; Scholars Press: Atlanta, Georgia, 1990.

Kittel, G. & Friedrich, G. (eds.) 1964–1976 *The Theological Dictionary of the New Testament*, 10 vols, ET by G. W. Bromiley; Wm. B. Eerdmans: Grand Rapids, Michigan, 1964–1976.

Klauck, H-J. 1981 *Hausgemeinde und Hauskirche im frühen Christentum*, Stuttgarter Bibelstudien 103; Katholisches Bibelwerk: Stuttgart, 1981.

Klauck, H-J. 1982 *Herrenmahl und Hellenistischer Kult: Eine religionsgeschichtliche Untersuchung zum ersten Korintherbrief*, Neutestamentliche Abhandlungen, Neue Folge 15; Aschendorff: Münster, 1982.

Klauck, H-J. 1984 *1. Korintherbrief*, Die Neue Echter Bibel; Kommentar zum Neuen Testament mit der Einheitsübersetzung, Band 7; Echter Verlag: Würzburg, 1984.

Knight, G. W. III. 1992 *The Pastoral Epistles: A Commentary on the Greek Text*, The New International Greek Testament Commentary; Wm. B. Eerdmans: Grand Rapids, Michigan; Paternoster: Carlisle, 1992.

Knoch, O. 1964 *Eigenart und Bedeutung der Eschatologie im theologischen Aufriß des ersten Clemensbriefes: Eine auslegungsgeschichtliche Untersuchung*, Theophaneia 17; Beiträge zur Religions- und Kirchengeschichte des Altertums; Peter Hanstein Verlag: Bonn, 1964.

Knox, J. 1950 *Chapters in a Life of Paul*, SCM Press: London, 1989, revised edition.

Knox, J. 1983 'Chapters in a life of Paul – A response to Robert Jewett and Gerd Luedemann', 339–364 in Corley (ed.) 1983.

Koester, H. 1982a *Introduction to the New Testament: Vol. 1; History, Culture and Religion of the Hellenistic Age*, Fortress Press: Philadelphia; Walter de Gruyter: Berlin and New York, 1982.

Koester, H. 1982b *Introduction to the New Testament: Vol. 2; History and Literature of Early Christianity*, Fortress Press: Philadelphia; Walter de Gruyter: Berlin and New York, 1982.

Kraabel, A. T. 1981 'The Disappearance of the "God-fearers"', *Numen* 28 (1981) 113–126.

Kraabel, A. T. 1986 'Greeks, Jews and Lutherans in the Middle Half of Acts', *HTR* 79 (1986) 147–157.

Kreissig, H. 1967 'Zur sozialen Zusammensetzung der frühchristlichen Gemeinden im ersten Jahrhundert u.Z.', *Eirene* 6 (1967) 91–100.

Kroeger, R. & Kroeger, C. 1978 'An Inquiry into Evidence of Maenadism in the Corinthian Congregation', SBLSP 14 (1979) vol. 2, 331–338; Scholars Press: Missoula, Montana, 1978.

Kuhn, T. S. 1970 *The Structure of Scientific Revolutions*, 2nd edn with postscript; The University of Chicago Press; Chicago, 1970.

Kümmel, W. G. 1966 'Review of J. C. Hurd, *The Origin of 1 Corinthians*', *ThLz* 91 (1966) 505–508.

Kümmel, W. G. 1975 *Introduction to the New Testament*, New Testament Library; SCM Press: London, 1975.

Kümmel, W. G. 1985 'Das Urchristentum II. Arbeiten zu Spezialproblemen, b. Zur Sozialgeschichte und Soziologie der Urkirche', *Theologische Rundschau* 50 (1985) 327–363.

Kürzinger, J. 1978 'Mann und Frau nach 1 Kor 11,11f.', *Biblische Zeitschrift* 22 (1978) 270–275.

Kyrtatas, D. J. 1987 *The Social Structure of the Early Christian Communities*, Verso: London and New York, 1987.

Lake, K. 1912 *The Apostolic Fathers*, vol. 1; I and II Clement; Ignatius; Polycarp; Didache; Barnabas; LCL, 1912.

Lampe, G. W. H. 1967 'Church Discipline and the Interpretation of the Epistles to the Corinthians', 337–361 in Farmer, Moule & Niebuhr (eds.) 1967.

Lampe, P. 1990 'Theological Wisdom and the "Word About the Cross". The Rhetorical Scheme in I Corinthians 1–4', *Int* 44 (1990) 117–131.

Lampe, P. 1991 'Das korinthische Herrenmahl im Schnittpunkt hellenistisch-römischer Mahlpraxis und paulinischer Theologia Crucis (1 Kor 11, 17–34)', *ZNW* 82 (1991) 183–213.

Lane Fox, R. 1986 *Pagans and Christians*, Viking; Penguin Books: Harmondsworth, 1986.

Lang, F. 1986 *Die Briefe an die Korinther*, Das Neue Testament Deutsch, Band 7; Vandenhoeck und Ruprecht: Göttingen und Zürich, 1986.

Lash, N. 1986 *Theology on the Way to Emmaus*, SCM Press: London, 1986.

Lassen, E. M. 1991 'The Use of the Father Image in Imperial Propaganda and 1 Corinthians 4:14–21', *TynBul* 42 (1991) 127–136.

Levinskaya, I. A. 1990 'The Inscription from Aphrodisias and the Problem of God-Fearers', *TynBul* 41 (1990) 312–318.

Liddell, H. G., Scott, R. & Jones, H. S. 1940 *A Greek-English Lexicon*, 9th edn; 2 vols; The Clarendon Press: Oxford, 1940.

Lietzmann, D. H. & Kümmel, W. G. 1949 *An die Korinther I, II*, Handbuch zum Neuen Testament, Band 9, Ergänzte 4. Auflage; J. C. B. Mohr (Paul Siebeck): Tübingen, 1949.

Lightfoot, J. B. 1890a *The Apostolic Fathers. Part I: S. Clement of Rome. A Revised Text with Introductions, notes, dissertations and translations, Vol. 1;* Macmillan: London and New York, 1890.

Lightfoot, J. B. 1890b *The Apostolic Fathers. Part I: S. Clement of Rome. A Revised Text with Introductions, notes, dissertations and translations, Vol. 2;* Macmillan: London and New York, 1890.

Lim, T. H. 1987 'Not in Persuasive Words of Wisdom, 1 Cor 2.4.', *NovT* 29 (1987) 137–149.

Lincoln, A. T. & Wedderburn, A. J. M. 1993 *The Theology of the Later Pauline Letters*, New Testament Theology; Cambridge University Press: Cambridge, 1993.

Lindars, B. & Smalley, S. S. (eds.) 1975 *Christ and Spirit in the New Testament: Essays in honour of C.F.D. Moule*, Cambridge University Press: Cambridge, 1975.

Lindemann, A. 1979 *Paulus im ältesten Christentum: Das Bild des Apostels und die Rezeption der paulinischen Theologie in der frühchristlichen Literatur bis Marcion*, Beiträge zur historischen Theologie 58; J. C. B. Mohr (Paul Siebeck): Tübingen, 1979.

Lindemann, A. 1990 'Paul in the Writings of the Apostolic Fathers', 25–45 in Babcock (ed.) 1990.

Lindemann, A. 1992 *Die Clemensbriefe*, Handbuch zum Neuen Testament 17; Die Apostolischen Väter, I; J. C. B. Mohr (Paul Siebeck): Tübingen, 1992.

Litfin, D. 1994 *St. Paul's Theology of Proclamation: 1 Corinthians 1–4 and Greco-Roman rhetoric*, SNTSMS 79; Cambridge University Press: Cambridge, 1994.

Llewelyn, S. R. 1992 *New Documents Illustrating Early Christianity, Vol. 6: A Review of the Greek Inscriptions and Papyri published in 1980–81, with the collaboration of R.A. Kearsley*, The Ancient History Documentary Research Centre: Macquarrie University, 1992.

Lohfink, G. 1985 *Jesus and Community: The Social Dimension of Christian Faith*, SPCK: London, 1985.

Longenecker, R. N. 1990 *Galatians*, WBC 41; Word Books: Dallas, Texas, 1990.

Lüdemann, G. 1983 'A Chronology of Paul', 289–307 in Corley (ed.) 1983.

Lüdemann, G. 1984 *Paul, Apostle to the Gentiles: Studies in Chronology*, SCM Press: London, 1984.

Lüdemann, G. 1989 *Early Christianity According to the Traditions in Acts: A Commentary*, SCM: London, 1989.

Lührmann, D. 1975 'Wo man nicht mehr Sklave oder Freier ist. Überlegungen zur Struktur frühchristlicher Gemeinden', *Wort und Dienst* 13 (1975) 53–83.

Lührmann, D. 1981 'Neutestamentliche Haustafeln und antike Ökonomie', *NTS* 27 (1981) 83–97.

Lund, N. W. 1942 *Chiasmus in the New Testament: A Study in the Form and Function of Chiastic Structures*, University of North Carolina Press, 1942; reprinted by Hendrickson Publishers: Peabody, Massachusetts, 1992.

Lyon, D. 1975 *Christians and Sociology*, Inter-Varsity Press: Leicester, 1975.

MacDonald, D. R. 1983 *The Legend and the Apostle: The Battle for Paul in Story and Canon*, The Westminster Press: Philadelphia, 1983.

MacDonald, D. R. 1987 *There is No Male and Female: The Fate of a Dominical Saying in Paul and Gnosticism*, Harvard Dissertations in Religion 20; Fortress Press: Philadelphia, 1987.

MacDonald, M. Y. 1988 *The Pauline Churches: A socio-historical study of institutionalization in the Pauline and deutero-Pauline writings*, SNTSMS 60; Cambridge University Press: Cambridge, 1988.

MacDonald, M. Y. 1990 'Women Holy in Body and Spirit: The Social Setting of 1 Corinthians 7', *NTS* 36 (1990) 161–181.

MacIntyre, A. 1981 *After Virtue: a study in moral theory*, Duckworth: London, 1981.

MacMullen, R. 1974 *Roman Social Relations 50BC to AD284*, Yale University Press: New Haven and London, 1974.

Maier, H. O. 1991 *The Social Setting of the Ministry as Reflected in the Writings of Hermas, Clement and Ignatius*, Dissertations SR vol. 1, Canadian Corporation for Studies in Religion; Wilfred Laurier University Press: Waterloo, Ontario, Canada, 1991.

Malherbe, A. J. 1983 *Social Aspects of Early Christianity*, 2nd edn; Fortress Press: Philadelphia, 1983.

Malherbe, A. J. 1987 *Paul and the Thessalonians: The Philosophic Tradition of Pastoral Care*, Fortress Press: Philadelphia, 1987.

Malherbe, A. J. 1989 *Paul and the Popular Philosophers*, Fortress Press: Minneapolis, 1989.

Malina, B. J. 1979 'Review of Theissen, *Sociology of Early Palestinian Christianity*', *CBQ* 41 (1979) 176–178.

Malina, B. J. 1981 *The New Testament World: Insights From Cultural Anthropology*, SCM Press: London, 1983.

Malina, B. J. 1982 'Social Sciences and Biblical Interpretation', *Int* 36 (1982) 229–242.

Malina, B. J. 1985 'Review of W. Meeks, *The First Urban Christians*', *JBL* 104 (1985) 346–349.

Malina, B. J. 1986 *Christian Origins and Cultural Anthropology: Practical Models for Biblical Interpretation*, John Knox Press: Atlanta, 1986.

Mann, M. (ed.) 1983 *The Macmillan Student Encyclopedia of Sociology*, Macmillan Press: London, 1983.

Marsh, P. 1978 'Life and careers on the soccer terraces', reprinted as 361–372 in Potter (ed.) 1981.

Marshall, I. H. 1980a *Acts*, Tyndale New Testament Commentaries; Inter-Varsity Press: Leicester, England, 1980; Wm. B. Eerdmans: Grand Rapids, Michigan, 1980.

Marshall, I. H. 1980b *Last Supper and Lord's Supper*, Paternoster: Exeter, 1980.

Marshall, I. H. 1983 *1 and 2 Thessalonians*, New Century Bible Commentary; Marshall, Morgan & Scott: London, 1983.

Marshall, P. 1984 'Hybrists Not Gnostics in Corinth', SBLSP 1984, 275–287; Scholars Press: Chico, California, 1984.

Marshall, P. 1987 *Enmity in Corinth: Social Conventions in Paul's Relations with the Corinthians*, WUNT (2nd Series) 23; J. C. B. Mohr (Paul Siebeck): Tübingen, 1987.

Martin, D. B. 1990 *Slavery As Salvation: The Metaphor of Slavery in Pauline Christianity*, Yale University Press: New Haven and London, 1990.

Martin, D. B. 1991a 'Ancient Slavery, Class, and Early Christianity', *Fides et Historia* 23 (1991) 105–113.

Martin, D. B. 1991b 'Tongues of Angels and Other Status Indicators', *JAAR* 59 (1991) 547–589.

Martin, D. B. 1995 *The Corinthian Body*, Yale University Press: New Haven & London, 1995.

Martin, R. P. 1986 *2 Corinthians*, WBC 40; Word Books: Milton Keynes, England, 1986.

Martin, W. J. 1970 '1 Corinthians 11:2–16: An Interpretation', 231–41 in *Apostolic History and the Gospel: Biblical and Historical Essays presented to F. F. Bruce on his 60th Birthday*, W. W. Gasque & R. P. Martin (eds.), Paternoster: Exeter, 1970.

Martins, H. 1974 'Time and Theory in Sociology', 246–294 in *Approaches to Sociology: An Introduction to Major Trends in British Sociology*, J. Rex (ed.), Routledge & Kegan Paul: London and Boston, 1974.

Marx, K. & Engels, F. 1957 *On Religion*, Foreign Languages Publishing House: Moscow, 1957.

Mayer, A. 1983 *Der zensierte Jesus: Soziologie des Neuen Testaments*, Walter-Verlag: Olten, 1983.

Mayes, A. D. H. 1987 'Idealism and Materialism in Weber and Gottwald', *Proceedings of the Irish Biblical Association* 11 (1987) 44–58.

Mayes, A. D. H. 1989 *The Old Testament in Sociological Perspective*, Marshall Pickering: London, 1989.

McDonald, J. I. H. 1980 *Kerygma and Didache: The articulation and structure of the earliest Christian message*, SNTSMS, 37, Cambridge University Press: Cambridge, 1980.

Meeks, W. A. 1972 'The Man From Heaven In Johannine Sectarianism', *JBL* 91 (1972) 44–72.

Meeks, W. A. 1974 'The Image of the Androgyne: Some Uses of a Symbol in Earliest Christianity', *History of Religions* 13 (1974) 165–208.

Meeks, W. A. 1982a 'The Social Context of Pauline Theology', *Int* 36 (1982) 266–277.

Meeks, W. A. 1982b '"And Rose up to Play": Midrash and Paraenesis in 1 Corinthians 10:1–22', *JSNT* 16 (1982) 64–78.

Meeks, W. A. 1983 *The First Urban Christians: The Social World Of The Apostle Paul*, Yale University Press: New Haven and London, 1983.

Meeks, W. A. 1993 *The Origins of Christian Morality: The First Two Centuries*, Yale University Press: New Haven and London, 1993.

Meggitt, J. 1994 'Meat Consumption and Social Conflict in Corinth', *JTS* 45 (1994) 137–141.

Merklein, H. 1984 'Die Einheitlichkeit des ersten Korintherbriefes', *ZNW* 75 (1984) 153–183.

Metzger, B. M. 1971 *A Textual Commentary on the Greek New Testament*, United Bible Societies: London; New York, 1971; corrected edn 1975.

Metzger, B. M. 1977 *The Early Versions of the New Testament: Their Origin, Transmission, and Limitations*, Clarendon Press: Oxford, 1977.

Meyer, B. F. 1979 *The Aims of Jesus*, SCM Press: London, 1979.

Michaels, J. R. 1988 *1 Peter*, WBC 49; Word Books: Waco, Texas, 1988.

Mikat, P. 1969 *Die Bedeutung der Begriffe Stasis und Aponoia für das Verständnis des 1. Clemensbriefes*, Arbeitsgemeinschaft für Forschung des Landes Nordrhein-Westfalen; Geisteswissenschaften, Heft 135; Westdeutscher Verlag: Köln und Opladen, 1969.

Milbank, J. 1990 *Theology and Social Theory: Beyond Secular Reason*, Blackwell: Oxford, 1990.

Milburn, R. L. P. 1945 'The Persecution of Domitian', *Church Quarterly Review* 139 (1945) 154–164.

Miller, D. E. 1979 'Sectarianism and Secularization: The Work of Bryan Wilson', *Religious Studies Review* 5 (1979) 161–174.

Mitchell, A. C. 1993 'Rich and Poor in the Courts of Corinth: Litigiousness and Status in 1 Corinthians 6.1–11', *NTS* 39 (1993) 562–586.

Mitchell, G. D. (ed.) 1979 *A New Dictionary of Sociology*, Routledge & Kegan Paul: London, 1st edn 1968, new edn, 1979.

Mitchell, M. M. 1989 'Concerning περὶ δέ in 1 Corinthians', *NovT* 31 (1989) 229–256.

Mitchell, M. M. 1991 *Paul and the Rhetoric of Reconciliation: An Exegetical Investigation of the Language and Composition of 1 Corinthians*, Hermeneutische Untersuchungen zur Theologie 28; J. C. B. Mohr (Paul Siebeck): Tübingen, 1991.

Moiser, J. 1983 'A Reassessment of Paul's View of Marriage with reference to 1 Cor.7', *JSNT* 18 (1983) 103–122.

Moltmann, J. 1974 *The Crucified God: The Cross of Christ as the Foundation and Criticism of Christian Theology*, SCM Press: London, 1974.

Morgan, R with Barton, J. 1988 *Biblical Interpretation*, Oxford Bible Series; Oxford University Press: Oxford, 1988.

Morris, L. 1956 'Καὶ ἅπαξ καὶ δίς', *NovT* 1 (1956) 205–208.

Morris, L. 1988 *The Epistle to the Romans*, Wm. B. Eerdmans: Grand Rapids, Michigan; Inter-Varsity Press: Leicester, 1988.

Mosala, I. J. 1989 *Biblical Hermeneutics and Black Theology in South Africa*, Wm. B. Eerdmans: Grand Rapids, Michigan, 1989.

Moule, C. F. D. 1953 *An Idiom Book of New Testament Greek*, Cambridge University Press: Cambridge, 1953.

Moule, C. F. D 1961 *Worship in the New Testament*, Lutterworth Studies in Worship, 9; Lutterworth Press: London, 1961.

Moule, C. F. D. 1981 *The Birth of the New Testament*, 3rd edn; A. & C. Black: London, 1981.

Moulton, W. F., Geden, A. S., & Moulton, H. K. 1978 *A Concordance to the Greek Testament*, 5th edn; T. & T. Clark: Edinburgh, 1978.

Moulton, J. H. & Howard, W. F. 1979 *A Grammar of New Testament Greek*, by J. H. Moulton, *vol. II: Accidence and Word Formation*; T. & T. Clark: Edinburgh, 1979.

Moxnes, H. 1988 'Sociology and the New Testament', 143–159 in Karlsaune (ed.) 1988.

Munck, J. 1959 *Paul and the Salvation of Mankind*, SCM Press: London, 1959.

Munck, J. 1963 '1 Thess I. 9–10 and the Missionary Preaching of Paul', *NTS* 9 (1962/63) 95–110.

Munro, W. 1983 *Authority in Paul and Peter: The Identification of a Pastoral Stratum in the Pauline Corpus and 1 Peter*, SNTSMS 45; Cambridge University Press: Cambridge, 1983.

Munro, W. 1988 'Women, Text and the Canon: The Strange Case of 1 Corinthians 14: 33–35', *BTB* 18 (1988) 26–31.

Munro, W. 1990 'Interpolation in the Epistles: Weighing Probability', *NTS* 36 (1990) 431–443.

Murphy O'Connor, J. 1976 'The Non-Pauline Character of 1 Corinthians 11:2–16?', *JBL* 95 (1976), 615–621.

Murphy O'Connor, J. 1977 '1 Corinthians, V, 3–5', *RB* 84 (1977) 239–245.

Murphy O'Connor, J. 1978a 'Corinthian Slogans in 1 Cor 6:12–20', *CBQ* 40 (1978) 391–396.

Murphy O'Connor, J. 1978b 'Freedom or the Ghetto (1 Cor., VIII, 1–13; X,23–XI,1.)', *RB* 85 (1978) 543–574.

Murphy O'Connor, J. 1980 'Sex and Logic in 1 Corinthians 11:2–16', *CBQ* 42 (1980) 482–500.

Murphy O'Connor, J. 1981 'The Divorced Woman in 1 Cor 7:10–11', *JBL* 100 (1981) 601–606.

Murphy O'Connor, J. 1982 'Pauline Missions before the Jerusalem Conference', *RB* 89 (1982) 71–91.

Murphy O'Connor, J. 1983 *St. Paul's Corinth: Texts and Archaeology*, Good News Studies vol. 6; Michael Glazier: Wilmington, Delaware, 1983.

Murphy O'Connor, J. 1984 'The Corinth that Saint Paul saw', *Biblical Archaeologist* (Sept. 1984) 147–159.

Murphy O'Connor, J. 1986 'Interpolations in 1 Corinthians', *CBQ* 48 (1986) 81–94.

Murphy O'Connor, J. 1987 'Pneumatikoi in 2 Corinthians', *Proceedings of the Irish Biblical Association* 11 (1987) 59–66.

Murphy O'Connor, J. 1990 'Another Jesus (2 Cor 11:4)', *RB* 97 (1990) 238–251.

Murphy O'Connor, J. 1991a *The Theology of the Second Letter to the Corinthians*, Cambridge University Press: Cambridge, 1991.

Murphy O'Connor, J. 1991b 'The Date of 2 Corinthians 10–13', *ABR* 39 (1991) 31–43.

Neyrey, J. H. 1986 'Body Language in 1 Corinthians: The Use of Anthropological Models for Understanding Paul and His Opponents', *Semeia* 35 (1986) 129–170.

Nickle, K. F. 1966 *The Collection: A Study in Paul's Strategy*, Studies in Biblical Theology 48; SCM Press: London, 1966.

Nineham, D. 1975 'A Partner for Cinderella?', 143–154 in *What About the New Testament? Essays in Honour of Christopher Evans*, M. Hooker and C. Hickling (eds.), SCM Press: London, 1975.

Nineham. D. 1976 *The Use and Abuse of The Bible: A Study of the Bible in an Age of Rapid Cultural Change*, SPCK: London, 1978.

Nineham, D. 1982 'The Strangeness of the New Testament World', Part I, *Theology* 85 (1982) 171–77; Part II, *Theology* 85 (1982) 247–255.

O'Brien, P. T. 1982 *Colossians, Philemon*, WBC 44; Word Books: Waco, Texas; Milton Keynes, England, 1982.

O'Neill, J. C. 1972 *The Recovery of Paul's Letter to the Galatians*, SPCK: London, 1972.

O'Neill, J. C. 1975 *Paul's Letter to the Romans*, Penguin Books: Harmondsworth, 1975.

Oates, J. F., Samuel, A. E. & Welles, C. B. 1967 *Yale Papyri in the Beinecke Rare Book and Manuscript Library*, American Studies in Papyrology vol. 2, no. 1; American Studies in Papyrology, 1967.

Odell-Scott, D. W. 1983 'Let the Women Speak in Church: An Egalitarian Interpretation of 1 Cor 14:33b–36', *BTB* 13 (1983) 90–93.

Odell-Scott, D. W. 1987 'In Defense of An Egalitarian Interpretation of I Cor 14:34–36', *BTB* 17 (1987) 100–103.

Orr, W. F. & Walther, J. A. 1976 *1 Corinthians: A New Translation, Introduction with a Study of the Life of Paul, Notes and Commentary*, Anchor Bible; Doubleday: Garden City, New York, 1976.

Osiek, C. 1984 *What are they saying about the social setting of the New Testament?*, Paulist Press: New York / Ramsey, 1984.

Oster, R. E. 1988 'When Men Wore Veils to Worship: The Historical Context of 1 Corintians 11.4', *NTS* 34 (1988) 481–505.

Oster, R. E. 1992 'Use, Misuse and Neglect of Archaeological Evidence in Some Modern Works on 1 Corinthians (1 Cor 7,1–5; 8,10; 11,2–16; 12,14–26)', *ZNW* 83 (1992) 52–73.

Outhwaite, W. 1990 'Agency and Structure', 63–72, 85–86 in Clark, Modgil & Modgil (eds.) 1990.

Padgett, A. 1984 'Paul on Women in the Church: The Contradictions of Coiffure in 1 Cor 11.2–16', *JSNT* 20 (1984) 69–86.

Padgett, A. 1994 'The significance of ἀντί in 1 Cor. 11:15', *TynBul* 45 (1994) 181–187.

Pagels, E. H. 1974 'Paul and Women: A Response to Recent Discussion', *JAAR* 42 (1974) 538–549.

Pagels, E. H. 1975 *The Gnostic Paul: Gnostic Exegesis of the Pauline Letters*, Fortress Press: Philadelphia, 1975.

Paulsen, H. 1980 'Einheit und Freiheit der Söhne Gottes – Gal 3. 26–29', *ZNW* 71 (1980) 74–95.

Payne, P. B. 1993 'Man and Woman in Christ: the text of 1 Cor 14.34–35 and οὐδέ in 1 Tim 2:12', Unpublished paper delivered to Cambridge New Testament Seminar 11.5.93 (see also Payne 1995).

Payne, P. B. 1995 'Fuldensis, Sigla for variants in Vaticanus, and 1 Cor 14.34–5', *NTS* 41 (1995) 240–262.

Payne, P. B. forthcoming *Man and Woman: One in Christ*, Zondervan: Grand Rapids.

Pearson, B. A. 1973 *The Pneumatikos-Psychikos Terminology in 1 Corinthians: A Study in the Theology of the Corinthian Opponents of Paul and Its Relation to Gnosticism*, SBLDS 12; Scholars Press: Missoula, Montana, 1973.

Peretto, E. 1989 'Clemente Romano ai Corinti. Sfida alla violenza', *Vetera Christianorum* 26 (1989) 89–114.

Perriman, A. C. 1994 'The Head of a Woman: The Meaning of ΚΕΦΑΛΗ in 1 Cor. 11:3', *JTS* 45 (1994) 602–622.

Petersen, N. 1986 'Pauline Baptism and "Secondary Burial" ', *HTR* 79 (1986) 217–226.

Phipps, W. E. 1982 'Is Paul's Attitude toward Sexual Relations Contained in 1 Cor 7.1?', *NTS* 28 (1982) 125–131.

Plank, K. A. 1987 *Paul and the Irony of Affliction*, SBL Semeia Studies; Scholars Press: Atlanta, Georgia, 1987.

Pleket, H. W. 1985 'Review of Meeks, *The First Urban Christians*', *VC* 39 (1985) 192–196.

Plummer, A. 1915 *A critical and exegetical commentary on the Second Epistle of St. Paul to the Corinthians*, ICC; T. & T. Clark: Edinburgh, 1915.

Polkinghorne, J. 1989 *Science and Providence: God's Interaction with the World*, SPCK: London, 1989.

Pomeroy, S. B. 1975 *Goddesses, Whores, Wives and Slaves: Women in Classical Antiquity*, Robert Hale: London, 1976.

Potter, D. (ed.) 1981 *Society and the Social Sciences*, Routledge & Kegan Paul: London and Henley; with the Open University Press, 1981.

Pred, A. 1982 'Social reproduction and the time-geography of everyday life', 157–186 in *A Search for Common Ground*, P. Gould and G. Olsson (eds.), Pion: London, 1982.

Radcliffe, T. 1990 'Paul and Sexual Identity: 1 Corinthians 11.2–16', 66–72, in *After Eve: Women, Theology and the Christian Tradition*, J. M. Soskice, (ed.), Women in Religion; Collins, Marshall Pickering: London, 1990.

Ranke, E. 1868 *Codex Fuldensis: Novum Testamentum Latine interprete Hieronymo ex manuscripto Victoris Capuani*, N. G. Elwert: Marburg & Leipzig, 1868.

Reiss, A. J., Eisenstadt, S. N., Lécuyer, B. & Oberschall, A. R. 1968 'Sociology', IESS, vol. 15, 1–53.

Remus, H. E. 1982 'Sociology of knowledge and the study of early Christianity', *Sciences Religieuses / Studies in Religion* 11 (1982) 45–56.

Richardson, P. 1980 'Pauline Inconsistency: 1 Corinthians 9:19–23 and Galatians 2:11–14', *NTS* 26 (1979/80) 347–362.

Richardson, P. 1983 'Judgment in Sexual Matters in 1 Corinthians 6:1–11', *NovT* 25 (1983) 37–58.

Richardson, P. 1986 'On the Absence of "Anti-Judaism" in 1 Corinthians', 59–74 in *Anti-Judaism in Early Christianity; Vol. 1. Paul and the Gospels*, Studies in Christianity and Judaism No. 2, P. Richardson with D. Granskou (eds.), Wilfred Laurier University Press: Ontario, Canada, 1986.

Richter, P. J. 1984 'Recent Sociological Approaches to the Study of the New Testament', *Religion* 14 (1984) 77–90.

Riis, O. 1988 'The Uses of Sociological Theory in Theology – Examplified [sic] by Gerd Theissen's Study of Early Christianity', 161–178 in Karlsaune (ed.) 1988.

Robertson, A. and Plummer, A. 1914 *A Critical and Exegetical Commentary on the First Epistle of St Paul to the Corinthians*, ICC; T. & T. Clark: Edinburgh, 1914, 2nd edn.

Robinson, J. A. T. 1976 *Redating the New Testament*, SCM Press: London, 1976.

Robinson, J. M. & Koester, H. 1971 *Trajectories through Early Christianity*, Fortress Press: Philadelphia, 1971.

Rodd, C. S. 1979 'Max Weber and Ancient Judaism', *SJT* 32 (1979) 452–469.

Rodd, C. S. 1981 'On Applying a Sociological Theory to Biblical Studies', *Journal for the Study of the Old Testament* 19 (1981) 95–106.

Rodd, C. S. 1990 'Sociology and Social Anthropology', 635–639 in *A Dictionary of Biblical Interpretation*, R. J. Coggins & J. L. Houlden (eds.), SCM Press: London; Trinity Press International: Philadelphia, 1990.

Rohrbaugh, R. L. 1984 'Methodological Considerations in the Debate over the Social Class Status of Early Christians', *JAAR* 52 (1984) 519–546.

Roloff, J. 1988 *Der erste Brief an Timotheus*, EKKNT 15; Benziger Verlag: Zürich; Neukirchener Verlag: Neukirchen-Vluyn, 1988.

Rowland, C. C. 1985a *Christian Origins: An account of the character and setting of the most important messianic sect of Judaism*, SPCK: London, 1985.

Rowland, C. C. 1985b 'Reading the New Testament Sociologically: An Introduction', *Theology* 88 (1985) 358–364.

Rowland, C. C. 1988 *Radical Christianity: A Reading of Recovery*, Polity Press: Cambridge, 1988.

Rowland, C. C. & Corner, M. 1990 *Liberating Exegesis: The Challenge of Liberation Theology to Biblical Studies*, Biblical Foundations in Theology; SPCK: London, 1990.

Russell, E. A. 1989 'Godly Concord: en homonoia (1 Clement 9.4)', *Irish Biblical Studies* 11 (1989) 186–196.

Ryan, A. 1981 'Is the study of society a science?' 8–33 in Potter (ed.) 1981.

Saller, R. P. 1982 *Personal Patronage under the Early Empire*, Cambridge University Press: Cambridge, 1982.

Saller, R. P. 1991 'Corporal Punishment, Authority, and Obedience in the Roman Household', 144–165 in *Marriage, Divorce, and Children in Ancient Rome*, B. Rawson (ed.), Humanities Research Centre: Canberra; Clarendon Press: Oxford, 1991.

Sanday, W. & Headlam, A. C. 1896 *A Critical and Exegetical Commentary on the Epistle to the Romans*, ICC; T. & T. Clark: Edinburgh, 1896.

Sanders, E. P. 1977 *Paul and Palestinian Judaism*, SCM Press: London, 1977.

Sanders, E. P. 1991 *Paul*, Past Masters; Oxford University Press: Oxford; New York, 1991.

Sanders, L. 1943 *L'Hellénisme de Saint Clément de Rome et le Paulinisme*, Studia Hellenistica; Catholic University of Louvain: Louvain, 1943.

Sänger, D. 1985 'Die δυνατοί in 1 Kor 1 26', *ZNW* 76 (1985) 285–291.

Savage, T. B. 1986 *Power through Weakness: An Historical and Exegetical Examination of Paul's Understanding of the Ministry in 2 Corinthians*, PhD thesis; Cambridge University, 1986.

Schmithals, W. 1971 *Gnosticism in Corinth: An investigation of the letters to the Corinthians*, Abingdon Press: Nashville, New York, 1971.

Schöllgen, G. 1988 'Was wissen wir über die Sozialstruktur der Paulinischen Gemeinden?', *NTS* 34 (1988) 71–82.

Schottroff, L. 1985 '»Nicht viele Mächtige«, Annäherungen an eine Soziologie des Urchristentums', 247–256 in *Befreiungserfahrungen: Studien zur Sozialgeschichte des Neuen Testaments*, Theologische Bücherei Band 82; Chr. Kaiser Verlag; München, 1990.

Schrage, W. 1991 *Der Erste Brief an die Korinther, 1. Teilband; 1 Kor 1,1–6,11*, EKKNT 7.1; Benziger: Zürich and Braunschweig; Neukirchener: Neukirchen-Vluyn, 1991.

Schreiber, A. 1977 *Die Gemeinde in Korinth: Versuch einer gruppendynamischer Betrachtung der Entwicklung der Gemeinde von Korinth auf der Basis des ersten Korintherbriefes*, Aschendorff: Münster, Westfalen, 1977.

Schütz, J. H. 1982 'Introduction to *The Social Setting of Pauline Christianity*', by G. Theissen (1982).

Schweitzer, E. 1967 *The Lord's Supper According to the New Testament*, Facet Books, Biblical Series 18; Fortress Press: Philadelphia, 1967.

Scott, J. M. 1992 *Adoption as Sons of God: An Exegetical Investigation into the Background of ΥΙΟΘΕΣΙΑ in the Pauline Corpus*, WUNT, 2. Reihe, 48; J. C. B. Mohr (Paul Siebeck): Tübingen, 1992.

Scroggs, R. 1972 'Paul and the Eschatological Woman', *JAAR* 40 (1972) 283–303.

Scroggs, R. 1974 'Paul and the Eschatological Woman: Revisited', *JAAR* 42 (1974) 532–537.

Scroggs, R. 1975 'The Earliest Christian Communities as Sectarian Movement', 1–23 in *Christianity, Judaism and Other Greco-Roman Cults*, Studies for Morton Smith at Sixty; Part Two: Early Christianity, J. Neusner (ed.), E. J. Brill; Leiden, 1975.

Scroggs, R. 1980 'The Sociological Interpretation of the New Testament: The Present State of Research', *NTS* 26 (1980) 164–179.

Sellin, G. 1982 'Das »Geheimnis« der Weisheit und das Rätsel der »Christuspartei« (zu 1 Kor 1–4)', *ZNW* 73 (1982) 69–96.

Sellin, G. 1987 'Hauptprobleme des Ersten Korintherbriefes', *ANRW* II.25.4, 2940–3044.

Sellin, G. 1991 '1 Korinther 5–6 und der "Vorbrief" nach Korinth', *NTS* 37 (1991) 535–558.

Semler, J. S. 1776 *Paraphrasis II: Epistolae ad Corinthos*, Halle, 1776.

Shaw, G. 1983 *The Cost of Authority: Manipulation and Freedom in the New Testament*, SCM Press: London, 1983.

Sherwin-White, A. N. 1963 *Roman Society and Roman Law in the New Testament*, Clarendon Press: Oxford, 1963.

Shoemaker, T. P. 1987 'Unveiling of Equality: 1 Corinthians 11:2–16', *BTB* 17 (1987) 60–63.

Sills, D. L. (ed.) 1968 *International Encyclopedia of the Social Sciences*, 17 vols; The Macmillan and The Free Press: USA, 1968.

Skocpol, T. (ed.) 1984 *Vision and Method in Historical Sociology*, Cambridge University Press; Cambridge, 1984.

Slattery, M. 1985 *The ABC of Sociology: A Series from New Society*, Macmillan Education Ltd: London and Basingstoke, 1985.

Smith, J. Z. 1975 'The Social Description of Early Christianity', *Religious Studies Review* 1 (1975) 19–25.

Smith, J. Z. 1978 'Too much Kingdom, Too little Community', *Zygon* 13 (1978) 123–130.

Sölle, D. 1974 *Political Theology*, translated and with an introduction by John Shelley, Fortress Press: Philadelphia, 1974.

Spicq, C. 1994 *Theological Lexicon of the New Testament*, 3 vols, translated and edited by J. D. Ernest, Hendrickson: Massachusetts, 1994.

Stambaugh, J. & Balch, D. 1986 *The Social World of the First Christians*, SPCK: London, 1986.

Stanley, D. 1984 'Imitation in Paul's Letters: Its Significance for His Relationship to Jesus and to His Own Christian Foundations', 127–141 in Hurd and Richardson (eds.) 1984.

Ste. Croix, G. E. M. de 1975 'Early Christian Attitudes to Property and Slavery', 1–38 in *Studies in Church History, vol. 12, Church, Society and Politics*, D. Baker (ed.), Basil Blackwell: Oxford, 1975.

Ste. Croix, G. E. M. de 1981 *The Class Struggle in the Ancient Greek World: from the Archaic Age to the Arab Conquests*, Duckworth: London, 1981, 2nd impression (corrected) 1983.

Stein, A. 1968 'Wo trugen die korinthische Christen ihre Rechtshändel aus?', *ZNW* 59 (1968) 86–90.

Stendahl, K. 1963 'The Apostle Paul and the Introspective Conscience of the West', 78–96 in *Paul among Jews and Gentiles*, SCM Press: London, 1977.

Stephenson, A. M. G. 1964 'Partition theories on II Corinthians', *Studia Evangelica* 2, 639–646, F. L. Cross (ed.), TU 87; Akademie-Verlag: Berlin, 1964.

Stephenson, A. M. G. 1965 'A Defence of the Integrity of 2 Corinthians', 82–97 in *The Authorship and Integrity of the New Testament*, K. Aland et al., SPCK Theological Collections 4; SPCK: London, 1965.

Stinchcombe, A. 1990 'Milieu and Structure Updated: A Critique of the Theory of Structuration', 47–56, 59–60 in Clark, Modgil & Modgil (eds.) 1990.

Stowers, S. K. 1984 'Social Status, Public Speaking and Private Teaching: The Circumstances of Paul's Preaching Activity', *NovT* 26 (1984) 59–82.

Stowers, S. K. 1985 'The Social Sciences and the Study of Early Christianity', 149–181 in *Approaches to Ancient Judaism, vol. 5, Studies in Judaism and Its Greco-Roman Context*, W. S. Green (ed.), Scholars Press: Atlanta, Georgia, 1985.

Stowers, S. K. 1990 'Peri men gar and the Integrity of 2 Cor. 8 and 9', *NovT* 32 (1990) 340–348.

Stowers, S. K. 1994 *A Rereading of Romans: Justice, Jews, and Gentiles*, Yale University Press: New Haven and London, 1994.

Stuhlmacher, P. 1975 *Der Brief an Philemon*, EKKNT; Benziger Verlag: Zürich; Einsiedeln; Köln; Neukirchener Verlag: Neukirchen-Vluyn, 1975.

Sturdy, J. V. M. 1979 'Review of *Redating the New Testament*, by J. A. T. Robinson', *JTS* 30 (1979) 255–262.

Sumney, J. L. 1990 *Identifying Paul's Opponents: The Question of Method in 2 Corinthians*, JSNTSup 40; JSOT Press: Sheffield, 1990.

Talbert, C. H. 1987 *Reading Corinthians: A New Commentary for Preachers*, SPCK: London, 1987.

Tannehill, R. C. 1967 *Dying and Rising with Christ: A Study in Pauline Theology*, Beihefte zur ZNW 32; Alfred Töpelmann: Berlin, 1967.

Taylor, N. H. 1991 'The Composition and Chronology of Second Corinthians', *JSNT* 44 (1991) 67–87.

Taylor, R. D. 1986 'Toward a Biblical Theology of Litigation: A Law Professor looks at I Cor.6.1–11', *Ex Auditu* 2 (1986) 105–116.

Theissen, G. 1974a 'Theoretische Probleme religionssoziologischer Forschung und die Analyse der Urchristentums', *Neue Zeitschrift für Systematische Theologie und Religionsphilosophie* 16 (1974) 35–56, cited from reprint in Theissen 1979b/1988a, 55–76 (ET now in Theissen 1993, 231–254).

Theissen, G. 1974b 'Social Stratification in the Corinthian Community: A Contribution to the Sociology of Early Hellenistic Christianity', German original in *ZNW* 65 (1974) 232–272; also in Theissen 1979b/1988a, 231–271; cited from ET in Theissen 1982, 69–119.

Theissen, G. 1974c 'Social Integration and Sacramental Activity: An Analysis of 1 Cor. 11:17–34', German original in *NovT* 16 (1974) 179–206; also in Theissen 1979b/1988a, 290–317; cited from ET in Theissen 1982, 145–174.

Theissen, G. 1975a 'The Sociological Interpretation of Religious Traditions: Its Methodological Problems as Exemplified in Early Christianity', German original in *Kairos* 17 (1975) 284–299; also in Theissen 1979b/1988a, 35–54; cited from ET in Theissen 1982, 175–200.

Theissen, G. 1975b 'The Strong and the Weak in Corinth: A Sociological Analysis of a Theological Quarrel', German original in *Evangelische Theologie* 35 (1975) 155–172; also in Theissen 1979b/1988a, 272–289; cited from ET in Theissen 1982, 121–143.

Theissen, G. 1975c 'Legitimation and Subsistence: An Essay on the Sociology of Early Christian Missionaries', German original in *NTS* 21 (1974/75) 192–221; also in Theissen 1979b/1988a, 201–230; cited from ET in Theissen 1982, 27–67.

Theissen, G. 1978 *The First Followers of Jesus: A Sociological Analysis of the Earliest Christianity*, SCM Press: London, 1978.

Theissen, G. 1979a 'Zur forschungsgeschichtlichen Einordnung der soziologischen Fragestellung', 3–34 in Theissen 1979b/1988a.

Theissen, G. 1979b *Studien zur Soziologie des Urchristentums*, WUNT 19; J. C. B. Mohr (Paul Siebeck): Tübingen, 1979 (see also Theissen 1988a).

Theissen, G. 1979c *On Having a Critical Faith*, SCM Press: London, 1979.

Theissen, G. 1982 *The Social Setting of Pauline Christianity*, edited and translated by John Schütz, T. & T. Clark: Edinburgh, 1982.

Theissen, G. 1983 'Christologie und soziale Erfahrung. Wissenssoziologische Aspekte paulinischer Christologie', 318–330 in Theissen 1988a; ET now in Theissen 1993, 187–201.

Theissen, G. 1985 'Review of W. Meeks, *The First Urban Christians*', *Journal of Religion* 65 (1985) 111–113.

Theissen, G. 1987 *Psychological Aspects of Pauline Theology*, translated by John Galvin, T. & T. Clark: Edinburgh, 1987.

Theissen, G. 1988a *Studien zur Soziologie des Urchristentums*, 2nd edn, 1983; 3rd edn, 1988; WUNT 19; J. C. B. Mohr (Paul Siebeck): Tübingen, 1988.

Theissen, G. 1988b 'Vers une théorie de l'histoire sociale du Christianisme primitif', *Études Théologiques et Religieuses* 63 (1988) 199–225; ET now (with slight additions) in Theissen 1993, 257–287.

Theissen, G. 1993 *Social Reality and the Early Christians: Theology, Ethics, and the World of the New Testament*, translated by Margaret Kohl, T. & T. Clark: Edinburgh, 1993.

Thiselton, A. C. 1978 'Realised Eschatology at Corinth', *NTS* 24 (1978) 510–526.

Thomason, B. C. 1982 *Making Sense of Reification: Alfred Schutz and Constructionist Theory*, Macmillan: London and Basingstoke, 1982.

Thompson, G. A. & Theodorson, A. G. 1970 *A Modern Dictionary of Sociology*, Methuen: London, 1970.

Thompson, J. B. 1981 *Critical Hermeneutics: A study in the thought of Paul Ricoeur and Jürgen Habermas*, Cambridge University Press: Cambridge, 1981.

Thompson, J. B. 1984 *Studies in the Theory of Ideology*, Polity Press: Cambridge, 1984.

Thompson, J. B. 1989 'The Theory of Structuration', 56–76 in Held & Thompson (eds.) 1989.

Thrall, M. E. 1962 *Greek Particles in the New Testament: Linguistic and Exegetical Studies*, New Testament Tools and Studies, B. M. Metzger (ed.), vol. 3; E. J. Brill: Leiden, 1962.

Thrall, M. E. 1975 'Christ crucified or second Adam? A christological debate between Paul and the Corinthians', 143–156 in *Christ and Spirit in the New Testament*, Essays in Honour of C. F. D. Moule, B. Lindars and S. S. Smalley (eds.), Cambridge University Press: Cambridge, 1975.

Thrall, M. E. 1978 'The Problem of II Cor. VI.14–VII.1 in Some Recent Discussion', *NTS* 24 (1978) 132–148.

Thrall, M. E. 1980 'Super-Apostles, Servants of Christ, and Servants of Satan', *JSNT* 6 (1980) 42–57.

Thrall, M. E. 1982 'A Second Thanksgiving Period in II Corinthians', *JSNT* 16 (1982) 101–124.

Thrall, M. E. 1994 *A Critical and Exegetical Commentary on the Second Epistle to the Corinthians*, ICC; T. & T. Clark: Edinburgh, 1994.

Thrift, N. 1985 'Bear and mouse or bear and tree? Anthony Giddens's reconstitution of social theory', *Sociology* 19 (1985) 609–623.

Tidball, D 1983 *An Introduction to the Sociology of the New Testament*, Paternoster Press: Exeter, 1983.

Tiryakian, E. A. 1985 'Review of W. Meeks, *The First Urban Christians*', *American Journal of Sociology* 90 (1985) 1138–1140.

Tomson, P. J. 1990 *Paul and the Jewish Law: Halakha in the Letters of the Apostle to the Gentiles*, Van Gorcum: Assen/ Maastricht; Fortress Press: Minneapolis, 1990.

Towner, P. H. 1989 *The Goal of Our Instruction: The Structure of Theology and Ethics in the Pastoral Epistles*, JSNTSup 34; JSOT Press: Sheffield, 1989.

Tracy, D. 1978 'A Theological Response to *"Kingdom and Community"'*, *Zygon* 13 (1978) 131–135.

Travis, S. H. 1973 'Paul's Boasting in 2 Corinthians 10–12', *Studia Evangelica* 6, 527–632, E. A. Livingstone (ed.), TU 112; Akademie-Verlag: Berlin, 1973.

Trible, P. 1993 'Treasures Old and New: Biblical Theology and the Challenge of Feminism', 32–56 in Watson (ed.) 1993a.

Troeltsch, E. 1931 *The Social Teaching of the Christian Churches, vol. 1*, George Allen & Unwin Ltd: London; Macmillan: New York, 1931.

Trompf, G. W. 1980 'On Attitudes Toward Women in Paul and Paulinist Literature: 1 Corinthians 11:3–16 and Its Context', *CBQ* 42 (1980) 196–215.

Trummer, P. 1975 'Die Chance der Freiheit. Zur Interpretation des μᾶλλον χρῆσαι in 1 Kor 7,21', *Biblica* 56 (1975) 344–368.

Tuckett, C. M. 1987 *Reading the New Testament: methods of interpretation*, SPCK: London, 1987.

Turner, J. H. 1974 *The Structure of Sociological Theory*, Dorsey Press: Homewood, Illinois, 1974.

Turner, J. H. 1986 'Review Essay: The Theory of Structuration', *American Journal of Sociology* 91 (1986) 969–977.

Turner, J. H. 1987 'Analytical Theorizing', 156–194 in Giddens & Turner (eds.) 1987.

Turner, J. H. 1990 'Giddens's Analysis of Functionalism: A Critique', 103–110, 112–114 in Clark, Modgil & Modgil (eds.) 1990.

Turner, N. 1963 *A Grammar of New Testament Greek*, by J. H. Moulton, *vol. III; Syntax*, T. & T. Clark: Edinburgh, 1963.

Unnik, W. C. van 1950 'Is 1 Clement 20 purely Stoic?', *VC* 4 (1950) 181–189.

Unnik, W. C. van 1970 '„Tiefer Friede" (1. Klemens 2,2)', *VC* 24 (1970) 261–279.

Unnik, W. C. van 1972 'Noch einmal „Tiefer Friede"', *VC* 26 (1972) 24–28.

Urry, J. 1982 'Duality of Structure: Some Critical Issues', *Theory, Culture and Society* 1, no. 2; A Symposium on Giddens, (1982) 100–106.

Vanhoye, A. (ed.) 1986 *L'Apôtre Paul: Personnalité, Style et Conception du Ministère*, Bibliotheca Epheridum Theologicarum Lovaniensium 73; Leuven University Press: Leuven, 1986.

Venetz, H-J. 1985 'Der Beitrag der Soziologie zur Lektüre des Neuen Testaments. Ein Bericht', *Theologische Berichte* 13 (1985) *Methoden der Evangelien-Exegese*, 87–121.

Verner, D. C. 1983 *The Household of God: The Social World of the Pastoral Epistles*, SBLDS 71; Scholars Press: Chico, California, 1983.

Vielhauer, P. 1975a *Geschichte der Urchristlichen Literatur*, Walter de Gruyter: Berlin, New York, 1975.

Vielhauer, P. 1975b 'Paulus und die Kephaspartei in Korinth', *NTS* 21 (1975) 341–352.

Vischer, L. 1955 *Die Auslegungsgeschichte von I. Kor. 6,1–11. Rechtsverzicht und Schlichtung*, Beiträge zur Geschichte der neutestamentliche Exegese 1; J. C. B. Mohr (Paul Siebeck): Tübingen, 1955.

Wagner, G. 1967 *Pauline Baptism and the Pagan Mysteries: The Problem of the Pauline Doctrine of Baptism in Romans VI. 1–11, in the light of its Religio-Historical "Parallels"*, Oliver and Boyd: Edinburgh and London, 1967.

Walker, W. O. 1975 '1 Corinthians 11:2–16 and Paul's Views Regarding Women', *JBL* 94 (1975) 94–110.

Walker, W. O. 1983 'The "Theology of Woman's Place" and the "Paulinist" Tradition', *Semeia* 28 (1983) 101–112.

Walker, W. O. 1987 'The Burden of Proof in Identifying Interpolations in the Pauline Letters', *NTS* 33 (1987) 610–618.

Walker, W. O. 1988 'Text-Critical Evidence for Interpolations in the Letters of Paul', *CBQ* 50 (1988) 622–631.

Walker, W. O. 1989 'The Vocabulary of 1 Corinthians 11.3–16: Pauline or Non-Pauline?', *JSNT* 35 (1989) 75–88.

Watson, D. F. 1991 *Persuasive Artistry: Studies in New Testament Rhetoric in Honor of George A. Kennedy*, JSNTSup 50; JSOT Press: Sheffield, 1991.

Watson, F. 1984 '2 Cor. x–xiii and Paul's Painful Letter to the Corinthians', *JTS* 35 (1984) 324–346.

Watson, F. 1986 *Paul, Judaism and the Gentiles: A Sociological Approach*, SNTSMS 56; Cambridge University Press: Cambridge, 1986.

Watson, F. 1992a 'Christ, Community, and the Critique of Ideology: A Theological Reading of 1 Corinthians 1.18–31', *Nederlands Theologisch Tijdschrift* 46 (1992) 132–149.

Watson, F. 1992b 'Strategies of Recovery and Resistance: Hermeneutical Reflections on Genesis 1–3 and its Pauline reception', *JSNT* 45 (1992) 79–103.

Watson, F. (ed.) 1993a *The Open Text: New Directions for Biblical Studies?*, SCM Press: London, 1993.

Watson, N. 1992c *The First Epistle to the Corinthians*, Epworth Commentaries; Epworth Press: London, 1992.

Watson, N. 1993b *The Second Epistle to the Corinthians*, Epworth Commentaries; Epworth Press: London, 1993.

Wedderburn, A. J. M. 1980 'Keeping up with Recent Studies: Some Recent Pauline Chronologies', *ExpTim* 92 (1980) 103–108.

Wedderburn, A. J. M. 1987 *Baptism and Resurrection: Studies in Pauline Theology against Its Graeco-Roman Background*, WUNT 44; J. C. B. Mohr (Paul Siebeck): Tübingen, 1987.

Weiser, A. 1983 'Die Rolle der Frau in der urchristlichen Mission', 158–181 in Dautzenberg, Merklein & Müller (eds.) 1983.

Weiss, J. 1910 *Der erste Korintherbrief*, Kritisch-exegetischer Kommentar über das Neue Testament begründet von H. A. W. Meyer, fünfte Abteilung, 9. Auflage; Vandenhoeck und Ruprecht: Göttingen, 1910.

Welborn, L. L. 1984 'On the Date of First Clement', *Biblical Research* 29 (1984) 35–54.

Welborn, L. L. 1987 'On the Discord in Corinth: 1 Corinthians 1–4 and Ancient Politics', *JBL* 106 (1987) 85–111.

Welborn, L. L. 1995 'The Identification of 2 Corinthians 10–13 with the "Letter of Tears" ', *NovT* 37 (1995) 138–153.

Wengst, K. 1987 *Pax Romana and the Peace of Jesus Christ*, SCM Press: London, 1987.

Wengst, K. 1988 *Humility: Solidarity of the Humiliated. The transformation of an attitude and its social relevance in Graeco-Roman, Old Testament–Jewish and Early Christian tradition*, SCM Press: London, 1988.

Westermann, W. L. 1943 'Slavery and the Elements of Freedom in Ancient Greece', *Quarterly Bulletin of the Polish Institute of Arts and Sciences in America* (1943) 1–16; cited from reprint in Finley (ed.) 1960, 17–32.

Westermann, W. L. 1955 *The Slave Systems of Greek and Roman Antiquity*, The American Philosophical Society; Independence Square, Philadelphia, 1955.

Whelan, C. F. 1993 'Amica Pauli: The Role of Phoebe in the Early Church', *JSNT* 49 (1993) 67–85.

Wiefel, W. 1991 'The Jewish Community in Ancient Rome and the Origins of Roman Christianity', 85–101 in Donfried (ed.) 1991.

Willis, W. L. 1985a *Idol Meat in Corinth: The Pauline Argument in 1 Corinthians 8 and 10*, SBLDS 68; Scholars Press: Chico, California, 1985.

Willis, W. L. 1985b 'An Apostolic Apologia? The Form and Function of 1 Corinthians 9', *JSNT* 24 (1985) 33–48.

Willis, W. L. 1991 'Corinthusne deletus est?', *Biblische Zeitschrift* 35 (1991) 233–241.

Wilson, B. R. 1961 *Sects and Society: A Sociological Study of Three Religious Groups in Britain*, Heinemann; London, 1961.

Wilson, B. R. 1963 'A Typology of Sects', 361–383 in *Sociology of Religion*, R. Robertson (ed.), Penguin: Harmondsworth, 1969.

Wilson, B. R. (ed.) 1967 *Patterns of Sectarianism: Organisation and Ideology in Social and Religious Movements*, Heinemann; London, 1967.

Windisch, H. 1924 *Der zweite Korintherbrief*, Kritisch-exegetischer Kommentar über das Neue Testament begründet von H. A. W. Meyer; part 6, 9th edn; Vandenhoeck & Ruprecht: Göttingen, 1924.

Winter, B. W. 1991 'Civil Litigation in Secular Corinth and the Church. The Forensic Background to 1 Corinthians 6.1–8', *NTS* 37 (1991) 559–572.

Winter, S. C. 1987 'Paul's Letter to Philemon', *NTS* 33 (1987) 1–15.

Wire, A. C. 1990 *The Corinthian Women Prophets: A Reconstruction through Paul's Rhetoric*, Fortress Press: Minneapolis, 1990.

Wisemann, J. 1979 'Corinth and Rome I: 228 BC – AD 267', *ANRW* II.7.1, 438–548.

Witherington, B. 1988 *Women in The Earliest Churches*, SNTSMS 59; Cambridge University Press: Cambridge, 1988.

Wolff, C. 1989 'Humility and Self-Denial in Jesus' Life and Message and in the Apostolic Existence of Paul', 145–160 in Wedderburn, A. J. M. (ed.), *Paul and Jesus: Collected Essays*, JSNTSup 37; JSOT Press: Sheffield, 1989. German original in *NTS* 34 (1988) 183–196.

Wong, D. W. F. 1977 'Natural and Divine Order in 1 Clement', *VC* 31 (1977) 81–87.

Wright, E. O. 1989 'Models of historical trajectory: an assessment of Giddens' critique of Marxism', 77–102 in Held & Thompson (eds.) 1989.

Wright, N. T. 1991 *The Climax of the Covenant: Christ and the Law in Pauline Theology*, T. &. T. Clark: Edinburgh, 1991.

Wuellner, W. 1973 'The Sociological Implications of I Corinthians 1: 26–28 reconsidered', *Studia Evangelica* 6, 666–672, E. A. Livingstone (ed.), TU 112; Akademie-Verlag: Berlin, 1973.

Wuellner, W. 1978 'Ursprung und Verwendung der σοφός-, δυνατός-, εὐγενής- Formel in I Kor I,26', 165–184 in *Domum Gentilicium*, New Testament Studies in Honour of David Daube, E. Bammel, C. K. Barrett & W. D. Davies (eds.), Clarendon Press: Oxford, 1978.

Wuellner, W. 1979 'Greek Rhetoric and Pauline Argumentation', 177–188 in *Early Christian Literature and the Classical Intellectual Tradition*, in honorem Robert M. Grant, W. R. Schoedel & R. L. Wilken (eds.), Théologie Historique 53; Éditions Beauchesne: Paris, 1979.

Wuellner, W. 1982 'Tradition and Interpretation of the "Wise-Power-ful-Noble" Triad in I Cor 1, 26', *Studia Evangelica* 7, 557–562, E. A. Livingstone (ed.), TU 126; Akademie-Verlag: Berlin, 1982.

Yoder, J. H. 1972 *The Politics of Jesus*, Wm. B. Eerdmans: Grand Rapids, Michigan, 1972.

Young, F. 1994 *The Theology of the Pastoral Letters*, New Testament Theology; Cambridge University Press: Cambridge, 1994.

Ziesler, J. 1989 *Paul's Letter to the Romans*, TPI New Testament Commentaries; SCM Press: London; Trinity Press International: Philadelphia, 1989.

Index of ancient references

Index of names

Index of subjects

anthropology 17, 27–29, 31, 33
apostles, apostolic image and lifestyle
5, 75–77, 130, 135, 144, 199–
216, 217, 219, 221–29, 231,
234, 283

banquets (see meals)
baptism 78–79, 82–86, 88, 117–
18, 144, 155, 170

collection, Paul's 90, 219, 225,
231–31, 297–98, 303–307
consequences, intended and
unintended 36–38, 49–50, 52,
63, 91, 125–26, 217–18, 233

diachrony (see synchrony)
dominant social order 42, 44, 56,
71, 73, 134, 137, 141–42, 156,
160, 181, 195, 197–98, 200,
233, 235–36, 257–58, 279,
282, 284, 293
domination 50–52, 55–59, 69, 72,
236, 258, 263, 268, 291–92

empire, Roman 64–73, 110, 127,
274, 289
eucharist (see Lord's Supper)
explanation 18–22, 25, 34, 36–37,
45, 287–88

freedpersons, freedmen 64, 67, 94,
99, 103, 111, 117, 160–61,
165–67

functionalism 28, 33–38, 126, 281,
313

hierarchy xiii, 57, 70, 72–73, 157,
167, 174, 176, 180–82, 184,
195–97, 236, 256–58, 260,
262–64, 268, 279, 282, 284,
286, 288, 292
history and sociology 1, 9, 21, 25,
26–31, 281
household (see also *paterfamilias*) 68,
76, 94, 96–99, 117, 129, 157,
159, 167, 176, 214, 247, 263,
265, 269, 271–72, 277, 287
household codes, *Haustafeln* 194,
263–71, 278, 280, 286

ideology xi, xiii, 4, 44, 50–52, 55–
59, 63, 69, 71, 73, 124, 126,
161, 176, 178, 180, 184, 195,
235–36, 250, 257–58, 262–63,
268, 273, 279, 281–82, 284,
286, 291–93, 295, 313
idol-food, idol-meat, idol-worship 79,
89, 105–109, 122, 142–50, 205
imitation of Paul, of Christ, *imitatio
Christi* 149, 204–205, 209, 218,
228, 230–31, 234, 236, 254,
283, 294
institutionalisation 287–88
interests 36, 44, 51–52, 55–59, 63,
124, 126, 157, 185, 195, 235–
36, 250, 257, 268, 271, 279,
281, 284, 290–92